EVANGELIZATION
AND IDEOLOGY

MATTHEW R. PETRUSEK

FOREWORD BY CARDINAL THOMAS COLLINS

EVANGELIZATION
AND IDEOLOGY

HOW TO UNDERSTAND
AND RESPOND TO THE
POLITICAL CULTURE

Published by the Word on Fire Institute, an imprint of
Word on Fire, Park Ridge, IL 60068
© 2023 by Matthew R. Petrusek
Printed in the United States of America
All rights reserved

Cover design by Rozann Lee, typesetting by Marlene Burrell,
and interior art direction by Nicolas Fredrickson

Scripture excerpts are from the New Revised Standard Version Bible:
Catholic Edition (copyright © 1989, 1993), used by permission of the National
Council of the Churches of Christ in the United States of America.
All rights reserved worldwide.

Excerpts from the English translation of the *Catechism of the Catholic Church*
for use in the United States of America copyright © 1994, United States
Catholic Conference, Inc.—Libreria Editrice Vaticana. Used by permission.
English translation of the *Catechism of the Catholic Church*: Modifications
from the Editio Typica copyright © 1997, United States Conference of
Catholic Bishops—Libreria Editrice Vaticana.

First printing, July 2023

ISBN: 978-1-685780-10-4

Library of Congress Control Number: 2021922708

CONTENTS

Foreword

Cardinal Thomas Collins

Many years ago, when I was a young priest, my bishop sent me to study Scripture. The biblical book that I studied most intensely was the Apocalypse, the book of Revelation, written in the last decade of the first century to strengthen the Christians of what is now Turkey. Some of them were thrown to the beasts in the arena because of their insistence that Jesus, not Caesar, is Lord. From the days of the Apocalypse to this present day, the disciples of Jesus have been willing to offer the ultimate witness of martyrdom. Each year many thousands of our brothers and sisters in Christ give up their homes, their freedom, and often their lives rather than deny Jesus, our Lord and God.

But many disciples of Jesus in the time of the Apocalypse were more like Christians in modern Western society: they would not be called upon to die for Christ, but they were called upon to live for Christ with integrity in an alien society. They were called to live as faithful citizens of the heavenly city Jerusalem, the city of God, while passing through godless Babylon, the city of man, which was under the spell of ideologies contrary to the Gospel. Yearning for the rock of Gospel reality, they were caught in the swamp of secular illusion.

That has been the challenge for Christians down through the ages. It is our challenge now. How do we effectively proclaim the life-giving reality of the Gospel of Jesus Christ in a society in which people are deluded by ideologies that, upon examination, are revealed to be both false and destructive? Yet these ideologies, though misguided, shape the thoughts and behaviors of citizens and the policies of governments. Popular culture is distorted by them, and increasingly, those who do not go along with them find themselves silenced and pressured to conform.

To survive in such a desert, and to bring the life of the Gospel of Jesus to our fellow human beings in the midst of it, we need to draw water joyfully from the wells of salvation (Isa. 12:3). We do that through prayer, the reception of the sacraments, and the practice of sacrificial love. But we also need to understand the workings of the negative ideologies with which we are confronted in our mission of evangelization.

Evangelization and Ideology: How to Understand and Respond to the Political Culture offers us invaluable assistance as we seek to fulfill the mandate entrusted to each of us in Baptism and Confirmation: to witness to the reality of the Gospel in our sadly deluded world, which too often is like a house of mirrors in which illusion seems to have triumphed over reality. The spiritually and intellectually fruitful insights of this book allow us to understand the society in which, by the providence of God, we are called and sent to witness to Christ, and they help us to communicate effectively the reality of the Good News in an environment distorted by deadly illusion.

CHAPTER I

Introduction:
The Politicization of the
Culture: A Challenge and an
Opportunity

"Politics and religion are best not discussed in polite company."

Whatever wisdom this adage may have once contained, only half of it is heeded anymore. Religion certainly remains verboten in public, yet politics is now all the rage. Indeed, it's difficult to find a social domain that has *not* been politicized: art, music, cinema, education, public health, literature, science—even coffee, cookies, canned beans, pillows, and toys[1]—are now battlefields

---

1. For example, there have been massive calls to boycott the CEO of the Hispanic food company Goya because he said positive words about former president Donald Trump (see David Goldman, "Goya Foods boycott takes off after its CEO praises Trump," CNN, July 10, 2020, https://www.cnn.com/2020/07/10 /business/goya-foods-boycott-trump/index.html). A young political activist gained national attention when he promised to found a new "progressive" pillow company to combat the success of the company "My Pillow," whose CEO was also supportive of President Trump (see Meryl Kornfield, "Parkland survivor David Hogg launches his own company in a 'pillow fight' against Mike Lindell," *The Washington Post*, February 9, 2021, https://www.washingtonpost.com/technology/2021/02/09/david-hogg-good-pillow-mike-lindell/); the activist ultimately abandoned the idea. The state of California recently banned retail stores from "gendering" their toy aisles with blue and pink colors (see Adam Beam, "California becomes first state to require gender-neutral toy aisles at large retail stores," *USA Today*, October 10, 2021, https://www.usatoday.com/story/news/nation/2021/10/10/california-mandate -gender-neutral-toy-sections/6082593001/). Oreo cookies are no longer always black and white; you can now purchase rainbow-themed cookies to "celebrate" LGBTQ+ "pride" (see Marika Gerken, "Oreo created limited edition rainbow cookies

of ideological warfare. The markers of political tribalism have become more pronounced in the process: Do you drive an F-150 or a Prius? Shop at Walmart or Whole Foods? Watch Fox News or MSNBC? Listen to AM talk radio or FM NPR? Own a gun (or two or three) or a yoga mat (or two or three)? Do you sip an insulated mug that proudly displays "Leftist Tears"? Or does yours declare "No Justice, No Peace"? Do ads for tactical flashlights and emergency food supplies pop up when you watch YouTube? Or are you interrupted by invitations to organic meal plans and portable juice blenders? Did you want to be seen without a mask during the 2020–2022 pandemic? Or did you wear yours with pride?

There is plentiful comedy in our hyper-politicized culture, an environment in which news can be difficult to distinguish from satire.[2] Yet fear and suffering lie just beneath the surface. Those who have lost their businesses to riots or their jobs to decade-old tweets don't find the politicization of the culture funny. Those who no longer feel comfortable exposing their children to public school curriculum but cannot afford private alternatives aren't in on the joke either. Nor are those who work full time, spend responsibly, but cannot make rent. Nor those who fear the government will force them to violate their conscience or be fired. Nor those who are branded "bigots" for wanting their daughters

to celebrate LGBTQ+ History Month," CNN, October 9, 2020, https://www.cnn .com/2020/10/09/us/oreo-rainbow-cookies-lgbtq-month-trnd/index.html). The coffee chain Starbucks has been accused of participating in a "war on Christmas" by refusing to include (secular) Christmas imagery on its "holiday-themed" cups (see Marisa Iati, "Starbucks holiday cups were once a flash point in a 'war on Christmas.' Now they're a meme," *The Washington Post*, November 4, 2021, https:// www.washingtonpost.com/history/2021/11/04/starbucks-coffee-holiday-cup -meme/). The list goes on.

2. The Babylon Bee is a comedy site that satirizes politics and the culture from a mostly politically conservative point of view. Despite the fact that the site openly identifies itself as producing satire, some "hard news" organizations have engaged in "fact checking" its claims. See, for example, "Fact Check– Satirical article by the Babylon Bee about Nancy Pelosi taken seriously," Reuters, https://www.reuters.com/article/factcheck-pelosi-satire-sacrifice/fact-check -satirical-article-by-the-babylon-bee-about-nancy-pelosi-taken-seriously -idUSL1N2MK1U2.

to compete against other biological females in school sports. Nor those who have no affordable access to medical care and are one illness away from bankruptcy. Nor those who fear errant bullets will pass through their windows and kill them while they sleep. Nor those who have lost a loved one to a drug overdose. Indeed, the more we obsess about politics, the more broken our common life seems to become.

But what does all this civic turmoil have to do with evangelization, especially since "religious" speech in public (still respecting the opening adage) continues to be shunned? Moreover, Americans and Europeans are leaving organized religion in droves nowadays, including the Catholic Church.[3] Many people, perhaps most people, just don't seem to care about God anymore. And many of those who do care, care in the same way a landlord cares about a squatter: they want religion kicked out from the public square once and for all. From this perspective, evangelization and the political culture would appear to be at odds. Whatever hope remains for the Church to evangelize society in the twenty-first century, it would thus seem that the best path forward would be to steer clear of the sociopolitical arena altogether.

Although it may sound counterintuitive, this book makes the opposite case: the hyper-politicization of society constitutes an opportunity for evangelization rather than an obstacle. In ways that may not have been possible in previous decades, when secularization trends were palpable but not yet dominant, the Church has a unique opening to re-enter the sociopolitical fray, re-engage the secular mind, and call the culture back to Christ—provided we can effectively understand and respond to the contemporary ideological battlefield.

3. See, for example, this recent polling by Gallup: Jeffrey M. Jones, "U.S. Church Membership Falls Below Majority for First Time," Gallup, March 29, 2021, https://news.gallup.com/poll/341963/church-membership-falls-below-majority -first-time.aspx.

There is a two-pronged reason for approaching evangelization this way. First, things are falling apart. Establishing an empirically sound causal relationship between the secularization and politicization of the culture and the decline of social and individual well-being is complex, but there are ample data points to raise concern. Even before the 2020–2022 pandemic, rates of anxiety, depression, suicide, drug overdoses, school dropouts, divorce, self-reported loneliness, and social isolation were already soaring. Moreover, as more children in the womb are killed— nearly 25 percent of all pregnancies in the US currently end in an abortion[4]—those who survive through birth are growing up to find themselves without siblings or substantive friendships. And even if we callously insist that these trends don't matter as long as society continues to progress economically and technologically, the stubborn fact remains that secular societies tend not to have enough children to perpetuate themselves in the long run, a phenomenon known as demographic death.[5] There is no guarantee that these destructive currents will spur a religious reawakening, but, like all suffering, they at least crack open the possibility for reconsidering the sacred. Evangelists thus must be ready to speak to the swelling number of the disenchanted with the possibility of another way of life.

The second reason is that, despite the common insistence that all religion, including Catholicism, is "irrational," the Church's social doctrines provide a more reasonable sociopolitical framework than secular alternatives. One of the greatest prejudices of our age is "presentism," or the blind assertion that the present is morally superior to the past simply because it is

4. Rachel K. Jones and Jenna Jerman, "Population Group Abortion Rates and Lifetime Incidence of Abortion: United States, 2008–2014," *American Journal of Public Health* 107 (2017): 1904–1909, https://doi.org/10.2105/AJPH.2017.304042.

5. See, for example, Damien Cave, Emma Bubola, and Choe Sang-Hun, "Long Slide Looms for World Population, With Sweeping Ramifications," *The New York Times*, May 24, 2021, https://www.nytimes.com/2021/05/22/world/global-population-shrinking.html.

more recent. Embedded within presentism is the belief that a society holds the views it does because it has passed through a moral and intellectual evolution. That is true on some issues, to be sure—ending the practice of slavery, striking racially discriminatory laws, and extending voting rights to women, for example. Yet it is not necessarily true on all questions. For instance, it used to be considered self-evident that every child deserves to be born to and raised by a loving mother and father. Yet today large numbers of people tag that once obvious conviction as "hateful" and even evidence of a "phobia" (even though *they* all have mothers and fathers). Is this a sign of moral evolution? Has the argument in support of the traditional family been rationally defeated? Has it been shown to be false? Setting aside the frustratingly frequent tendency of being informed, in one breath, that there is no such thing as "moral objectivity" while, in the next, being scolded for holding the wrong point of view, the question of truth, the question of rightness and wrongness, is as alive today as it ever has been. So, again: Are *all* our values really better than our predecessors', including the new definition of "family"?

Answering that question requires determining what "better" means, which points to the question of what "good" means, which, in turn, points to the question of what is "true."[6] What should we believe as true, then? What is believable? On what grounds do we believe it? According to what standard of rationality? It may come as a surprise to Catholics—and this is a sad reflection of the Church's efforts to evangelize itself—but Catholicism has deep, systematic, comprehensive, coherent, and rationally sound responses to these questions, as they relate to both the definition

---

6. Rejecting a rational connection between "what is true" and "what is good" would mean that we could claim that there are false ideas that are also good ideas. At some level, every moral theory must be grounded in some connection of what it takes to be "objectively true." Even a utilitarian theory that would say that lies are "good" in some instances also believes that its conception of the good—the greatest good for the greatest number—is *true*. This book will explain the relationship between competing conceptions of goodness and truth in depth.

of the family and everything else in the sociopolitical sphere. In other words, Catholics are well equipped to talk about politics *as Catholics* and to make the case for the comprehensive Catholic view of moral reality. The Church holds a trove of good arguments that, despite having existed for thousands of years, have been mostly absent from contemporary public debates—arguments that are superior to competing political philosophies, not despite being grounded in a doctrine of God, but precisely *because* they are grounded in a doctrine of God.

OUT OF BOUNDS?

But wait. Doesn't this approach to evangelization contravene the first commandment of all secular ideologies, that thou shalt not mix God and politics? Wouldn't it be a violation of the separation of church and state? Wouldn't it be an imposition of the Church's beliefs on others? And wouldn't that, in violation of secularity's second commandment, be intolerant? And doesn't being intolerant mean that you are full of hate?

In an age in which political discourse has been reduced to bumper-sticker soundbites whose moral authority depends on how well the words rhyme (e.g., "Keep Your Rosaries off My Ovaries," "Silence is Violence," "Hey Hey, Ho Ho, [enter target of opprobrium] Has Got to Go," or, less felicitously, "Pigs in a Blanket, Fry Them Like Bacon"), answering these questions requires extensive conceptual disentangling and a journey back to the proverbial drawing board. First, all who insist that appeals to religious principles have no place in political debates necessarily position themselves in opposition to the arguments of Martin Luther King Jr. and much of the moral logic of the American civil rights movement more broadly. This is not a cheap shot against secularism. It is a statement of fact: there is no intellectually responsible way to disaggregate some "religion-free" nugget of moral truth from the body of Martin Luther King's case for racial equality.

Take, for example, these passages from one of Martin Luther King's most renowned writings, "Letter from a Birmingham Jail":

> The question is not whether we will be extremist but what kind of extremist will we be. Will we be extremists for hate or will we be extremists for love? Will we be extremists for the preservation of injustice—or will we be extremists for the cause of justice? In that dramatic scene on Calvary's hill, three men were crucified. We must not forget that all three were crucified for the same crime—the crime of extremism. Two were extremists for immorality, and thusly fell below their environment. The other, Jesus Christ, was an extremist for love, truth and goodness, and thereby rose above his environment.[7]

> Whenever the early Christians entered a town the power structure got disturbed and immediately sought to convict them for being "disturbers of the peace" and "outside agitators." But [the Christians] went on with the conviction that they were a "colony of heaven," and had to obey God rather than man. They were small in number but big in commitment. They were too God-intoxicated to be "astronomically intimidated." They brought an end to such ancient evils as infanticide and gladiatorial contest.[8]

> One may well ask, "How can you advocate breaking some laws and obeying others?" The answer is found in the fact that there are two types of laws: there are *just* and there are *unjust* laws. I would agree with Saint Augustine that "An unjust law is no law at all." ... A just law is a manmade code that is out of harmony with the moral law. To put it in the terms of Saint Thomas

---

7. Martin Luther King Jr., "Letter from a Birmingham Jail," in *I Have a Dream: Writings and Speeches that Changed the World*, ed. James M. Washington (San Francisco: Harper, 1992), 95.

8. King, 97.

Aquinas, an unjust law is a human law that is not rooted in the eternal or the natural law.[9]

And in case there is any doubt that Martin Luther King Jr. employed *religious* language to address a *public* audience, note these excerpts from his 1963 "I Have a Dream" speech delivered at the Lincoln Memorial in Washington, DC:

> Now is the time to make real the promises of democracy; now is the time to rise from the dark and desolate valley of segregation to the sunlit path of racial justice; now is the time to lift our nation from the quicksands of racial injustice to the solid rock of brotherhood; now is the time to make justice a reality for all God's children.[10]

> With this faith we will be able to work together, to pray together, to struggle together, to go to jail together, to stand up for freedom together, knowing that we will be free one day. This will be the day when all of God's children will be able to sing with new meaning—"my country 'tis of thee; sweet land of liberty; of thee I sing" . . . and if America is to be a great nation, this must become true.[11]

> [W]hen we allow freedom to ring, when we let it ring from every village and hamlet, from every state and city, we will be able to speed up that day when all God's children—black men and white men, Jews and Gentiles, Catholics and Protestants—will be able to join hands and sing in the words of the old Negro spiritual, "Free at last, free at last; thank God Almighty, we are free at last."[12]

9. King, 89.
10. Martin Luther King Jr., "I Have a Dream," in *I Have a Dream*, 103.
11. King, 105.
12. King, 105-106.

There is, in short, no way to shuck the shell of religion from Martin Luther King Jr.'s arguments and end up with some secular nugget intact. Remove God—indeed, remove the Bible—from King's moral vocabulary, and you lose King himself and the movement he represented.

The public appeal to religion is not a relic of history, moreover. Politicians across the ideological spectrum continue to invoke the divine to explain and defend their positions (though we may question whether their appeals are as authentic as King's). "Red State" Republicans are well known for speaking about God publicly. Yet "Blue State" Democrats commonly employ theological language as well. For example, former Speaker of the House Nancy Pelosi—in diametric contradiction to Catholic teaching—once declared that abortion rights are "sacred ground."[13] President Joe Biden, who excoriated his predecessor for "using" religion to advance his agenda,[14] has also identified his belief in God as the core theological framework out of which flow his fundamental governing principles.[15] Even self-declared socialist Bernie Sanders has shared that "religious principles" have deeply shaped his political values.[16] These are a few prominent examples of many. In short, though the United States may be growing less religious, most people still have no problem voting for candidates who employ "God talk" regularly in their stump speeches.

13. See "Pelosi On Abortion: 'As A Practicing And Respectful Catholic, This Is Sacred Ground To Me,'" Real Clear Politics, June 13, 2013, https://www.realclear politics.com/video/2013/06/13/pelosi_on_abortion_as_a_practicing_and _respectful_catholic_this_is_sacred_ground_to_me.html.

14. See Christina Wilkie and Amanda Macias, "Biden slams Trump's response to George Floyd protests: 'More interested in power than principle,'" CNBC, June 2, 2020, https://www.cnbc.com/2020/06/02/george-floyd-protests-biden-slams -trump-over-st-johns-church-photo-op.html.

15. See Asma Khalid, "How Joe Biden's Faith Shapes His Politics," NPR, September 20, 2020, https://www.npr.org/2020/09/20/913667325/how-joe-bidens -faith-shapes-his-politics.

16. See Eugene Scott, "Bernie Sanders, America's most prominent 'unaffiliated' politician, still says religion shaped his values," *The Washington Post*, February 7, 2020, https://www.washingtonpost.com/politics/2020/02/07 /bernie-sanders-religion-values-how-both-shape-his-politics/.

Second, the secular insistence that there exists a bright conceptual line between "religious" beliefs and principles and "nonreligious" beliefs and principles is more myth than reality. Take, for example, the claim that "all human beings are equal," which is something that (at least for the time being) no politician would dare deny openly. It certainly sounds good. Yet what is the justification for this belief? What distinguishes it from sheer superstition, blind appeal to authority, or even fanciful delusion? Why is it reasonable? Whatever the answer, the belief in universal moral equality certainly isn't justified from a scientific or empirical perspective for at least two reasons: (1) "moral equality" cannot be empirically identified, and (2) there is nothing empirically observable in human beings that is both unique to humanity *and* that exists in absolute equality among all humans without exception.[17] Consider some possible observable characteristics that might be relevant to justifying the existence of human dignity: IQ, self-awareness, the capacity to feel pleasure and pain, the capacity to form relationships, the capacity to communicate, the capacity to create art, the capacity for self-directed action, etc. Which of these, or any other attribute, are *both* universally present in all human beings without exception *and* universally present in all human beings to the same degree? The answer is none. And even if, in a philosophical move related to the thought of Enlightenment philosopher Immanuel Kant, we seek to ground equal human worth in some abstract conception of "autonomy" (being a law unto oneself), we are still talking about a human capacity and, therefore, still talking about something that is unequally distributed across the human population and, indeed, across human individuals throughout the course of their own

---

17. As I'll argue in more depth below, human DNA is insufficient to establish human dignity because every other species also has its own unique DNA markers, and it would be morally arbitrary to claim that our uniqueness is somehow more "special" than the uniqueness present in other species purely on biochemical grounds.

lifetimes. In short, even a quick examination of the question shows that it is far from clear that a purely secular epistemology, completely devoid of any conception of God, could coherently justify the belief that "all human beings are equal."

So, then, does believing in human dignity make you a religious fanatic or a superstitiously credulous looney? Does it make you, to use the words of atheist cultural critic Bill Maher, a "[blank]ing nut" (language he used to describe Catholic Supreme Court Justice Amy Coney Barrett)?[18] If so, we should all inform our political class (and the Declaration of Independence) immediately, so they'll cease all this religious claptrap about "human equality." If not—if the belief in universal moral value is not something we are willing to jettison (yet)—then perhaps we can admit that the lines between "faith" and "reason" may not be as bright as secularism has been insisting. This is not to say that we cannot make meaningful distinctions between what pertains to the domain of "religion" and what pertains to the domain of "rationality." (It is also *not* to say that universal human equality is irrational.) However, it *is* to recognize—again, contra secularism's self-soothing mythmaking—that the relationship between "religious beliefs" and "rational beliefs," especially in moral matters, is immensely complex. We should stop pretending otherwise.

Finally, and most importantly for this book, the Catholic social thought tradition can and does make moral arguments without explicitly appealing to "faith" or what the tradition also calls "revelation." Indeed, the basic epistemic presupposition of Catholic social ethics is that it is intelligible to all human beings, no matter what explicit religion they may or may not profess. It is for this reason that papal encyclicals and exhortations on social questions are addressed—explicitly since the papacy of Pope St.

18. See Ross A. Lincoln and Phil Owen, "Bill Maher Says Amy Coney Barrett Is 'a F–ing Nut,'" *The Wrap*, September 25, 2020, https://www.thewrap.com /bill-maher-says-amy-coney-barrett-is-a-f-ing-nut/.

John XXIII and implicitly before then—to "all people of good will." "All people of good will" means all people who are open and willing to seek truth and to do to their best to abide by it, even if there are disagreements along the way. The moral arguments that constitute Catholic social thought do not presuppose that one has accepted Jesus Christ as one's Lord and Savior, that the Eucharist is the Real Presence of Jesus Christ, that Mary was bodily assumed into heaven, or that God is one God in three persons (Father, Son, and Holy Spirit). They only presuppose that you are willing to use the natural light of reason and follow wherever it leads. This is not to say that the dogmatic truths that come to us in revelation—the deposit of faith that God has communicated to the Church in Scripture and Tradition—are against reason or not open to rational engagement. It is to say, however, that believing in the content of revelation is not an epistemic precondition for understanding and rationally evaluating the validity and soundness of Catholic social teaching.

Highlighting Catholic social thought's appeal to epistemic universality is important not only for identifying how the tradition seeks to make its case but also for nipping the "imposing your values" objection in the bud. It shows the objection to be a red herring. First, it is not clear what "imposing" means. If it means coercing someone to do something that they disagree with (or not allowing them to do something they want to do), then any and every law is an "imposition" on someone's beliefs. And Catholicism, of course, is not a legislative or executive or judicial body; it cannot make or enforce any civil law. The most it can do is make arguments in the public square about what it takes to be morally right, just like every other individual and group. In this sense, the Church cannot "impose" its vision of the good more than any other group in society.

If, on the other hand, "imposing" means making moral claims that other people disagree with, then all people who make public arguments, whether "religious" or not, are guilty of "imposing" their beliefs on others. In this case, "being imposed on" simply means "being exposed to." Consequently, the only way to prevent "imposing one's beliefs" on others from this perspective would be for everyone to agree to remain silent about all moral and political matters in the civic sphere. That may sound preferable to our current politics; however, in addition to paralyzing democratic decision-making, it's not a truce, I suspect, that would last very long.

In sum, it's ultimately not important or even relevant whether an argument is "religious" or "nonreligious" or whether someone might think that it constitutes an "imposition." The only thing that matters, in the end, is how well the argument holds up under scrutiny. This book will be making the case that the Catholic argument—the *big* argument on the best understanding of the nature and purpose of politics—holds up very well indeed, especially when examined in relation to secular alternatives.

WINNING MINDS OR SAVING SOULS? YES.

But even if it is the case that Catholic social teaching provides a better political paradigm, what evangelical purpose does political argument serve? What relationship could it possibly have to the Good News of Jesus Christ or to the call to conversion and repentance? The evangelical strategy is twofold.

First, the book's proximate goal is to show how political debate, done with the right tools, can help win minds to a conception of the good that is, in fact, *good*, one that establishes a moral and political framework that gives us the best shot at creating a civil environment that engenders individual and communal flourishing, to the extent it's possible in a fallen world. In other words, the first goal is to equip evangelists—and *every* baptized Catholic is called to be an evangelist—to make the strongest possible case for the natural-law alternative to secular politics.

Yet within and beyond this goal lies an invitation to something deeper—much deeper—than debate about the political order and advocacy for a particular sociopolitical structure. The final goal is not ultimately about "winning an argument" or even working to establish and maintain an authentically just society, as noble as that is. The greater goal, the goal behind the goal, is to offer the culture an escape from hyper-politicization by presenting an alternative to thinking—and acting—ideologically altogether. It is to invite the culture into a relationship with a man who calls everyone to do everything possible to fix the world while also unambiguously declaring, "My kingdom is not from this world" (John 18:36).

In short, the social teachings of the Catholic Church rationally stand on their own. But that rationality points through itself to its foundation—the Logos—who is, simultaneously, *Agape*, unconditional love. It points to Jesus Christ. Indeed, as the Gospel of John reveals, the ground of truth itself—"In the beginning was the Word, and the Word was with God, and the Word was God. . . . All things came into being through him, and without him not one thing came into being" (John 1:1–3)—is one and the same as the man who declares, "I came that they may have life, and have it abundantly" (John 10:10). In sum, if evangelists can make a convincing case that the Church has a good vision of politics, a vision grounded in objective truth, then we at least open the door for considering whether the Church might have a good vision of religion as well—a vision founded in objective love. This approach to evangelization does not transform politics into religion or religion into politics. Much the opposite: it allows us to present the two in right relationship to each other and put both in service of God and the authentic human good.

BUILDING A FRAMEWORK

Evangelization and Ideology is divided into two parts comprised of ten chapters, including this introduction (chapter 1). Part 1 develops a methodology for employing Catholic social thought to debate secular ideologies. Drawing on the writings of Bishop

Robert Barron and the Catholic philosophers Peter Kreeft and Fr. Ronald Tacelli, SJ, chapter 2 of part I, "Stop Fighting—and Start Arguing," identifies how to engage in political discussions by identifying the fundamental principles of moral argumentation. Chapter 3 of part I, "Getting Your Bearings: Locating the Sources of Political Disagreement," discusses *where* to engage in political discussion—not geographically but conceptually. As the chapter explains, most sociopolitical disagreements are not fundamentally about different laws or policies; rather, they are about competing theories of justice (morality and applied morality), knowledge (epistemology), human nature (anthropology), and/or the nature of existence (metaphysics or ontology). Finally, chapter 4 of part I, "From How to Debate to What to Say: The Comprehensive Toolbox of Catholic Social Thought," explains the features of Catholic morality that are most relevant to challenging secular ideologies. These features include moral truth, moral progress and its limits, moral hierarchies and the common good, human dignity, and free speech, all of which are paradigmatically present in the life and thought of Pope St. John Paul II.

Part II of the book turns to analyzing diverse secular ideologies, showing how Catholic social thought provides a better alternative to each. Chapter 5, "Totality without Transcendence: The Anatomy of an Ideology," identifies the basic constitutive moral logic of all "ideologies" per se, notwithstanding their otherwise profound differences. Having established a basic definition of ideology as idolatry, the following chapters critically consider four secular ideologies by identifying their foundational principles, examining one or more contemporary representatives, and then arguing how Catholic social thought addresses their respective shortcomings. Chapter 6 engages utilitarianism ("The God of Pleasure"), chapter 7 engages classical liberalism and libertarianism ("The God of My Self"), chapter 8 engages progressivism, also known as "wokeism" ("The God of My Tribe"), and chapter 9 engages non-theistic conservativism ("The God of Fortune").

The final chapter, chapter 10, offers practical advice on how to apply the book's arguments to evangelize all who are willing to listen in the political sphere.

It is important to note that part I can function independently of part II, meaning that readers can "get" the book's primary points by reading part I alone. Part II seeks to complement part I by offering those who are interested a deeper dive into the philosophical foundations of our age's reigning secular ideologies and how the Catholic social thought tradition can constructively respond to each. The book's conclusion, in turn, serves to tie together both parts I and II.

MARKING BOUNDARIES AND MOVING FORWARD

A few parameters before diving in. First, this book is not about specific political issues. That doesn't mean that issues are un-important; indeed, some issues, like abortion and euthanasia, are matters of life and death. However, "issues" are only "issues" insofar as they have their grounding in a comprehensive vision of what is good and bad, right and wrong. Thus, to "win" on the issues in any meaningful and durable sense, we must "win" at the deeper levels of moral reality.

Second, this book is meant to serve as an introduction to Catholic social thought and to the rival political theories it engages. There is great complexity both within Catholic socio-political ethics and its competition. This book does not provide a comprehensive explanation or assessment of that complexity. Many very thoughtful people both inside and outside the Church have devised intricate political theories that defy facile catego-rization. The principles in these pages are meant only to mark out and critically evaluate general territories in the sociopolitical landscape, taking a thirty-thousand-foot view. My hope is that these generalizations provide accurate and useful maps that enable and—in the case of Catholic social thought—*inspire* readers to take a closer look.

Third, the book will examine secular political ideologies primarily from a US perspective. What a "conservative," "liberal," "utilitarian," "progressive," "green," etc. looks like can vary depending on the unique political culture of a region, each of which has its unique history and culture. As noted, there are many important nuances to consider when engaging in political debates. Context always matters. That said, many of the characteristics of secular ideologies do indeed transcend national, cultural, and historical boundaries. Those cross-cultural characteristics will be the focus of the analysis.

Fourth, while there are some sociopolitical questions on which faithful Catholics cannot disagree—for example, on when life begins (at conception), when life ends (natural death), and what defines a marriage (a lifelong union between a biological woman and a biological man that is open to procreation)—there are some questions on which disagreement is not only morally legitimate but also desirable because it leads to better laws and public policies. Questions related to economic, environmental, defense, and security policies often fall into this category. In explicating and defending the principles of Catholic social thought this book thus does not take a stand on any prudential sociopolitical judgment—that is to say, judgments related to questions on which people of good will and sound reasoning can legitimately differ. Relatedly, it does not endorse any political party, though some party platforms are clearly more consonant with Catholic teaching than others (and some party platforms entirely contradict Catholic teaching). Moreover, as the chapter on Catholic social thought will highlight specifically, a productive tension exists within the heart of the Catholic view of politics, found, paradigmatically, in the tension between the political thought of St. Augustine and St. Thomas Aquinas. This tension is not a problem to be fixed but rather a paradox to be embraced.

Leveraging political debate to invite the culture to consider a Catholic worldview is not, of course, the only way to practice evangelization. There are as many ways to evangelize as there are individuals, and no way is superior to another so long as they all lead to Christ and his Church. Yet engaging in political debate is certainly *one* way to evangelize, and it is a way, this book will argue, that is becoming increasingly necessary as society becomes more politicized. In the end, evangelizing always requires going to where the people are, and where many people are today is stuck in a morass of increasingly aggressive political ideologies, each one seducing its adherents down varied paths to the same dead end: moral, spiritual, and yes, political futility. There is a better option.

PART I

Foundations

CHAPTER 2

Stop Fighting—and
Start Arguing

Getting into a fight is easy. Getting into an argument—that takes work. Moreover, despite the common conflation of "arguing" with "fighting"—an understandable conflation for those who watch YouTube and cable TV news—the fact is that we'd be fighting less if we were having *more* arguments with each other. The reason is because learning how to disagree is essential for reaching a durable agreement.

This theme, restoring the lost art of disagreement, forms one of the pillars of Bishop Robert Barron's evangelization work, which he develops in *Arguing Religion: A Bishop Speaks at Facebook and Google*. In this short book, Barron lays out a rhetorical framework for engaging in moral, philosophical, and religious argumentation, especially with those who identify as "nones" (those who eschew all religious traditions). The framework enables constructive debate among individuals who hold, or appear to hold, profoundly different worldviews.

Barron's first two principles—paraphrased, "Do not pit reason against faith" and "Overcome scientism"—identify two epistemological foundations to productive disagreement. As noted previously, the contemporary assertion that "faith" is, at best, independent of reason and, at worst, repugnant to reason is, in fact, *unreasonable*. As Barron writes,

Authentic faith is not ... infrarational; it is suprarational. The infrarational—what lies below reason—is the stuff of credulity, superstition, naiveté, or just plain stupidity, and no self-respecting adult should be the least bit interested in fostering or embracing it. It is quite properly shunned by mature religious people as it is by scientists and philosophers. The suprarational, on the other hand, is what lies beyond reason but never stands in contradiction to reason. It is indeed a type of knowing, but one that surpasses the ordinary powers of observation, experimentation, hypothesis formation, or rational reflection.[1]

In short, constructive debate requires refraining from playing "epistemic gatekeeping" with debate participants insisting, for example, that no "religious arguments" can be used to make one's moral and political case. Twentieth-century philosophers like John Rawls and Jürgen Habermas dedicated much of their careers to defending such gatekeeping by contending that all public claims (e.g., explaining why you oppose a law) must be free from "religious" content. Yet their arguments ultimately fall flat for two reasons. First, as noted earlier, they cut against the historical experience of "religious language" effectively producing moral progress in society, which we see paradigmatically in figures like Abraham Lincoln, Dorothy Day, Martin Luther King Jr, and Cesar Chavez; and second, what counts as "rational" in civil debate is, or at least should be, *part of the debate itself.* (I will further develop this point in the next chapter.) In recasting the relationship between "faith" and "reason" as potentially complementary, Bishop Barron is thus highlighting that constructive debate necessitates opening the mind to *all* possible forms of evidence and being willing to use *all* tools at our disposal, including tools that do not fall neatly

---

1. Robert Barron, *Arguing Religion: A Bishop Speaks at Facebook and Google* (Park Ridge, IL: Word on Fire, 2018), 7–8.

into narrow secular definitions of "rationality." To be sure, some viewpoints will, indeed, emerge as "infrarational"—as contrary to reason—in the process, but that's the point: we have to get all the positions on the table before we can start the sorting.

This leads to Bishop Barron's second condition for constructive debate: overcoming scientism. Scientism, according to Barron, is "the reduction of all knowledge to the scientific form of knowing."[2] The consequence of this viewpoint is that all knowledge that falls outside the scope of empirical verifiability is epistemically indistinguishable from irrational emotive assertion (i.e., "I believe it because I feel it"). Scientism has become dominant in secular culture, especially among young people, a reality captured in the popular internet meme, "Dude, do you even science?" (or its variant, "Do you even science, bro?"). The meme encapsulates the sentiment that only an idiot would believe something that isn't "scientific."

Unfortunately for the bros (and brosettes) who think this way, scientism is logically incoherent and self-defeating. As Bishop Barron points out,

> The entire program of scientism rests squarely upon a contradiction. The principle is that the only meaningful statements are those that can be confirmed through empirical observation and experimentation; and yet, that very principle is not confirmable in such a manner. Where or how does one observe or experimentally verify that meaningfulness is reducible to that which can observed through the senses?[3]

In other words, the claim "only scientific knowledge is meaningful knowledge" is not possible to defend empirically. This is for two related reasons. First, the meaning of the terms

2. Barron, 17.
3. Barron, 20–21.

themselves, both individually and in relation to each other, are not raw pieces of empirical material reality; they are *interpretations* of empirical material reality and, as such, do not exist "purely" as empirical reality itself. That may sound abstract, but think of it this way: How, from an empirical perspective, would it be possible to observe and, even less, quantify and test "meaningfulness" or "knowledge" or "science-ness" in and of itself? The whole enterprise would depend on adopting an a priori—that is, prior to observation—definition of the content of each term, which means that empiricism is not sui generis or self-justifying but rather conceptually relies on non-empirical rational categories. Put more colloquially, you must define what you seek to observe before you can go about observing it. (For those with interest in the history of philosophy, this is similar to the case that rationalist philosopher extraordinaire Immanuel Kant made against the self-described empiricist David Hume, which we will examine in later chapters).

Second, even if we could empirically define each term in the claim that "only scientific knowledge is meaningful knowledge," we would still have no scientific means to determine whether such a claim is, in fact, empirically true. The reason is that, methodologically, there is no way to set up an experiment that could test the empirical validity of the statement, because *such a statement cannot possibly be falsified*, which is the sole standard for determining scientific truth.

Falsifiability, in the scientific method, means being able to imagine an outcome in which your hypothesis could turn out to be false. So, for example, past medical practitioners seeking to empirically verify the cause of why some of their patients had yellow eyes must have said to themselves, "I hypothesize that the cause of yellow eyes is in the eye itself; however, it is at least possible that the cause may lie elsewhere in the body." This "it is possible that the cause lies elsewhere in the body" is the introduction of falsifiability into the practitioners' scientific reasoning. Indeed, this example—using experimentation to discover the true cause of jaundice—shows the power of the scientific method in action: precisely because doctors were conceptually able to imagine that the cause of yellow eyes could lie outside the eyes, even if that seemed counterintuitive at the time, they were able to conduct experiments that eventually led them to identify a liver deficiency, not an eye deficiency, as the culprit. Falsifiability, in other words, eventually led them to the truth.

The problem with the claim that "only scientific knowledge is meaningful knowledge," however, is that it cannot be falsified using the scientific method. Indeed, scientifically testing the claim would be like a scientist saying, "I am going to conduct an experiment to see whether the color 'pure white' exists in nature by using these red-tinted glasses." Given the nature of the question and the method chosen to pursue it, the "result" to the experiment is already contained within the experiment itself.

We can see this issue with empiricism more directly by setting it up in the form of a syllogism or structured argument (I'll say more about the structure of arguments later in this chapter):

Premise 1: Only knowledge acquired by the senses is meaningful.

Premise 2: Science is the only means by which we acquire knowledge by the senses.

Conclusion: Therefore, only knowledge acquired by science is meaningful.

Expressed this way, scientism provides a paradigmatic example of begging the question. In the language of logic, "begging the question" means avoiding the central issue at stake. The central issue in this context, the issue we must settle before moving on to any other issue, is *whether it is true* that only knowledge acquired by the senses is meaningful. It certainly may be accurate to claim that science, broadly speaking, represents the only means by which we (reliably) acquire sensory knowledge (the second premise in the argument); yet that statement alone tells us nothing about the truth status of the first premise, the claim that only sensory knowledge is meaningful. And the problem is that we cannot coherently use "science" to provide an answer to that without engaging in circular reasoning.

A classic example of begging the question uses the Bible to drive home the fallacy at play here (and, by the way, this is *not* the reasoning the Church employs to defend the Bible's authority). One person asks, "Is the Bible true?" to which the other responds, "Yes." "Why?" says the first. "Because the Bible says so," responds the second. The "reasoning" embedded in this statement rightly drives science-loving people nuts. They could reply, "But we need something *outside* the Bible to determine whether what the Bible says about itself is true—something can't just appeal to itself to justify its own authority!" That is an excellent point. Yet shouldn't we also therefore conclude that science cannot appeal to itself to justify its own authority and, even less, to justify the claim that nothing "outside of science" is objectively meaningful?

This, ultimately, is the problem with scientism. The reduction of all meaningful knowledge to the domain of the empirical is, translated, the same as asserting "the scientific method is the only way to determine what is true because only the scientific method can determine truth." Adopting this position is, analogously, no different from adopting the position that the Bible is true because the Bible says so. It is a sheer, circular appeal to asserted authority.

As Bishop Barron emphasizes, however, critiquing scientism is *not* a critique of science itself. The scientific method can, indeed, give us bountiful information about the workings of the universe and has been indispensable in vastly improving standards of living across the globe. But science is strictly methodologically limited and, as such, can neither justify its own existence nor serve as the sole epistemic foundation for argumentation, especially moral argumentation. It is a tool, not a totality, and, as such, can be *one* of the resources at our disposal when engaging in debates—but only one.

Another presupposition for constructive debate is Barron's principle "Avoid voluntarism." Voluntarism is "the trumping of the intellect by the will" and the view that "things are true because I want them to be true."[4] Voluntarism rivals scientism's influence in secular culture. Unlike scientism, however, voluntarism does not even feign rationality and, as such, is much more poisonous to civil discussion. Scientism can at least argue about science with rational authority; voluntarism, on the other hand, denies the existence of objective, universal rational principles altogether and thus cannot make a rational case for anything. This viewpoint appears in the commonplace assertions, "You have your truth, I have mine"; "Who are you to judge?"; "All values are relative"; "No culture is superior to another"; and "I want my outside to match my inside," which encapsulates the voluntaristic belief that individuals can, by sheer acts of will, define the nature, meaning, and purpose of their physical body independently of objective (including scientific) reality, especially in matters of gender and sexual behavior (though curiously, given the logic of the position, not in race, age, disability, class, privilege, etc.).

Voluntarism is completely incoherent; to assert that there is no universal truth beyond an individual's own definition of truth is to embrace a universal truth. Moreover, as we will see in the chapter on progressivism, it is distinctively destructive when socialized and repackaged as a political ideology. However, here it is sufficient to observe that adopting a voluntaristic position sabotages the possibility of debate even before the first word has been uttered. As Bishop Barron puts it, "When voluntarism holds sway, there is no room for argument, for truth has become utterly individualized and relativized."[5] It is important to stress that

4. Barron, 37.
5. Barron, 44.

rejecting voluntarism as a condition for debate is not to impose any limitations on the method or content of the conversation. Quite the opposite, it is to make the exchange of ideas possible in the first place. Without stipulating as a minimal requirement for civil discussion that all parties must be willing to offer *reasons* to support their viewpoints beyond a self-righteous "because I say so," there is no way to rationally apprehend and, even less, evaluate each other's positions. The best that voluntarism can produce is performative public tantrums.

The final conditions Bishop Barron identifies can be summarized as *dispositions* for constructive debate. They include seeking to understand your opponent's position and being intolerant of toleration. What unites both is an idea that may sound quaint to contemporary ears but nevertheless still undergirds all worthwhile public (and much private) discussion: *seek the truth.* Understanding your opponent's position serves two interrelated functions in this regard: It enables you to comprehend the other's point of view on its own terms while, in the process, spurring you to refine your position in response. Barron draws on St. John Henry Newman to highlight the importance of this "back and forth" among competing positions:

> When we take an idea in, we do not dumbly receive it, but instead, we turn it over, look at it from different angles, tease out its implications, etc. And then, in a manner of a game, we toss it back to a fellow player, who does much the same thing. In this sifting process, all of an idea's aspects are allowed to come into the light. Jumping on a question or a challenge with a put-down or a quip or a canned argument simply shuts down this indispensable process.[6]

6. Barron, 47–48.

Central to playing the game of truth-seeking is knowing the opponent's position at least as well, if not better, than he or she does. This is important not only, or even primarily, so that you can end up "winning" the debate, but rather so that you can confirm *to yourself* that you hold the position you do not because it's "yours" but because it is the best—that is to say, most truthful—position as far as you can discern.

This commitment to an ongoing, ever-refining confirmation that one's beliefs can withstand the highest levels of scrutiny points to the other disposition: being intolerant of toleration. Some beliefs are mutually exclusive: God either exists or does not; humans either have an immortal soul or they don't; there is either a universal human good or there isn't. As Barron bluntly observes, "Someone has to be wrong."[7] While toleration is an indispensable principle in a pluralistic society, it cannot be the only and, even less, the foundational principle because there must be *some* shared conception of truth that unites society—that makes it a "society" at all—in the first place. We don't have to agree on everything, but we do have to agree on something, and merely "agreeing to disagree" won't cut it when it comes to the constitutive laws and values of a society. "Toleration," in short, cannot sustain itself either in principle ("toleration" would have to tolerate all forms of "intolerance") or in practice ("toleration" would have to tolerate all attempts to destroy it).

Pointing out the limits of toleration is not to justify violence or the threat of violence as a means to advance one's viewpoint. Again, much the opposite, it is to give life to the purpose of argumentation itself, which is, ultimately, not merely to *seek* a common truth but to *practice* a common truth, a truth that is not reducible to individual or group preference and, as such, protects both individuals and groups from the tyranny of other individual and group preferences. In this sense, transcending

7. Barron, 33.

toleration in the name of shared principles is the best hope we have of establishing and maintaining a peaceful society. As Bishop Barron puts it, "Argument is the way to turn even fierce opponents into allies."[8] I would add that it's the *only* way. The lone alternative to argument in the pursuit of truth is aggression in the pursuit of power.

THE ANATOMY OF AN ARGUMENT

It's one thing to recognize the conditions that make constructive debate possible. But what about the arguments themselves? How can anyone go about making a determination on the intellectual merits of what another is claiming? Doesn't it all come down to opinion in the end?

No—and a brief anecdote helps show why. Around fourth grade, our children began being taught the difference between a "fact" and an "opinion" as part of the instruction on how to write elementary essays. This knowledge, they believed, seemed to endow them with superpowers, for with it they could immediately disarm their parents of moral authority. Here's an example:

Child: Can I sleep downstairs in front of the TV tonight?

Mom and Dad: No.

Child: Why not?

Mom and Dad: Because you are always grumpy the next day and unpleasant to be around.

Child: No, I'm not.

Mom and Dad: Yes, you are.

Child: No, I'm not. It's just your opinion that I get grumpy, and you can't force your opinion on anyone.

8. Barron, 36.

Mom and Dad: [in our heads: *oh yes we can*] Okay, but it's just your opinion that it is our opinion that you get grumpy—and that's a fact.

Child: [confused; after extended pause] Okay, what if I put away all the laundry on the couch.

Mom and Dad: Deal.

The "fact" vs. "opinion" distinction is a good learning tool and helpful heuristic for thinking through an issue in dispute (What here is "fact," what here is "opinion"?). But, of course, the distinction between "fact" and "opinion" itself rests upon a claim that there actually *is* a difference between fact and opinion in the first place. Is that claim a fact? Or is it an opinion? Can an opinion be factual? Can something factual just be someone's opinion? How in the world can we begin to sort any of this out?

The answer is that we isolate the argument being made, break it up into its parts, and then critically evaluate each component both individually and in relation to the other components. The eminent Catholic philosopher Peter Kreeft has made a wealth of arguments in support of the intellectual integrity of Catholicism, but one of his most valuable contributions is his breakdown of the anatomy of an argument itself. Arguments can be immensely complex. However, the criteria to understand and assess arguments, both individually and knitted together into complex systems, are relatively simple. In *Handbook of Catholic Apologetics: Reasoned Answers to Questions of Faith*, Kreeft and his co-author, Fr. Ronald Tacelli, SJ, lay the foundation for apologetics (reasoned defense of the truth of Catholicism) on three basic concepts, which the authors call the "three acts of the mind," and three corresponding *modes of expression* of those acts of the mind. The acts of the mind are understanding, judging, and reasoning, and the corresponding modes of expression are terms, propositions, and arguments.[9] (So, understanding relates to terms, judging to propositions, and reasoning to arguments.)

The argument about arguments is straightforward, but it is easy to get tripped up on the terminology, so let me start with an example. Here is a simple syllogism—that is, a deductive argument—against abortion:

Premise 1: It is wrong to kill innocent human life.

Premise 2: Humans in the womb are innocent human life.

Conclusion: Therefore, it is wrong to kill humans in the womb.

The terms in this syllogism are the words that exist in the two premises and conclusion, including "kill," "innocent," "human," "life," "womb," etc. The propositions are the statements in the two premises that bind the terms together—i.e., "It is wrong to kill innocent human life" and "Humans in the womb are innocent human life." The argument is the *relationship* between the premises (the propositions) that leads to the conclusion "Therefore, it is wrong to kill humans in the womb." Connecting this to the three operations of the mind, it is the rational power of understanding that evaluates terms, the rational power of judging that evaluates propositions, and the rational power of reasoning that evaluates arguments.

There is one more tool we need to add here: the *criteria* that the powers of the mind employ to assess terms, propositions, and arguments. The criterion for assessing terms is clarity—that is, is the meaning of the term clear or unclear, or, in other words, has the term been defined unambiguously? The criterion for assessing propositions is truth and falsity—that is, is the statement (the

---

9. Peter J. Kreeft and Ronald K. Tacelli, *Handbook of Catholic Apologetics: Reasoned Answers to Questions of Faith* (San Francisco: Ignatius Press, 1994), 17.

collection of terms) being made true or not true? Finally, the criterion for assessing argument is validity—that is, determining whether the conclusion resulting from the propositions necessarily follows.

A bit more detail is helpful for explaining the last criterion before returning to our abortion example. Here is a classic example of a *valid* argument, meaning an argument whose conclusion necessarily follows from its premises (and by "necessarily" I mean that our mind cannot conceive of another possibility, in the same way that, logically, our mind cannot conceive of 0 + 0 equaling anything other than 0):

Premise 1: All humans are mortal.

Premise 2: Matthew is a human.

Conclusion: Therefore, Matthew is mortal.

This is a *valid* argument; the conclusion necessarily follows from the premises. Here, however, is an example of an *invalid* argument:

Premise 1: All humans are mortal.

Premise 2: Matthew is a human.

Conclusion: Therefore, Matthew is worthy of respect.

Note that despite the fact that each proposition in this argument is true and, at least for the sake of illustration, there is no ambiguity in the terms, this second argument is *invalid*—the conclusion does not necessarily follow from the premises. Indeed, we could call it a *non sequitur* (Latin for "it does not follow"). There is nothing about the propositions in and of themselves that logically leads to the conclusion about humanity conferring "respect" on any given human, including "Matthew." We would need additional premises, additional propositions, to establish that causal relationship validly. Invalid arguments, logically speaking, are indistinguishable from nonsense.

There's one more block to lay in the foundation here. An argument being valid in and of itself is not logically sufficient to induce assent (meaning to compel your mind to agree with it) for this reason: An argument can contain both ambiguous terms and contradictory propositions and still be valid. Here's an example drawn from contemporary events:

Premise 1: Violence in service of a good cause is peaceful.

Premise 2: Tearing down the system is a good cause.

Conclusion: Therefore, violence in service of tearing down the system is peaceful.

What? You might say. *This makes no sense.* You're right—it doesn't. Not only does the syllogism contain ambiguous terms (What, for example, do "good cause" and "tearing down" and "system" mean specifically here?), but the first proposition is contradictory: violence, by definition, is *not peaceful*. It may be warranted to claim that violence is necessary to protect or restore peace; however, the claim here is that violence = peace and peace = violence. It is an example of pure sophistry. And yet, the argument remains valid, notwithstanding the problems with the terms and propositions, because the conclusion still follows from the premises.

The point, therefore, is that having a valid argument is a *necessary but insufficient condition* for making a rationally persuasive case. The standard we're ultimately aiming for is called *soundness* in the language of logic. A sound argument is a valid argument that also has true propositions, which, in turn, also have unambiguous terms. And here's the most important takeaway from all these terminological distinctions: If an argument is, indeed, sound, then the human mind cannot rationally account for why it would disagree. In other words, disagreeing with a sound argument is *irrational*. It would be a form of voluntarism (i.e., "I don't believe it because I don't want to believe it").

With all this on the table, let's return to the abortion argument to tie the pieces together and see why understanding the components of an argument matters. The argument, again, is:

Premise 1: It is wrong to kill innocent human life.

Premise 2: Humans in the womb are innocent human life.

Conclusion: Therefore, it is wrong to kill humans in the womb.

Is this a good argument? Is it worthy of rational assent? Let's apply Kreeft's and Fr. Tacelli's tools. First, are the terms clear? It seems so. It's fair to say, I believe, that anyone reading this argument who understands English would have a shared, if basic, comprehension of the definitions of "is-ness," "wrongness," "killing," "innocence," "human-ness," "life," prepositionally being "in" something, and "womb." So, at least in a basic sense, the argument seems to pass the clarity tests. There does not appear to be any significant ambiguity.

How about the propositions? Recall, the criterion of assessment for propositions is truth and falsity. This can be trickier to evaluate because it requires a deeper dive into the grounds and justification not only of "truth" per se but of "moral truth" in particular. Yet we can still make a tentative judgment this way: What are the implications if the claim "It is wrong to kill innocent human life" were *not* true? Applying the logical principles of noncontradiction (something cannot be true and false at the same time in the same way) and the excluded middle (something must be either true or false), it would mean, expressed negatively, that it is *not* wrong to kill innocent human life or, expressed positively, that killing innocent human life is morally acceptable. This is a position someone could take (and some abortion extremists do take); however, it logically commits the person who adopts this view to accepting that human life can justifiably be snuffed out even if the human is innocent—that is, even if, as is implicit in the definition of "innocence," the human is not a threat and has not committed a crime. Even utilitarian philosophers and real-politick just-war theorists who argue that the killing of innocent life may sometimes be justified in order to save other innocent lives (which is not the Catholic position, it is important to stress) still recognize the truth of the general moral principle "killing innocent human life is wrong." Indeed, it is this principle, they would argue, that supplies the exception to the general moral rule itself (i.e., they recognize there are exceptions to the immorality of killing innocent human life in order to protect innocent human life). Rejecting the truth of the premise "It is wrong to kill innocent human life" is thus extremist, to say the least. Consequently, the truth of the first premise is at least rationally plausible.

How about the second premise—"Humans in the womb are innocent life"? Is this premise true or false? Again, the assessment can get complex because of the difficulty of identifying and justi-fying the grounding of moral truth. But we can make a tentative judgment here as well. To say that the proposition "Humans in the womb are innocent human life" is *false* would require denying one or more of the following: (1) humans in the womb are, in fact, human (if not human, what are they?), (2) humans in the womb are, in fact, "life" (if they are not alive, what could possibly define "life"?), and/or (3) humans in the womb are, in fact, innocent (if not innocent, what could they possibly be guilty of and what human could possibly be categorized as *more* innocent than an unborn child?). Again, we can find people who take these positions, including those who are willing to call unborn babies "parasites" to protest abortion restrictions.[10] However, adopting this viewpoint would entail embracing a radical re-definition of

10. See, for example, Dan MacGuill, "Did Pro-Choice Protesters Carry a Sign that Likened Fetuses to 'Parasites'?" Snopes, June 12, 2019, https://www.snopes.com/fact-check/parasites-rights-abortion-sign/.

basic biology (i.e., life in the womb is not a living human) and morality (life in the womb is not innocent). The second premise thus can also plausibly claim the mantle of being true.

At this point, let's say, for the sake of illustration, it is justified to conclude both that the terms in the propositions are clear (unambiguous) and that the propositions themselves are true. The argument is passing rational muster up to this point. Yet what about the argument's *validity*? Does it necessarily logically follow that if it is wrong to kill innocent human life and if humans in the womb are innocent human life then it is wrong to kill humans in the womb? Although we could again ask deeper philosophical questions about both the nature of logic and why our minds function the way they do, it's not clear how we could reach any other conclusion. By the sheer authority of the rules of rational deduction, denying that the first two premises of the argument lead to the conclusion "It is wrong to kill babies in the womb" would be rationally analogous to denying that $0 + 0 = 0$. To be sure, someone could say that he denies the validity of the argument, just as I could say that I was born without biological parents. Yet—and this sounds revolutionary to contemporary secular culture—*saying* something does not make it so. If an argument is valid, it is valid no matter what we feel about it. And, in the case of this argument, it's not clear how we could rationally conclude that it is not valid.

So let's put it all together: If the terms are clear, the propositions are true, and the relationship between the propositions and the conclusion is valid, what, then, do we have before us? The answer is a *sound argument*—an argument that can only be denied on pain of self-contradiction. *If* I believe that it is wrong to kill innocent human life *and* that humans in the womb are, in fact, innocent human life, *then* I cannot *not* believe—"believe" in the sense of rationally assent to—that it is wrong to kill innocent humans in the womb, which is another way of saying that abortion is wrong.

THE RECALCITRANT WILL CAN'T KILL
THE OBEDIENT MIND

Applying Kreeft's and Fr. Tacelli's principles to the abortion example, even in its highly simplified form, shows the enduring power of rationality to formulate, communicate, and defend a point of view and, conversely, to identify flaws in competing views. One of the "settled truths" of contemporary secular culture is that there is no rational way to settle political questions because "rationality" is subjective and open to infinite interpretations. Yet a quick examination of how it functions in and through the actions of the mind reveals how false this "privatized" definition of rationality is. Reason can, indeed, guide us to common moral principles.

To be sure, we are all tempted to cling to beliefs on the voluntaristic grounds that we want them to be true because they align with our (misdirected) desires. The "dear self" in all of us, as Immanuel Kant called it, is, indeed, a vacillating despot who wants to treat the truth as if it were a lump of wax whose only purpose is to bear our covetous seal, reality be damned. Yet one of the abiding gifts of human nature is that we can never extinguish the light of reason, desperately try as we may. We can bury it under sundry sedimentary layers of (self) deceit, (self) manipulation, (willful) ignorance, sophistical misinformation, propaganda, sloganeering, and the like; we can, to shift the metaphor, blow and blow and blow in frantic attempts to extinguish the flame so that we can finally do whatever the hell we want in the dark, delusionally thinking, like a two-year-old covering his eyes (or Adam and Eve hiding in the garden), that the truth can't see us because we've made ourselves blind. But, in the end, trying to kill reason only reaffirms its invulnerability. Just as the condition for the possibility of telling a lie is the existence of the truth, so too the condition for the possibility of *denying* the existence of reason is the existence of reason itself. To say and understand the words "There is no such thing as rationality" or "Rationality has no authority," we must be eminently rational beings, whether we like it or not.[11]

Kreeft and Tacelli aptly summarize the power of a good rational argument:

> Arguments are like eyes: they see reality. . . . To disagree with the conclusion of any argument, it must be shown that either an ambiguous term or false premise or a logical fallacy exists in that argument. Otherwise, to say "I still disagree" is to say "You have proved your conclusion true, but I am so stubborn and foolish that I will not accept this truth. I insist on living in a false world, not a true one."[12]

Avoiding living in a false world may sound academic and detached from everyday concerns. But that assessment rapidly changes the moment someone or some group comes along and tries to conscript you into their ideological fantasy. Once you discover they are not going to leave you alone and are intent on you joining their cause (or else), it becomes clear that there are only four options to respond: You can run. You can submit. You can bloody your knuckles. Or you can craft a better argument and make your case boldly.

If the last option sounds awkward and burdensome, consider the alternatives.

11. Put differently, saying, "I don't believe in reason," is analogous to saying, "I don't believe I was born"—in both cases, the condition for the possibility of the statement is the existence of that which the statement is denying.

12. Kreeft and Tacelli, *Handbook of Catholic Apologetics*, 18.

CHAPTER 3

Getting Your Bearings: Locating the Sources of Political Disagreement

Most political conflicts have little to do with politics. They are rooted in more fundamental disputes about moral values, moral knowledge, the definition of the human being, and even metaphysics. Politics, in other words, is inescapably conceptual and theoretical. We may do most of our quarreling downstream in the social and civic floodplains (or, better, swamps), where conflicting worldviews dump out and stagnate, but the *real* source of conflict lies far above in the rarefied mountains of philosophy and theology.

The use or misuse of the word "harm" and its corollary "safety" in contemporary political debates illustrates this point. Positions broadly associated with the progressive left in the United States are increasingly appealing to "harm avoidance" as a reason, if not *the* reason, to justify their positions on diverse policies, especially those related to race, gender, sexual behavior, and, increasingly, free speech. Once again, we can simplify the issue by breaking it down into syllogisms. Here is an argument related to "harm" and "safety" advanced by political progressives:

> Premise 1: Governments have a duty to protect their citizens from harm.

Premise 2: Protecting citizens from harm requires keeping them safe.

Premise 3: Some points of view make some citizens feel unsafe.

Conclusion: Therefore, governments have the duty to protect some citizens from some points of view.

We could also construct a similar syllogism using gender identity ideology:

Premise 1: Governments have a duty to protect their citizens from harm.

Premise 2: Protecting citizens from harm requires keeping them safe.

Premise 3: Being called the "incorrect" pronoun makes some citizens feel unsafe.

Conclusion: Therefore, governments have a duty to protect some citizens from being called the "incorrect" pronoun.

These are simplified versions of the arguments, of course, and there are other syllogisms with other terms and propositions that could do the same work (for example, using the language of "rights" or "autonomy" or "self-determination," etc.). But these will serve our purposes for understanding how and why political disagreements have much deeper origins than politics.

The first point to highlight is that both arguments are valid—the conclusion necessarily follows from the premises. Also, political conservatives—or, more broadly, those who disagree that there should be government-imposed limitations on speech or that the government should have the authority to compel speech by mandating "correct" pronouns—would likely *agree* with the first two premises in each argument: (1) Governments have a duty to protect their citizens from harm, and (2) Protecting citizens from harm requires keeping them safe. Indeed, they would likely also agree, from a descriptive perspective (meaning as a description of empirical fact), that some people do, indeed, "feel" unsafe when hearing certain points of view or not being called by the pronoun of their choice. So where, then, is the disagreement? If these are valid arguments, why don't conservatives and progressives unite to declare a right to be shielded from certain points of view and a right to be called whatever pronoun one desires?

The reason is that they fundamentally disagree on the meaning of the *terms* in the propositions and, in turn, the concepts underpinning those different meanings. For progressives in this example, "harm" means whatever makes one *feel* unsafe; for conservatives, "harm" means whatever actually *is* harmful, independently of what one may feel. In other words, the progressives have a *subjective* definition of "harm," while the conservatives have an *objective* definition of harm. For conservatives, the above arguments are valid but not sound, precisely because, for them, there is a false definition of "harm" and, consequently, "safety" at play, which thus generates a false conclusion.

Reaching a consensus on the issues of the regulation of speech and coercive protections for gender identity would thus require first finding common ground on the definition of "harm." Yet how is that possible, given each side's different understandings of the *justification* for their respective definitions? Progressives, in this example, understand "feeling," or, as they often also put it, "lived experience," as the ground for their definition; conservatives understand some version of "objective reality" as the ground for their definition. In other words, what we have here is not really a disagreement about free speech and transgender rights. Rather, we have a disagreement about the basis of moral knowledge, the definition of the human person, and the structure of reality itself. Minimally, even to have hope of settling the debate, the disagreeing parties would have to come to a common answer to the question, "Are one's 'feelings' a sufficient foundation for identifying principles that can be given the force of law?" Otherwise, debating about what specific ways the government should protect its citizens from "harm" is inevitably futile.

YOU ARE HERE

This example indicates how difficult it can be to identify the source of political disagreement, notwithstanding the difficulty of then settling the disagreements. The first response might be, "But that sounds too complicated, especially when there is so much important work to be done to convince others to support my cause." Fair enough—it can, indeed, be complicated. Yet without pinpointing where the conflict originates, there can be no authentic debate; the disagreeing parties will simply be talking (or, more likely, shouting) past each other. Knowing where and why you disagree with your interlocutors is the condition for the possibility of ever reaching an agreement.

But how do we go about doing it? Below are two "maps" designed to help cut through the noise of political conflict and diagnose the source of the dispute on any given issue, big or small. The two maps take different shapes, one in 2D concentric circles, the other in a 3D pyramid. However, they are intended to convey the same information about the conceptual relationships among the different components of moral argumentation. As I tell my students, everyone already knows how these maps work because we appeal to them constantly to make big and small moral decisions in our lives, even if we are not explicitly aware of the fact that we are doing so. Essentially, the maps are putting the natural process of moral reasoning into a visual form; and just like everyone naturally knows how to breathe, everyone—at least everyone who has the capacity to act voluntarily—naturally knows how to perform moral reasoning. Yet, also like breathing, what we already know how to do we can learn how to do better. That's the purpose of the maps below.

Here's the first one:

THINKING IN CIRCLES

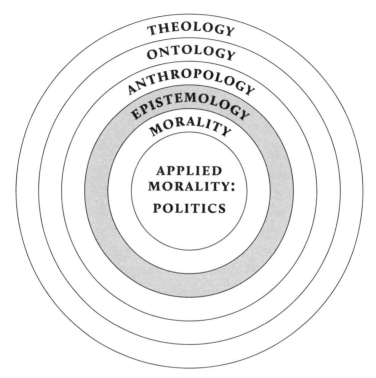

This map is made of concentric circles, with "politics" at its core. The positioning of circles (circles within circles) is meant to communicate relationships of hierarchical contingency or, put differently, what must conceptually exist in order for something else to exist. The closer the circle is to the center of the diagram, the more conceptually dependent it is on the surrounding concepts; conversely, the further out the circle is from the center, the more conceptually foundational it is to the more interior concepts. (Note that "epistemology" is shaded, unlike the other circles. I'll explain why later.)

The terminology corresponding with each circle has a specific definition in this context. The best way to capture the definition of each is to identify what basic question(s) it is seeking to answer:

- **Politics**: How should we civilly apply the true definition of the human good (i.e., what laws and policies should we implement and how should we implement them)?

- **Applied Morality**: How should we implement the true definition of the human good in the different spheres of human life, including individually, in families, socially (civilly and non-civilly), and professionally, among others?

- **Morality**: What is the true nature of the human good?

- **Epistemology** (from the Greek *episteme* meaning "systematic knowledge"): What can human beings know and how can we know it? (This includes knowledge of the human good.)

- **Anthropology** (from the Greek *anthrōpos* meaning "human"): What is the nature of the human being as such (that is, abstracted from individual and social particularities that are incidental to the meaning of "human being")?

- **Ontology** (from the Greek *óntos* meaning "reality"): What is the nature of being, or existence, as such (that is, existence both in its parts and its totality)?

- **Theology** (from the Greek *theós* meaning "God"): What is the nature of ultimate reality, or, put differently, what is the condition for the possibility of existence itself?

We can now get a sense of what the map is conveying. Let me first explain the relationship among the circles by starting in the center and moving outward. "Politics" is an *applied* domain; it is answering the question, "What laws and policies should we implement right here and right now in this particular place?" Formulating and then applying a specific law, whatever it may be, presumes that you already possess a general sense of morality that you wish to enact in the civil domain. Politics is thus one instance of applied morality. Other examples are morality as it pertains to individual behavior, to social organizations, or to a professional arena such as medicine, science, law, etc. However, what unites all instances of applied morality is that they are *applied*, meaning they depend upon a prior, more general conception of the good. For this reason, the circle of "politics" is inside "applied morality" and "applied morality" is inside "morality."

Yet what is "morality"? What is good? What is bad? What should humans do? What should humans avoid doing? What, more broadly, is the purpose of human life? These are all questions embedded within the domain of "morality." The basic insight captured in moving from "politics" to "applied morality" more generally and then to "morality" even more generally is that there is a conceptual hierarchical relationship of contingency already in play: If you don't possess a general moral theory—a comprehensive understanding of the nature of the good—then there is *nothing to apply*, no vision to implement at the applied level, including within the domain of politics. The opposite, it is important to note, is not the case: it is conceptually possible to think about and even define morality without thinking about and defining applied morality. This, again, is why "morality" is more basic, more fundamental, and "wider" than applied morality and, in turn, politics. Politics needs morality to exist in a conceptual sense (that is, to have any content), but morality does not need politics.

At this point, one could object that marking a fine distinction between "morality" and "applied morality" (and, by extension, "politics") is useless academic hairsplitting. Is there really such a significant difference between possessing a moral theory and applying that theory by putting it into practice? Potentially, very much so. Let's say, for example, that you decide at the level of "morality" that your whole moral theory, the theory you employ to organize all of your actions, will be based on a version of the

Golden Rule: "Treat others as you would want to be treated if you were in their shoes." Acting in accordance with this moral principle would thus take the form of sympathetically imagining yourself to be in the circumstances of everyone whom you encounter and acting in accordance with what you would want if you were that person. Simple, right?

Not necessarily. To be sure, the Golden Rule serves as a necessary bulwark against our egotistical tendencies. However, it quickly runs into difficulties when applied to different circumstances. Let's say, for example, that you are a police officer who has just pulled over a vehicle that was swaying from lane to lane. Upon approaching the car, a plume of pungent smoke rushes out of the driver's window. Drawing closer, you see a glass pipe and empty half pint of vodka resting in the passenger seat. The driver's slurred speech, fraternity-floor breath, and bloodshot eyes confirm that the scene is as innocent as it looks. But before instructing the driver to exit the vehicle and put his hands behind his back you suddenly remember, "Ah yes! I am a devotee of the Golden Rule: If I were this man (who has now just vomited on himself), what would I want done unto me?" With a touch of serene self-satisfaction, the conclusion arrives: I would want to continue on my way without getting arrested. And so, in the name of righteous consistency, you let the driver go, offering a friendly wave and "Have a safe drive home!" as the car squeals and lurches back into traffic.

As this example suggests, it's not as easy to apply the Golden Rule as it first appears. To be sure, it's an excellent principle to consult when determining how many slices of pizza you should take from a communal pie, or whether you should leave your garbage bin out on the curb all week, or whether, more seriously, you should engage in wanton gossip. But police officers, prison guards, teachers, pediatricians, and parents, among others, would, in fact, be acting *immorally* if they were to live according to the Golden Rule alone. The point here is that it's one thing to adopt a moral theory and another thing to apply it, and the former does not always clearly indicate how to do the latter. Additional reasoning is usually necessary to move from theory to application. It is for this reason that "morality" and "applied morality" and, even more specifically, "politics" have their own circles.

Now back to the map itself. At this point, we now stand at the level of "morality," asking and seeking to answer fundamental questions about the nature of the human good. However, this set of questions immediately points to a related but conceptually distinct set of questions: How do I know what is good and what is bad? Indeed, how do I know anything at all? These are *epistemological* questions, which point to the next circle moving outward. At the level of epistemology, the same analogous relationship holds between "epistemology" and "morality" as between "morality" and "applied morality": Asking and answering the question "How do I know what I know?" is the condition for the possibility of asking and answering the question "What is the nature of the human good?" It is conceptually impossible to identify and adopt a moral theory (and apply it) without knowing how and why you know that moral theory is, in fact, true. In other words, we can't talk about morality without first talking about epistemology. The opposite, however, is not the case—we can conceptually talk about epistemology without talking about morality. For that reason, morality depends on epistemology, and, therefore, epistemology is "outside," occupying a "bigger circle" than morality.

So, to sum up at this point: We cannot talk about politics without talking about applied morality, because applied morality depends on the existence of morality. Likewise, we cannot talk about morality without talking about epistemology, because morality depends on having knowledge, including (though not limited to) moral knowledge. But it doesn't stop there. The next circle moving outward is "anthropology," which means, conceptually, that anthropology (which answers the question "What is the nature of human existence?"), is the condition for the possibility of doing epistemology. In other words, epistemology depends upon anthropology. Why? Because in order for there to be human knowledge, there must first be a human being who possesses knowledge yet who is not reducible to the knowledge she or he possesses. Moreover, the answer to the question "What is a human being?" is not self-evident. For example, we need to determine whether humans are even capable of ascertaining moral knowledge at all or whether, like animals, we can only reason about the means to pursue goals (like survival and reproduction) but not the goals themselves. A full anthropology also needs to ascertain whether humans are fundamentally individualistic or fundamentally social (and, if both, how the two traits are related); whether we are bellicose or peace loving; egotistical or altruistic; docile or prone to rebellion; lovers of order or lovers of chaos—and, if all of the above, whether our nature also contains the free will to act in accordance with some traits rather than others. All this and more falls within the domain of the anthropological. And if we don't answer the question "What are we?" then we cannot ask and begin to answer the subset question "What can we know?"

The line of questioning doesn't end here, either. For outside of the circle of anthropology lies an even conceptually larger circle, a circle that contains within it all the other circles up to this point. This is the domain of "ontology," the domain that answers the question "What is the nature of existence itself?" Following the same logic, the reason that anthropology is "inside" ontology is because the condition for the possibility of human existence is for there to be an existence as such. Yet what is the nature of that existence? Is it fundamentally chaotic and random in its composition, or is it structured and ordered? Are there objective laws of nature and natural laws, or are those only illusory human social constructions? Is there anything like a hierarchical "chain of being" in which metaphysically "lesser" beings depend upon "higher beings" for their existence? Or is existence ultimately metaphysically "flat"? Is matter all there is? Or are there also non-material substances in existence? If the former, what, if anything, organizes matter and brings about its potentialities? If the latter, what, if anything, governs the relationship between material and non-material being? Etc. In short, since "human existence" is an ontological subset of "existence itself," we cannot say what defines "human beings" if we don't first have some ideas of what defines "being." Thus, ontology contains anthropology.

We're nearly to the outermost ring on the map, but let's briefly retrace how we've gotten this far. In order to identify and implement a law at the level of politics, we first need to have a general understanding of how to apply morality more broadly. Yet in order to apply moral principles at all (including in the domain of the political), we first need an understanding of what defines morality as such, including what defines "good," "bad," "right," and "wrong." Yet in order to define these terms, we first need to determine how we can know anything at all, including how we can have moral knowledge. However, in order to define what we can know, we must first define what "we" means, that is, what it means to be human. And finally, in order to define what "human existence" is, we must first define what existence as such is, because human existence is contingent on existence itself.

This conceptual chain finally points us to the last (or, depending on how you look at it, first) conceptual circle, the circle within which all other circles exist and the condition for the possibility of every other domain of existence: theology. The theological domain seeks to answer the question "What is the nature of the *ground* of all existence?" The difference between ontology and theology can be subtle, but the difference is still important to mark. The theological asks the question, "Is existence itself—the totality of the universe and everything in it—all there is, or is there something metaphysically 'outside' that makes the existence of the universe possible?" In other words, the domain of the theological seeks to answer the question beyond which there is no other question: the question of whether God exists and, if so, what defines God's nature both in itself and in relation to the universe. The question of God is, of course, a philosophical question; yet, insofar as it seeks to formulate an answer to ultimate reality, it escapes strictly rational reflection and, for that reason, falls more broadly into the domain of theology.

Before offering a concrete example to illustrate the map in action, it is important, finally, to explain why only epistemology is shaded among the other circles. To be sure, epistemology conceptually depends upon anthropology, ontology, and theology; likewise, morality and applied morality are conceptually after epistemology. Nevertheless, epistemology has the unique status of serving as the interpretive key that unlocks the content of all the other domains. What can we say about the definition of morality, for example? It depends on what we can know and how we can know it. Yet that's also the case for what we can say about human existence (anthropology), the universe and everything in it (ontology), and the ultimate ground of existence (theology). In short, *the* primordial question in assessing any issue—whether political, moral, epistemological, anthropological, ontological, or theological—is *What is the truth and on what grounds do I believe it to be true?* It is for this reason that epistemology deserves distinctive attention in formulating a viewpoint on politics or anything else. If we are wrong about what we can know and how we can know it, then our understanding of everything will be skewed. Theology may be the most conceptually foundational domain of inquiry, but it, and every other domain, is substantively empty without epistemology. This, once again, points to the importance of putting everything on the table (including the "table itself") when assembling our view of the sum total of reality and how it's all related—which, in turn, is a reminder not to pit reason and faith against each other.

MOVING INSIDE OUT

The domains of inquiry and the relationship among these circles can be challenging to grasp in the abstract, so let me offer a concrete example of how the map works in action. I'll start with an example moving from the "inside out" and then offer one from the obverse perspective, moving from the "outside in."

Let's say, for example, that a hypothetical "you" is a free speech supporter who is advocating for the passage of a law that protects employees from being fired for speech they engage in while not at work. Let's call it the "Free Speech Job Protection Act," or the FSJPA. This proposed law would fit in the center of the map's "politics" domain. The first question to ask, however, is *why* you believe passing this law is a good thing to do. One obvious answer is that you believe that a right to free speech is good, and because you believe this, you believe individuals should be protected from losing their livelihoods on account of saying what they believe. In other words, you are applying the moral belief "Free speech is good" to a civil context, which means you have already moved conceptually "outward" in the justification of your political beliefs into the territory of applied morality. Note, here, that the political domain is only one of many applied domains in which the belief "Free speech is good" could be put into practice; it could also be applied in the private domain of your personal life, in social settings, or in the professional domain by advocating for free speech policies in a career field (say, medicine, law, entertainment). The point is that all these examples are applied; the fundamental question is one of implementation ("How do I put my belief about free speech into action most effectively?").

The next question to ask, however, is "*Why* do I believe that free speech is good?" This question pushes you further outward into the larger circle of "morality"; the question here is not fundamentally about implementation but rather *justification*, and, in particular, justification in relation to a hierarchy of values. The question of why you believe free speech is good opens many related questions. What else do you believe is good, and why? What, if anything, is more important than free speech in your hierarchy of values? For example, if you had to choose between free speech and a society in which pornography would be prohibited, which would you choose and why? Or between free speech and national security? Or between free speech and permitting the existence of extremist groups? Or between free speech and intellectual property rights? In thinking through these and related questions, you will develop a moral theory that enables you to weigh competing goods—or, at least, goods in tension—and put them into what you take to be the correct value ordering.

Let's say, then, in going through this process of rational refinement, you come to the conclusion that your foundational moral value is something along the lines of "equal human dignity," which is an intrinsic good that supersedes all other values because it is the ground of all other values. "All humans have a right to free speech," you tell yourself (and others), "because all humans have equal dignity; and having the right to speak your beliefs is a necessary implication of having human dignity, which, in turn, means that no institution, whether public or private, can punish you for exercising that right." In other words, the thinking goes:

- Possessing dignity is the most foundational good.

- That foundational good (human dignity) includes the derivative good of having a right to free speech.

- The derivative good of having a right to free speech includes the derivative good of being able to speak your mind off the job without the fear of getting fired.

This chain of reasoning has already reached significant conceptual depth. You are now at the heart of the domain of "morality" in the conceptual map, and from that heart you are explaining how and why you act on your moral beliefs at the level of applied morality and, ultimately, politics.

But here's the question you have to ask yourself now: How do I *know* that human beings have equal dignity and, in particular, dignity that justifies the right to freedom of speech? Welcome to the domain of the epistemological. Things get especially complicated here. For example, as noted in the introduction, it's not self-evident how to justify a belief in universally equal dignity. Scientific or empirical observation can't do it alone, nor can a non-theistic rationalism (for example, like we see in Immanuel Kant). Sources of revelation like the Bible can certainly contribute, though they, too, will need epistemic validation. Let's say, therefore, that after thinking the question through you come to the conclusion that you know (that is, you have justified reason to believe) that humans have equal dignity because you believe that it is possible to discern, based on all sources of evidence available, that human beings have an eternal soul in addition to a body. By virtue of the unity of body and soul, you thus tell yourself (and others), humanity as a whole and human individuals in particular have irreducible and equal dignity; this dignity, in turn, invests human beings with certain rights, one of which is the right to speak one's beliefs without fear of pecuniary reprisal.

This epistemic conclusion, however, already points to the next rung outward: the domain of the anthropological. First, believing humans have souls implies that humans actually *have* souls. That is a foundational anthropological claim. There are additional anthropological claims embedded in the chain of reasoning thus far as well. To say humans have a right to free speech, for example, implies that humans have the capacity to speak freely, which, in turn, implies that humans have some degree of free will. That, too, is a foundational anthropological claim. Moreover, the definition of humanity as a unity of body and soul implies that humans are rational beings insofar as the definition implies that it is possible for humans to know their true nature. Moreover, the affirmation that we have both dignity and, derivatively, rights implies two additional characteristics of human nature: On the one hand, having dignity implies that we have inherent worth, which, in turn, implies that we are inherently good; yet, on the other hand, saying that we have rights implies that we need rights, which, in turn, implies that human dignity needs protection from those who might violate those rights—all of which means that we are also something less than fully good (that is, that we are fallen). In short, the moral and epistemic theories, up to this point in the chain of reasoning, presuppose a complex anthropological theory as well—a theory that must be true in order for the epistemic and moral theories to be true.

Yet how is it possible for a human being so defined to exist? What must first exist? You have now pushed into the ontological domain of inquiry. And just as your epistemology contains necessary anthropological presuppositions, your anthropology will contain necessary ontological presuppositions. For example, to affirm that human beings have souls is to affirm the existence of at least one non-material substance in reality. Yet where does that substance come from? Could human souls be sui generis (that is, could they originate from themselves)? It's not clear how that could be the case, for it's not clear how anything in the universe can create itself in an absolute sense. The immaterial soul, then, must come from something that is not only metaphysically "outside" the human soul but is both immaterial itself and capable of creating new immaterial substances. Moreover, because, at the anthropological and epistemological levels, you have affirmed that human beings are both good and rational, the same metaphysical reasoning—that humans are not self-creating—implies that "the good" and "the true" are not confined to or derived from human beings but are rather "out there" in existence. In other words, in order to support your views at the anthropological level, you must also affirm that objective truth and objective goodness exist metaphysically independent of human beings.

There is, however, a final circle of analysis to address. It's one thing to have a comprehensive definition of reality as such. It's another to have an explanation, a "how" and a "why" for how reality, so defined, both can and does exist. This question pushes past ontology to the domain of the theological, the domain that seeks to answer the greatest, most comprehensive, most "meta" question possible: the question of God's existence, nature, and relationship to the universe. To be sure, operating in this domain includes the use of philosophical modes of knowing, those that we might term as strictly "rational." However, insofar as God, even abstractly defined, cannot be limited to what is accessible to our rational capacities alone, every resource is on the table, insofar as the object of understanding is the condition for the possibility of existence itself.

Let's say, therefore, that because you have adopted a vision of material and immaterial reality that is structured, ordered, intelligible, and contains moral objectivity, you eventually reach the conclusion, based on extensive reading in philosophy, theology (especially Scripture), the sciences, and even art and literature, that the best explanation for the sum total of reality is to affirm the existence of a transcendent God who has created the universe and everything in it, including humans who have the unique nature of being a unity of body and soul. In other words, to sum it all up, the reason that you ultimately believe in the Free Speech Job Protection Act is *because you believe in God.*

Expressed this way, the connection between the practical (advocating for the passage of the FSJPA) and the theoretical (believing God exists) may sound absurdly, even comically, stretched. Yet bridging the two beliefs—indeed, showing that there is ultimately no disconnect between the theoretical and the practical—is precisely the purpose of the conceptual map. Let me try to drive home the point by summarizing the "inside out" reasoning one final time:

- Hypothetical "you" supports the FSJPA.

- Yet in order to explain why you support the law, you have to explain why you think that this specific civil application of your understanding of morality is, in fact, good.

- Yet in order to explain why you think this application of your understanding of morality is good, you have to explain both what defines your comprehensive moral framework (including your hierarchy of values) and why you believe that moral framework to be worthy of believing in and acting on.

- Yet in order to explain why your moral framework is worthy of believing in and acting on, you must explain how and why you know that your moral framework is true, and—especially since you are advocating for a public policy—not just "true for you" but true for everyone, that is, objectively true.

- Yet in order to explain how it is possible for you to both know objective truth and be able to implement that truth through action, you must be able to explain what it is about human nature that makes it possible to both know objective truth and act on it.

- Yet in order to explain how it is possible for humans to exist as you have described them (rational and capable of free, good action), you must be able to explain what it is about existence itself that makes it possible for humans to exist in this way.

- Yet, finally, in order to explain what makes it possible for reality to exist as you have described it, you must be able to explain what the condition for the possibility of such existence is—in other words, you must ask and answer the question of God.

It is important to stress that the conceptual map does not by itself give you the right answers to the questions in each domain of inquiry. The map also does not serve as an argument for demonstrating God's existence (though, as we'll see below, it can be helpful for identifying the implications of believing in God or not). Moreover, the chain of reasoning "you" used in the above example could very well have been different. Another "you" could potentially reach significantly different conclusions about the nature of morality, knowledge, humanity, existence, and God. In other words, the answers to the questions that each domain asks can and do vary substantially, even radically, from person to person and from group to group—which, as we'll see later, is why there are substantial, even irreconcilable, differences among political ideologies.

Yet while the answers to the questions in the domains of inquiry can and do change, it is important to remember this: the domains of inquiry themselves, and the conceptual relationships among them, remain the same. No matter what the content of a belief system is, it always contains a conceptual hierarchy, and not just any conceptual hierarchy but one that takes the form of concentric circles that the map represents. Before moving on to illustrate how the map can also work from the "outside in" (and why all of this matters for engaging in political arguments), here is another illustration that communicates the same conceptual information as the concentric circle map in a 3D pyramidal format:

Politics:
How should we implement the definition of the human good civically?

Applied Morality:
How should we implement the definition of the human good?

Morality:
What is the nature of the human good?

Epistemology:
What is the nature of human knowing?

Anthropology:
What is the nature of human existence?

Ontology:
What is the nature of existence itself?

Theology:
What is the nature of the ground of all existence?

Seen from this perspective, and applying a bit of "gravity" to the model, we can once again see how the concepts relate to each other hierarchically. Imagine it as a conceptual skyscraper: If you were to pull out one of the "floors," everything above it would collapse while everything below it would stay intact. So, for example, we could pull out morality and, though applied morality and politics would collapse (they would lose their foundation), epistemology and everything below it would remain in place, conceptually unperturbed. So too, pulling out anthropology: Removing human beings would remove human knowledge, the human good, and the applied human good, but the universe (ontology) would presumably continue to get along just fine. The same conceptual logic explains why theology lies at the bottom of it all. If we take that away—if we have no ultimate explanation, at least tentatively, for how and why existence is the way we discern it to be—then everything tumbles into a nihilistic abyss. Or to return to the initial simile, trying to build a theory that explains what you believe about existence, humanity, knowledge, and morality without a theological foundation is like trying to construct a skyscraper out of thin air atop thin air.

OUTSIDE IN

The Free Speech Job Protection Act example sought to illustrate how starting with the question of how to justify a political position necessarily leads to ever-deepening moral, epistemological, anthropological, ontological, and theological questions. From this "inside out" perspective, it becomes evident that every political issue is, ultimately, grounded in a comprehensive view of reality. Yet we can also use the map to see the reverse—that is, that every comprehensive view of reality necessarily has political implications—by starting at the outside and moving inward (or, with the pyramid model, starting at the bottom and moving upward).

Let's say, for example, that you decide to be a consistent atheist who, like the man in Friedrich Nietzsche's famous anti-parable "The Parable of the Madman," chooses to believe in and live according to all the implications of denying God's existence. Along the contours of the outermost circle, theology, you thus mark a dark dot and write next to it, "There is no God" (or as Nietzsche famously puts it, "God is dead."). That is your final answer to the theological question.

Yet given that you believe that statement to be true, what then are the ontological implications? What must be true about the universe and everything in it? Minimally, you would have to embrace some form of materialism, or the view that matter is all that exists (meaning there is no such thing as immaterial or spiritual reality). You would also have to abandon the idea that there is any meaningful order, structure, or purpose in existence; any patterns that you might think you detect may or may not be there (they might just be the sheer invention of the human mind seeking to impose order on an otherwise chaotic existence), but, either way, you would have to understand the patterns as accidental and arbitrary both in origin and in movement. Finally, believing in anything resembling moral objectivity or moral realism would certainly be prohibited, because goodness could not exist in the universe beyond haphazard human invention.

If, in turn, all this is ontologically true about the nature of existence, what must consequently be true about human existence in particular? First, you would have to conclude that human life has no more value than a bacterium or virus. Human beings have no special place in the universe because nothing has a special place in the universe. Likewise, you would have to discard the existence of an immaterial soul or even consciousness because, you believe, only material things exist and there is no such thing as a "consciousness" particle. The same goes for free will: free will is not stuff or even a collection of different stuff, and, thus, you would have no reason to affirm its existence (despite the fact that you presumably chose to become an atheist). Moreover, the meaning of the life of any given individual or any given people, culture, nation, or history would drown in the indiscriminate cosmic wash. Sure, you and/or some group could exercise "power" (assuming you could justify a stable definition of what power is within this framework), but all use of power, no matter what its purported goal, would be equally arbitrary, equally nonsensical. Life and death, for humanity and for everything else, would be morally indistinguishable.

If all this is true about human existence, what, then, defines human knowledge? When honest with itself, atheistic epistemology can only apprehend one truth no matter what methodology it embraces: there is no truth. Every discovery, every "break-through," every paradigm shift is merely another permutation of the primordial conclusion that there is, in the end, nothing to say but that there is nothing to say. Indeed, pushed to its logical limits, it's not clear how even science can withstand atheistic rational scrutiny. Science presupposes that the universe is intelligible, that it contains fixed patterns that make systematic observation and the conclusions we infer from it reliable (that is, "real" in some non-imaginary sense). However, if there is no reason to believe that there is an *intelligence* that makes the universe *intelligible*, then that intelligibility, too, dissolves into cosmic dust, as does the language we use to seek to understand and act in relation to the universe. Moreover, the materialism inherent within atheistic epistemology means that, properly speaking, we can only know "stuff." But "science" is not a "stuff," and so it's not clear what rational authority it could hold. Indeed, it's not clear how you, or anyone else, could know anything at all.[1]

This epistemic darkness will (again, if you are consistent) also swallow up the domains of morality and applied morality. Drawing on Nietzsche again, there is no good and evil in human life in the absence of an objective good, a conclusion he unpacks in his book *Beyond Good and Evil*. The base philosophical insight in the text is that there is no "good" and "evil" in existence— that is, neither good nor evil objectively exist. Consequently, humans must look beyond these false categories to create their

---

1. Nietzsche is, perhaps, the most consistent atheist to have ever lived, but even he doesn't seem willing to accept these epistemic implications. His madman tells the amazed onlookers, those who are not yet ready to accept the consequences of their unbelief, "must not lanterns be lit in the morning?" His point is that now that God is dead (meaning that, in his view, modernity has finally killed off the false idea of God's existence), human beings must be willing to create their own light and light their own path in the existential darkness. That may sound poetically noble, but it's actually an act of philosophical cowardice, which Nietzsche otherwise usually avoids. The truth is that if there is no God then there is no light anywhere, including in human beings, to kindle the fire of rational reflection; there is nothing to light your lamp with. It is all darkness all the time, and the best the human mind can do is slip deeper and deeper into the abyss.

own purpose in existence. Nietzsche's examination of what it means to live "beyond morality" is complex, richly so. Yet the basic conclusion is that those who are strong enough to do so (and most aren't) should become an *Übermensch* or "great man" who employs his will to power to create something new, no matter what the cost to himself and others. Despite many contemporary atheists extolling the virtues of "secular humanism," living according to atheistic morality means doing whatever you want to do (assuming you actually know what you want to do, which atheism actually makes figuring out difficult to do) if you calculate you can get away with it. It was the utilitarian Jeremy Bentham who famously called human rights "nonsense on stilts" (more on that in a later chapter). But, following the logic of atheism, it's not just rights that you would believe are nonsense—it's morality itself.

To complete the chain of reasoning, you, the hypothetical consistent atheist, would finally have to conclude that since no objective moral principles exist in the domain of morality, then there is, ultimately, *nothing to apply* in the domain of applied morality. Every action, including actions in the domain of the political, is equally arbitrary, and, consequently, your support of this law or that law, this candidate or that candidate, this policy proposal or that policy proposal, is rationally analogous to picking marbles out of a jar while blindfolded—whatever you choose you choose, but there's no *reason* you chose one over another beyond sheer chance.

In sum, this "outside in" example is meant to illustrate how adopting a belief at one level of the conceptual circle has necessary implications for the beliefs you can consistently adopt in the smaller circles. In this case, if you adopt the belief "There is no God" in the theological domain, then every other domain of inquiry must reflect the consequences of that belief. The basic pattern of reasoning goes like this: Given that I believe this is true, what must therefore also be true? This is the mirror image of the chain of reasoning at play in the previous "inside out" example, which is "What must be true in order for this to be true?" Again, the map, either in its circular or pyramidal form, cannot tell you what is true within any given domain of inquiry. However, it can serve as a guide to determining what the relationships among beliefs are, starting at the center (or top), the outside (or bottom), or anywhere in between.

FULL CIRCLE—HOW TO USE THE MAP IN DEBATE

At the beginning of this chapter, I used the example of free speech as it relates to the definition of "harm" to introduce how political disputes often have their roots in much deeper disagreements about the nature of morality, knowledge, the human person, reality, etc. Hopefully, it is now clearer how the conceptual map can both help identify the true source of these disagreements and serve as a tool for reaching possible consensus. More specifically, employing the map to analyze competing positions reveals that what people believe politically is often inconsistent with beliefs they hold in the more fundamental domains of inquiry. For instance, drawing on the above atheist example, if someone says "I don't believe in God" and "You are a bad person if you vote for

_____ for president," then that person is being inconsistent with his own beliefs (his theological position contradicts his political position). Likewise, if someone says "I only believe in what science can tell us" and "Voter ID laws are unjust," then that person, too, is being inconsistent with her beliefs (her scientistic epistemology cannot coherently support her applied moral conclusion). Or if someone says "I believe humans are merely a collection of random molecules" and "I believe all people should be treated according to their inherent equal moral worth," then that person, too, is being inconsistent (his anthropology cannot account for his morality because molecules cannot coherently account for the existence of moral equality).

Consistency testing, in short, is an indispensable tool in political debate. It equips you to ask your interlocutor not only "Is what you are saying *true?*" but also "Is what you are saying *consistent* with your other beliefs?"[2] If, in utilizing the conceptual map, you can find either untrue statements or inconsistent reasoning in your interlocutor's positions, then you have opened up fertile ground for facilitating a change of mind (and, perhaps, heart). This can happen, for example, when someone who really wants to believe in her cause of, say, making clean drinking water accessible for every child, realizes, in trying to persuade others to support her cause, that she must tell them that providing drinking water for all children is really and truly *good*, and that, in order for it to be really and truly good, there must exist some form of objective morality. And in order for there to exist some form of objective morality, there must be . . .

You get the idea.

The desire to be authentically and consistently moral (in addition to the desire to be seen as moral) lies deep within the human heart. Showing others what must be true in order for their moral beliefs to be true opens up ever-fresh possibilities for constructive engagement between people who might, in fact, be able to reach an agreement if they could just figure out why they are disagreeing in the first place. Likewise, pointing out to others that their political views have the same rational consistency as a two-year-old "arguing" his case by thrashing on a grocery store floor exposes intellectual fraud. In short, using the map to engage in political debate doesn't just help you find heretofore hidden moral and political allies;[3] equally important, it identifies those who have no interest in holding intellectually consistent and, even less, true beliefs—those otherwise known as bullies and tyrants.

2. Note, here, the overlap with the anatomy of argument from the previous chapter; making a sound argument requires both true premises and consistency between the premises and the conclusion.

3. It is important to note that the only durable form of consensus is consensus based on *principle*. People of different ideological stripes may happen to agree on a particular policy from time to time, which is great as far as it goes. Yet unless there is work to attain consensus at the deeper levels of morality and political principle, that consensus will always be fragile and temporary.

CHAPTER 4

From How to Debate to What to Say: The Comprehensive Toolbox of Catholic Social Thought

Up to this point, we've been examining how to formulate and assess arguments. Hopefully, it has become clear how these methodological tools can assist you in both developing your own comprehensive and internally consistent vision of reality, including moral reality, and comprehending and critiquing competing visions. However, knowing how to develop and evaluate an argument, though necessary, is not sufficient for effectively engaging in political debate. You must know what to say, as well, what positions to propose and to defend in the marketplace of ideas. The Catholic social thought tradition supplies this "what" in spades.

This extended chapter identifies, explains, and advocates for the fundamental principles in Catholic social thought, those that are essential to understanding the comprehensive Catholic view of the nature and purpose of the sociopolitical order. It is important to note upfront that there is an extended conversation within Catholic intellectual circles about what precisely defines the tradition and when it begins. The discussion can indeed get complex, but the short answer is that the tradition, which is as old as the Church herself, is defined by *all* of the Church's teachings that have sociopolitical relevance. That said, most scholars, including those working within the Magisterium of the Church (the official, irreducibly authoritative promulgator of the Church's teachings on faith and morals), recognize Pope Leo XIII's 1891 encyclical *Rerum Novarum* ("On New Things"), which laid out the Church's position on the relationship between capital and labor, as marking the modern "beginning" of what would later be identified as the "social thought tradition." The *Compendium of the Social Doctrine of the Church*, published by the Vatican's Pontifical Council for Justice and Peace, explains the origins of Catholic social thought in *Rerum Novarum* and its development in successive generations this way:

> The term "social doctrine" goes back to Pope Pius XI and designates the doctrinal "corpus" concerning issues relevant to society which, from the Encyclical Letter *Rerum Novarum* of Pope Leo XIII, developed in the Church through the Magisterium of Roman Pontiffs and the Bishops in communion with them. The Church's concern for social matters certainly did not begin with that document, for the Church never failed to show interest in society. Nonetheless, the Encyclical letter *Rerum Novarum* marks the beginning of a new path. Grafting itself onto a tradition hundreds of years old, it signals a new beginning and singular development of the Church's teaching in the area of social matters.[1]

Bishop Robert Barron, whose Word on Fire apostolate has published the *Catholic Social Teaching Collection*, also locates the foundations of social thought in *Rerum Novarum* and subsequent papal encyclicals. He additionally emphasizes that the tradition's roots reach not only into Scripture and the Church Fathers but also into the teachings and biographies of the Church's saints,

---

1. *Compendium of the Social Doctrine of the Church* 39.

doctors, and moral exemplars, including St. Thomas Aquinas, Bartolomé de las Casas, St. Peter Claver, St. Vincent de Paul, St. Damien of Molokai, Servant of God Dorothy Day, St. Teresa of Kolkata, and St. Óscar Romero, among others.[2]

The social thought tradition has a rich, variegated, and internally complex character indeed. However, this chapter's focus is to distill the tradition's most basic principles and to illustrate how they can serve as intellectually and morally potent tools in defining and defending the Catholic view of the nature and purpose of politics. The organization of the arguments below takes the form of identifying a basic problem that all political philosophies must address and then showing how the Catholic social thought tradition provides the most persuasive response. These include (1) the problem of moral foundations (which includes the problem of truth), (2) the problem of defining and building the "perfect" society, (3) the problem of defining and defending human dignity, (4) the problem of building moral hierarchies, and (5) the problem of free speech. In the final section, the chapter briefly highlights Pope St. John Paul II, who provides a distinctively compelling embodiment of the principles of Catholic social thought in action.

Let's turn, then, to the first and, perhaps, most difficult problem Catholic social thought confronts: the problem of truth.

NOTHING BUT THE TRUTH: THE PROBLEM OF MORAL FOUNDATIONS

Tell me if this sounds familiar. A politician gets up before a crowd of admirers and delivers the following lines or a variation of them (and feel free to choose your own folksy accent): "Look, I'm here to solve problems, not to engage in partisan bickering. I'm here to make the changes we need to move forward, not to waste your time fighting about who's right and who's wrong. I'm here to tell

2. See *Catholic Social Teaching Collection*, ed. Matthew Becklo and Daniel Seseske (Park Ridge, IL: Word on Fire Classics, 2020).

you that the only thing I care about is getting results—results for *you*, the American people, folks just like me, interested in progress, not in cross-aisle squabbles."

This "aw shucks" ploy to portray oneself as "above the fray" may sound like just another superficial (and smarmy) ploy to win votes, but it actually reflects a school of thought that, historically, has been profoundly influential in American social philosophy: pragmatism. Like all philosophical schools, pragmatism is internally complex and requires serious engagement to understand and evaluate its nuances. However, its basic premise is this: The way to solve moral and political disputes in society is to dispense with the question of truth and, in its place, pursue the path of what is useful, defined as what most effectively leads to societal progress. Hence the name "pragmatism," which we also see captured in the colloquial meaning of the word "pragmatic": just do what you need to do to get things done.

Pragmatism is a seductive ideology; especially in times of intense political and social conflict, it can sound like a siren-song solution to break the deadlock, which is one of the reasons politicians are wont to embrace it when they find it, well, pragmatic to do so. Talk of "usefulness" and "progress" sounds much more palatable than talk of "truth" or "rightness," especially to a secular population that is highly suspicious of speech about morality.

So why don't we all just agree to be pragmatists, to set aside our differences and work together for a better future? The problem is that pragmatism is both self-defeating and empty of any substantive content, and the reason is precisely because it avoids the question of truth. Think of it this way: The pragmatist says we should pursue what is useful rather than what is good because we cannot find any consensus on what is good. "Sounds nice," we say in response. "But what does 'useful' mean?" "What is useful," the pragmatist replies, "is that which is conducive to societal progress." "Fantastic!" we say. "But how do we define progress?"

"Ah, easy," replies the pragmatist. "Progress is that which we achieve when we act pragmatically."

The problem, as seen here, is that the argument for pragmatism is ultimately circular—in trying to define it, we end up right back where we started, not having clarified anything along the way. Put more directly, pragmatism cannot provide an answer to what progress is without appealing to what is useful; and it cannot define what is useful without appealing to what is good; and it cannot appeal to what is good without appealing to what is true. In other words, pragmatism cleverly thinks that it can propel human beings forward by sidestepping the question of truth, when in reality it's like a car accelerating on a treadmill, revving its intellectual engine as it stays perennially stuck in the same place.

That's the first point to emphasize in addressing the problem of moral foundations in sociopolitical discourse: despite what any honey-mouthed politician may say, there is no escaping the question of truth when it comes to identifying and living according to moral principles. The question at hand, then, is not *whether* we speak about pursuing truth when talking about politics but rather *which form of truth* we embrace. Let's turn to that question now.

Generalizations must always be made with caution, but, as we'll see in greater depth in part II of this book, most political ideologies, despite their vast differences, fall within two broad epistemological camps—that is, two schools of thought on how to identify moral truths. These, in turn, become the respective foundations for their different views of politics. We can call one "materialistic empiricism" and the other "transcendental rationalism"—which, it is important to note, is different than *transcendent* rationalism. People ranging from David Hume to Jeremy Bentham to Karl Marx to animal rights philosopher Peter Singer fall into the first category; people like Immanuel Kant, John Rawls, and perhaps the contemporary cultural commentator Ben

Shapiro are in the second category. Materialistic empiricism is generally tied to forms of utilitarianism or majoritarian ethics; transcendental rationalism, in contrast, is generally tied to different forms of classical liberalism and libertarianism. There is also a third epistemic alternative, which I'll explain in more detail below; we can call it transcendent moral realism, and that's what lies at the heart of Catholic social thought.

A quote from the Scottish Enlightenment philosopher David Hume aptly captures the nature of the first epistemological option, materialist empiricism. Hume ends his watershed 1748 treatise *An Enquiry Concerning Human Understanding* bombastically declaring,

> If we take in our hand any [book]; of divinity or school metaphysics, for instance; let us ask, does it contain any abstract reasoning concerning quantity or number? No. Does it contain any experimental reasoning concerning matter of fact and existence? No. Commit it then to the flames: for it can contain nothing but sophistry and illusion.[3]

By my lights, there is no better summation of materialist empiricism than these lines. If you can't see it, if you can't sniff it, or taste it, or rub it between your fingers—if you can't measure and experiment on it—then you can't really know it. And if you can't really know it, *burn it.* So what exactly should get torched according to Hume and Hume's legacy? All metaphysical inquiry into the nature of existence, including the existence and nature of God and all forms of morality that find their origin in this, must go. That basically leaves us with science and math, or, in contemporary terms, STEM, to do our thinking about reality and morality. We might call this Hume's bonfire of the humanities.

---

3. David Hume, *An Enquiry Concerning Human Understanding* (London: J.B. Bebbington, 1861), 120.

Hume's intellectual legacy is formidable and his contribution to the history of philosophy undeniable, something we will explore in greater depth in part II of the book. Yet there are two fundamental problems with his epistemology and the materialist empiricism standard of truth more broadly. First, like pragmatism, it cannot give an account of its own foundational principles, or, put differently, it assumes rather than demonstrates the truth of its most basic claim—namely, that only empirical knowledge is true knowledge. In this way, it traps itself in a vicious circularity: How do we know both that empirical knowledge is true and that *only* empirical knowledge is true from this point of view? By conducting empirical analysis. See the problem? As noted earlier, that's akin to saying you are going to conduct a scientific experiment to determine whether scientific experiments produce true knowledge, in which case you are using the tool you are testing to determine if the tool itself works. Despite Hume's supreme confidence in this theory, this is not a stable way to establish confidence in the validity of one's beliefs.

For our purposes—examining the foundations of morality, especially as it relates to politics—materialist empiricism has an even bigger problem: it cannot produce a prescriptive morality, meaning, it cannot tell us what we should and shouldn't do. Describing reality using only the empirical method can only tell us what *does* happen in the world, not what *should* happen. The reason is because it cannot establish rational necessity in existence, which means there are no possible moral contradictions from a materialist empiricist point of view. So, we might observe, for example, that humans tend to seek pleasure and avoid pain; however, there are plenty of people who seek pain and eschew pleasure or, even, seek pain as a kind of pleasure. We might also observe that most people are peaceful most of the time, but that observation, of course, has incalculable exceptions. Likewise, we might observe that most people are willing to sacrifice some degree of personal freedom for societal peace; however, not

everyone is. The problem with empiricism, in other words, is
that it cannot tell us which of these descriptive observations
about human beings is the better (meaning *truer*) way to be
human, because it has no fixed, rationally necessary standard
of comparison. Whatever humans do is, by definition, "human
behavior" from an empirical point of view; therefore, there is no
mechanism for distinguishing what we *do* do from what we *should*
do—no way, put more starkly, to morally differentiate between
Stalin and Mother Teresa. In short, empiricism can't coherently
provide the grounds for any political principles because it doesn't
have the intellectual resources to establish any moral principles
in the first place.

These weaknesses in materialist empiricism were not lost on
the Enlightenment philosopher Immanuel Kant, a great admirer
of Hume but also one of his greatest critics. Even more so than
Hume, Kant's philosophy is profoundly complex and has had an
indelible influence on the history of ideas, including political philosophy. Kant rejected empiricism as a reliable epistemic ground
and turned instead to *transcendental rationalism*. Rather than
acquiring knowledge from the senses, transcendental rationalism
examines the conditions for the possibility of knowing anything
at all, including knowledge from the senses. This marks Kant's
famous turn to the subjectivity of the individual as the source
of both knowledge and reality, which has been called Kant's
Copernican revolution in philosophy.

The inner workings of Kant's argument are some of the
densest and most intricate in philosophy, but his basic insight
is that there are certain principles that the human mind cannot
not know and that these principles form the basis of a shared
epistemic and moral human reality. Kant's most famous ethical
principle, derived from this conception of rationality, takes the
form of the categorical imperative. Translated into contemporary
language, it states, "Treat every single person, including yourself,
as an autonomous individual capable of directing and guiding his

or her own life." Although Kant didn't use these specific terms, the ideas they contain establish the foundation of classical liberalism and libertarianism, which we will also examine in greater depth in part II of the book. Basically, this branch of political philosophy maintains that individuals reign supreme in society and that all people should be able to pursue any definition of the good they desire so long as they do not violate the rights of others in the process of doing so.

Kant certainly deserves his place in the pantheon of great thinkers. However, without detracting from his brilliance, his work reinvents a moral wheel that has existed, at least in latent form, within Catholic social thought from its inception—namely, the idea that human beings are irreducibly valuable and, therefore, cannot be treated as if they were not. I'll develop this theme more in a subsequent section, but here let me note three problems with the Kantian transcendental rationalist epistemology before concluding with how the Catholic social thought tradition corrects these deficiencies.

First, moral foundations built upon autonomy are, by definition, limited to autonomous people. Autonomy—being able to identify your own goals and act in pursuit of them within rational confines—is a capacity, which means it is not something that all individuals universally and equally possess. Consequently, if justice is based exclusively on autonomy, and autonomy is not something that all individuals equally share, then justice, by definition, will not apply to all individuals equally. We see the danger of this form of thinking in contemporary abortion and euthanasia debates.

Second, autonomy defines the pursuit of the good completely independently of human nature. This can seem like merely an academic point, but it has enormous ethical implications. The only principle of autonomy that ultimately unites human beings is consent. That means that if two or more people agree to do something, or if you just agree with yourself, then the action

is, by definition, morally permitted. That sounds fine—until
we realize that it can lead to some disturbing moral outcomes.
For example, autonomy not only morally authorizes men and
women to disfigure their bodies to "change their sexes," but also,
following the logic to its end point, permits self-identified "trans-
abled" individuals to have their spinal cords surgically severed
because they believe themselves to be disabled persons trapped
in able-persons' bodies. At the level of sexual ethics, autonomy
means not only that individuals can have sex with whomever they
want whenever they want (and note: biological sex is no longer a
morally real category according to this line of thinking) but also
that individuals can form polyamorous relationships and even
engage in sexual relations with members of their own biological
families. From a broader point of view, autonomy can make no
moral distinction between a life spent smoking pot in your mom's
basement and a life spent seeking cures for cancer. Both are freely
chosen and therefore morally indistinguishable. Advocates for
autonomy usually don't like to see these implications brought
to light, but they are the inescapable consequences of a view
that rejects the existence of an objective human good rooted in
human nature.

Third, transcendental rationalism cannot effectively answer
the problem of moral motivation. Every moral theory must answer
at least two questions: (1) How can people know what is good? and
(2) How can people be motivated to act in accordance with the
good? The Kantian position is that rationality itself is sufficient
to motivate people to act rationally. But here's a question: Do you
think that's true about people? Do you think that's true *about
yourself*? Have you ever known something to be right and done the
exact opposite? (Yeah, me too.) But admitting that is an enormous
problem for transcendental rationalism; if its whole account of
moral motivation is that people will do what is right because it
is right, and then there are countless instances in which we see

people acting differently, then there is good reason to go back to the drawing board on the validity of the moral theory itself.

So, where does this all lead us? On the one hand, we cannot escape the question of truth in establishing a ground for morality in general and social morality in particular. On the other hand, both materialistic empiricism and transcendental rationalism fail to provide that foundation for the reasons noted above. Happily, there is a third alternative: transcendent realism, and this is what defines the foundation of Catholic social thought.

This theory of knowledge combines the best of its competitors without falling prey to their flaws. For example, like transcendental rationalism, the Catholic recognition of a universal natural law provides rationally necessary moral principles that can coherently and objectively identify what kinds of actions are good and what kinds of actions are bad. Within the natural law framework, we also find a principle of human dignity that recognizes irrevocably objective worth inhering in every human being, which can consistently be translated into the language of human rights. Yet the Catholic view attains these goods without the drawbacks of the Kantian position; because human worth is grounded in dignity and not in autonomy, we can coherently say that the Catholic position applies equally to all human beings, including those who have diminished (or non-existent) capacities to act autonomously. Likewise, since the Catholic position is grounded in reality as such, it does not run into the problem of defining the human good only according to consent. Consent is certainly good from a Catholic position; however, it is qualified by taking place in response to what is objectively good, which means, among other things, that Catholic thought would never sanction an individual surgically mutilating himself in the name of autonomy or, even less, a social movement that seeks to celebrate such mutilation and enshrine it into law. Finally, the Catholic position is able to address the problem of moral motivation by recognizing that human beings must habituate themselves—and be habituated—both to perceive the fullness of what is good and to act on its behalf. In other words, Catholicism recognizes the necessity of taking into account both reason *and* desire in explaining how we should act, both individually and socially.

Like materialistic empiricism, in turn, the transcendent realism of Catholicism readily turns its attention to the physical world to learn more about the nature of existence and how we should act in relation to each other. However, the empirical, from a Catholic view, serves the function of teaching us how to *apply* the good we find in natural law; it does not give us principles of the good itself. In this way, Catholicism does not fall prey to empiricism's inability to mark an objective difference between good and evil—and, as a bonus, it does not flatten human knowledge into relying on the senses alone. In other words, we get the humanities back.

This all, in sum, points to the virtuosity of the Catholic position in synthesizing what on the surface appears to be an irreconcilable duality, i.e., that we must choose between empiricism and rationalism to ground moral and thus political principles. It is precisely in the coherence of this synthesis at the level of moral knowledge that we avoid the false mutual exclusivities that give rise to ideological forms of thinking. To the questions "Is truth rationally abstract or empirical?", "Are individuals autonomous or do they have a normative nature?", and "Do humans act rationally or do they need to be habituated to do so?", Catholicism can confidently answer "yes." This both/and at the heart of Catholic moral thought in general and Catholic social thought in particular, as we will continue to see, solves many other problems, including the problem of defining, creating, and maintaining a "perfect" society.

MY KINGDOM IS NOT OF THIS WORLD: THE PROBLEM OF THE PERFECT SOCIETY

Imagine a "perfect" community, like a luxurious gated neighborhood full of amenities or an idyllic small town where everybody knows your name. On the one hand, such places serve as a model of the ideal human society—a taste of a life of material abundance and social concord. On the other hand, they can feel creepy and even paradoxically dystopian. It's not only the fact that creating and maintaining such places, like making sausage, requires a messy agglomeration of not-so-pleasant ingredients (like negotiating bickering neighborhood boards, managing contentious labor contracts with those hired to keep everything looking impeccable, being under surveillance by one's neighbors, the generation and disposal of trash, and, let's not forget, the high price of it all); it's that the implementation of perfection itself can feel stifling, oppressive, menacing, and unnatural, occupying a place in our psyche where comfort and contempt can be difficult to distinguish.

This says something strange about human nature—that we are capable of loving and loathing the same ideal—and also, more broadly, about human societies, especially as they relate to the pursuit of perfection. Is it really the case, as the cliché goes, that the perfect is the enemy of the good? If so, then why pursue social perfection at all? On the other hand, if we abandon the idea of perfection, do we not also abandon the possibility of social prog-ress, of, in a generic sense, making society more just and humane? On the other hand again, we must recall that, historically, the societies that have most trumpeted their own perfection have turned out to be the most oppressive and murderous in history, as we saw previously with the Soviet Union and see today in Communist North Korea and China.

This, then, appears to be the central problem: To what degree, if any, should society pursue an ideal of perfection at all? Note there are two interrelated questions at play. The first is "Can the perfect society be defined?" and the second is "Can the perfect society be achieved?" It is important to note up front that answering "yes" to the first question does not necessarily entail answering "yes" to the second question; it is conceptually possible to define the perfect society while denying that such a society could ever come into temporal existence. At the same time, answering "no" to the first question makes the second question moot; if we cannot define the perfect society, then we necessarily exclude the possibility of ever knowingly achieving it.

With these conceptual boundaries in place, let's set up a framework for examining different approaches to answering the question. Employing a graph to visualize the different possibilities is helpful in doing so. Imagine two axes, a horizontal "x" axis and a vertical "y" axis. The "x" axis represents time or history; the "y" axis represents the level of perfection. Now add one more line to the graph, another straight horizontal line high up on the "y" axis. This line represents maximal social perfection, or "MSP" for short, which, it is important to emphasize, only pertains to perfection in time and space in this context—not in eternity.

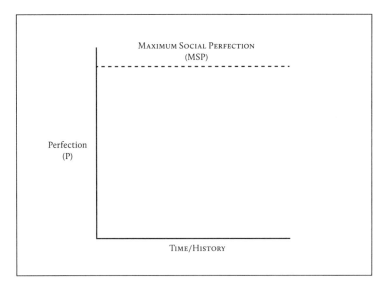

To this graph we can now add a line that signifies movement toward maximal perfection in history.

It is an interesting question to ask where, on the scale of perfection, the starting point should be. The Catholic view, for example, is that human beings, in their naturally created state, were without moral or physical blemish before original sin, and so, with that model, we would start at maximal moral and social perfection at the beginning of time and then see a precipitous drop on the "y" axis sometime soon after, followed by an uneven climb back toward perfection in salvation history. For our purposes, though, we don't need to settle how perfect humanity was at the beginning of history; rather, we only need to recognize that, however morally perfect we might have been, we are not currently perfect. The fundamental question at hand, in other words, is whether and to what extent human beings can form a perfect society *in the future.*

This points to the first model, the relativist or nihilist model. In this conception of social perfection, the underlying presupposition is that "perfection" cannot be objectively defined because no definition is any truer—any closer to the actual nature of things—than any other. This view may recognize that societies *believe* themselves to be acting according to a principle of perfection; however, such societies would all be wrong because every definition of perfection is equally arbitrary. The relativist-nihilist model thus looks something like this:

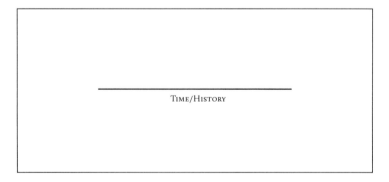

Note that there is no "y" axis here. That is because, following the logic of the position, there is no objective definition of the good, and therefore no definition of the "best," and consequently no definition of "perfect." At the same time, however, we can preserve the "x" axis because, at least for the sake of argument, even relativists and nihilists recognize the existence of time.

So, what, then, would "progress" toward perfection look like according to this model? Something like this:

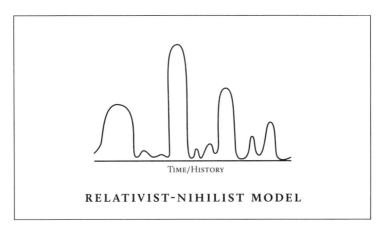

TIME/HISTORY

RELATIVIST-NIHILIST MODEL

The idea is that, because there is no objective definition of perfection, there is, consequently, no way to track progress toward that standard. There are, then, just random movements throughout history, all of them neither moral nor immoral. There is no progress. Indeed, there aren't even any historical "events," in the sense of moments in time that are more significant than other moments in time.

This is a terrifying view of morality. Despite the hesitance of contemporary relativists and nihilists (which, ultimately, are the same thing) to admit the implications of their view, denying the existence of an objective moral standard for societies renders moral progress impossible to define and, therefore, impossible to pursue. From this standpoint, eradicating slavery would, morally speaking, not be any different from the institution of slavery in the first place; the building of Auschwitz and the liberation of Auschwitz took place at different times, but we cannot mark one event as morally superior to the other. Likewise with the invention of electricity, vaccines, and water purification systems. Many fewer people perish from early death because of these inventions, but the relativist/nihilist can only respond with a shrug. In short, this model cannot be the basis for societal perfection because it cannot be the basis of *any* conception of morality.

There is another model to consider at the other end of the spectrum: the utopian-optimist model. In this version, the "y" axis happily returns, as does the horizontal line of maximal social perfection. What is unique to this model is that it affirms both that social perfection has an objective definition—which is what fundamentally distinguishes it from the relativist-nihilist model—*and* that social perfection can be attained in time and space. The graph looks something like this:

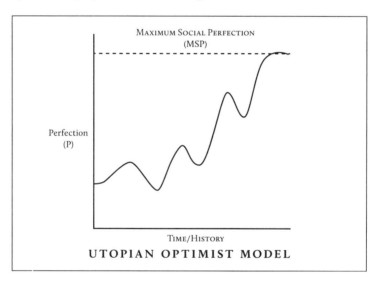

Note that this model can coherently account for moral fluctuations; things can get better and then worse and then better again moving through time. However, the most salient feature of this model is that it holds that humans have the capacity eventually to attain social perfection—that is, to use secularized theological language, to create a heaven on earth.

There are two great virtues to this model, especially in comparison to the previous one. First, its embrace of the possibility of an objective standard of perfection establishes a moral principle that can do the work of gauging whether any given society—or, even, the world as a whole—is moving closer to or deviating away from that standard. In other words, it enables us to coherently speak about moral progress or the lack thereof. Second, affirming that social perfection can be attained can motivate individuals and communities to work to improve society. As we will see shortly with another model, simply being able to define perfection does not by itself supply sufficient motivation to pursue it.

On the other hand, the utopian-optimist model is also, well, too utopian. It is instructive that the word "utopia" comes from a 1516 text of the same name by St. Thomas More, who famously chose martyrdom rather than sanction the illicit divorce and re-marriage of the tyrant King Henry VIII. The work is a masterpiece for many reasons, but one of the most important is that it can be difficult to distinguish between St. Thomas More the Catholic political theorist and St. Thomas More the Catholic satirist. The name of the island of Utopia in the book comes from the Greek words for "no" and "place." In other words, utopia is nowhere; and seeking to build such a society is thus equivalent to constructing an illusion—that is, a deviation from the true nature of reality.

This points to the first flaw in the utopian-optimist model of perfection: it ignores the reality of sin, both individually and socially. Catholicism recognizes that sin is neither the result of ignorance nor coercion by external forces. Rather, sin is the free use of our reason and will to act contrary to what we otherwise know to be good. At the heart of Christian anthropology is the doctrine of original sin, which is the recognition that all human beings are sinners, or, put again, that no human being is or can be perfect in this life (with the exception of Mary, the mother of Jesus Christ).

It is hard to dispute the universality of this human characteristic. As the Catholic apologist and humorist G.K. Chesterton wrote, "Original sin . . . is the only part of Christian theology which can really be proved."[4] If it is indeed true that all humans have a taste for destruction, both of others and of ourselves, then it's consequently true that everything we build—every civil institution, from courts to cabinets to entire governments—will be tainted with that sin as well, no matter how hard we try to make it perfect. That is not to say that all societies and forms of government are morally equal; it is only to recognize that even the noblest social and political institutions have lurking within them the impatient temptation to be used for less than noble ends, to become tools of domination, exploitation, self-aggrandizement, and good old-fashioned greed. The utopian-optimist model is either dangerously naïve or, more alarmingly, cynical about this reality. Either way, living according to this model would be immoral precisely because it does not adequately account for the unlimited human capacity for immorality itself.

There is another related flaw to this model captured in an answer to this question: "Has this idea ever been tried and found to be successful?" In response, the historical record is clear. All utopian projects in history—projects based on the premise that the perfect society can be not only defined but also achieved—have failed miserably by their own standards and caused unfathomable misery in the process. Limited to Nazism, Marxist Stalinism, and Maoism alone, the body count is in the tens of millions, including both those directly murdered by the state and those killed indirectly by economic mismanagement. Utopianism always runs into this conundrum. If people were capable of being perfect on their own—that is, if they weren't sinners—then there wouldn't be any need to enforce perfection. However, people are not perfect on their own, and yet utopian projects, by definition, still believe that social perfection is possible. What's the only alternative for the utopian architect, then? *Coercing perfection*, which includes everything from re-education camps like we see in contemporary

---

4. G.K. Chesterton, *Orthodoxy* (Park Ridge, IL: Word on Fire Classics, 2017), 8.

China to the concentration camps we saw in World War II. These are not bugs in the system; they are the system itself, an essential feature, not an accident. If you set out under the presumption that you and your group are going to construct the perfect society, then you better be ready to recognize that such a project will require nothing less than gaining total control of the population you intend to save from itself.

Overemphasizing the imperfectability and wickedness of humanity, however, can also get us into trouble, which we see in turning to a third model of perfection. Like the utopian optimist model, this model recognizes the possibility of objectively defining perfection. However, in direct contrast to the utopian-optimist model, it maintains that no progress can be made toward attaining that perfection (or at least any lasting progress). We'll call this the pessimist model of social progress, and it looks like this:

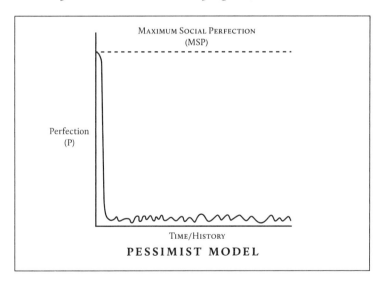

As the graph shows, the model recognizes that there can be some nominal movement toward perfection in time. However, that gain eventually, usually quickly, vanishes, either due to losing whatever progress society had attained in the first place or by the development of another social movement that counteracts the growth toward social progress—for example, by society embracing human rights, which, by itself, is a good development, but then appealing to those rights to justify the mass slaughter of the unborn, which is a monstrous step backward. Two steps up, three steps down, and then another up, and another down. The overall pattern that emerges over time is thus nearly a flatline hovering at the bottom.

One of the virtues of this model, in contradistinction to the utopian-optimist model, is that it is honest about the lack of virtue among human beings. As such, it is highly suspicious of grand initiatives to perfect society. Think of it this way: if the utopian-optimist model of perfection is the rusty, dilapidated playground of communists, socialists, and other sundry communitarians, then the pessimist model is the glistening playground—privately funded and surrounded by a double-locked gate—of libertarians and like-minded hyper-individualists. If the anthem of the former is a gauzy "We are all in this together," the anthem of the latter is a steely "Don't tread on me."

There is, no doubt, some nobility in this rugged pessimism, and it can serve as a welcome check on tyranny. The problem, though, is that pessimism is a double-edged sword when it comes to organizing society. To be sure, it can act as a bulwark against excessive governmental encroachment. But it can have the opposite effect as well. Based on the premise that human beings are irredeemably wicked, governments can soon find themselves justifying invasive social controls in the name of security, telling themselves and their citizens that keeping evil in line requires dabbling in a little darkness oneself. And hence we end up with the strange bedfellows of communism and fascism, bitter ideological enemies on their own terms yet finding agreement on the principle that making good social omelets requires breaking some individual eggs.

We can also say that the pessimist model is, well, *too pessimistic*. Think, for example, of all the people who used to say,

"Sure, slavery is bad—but there's nothing we can do to stop it"; or, "Sure, women should be able to vote, but you know these kinds of things can't be changed"; or, "Sure, people of all colors should be able to eat at the same dining counter, but, well, human nature is human nature." Operating from the standpoint of pessimism, none of these changes, none of these markers of authentic social progress, would have ever been achieved. While humans have a taste for evil, we also have a proclivity for good, which, when combined with the always surprising interventions of grace in human history, can accomplish levels of justice in society that were unimaginable in previous generations. The pessimistic model, however, precludes this kind of progress and in so doing saps individuals and communities of the motivation to fight for genuine moral improvement.

The failures and successes of these models ultimately point to a fourth option, which we can call the hope model. Note the distinction here between hope and optimism—unlike optimism, hope recognizes both the *possibility* and the *limits* of moral progress. It embraces both the promise of authentic movement toward a more just, more humane, more flourishing society *and* the lethal dangers of the conceited idea that a broken humanity has the power to fix itself. Visualized, the model looks something like this:

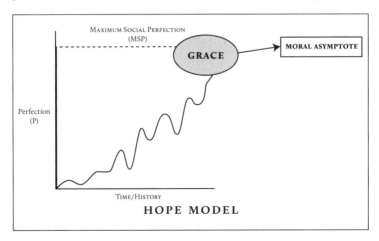

87

In the hope model, like the utopian-optimist and pessimist models, there is an underlying assumption that it is indeed possible to identify an objective standard of perfection, which, in turn, provides a means for determining whether any given society (or even humanity as a whole) is moving closer or further away from that standard. In other words, the hope model provides both a definition of moral progress and the possibility of moving toward that definition in history. At the same time, the hope model categorically rejects key features of utopianism and pessimism. Against the utopian-optimist model, it denies that establishing a secular heaven on earth is or ever will be possible; against the pessimist model, it denies with equal vehemence that the fallen state of human beings means that we can never approximate a higher standard of justice and hold onto it.

In other words, what ultimately defines the hope model is that it envisions social perfection *asymptotically.* Asymptotes, recall from middle-school math, describe movement toward a fixed line that can get closer and closer to that line while never being able to cross it. Translated into moral terms, an asymptotic model recognizes that human beings can potentially reach higher and higher levels of social perfection (by, for example, rectifying major sources of injustice) while concurrently holding that it is folly to believe that we could ever eradicate all injustice—and, indeed, that it would be an injustice itself to try to do so.

This, in the end, is the model of perfection paradigmatically present in Catholic social thought. Catholicism affirms both that human beings are broken *and* that we can labor to diminish the effects of sin; it affirms that all human beings are called to fight for ever greater justice while recognizing that the Christ who demands that every person, individually and communally, feed the poor, give drink to the thirsty, and clothe the naked (cf. Matt. 25:35–36) is the same Christ who says, "My kingdom is not from this world" (John 18:36). It affirms that we can indeed know what perfection looks like—a world without violence, a world without hunger, a world without lying and cheating and backbiting and domination—while concurrently maintaining that it is God's grace alone that can usher in the reign of such a kingdom. In this way, Catholic social thought protects us from the pitfalls of ideological thinking, which, as we will see in greater detail in part II of this book, alternately either condemn humankind to the nightmare of recalcitrant moral stagnation or to the equally terrifying nightmare of ravenous unlimited moral progress. To both ideological camps, the Church says these motivating and sobering words: "Strive first for the kingdom of God and his righteousness, and all these things will be given to you as well" (Matt. 6:33).

The hope model is not without its tensions, however. Two theological pillars support the Catholic conception of salvation history: (1) God created everything in existence good, including human beings, and (2) human beings freely *rejected* the goodness of creation, which forever (in a temporal sense) altered human nature in the form of original sin. It is for this latter reason that the Church calls humanity "fallen" and in need of salvation—salvation that God offers in and through the second person of the Holy Trinity, Jesus Christ. This tension between humanity's fundamental goodness and inescapable brokenness generates a basic question regarding the meaning and purpose of the civil order: Is civil government *natural*—that is, an extension of our nature as God created it? Or is civil government merely *necessary*—that is, a consequence of human sin?

Humanity, the Church teaches, would certainly still live in community even if there were no sin. The reason is because God created us social by nature; every person depends upon others to attain her/his full individual potential. As the *Catechism of the Catholic Church* explains,

> The human person needs to live in society. Society is not for
> him an extraneous addition but a requirement of his nature.

Through the exchange with others, mutual service and dialogue with his brethren, man develops his potential.[5]

However, the specific meaning of "society" is open to interpretation. Were it not for sin, would we need to belong to a society that includes legislatures, executives, judiciaries, treasuries, departments of state, departments of justice, and (directly to the point) departments of defense? Two doctors of the Catholic intellectual tradition, St. Augustine and St. Thomas Aquinas, answer this question differently.

St. Augustine (354–430 AD), for example, affirms with the *Catechism* that human beings are social by nature. Being social and living in community, however, does not necessarily entail creating governments. Indeed, Augustine argues that humanity in its naturally created, unfallen state would not have needed civil authority because "authority," in a political context, implies the use of power over others, which, Augustine believes, is only necessary when sin enters into human history.[6] As he writes in his classic tome *The City of God*,

> [God] did not intend that His rational creature, who was made in His image, should have dominion over anything but the irrational creation—not man over man, but man over the beasts. And hence the righteous men in primitive times were made shepherds of cattle rather than kings of men, God intending thus to teach us what the relative position of the creatures is,

---

5. *Catechism of the Catholic Church* 1879.

6. For an excellent analysis of St. Augustine's conception of the origins and purpose of civil government, see Paul Weithman, "Augustine's Political Philosophy," in *The Cambridge Companion to Augustine*, 2nd ed., ed. David Vincent Meconi and Eleonore Stump (Cambridge: Cambridge University Press, 2006), 234–250.

and what the desert of sin; for it is with justice, we believe, that
the condition of slavery is the result of sin.[7]

For Augustine, slavery—the absolute power of one human
being to impose his will on another—is a direct consequence of
sin. It is unnatural. However, Augustine additionally believes that
all coercive power—i.e., "dominion"—over others, which includes
the power of governments, is a result of the fall as well. Civil
government, in other words, is adventitious to human nature.
At best, the state exists as medicine to mitigate a sickness of our
own creation.

This correlation between sin and the political order also
underpins Augustine's conception of what he calls the "City of
Man" and the "City of God." Humanity, post-fall, divides itself
into two communities defined by what the individuals in those
communities love above all else. Those who love God as their
highest good—which is what we were created to love and, as such,
constitutes our happiness properly understood—abide in the City
of God; those who love something other than God as their highest
good, which is another way of saying those who practice idolatry,
reside in the City of Man. These communities are exhaustive and
mutually exclusive (that is, there are only two options, and you are
in either one or the other). However, they are also intermingled
in what Augustine calls the *saeculum*, or the period of history
between the fall and the eschaton (the Final Judgment). People
of the City of God do not live in one part of town and people of
the City of Man in another. Rather, the denizens of the two cities
work and live side by side. The only thing that distinguishes one
from the other is what defines the final object of their love—that
is, what they worship. As such, even belonging to the institutional
Church does not necessarily entail membership in the City of

7. Augustine, *City of God* 19.5, in *Nicene and Post-Nicene Fathers*, First Series,
vol. 2, trans. Marcus Dods, ed. Philip Schaff (Buffalo, NY: Christian Literature,
1887), newadvent.org.

God; there are many people, Augustine observes, who claim to be Christian yet are raging egoists on the inside.

St. Augustine's conception of the two cities is rich, nuanced, and perennially relevant. For our purposes, however, the dimension to highlight is the limits this interpretation of sin in relation to the civil order imposes on the capacity for government to contribute to the authentic human good, both temporally and spiritually. To be sure, Augustine believes that the two cities can cooperate to work for temporal peace, which he defines as the "tranquility of order." However, as the definition suggests, "peace" means the absence of overt violent conflict, not harmony or solidarity. That latter form of peace is reserved for heaven and heaven alone. Thus, the best we can hope for in this life, politically speaking, are decent roads, a satisfactory economy, a functioning military, and only modestly corrupt politicians.

It is ultimately for this reason that Augustine describes the Christian's place in the world as being a "pilgrim" rather than a "resident." Both pilgrims and residents need food, shelter, security, and functioning thoroughfares to go about their business. Yet residents believe they are here to stay. Pilgrims know they're just passing through. Unlike the residents of the City of Man who worship the world as if it were God, those who belong to the City of God know the truth about the finite and fallen nature of this life and live accordingly. They do the best they can to foster peace and prosperity but know it isn't going to last. As Augustine writes,

> The heavenly city, therefore, while in its state of pilgrimage, avails itself of the peace of earth, and, so far as it can without injuring faith and godliness, desires and maintains a common agreement among men regarding the acquisition of the necessaries of life, and makes this earthly peace bear upon the peace of heaven.[8]

8. Augustine, 19.17.

In short, St. Augustine's civil institutions are like hotels. Some are dimly lit and roach-infested, have suspicious stains on the mattresses, and are full of unsavory characters. Others are bright, tidy, capacious, and brimming with amenities and friendly faces. Humans have limited but real freedom to choose what kind of communal lodging we build in this life, and Augustine affirms that Christians have the duty, grounded in the love of God and neighbor, to fashion that lodging as closely to the ideal of the kingdom of God as possible. But, in the end, it's just a temporary dwelling, one that will inevitably fall into disrepair and collapse. God never intended the civil order to come into existence in the first place or, post fall, to save us from sin. St. Augustine thus counsels Christians to set their beliefs about what government can accomplish accordingly. Don't expect too much of the state, and maybe you won't be disappointed—though you probably will be anyway.

St. Thomas Aquinas (AD 1225–1274) drew deeply on the thought of St. Augustine, and there is certainly more in common between their theologies than differences. Yet, in part because of his engagement with the philosophy of Aristotle, Aquinas' conception of the origin, meaning, and purpose of the political order diverges from Augustine's. Unlike Augustine, for example, Aquinas views the origins of government within human nature as God originally created it. In other words, humans would have formed civil government even if it were not for the effects of original sin. He writes in the *Summa theologiae*,

> There is in man an inclination to good, according to the nature
> of his reason, which nature is proper to him: thus man has
> a natural inclination to know the truth about God, and to
> live in society: and in this respect, whatever pertains to this
> inclination belongs to the natural law; for instance, to shun

ignorance, to avoid offending those among whom one has to
live, and other such things regarding the above inclination.[9]

It is important to emphasize that Aquinas explicitly connects
humanity's "natural inclination to know the truth about God"
to our equally natural inclination "to live in society"—and both
inclinations inhere within natural law. These are not independent
principles; rather, there is, for Aquinas, a deep sense in which
rightly knowing God is at least partially *dependent upon* living in
a properly ordered society—that is, a society governed by natural
law by proper human authorities. In this sense, for Aquinas, we
are not only social by nature (in agreement with Augustine) but
also *political* by nature (in disagreement with Augustine).

This feature of Aquinas' theological anthropology lays the
foundation for a significantly more sanguine view of political life
than we see in Augustine. To be sure, Aquinas, like Augustine,
recognizes the destructive consequences of sin on individuals and,
by extension, the communities they form. His own native Italy
(like the crumbling Roman Empire of St. Augustine's time) was
in constant political turmoil. However, Aquinas' view of human
nature after the fall is not as bleak as Augustine's. Aquinas writes,
for example,

> In no man does the prudence of the flesh dominate so far as to
> destroy the whole good of his nature. And consequently there
> remains in man the inclination to act in accordance with the
> eternal law.[10]

Augustine may agree with this observation in theological principle (humanity cannot completely destroy what God has created),
but he believes it is the rare person indeed who acts in accordance

9. Thomas Aquinas, *Summa theologiae* 1-2.94.2.
10. Thomas Aquinas, 1-2.93.6 ad 2.

with this inclination without God's direct gracious intervention. Aquinas, however, is more willing to give humanity the benefit of the doubt and in so doing lays the theological foundation for a much more positive view of political life. He categorically rejects the possibility of humanity being able to build heaven on earth, yet he also believes that the "common good"—which is far more substantive than Augustine's "tranquility of order"—is, in fact, possible to instantiate in this life, even if imperfectly. Indeed, *all* humans have both the capacity and inclination to act in the service of the common good, which Aquinas identifies as the cardinal virtue of "justice"—a virtue that every person, by nature, has the desire to practice. As he writes,

> Justice . . . directs man in his relations with other men. . . . It
> is evident that all who are included in a community, stand in
> relation to that community as parts to a whole; while a part, as
> such, belongs to a whole, so that whatever is the good of a part
> can be directed to the good of the whole. It follows therefore
> that the good of any virtue, whether such virtue direct man in
> relation to himself, or in relation to certain other individual
> persons, is referable to the common good, to which justice
> directs: so that all acts of virtue can pertain to justice, in so
> far as it directs man to the common good. It is in this sense
> that justice is called a general virtue.[11]

In short, St. Thomas Aquinas affirms that acting justly in pursuit of the common good, that is, engaging in politics for more than purely selfish reasons, is not restricted only to those who belong to the City of God. It remains a part of our common human nature, even after the fall.

So who, then, is right? Is St. Augustine correct to frame the political order as a clumsy tool that temporarily mitigates the

11. Thomas Aquinas, 1-2.58.5.

worst consequences of sin? Or is St. Thomas Aquinas correct that the political order, though tainted by sin, can, when properly ruled by natural law, assist human beings in knowing and living according to the divine will? The Church's response to what sounds like an "either/or dilemma" is ultimately a "both/and." Catholic social thought teaches that we must never forget that every individual and community is sinful, which means we must be vigilant to the ways the civil sphere can (and will) become corrupted into an instrument of domination and self-interest. *And* Catholic social thought teaches that humans were not only created good but remain good; consequently, we can and should follow our natural inclination to build, protect, and improve civic institutions that instantiate and support our natural integrity. This two-fold strategy, in the end, is the best way to make authentic and durable moral progress in history. We should be inspired by St. Thomas Aquinas and sobered by St. Augustine and, in the unity of the two, aim for the best while preparing for the worst.

THE (IN)VULNERABLE SOUL: THE PROBLEM OF HUMAN WORTH

One of the greatest (if not *the* greatest) biblical contributions to morality is human dignity. Dignity permeates the Christian theological tradition and has its roots in the first chapter of the first book of the Bible: "Let us make humankind in our image, according to our likeness" (Gen. 1:26). But what does this claim mean, exactly—that God formed us in his image and likeness? First, it means that we are *made,* which necessarily implies that we do not create ourselves. We are not God. That should be the most obvious fact in the history of facts, yet it is one that each person and each society chooses to forget in one way or another. However, the *imago Dei,* as it is often referred to, is not only a negation; it is also an affirmation, a recognition that being human entails not only having an orientation to God as Creator but, so much more, sharing in God's very being and nature, possessing the divine imprint within us in a way different from everything else in creation. We are not merely animated matter; we are the unity of body and soul, which means we have a spiritual nature that lives eternally. And we are not merely passive recipients of God's activity in the world—we possess the divinely-gifted capacities of reason (in the form of being able to identify and comprehend truth) and free will (in the form of being able to respond to the truth without extrinsic control). These two features of humanity—being a composite of body and soul and possessing reason and free will—form the foundation of the biblical concept of human dignity, which, in turn, lies at the heart of Catholic social thought.

To understand why this matters, let me begin by quoting from Thomas Hobbes, the seventeenth-century English political philosopher who is most known for arguing that human beings, in a state of nature, live in a "war of all against all." Hobbes observed this about human dignity:

> The public worth of a man, which is the value set on him by the commonwealth, is that which men commonly call "dignity." And this value of him by the commonwealth is understood by offices of command, judicature, public employment; or by names and titles introduced for distinction of such value.[12]

In this passage, Hobbes succinctly describes the utilitarian definition of human worth, that the value a person has depends upon the usefulness she or he provides to society. For Hobbes, people with money and power—those we might call "the elite" today—have a high value because they are useful to others; they are the ones who offer the material and social benefits. Yet the elite are relatively few in number, the tiny peak on the top of the

---

12. Thomas Hobbes, *Leviathan* (London: George Routledge & Sons, 1886), 48.

social pyramid. Beneath them stack subsequent layers of society that, as we move downward, increase in number while proportionally decreasing in value until you get to a wide, dense base packed with people who basically can't give anything valuable to anyone and are therefore useless and consequently worthless. We might call them the "deplorables" in today's political language.

"What a repugnant understanding of human dignity!" you might think. And you'd be right. But why is Hobbes wrong? Why shouldn't we say he's just being honest, just being realistic, just cutting through our artificial pieties to tell us something we all already know and, in fact, practice every day? Indeed, isn't this precisely the thinking operative in the "pro-choice" movement? Isn't the underlying presupposition that the unborn baby only has value if the child is wanted—that is, if she or he can provide a psychological or material benefit to the parents? Depending on the poll, nearly half the people in the United States claim to think this way. So is Hobbes right after all?

No. But if we really want to reject the Hobbesian model, we need to establish a conception of human worth that is not reducible to an individual's utility to others. The moral stakes could not be higher. Failing to establish an objective, universal grounding for human dignity leads to the evaporation of the justification for human rights, for it is only because humans putatively have worth that we can coherently say they have rights *solely by virtue of being human*. A moral landscape devoid of human rights, in turn, means there are no moral limits to what people can do to each other. If that's the case, Hobbes' "war of all against all" is not far off the mark. Human dignity, we can say without exaggeration, is the first and last bulwark against this fate for humanity.

The question, therefore, is "How do we derive such an account of dignity?" The task becomes even more complex once we recognize that a morally functioning concept of worth must possess two fundamental characteristics. On the one hand, we must define dignity as invulnerable to harm, meaning that it cannot in any way be degraded, diminished, or extinguished. The reason is because moral invulnerability is a necessary condition for being able to claim that human dignity is both universal (meaning it applies to all beings otherwise defined as human) and equal (meaning it applies to all humans in the exact same degree). If, in contrast, we define dignity as vulnerable to moral harm, then we are recognizing that dignity can indeed be degraded and possibly even obliterated. Allowing for this possibility, however, would consequently mean that we could no longer define dignity as universal and equal. Why? Because recognizing that individuals' worth can be diminished means that some people can have more or less worth than others or even no worth at all. If this is the case, dignity is neither equal nor universal.

But this raises a new problem. If dignity is in fact invulnerable to harm, then doesn't it become a moot moral concept? In other words, if dignity cannot be attacked, at least successfully, then what's the point of acknowledging it in the first place? What moral work could it possibly do? Indeed, if human dignity is the justification for human rights, and the corresponding function of human rights is to protect human dignity, then wouldn't defining dignity as invulnerable pull out the rug from both the meaning and purpose of rights?

This is the great paradox that lies at the heart of the problem of human worth. On the one hand, we need a definition of dignity that is invulnerable to harm in order to warrant its universal equality; on the other hand, we need a definition of dignity that is vulnerable to harm in order to warrant the existence and purpose of rights. We need, in other words, a definition that recognizes dignity as both invulnerable and vulnerable at the same time. That sounds like a flat-out contradiction. Is such a conception of dignity even possible?

Happily, yes. But let's first examine some conceptions of dignity that *fail* to meet the criteria. First, consider autonomy, a concept at the heart of Enlightenment philosopher Immanuel

Kant's thought. The basic idea Kant advances, as we touched on previously, is that human beings can and should be conceived of as ends in and of themselves because they are capable of acting autonomously—that is, capable of appropriating a universal law of reason to guide their actions as they freely seek their own goals and purposes in life. As I noted before, the Kantian ethical framework is remarkably rigorous and philosophically rich. For what it's worth, I do think that he effectively establishes a framework for justifying *some* conception of dignity, one that does indeed rationally inhere in all autonomous human beings.

But, you see, that's the problem. If autonomy is a condition for dignity, then, by definition, those who are not autonomous—those who cannot appropriate a universal law of reason because of handicap, injury, incapacitation, or simply being too young—do not have full dignity. And merely adding that having the potential for autonomy suffices for ascribing dignity to all people doesn't fix this problem, since not all individuals equally have such a potential. Although this was certainly not Kant's intent, this moral gap in his philosophical system—and every other system that founds dignity on autonomy—thus ends up kicking many, many human beings off the boat of human worth.

This, it is crucial to note, applies to every single other conception of dignity based on human capacities. Whether it is consciousness, self-awareness, IQ, the ability to form friendships, the capability to fall in love or create art, or even the capacity to suffer—which, even if universal, is not equal among humans—you will never find a capacity that all human beings share in absolute equality because capacities and their exercise are as diverse as human beings themselves. As such, they can never coherently account for a universally equal conception of human worth.

If not autonomy or some other human capacity, what are we left with? What about the human body? Nope. To be sure, we all have bodies, but no two human bodies are equal in all respects. What, then, about human DNA? Isn't that something we all equally share? This option may sound promising on the surface; it is indeed true that we are united as a species in sharing the same biochemical coding, no matter what other differentiations we may possess. Yet every other living thing on the planet also has a unique DNA coding, which means, if we follow the same logic of dignity conferring rights, that every living thing would have equal rights. To put it bluntly, that's not going to work, unless we want to criminalize eating. Moreover, the "uniqueness" of DNA is itself an interpretation of a collection of elements that are common to all life (e.g., carbon); thus, even DNA is not irreducibly "real" in an absolute sense and, as such, could not explain the ontological uniqueness of anything in existence, especially in a way that would confer dignity.

What, then, are we left with? The book of Genesis has a suggestion: the image and likeness of God. This model, unlike all secular contenders, solves the riddle of how dignity can coherently be conceived of as invulnerable and vulnerable to moral harm at the same time, and it does so in a way that also establishes sound principles for defining the right relationship between the individual and society. How so?

First, recall that one of the fundamental characteristics of the *imago Dei* is that human beings, unlike everything else in existence, are a composite of body and rational soul. It is the existence of the soul in particular that provides the ground for claiming that all human beings are morally equal by virtue of being human. While bodies can and do differ, the biblical conception of the soul recognizes each person as having a unique spiritual identity only in the sense of being individuated. In other words, each one of us has a soul that is particular to us; however, no one's soul, at the most fundamental level of being, is ontologically or morally different than anyone else's. Thus, we can coherently say that all human beings are morally equal because all human beings equally possess an immaterial soul.

It is vital to add that grounding dignity in the soul consequently puts it out of reach of anyone or anything that would seek to do it harm. Precisely because the soul is immaterial and has its origins in the immaterial God who created and sustains it, nothing in the world—no matter how cruel, tortuous, disfiguring, or wicked—can affect, less diminish, less destroy, its integrity. Indeed, even trying to harm our own souls is as futile as trying to make ourselves unborn. The soul is not our creation and thus it is out of our power to injure. And it is precisely this invulnerability, this imperviousness to the material world, that accounts for the invulnerability of our moral equality, which, in turn, justifies the claim that human dignity is universally equal.

At the same time, though, we must recall that the image and likeness of God not only pertains to who we are; it also pertains to who we are to become. The *imago Dei* is not merely a static immaterial substance; it is also a potentiality that is capable of moral growth toward the perfection of its being. In Catholic terms, the soul possesses the possibility of *sanctification*, which means, in cooperation with God's grace, becoming more Christlike, which, in turn, is the same as becoming more fully human. Human worth is thus not only inherent but also attained. It is a gift that comes into its fullness of being when activated by our individual, free decisions to employ our reason and will to live in right relation with God and each other.

This dimension of the *imago Dei* illuminates how dignity can be conceived of as both invulnerable and vulnerable to harm without contradiction. Think of it this way: The gift of an eternal soul to every human being is a gift that nothing in the world can revoke or stain, and it is a gift that every human receives in absolute equality. At the same time, the soul contains within it a dynamic nature, which we see, for example, in the New Testament distinctions between "soul" and "spirit," as, for instance, when Our Lady says in the Gospel of Luke, "My soul magnifies the Lord, and my spirit rejoices in God my Savior" (Luke 1:46–47).

Though the relationship between the two is complex, our spirit is that within our immaterial soul that responds to God's call to be in relationship. Moreover, as Pope St. John Paul II lays out in his theology of the body, and as we also see in the theology of St. Thomas Aquinas, how we use our bodies plays an essential role in making our free response to God. How we act—and how we are acted upon—affects the integrity of our spirit, which, in turn, determines the integrity of our response to God's offer of relationship.

This may sound like an abstract theological matter, but it has profound moral consequences. Defining the soul as both a fixed ontological reality *and* a potentiality that can be realized (or fail to be realized) depending upon our actions explains why human worth is vulnerable to harm and how vulnerable it really is. What we do both to ourselves and to each other can and does deeply influence our respective capacities to respond to God's universal offer of relationship and become fully human. All other things being equal, for example, a child who is brought into the world in a loving family and who is taught to live according to the cardinal virtues of justice, prudence, temperance, and fortitude has a much greater likelihood of growing into a morally flourishing person who is capable of receiving and giving love than another child who is born addicted to drugs and raised in a materially poor and physically abusive environment. The Catholic conception of human worth recognizes a grave injustice that calls out for rectification in this latter situation precisely because it perceives, rightly, both that the abused child has indelible worth *and* that the realization of that worth is in severe danger. The abused child, in other words, is being morally injured, which, consequently, is undermining her capacity to become fully human, fully alive.

To be sure, this does not mean that individuals or communities can determine whether someone is saved or not. That choice is and always ultimately remains God's and God's alone. Recognizing our vulnerability to others also does not mean that we as individuals cease to be responsible for our own moral integrity. However, it does mean that we are responsible for fostering as much as we can the conditions to support every person's capacity to freely choose to become the fullness of who he or she is and is called to be: a unique gift of God's love made for eternal life with our Creator.

It is crucial to add that this moral vulnerability and our response to it also lays the foundation for recognizing the existence of and demanding respect for human rights. From the Catholic perspective, we have equal human rights because we have imperviously equal individual worth, and we need those rights to protect us from the actions of others that could undercut the growth of that worth into full, flourishing humanity.

In the end, this vision of human worth—a worth that is both vulnerable and invulnerable, inherent and attained, individual and social—serves as a comprehensive rebuttal to Thomas Hobbes' utility-based view of dignity, solves the conceptual riddles outlined earlier, and lays the foundations for establishing the right relationship between the individual and society.

To all ideologies that seek to define the human person merely as a product of the state or social community, as a piece of wax to be shaped into the right kind of "citizen" to carry out the state's purposes, the Catholic conception of human worth marks an irrevocable and inalienable boundary around the human person, affirming that the individual always precedes the state and that the state must therefore understand itself as profoundly limited in what it can do in the name of progress. In contrast to all ideologies that seek to define the human person solipsistically, as islands of autonomous sovereignty with no underlying moral connection to other people, the Catholic conception of human worth reminds us that, as the poet John Donne wrote, no man is an island. The moral integrity of every one of us is vulnerable to the individual and communal actions of others, and that vulnerability cuts directly to the final integrity of our soul. As such, it matters profoundly what society looks like—whether people can find work or are relegated to poverty; whether the courts are impartial or favor particular groups; whether elections are free and fair or manipulated to serve a party's interests; whether the schools provide the needed skills for social advancement or are merely a means of public employment; whether the most vulnerable find assistance or are allowed to fall through the cracks; whether the air and water are clean for all or living in the wrong zip code condemns you to drink and breathe poison. All these features of society matter morally for everyone because they form the conditions, the soil, as it were, within which the indestructible seed of each person's humanity takes root and either grows or withers. The Catholic view of human worth, in short, affirms that we are responsible for each other and that the integrity of our own individual souls depends upon embracing that responsibility.

To be made in the image and likeness of God, in the end, means not only that we are made of something but that we are made *for* something—for God, yes, and, as we see in the unity of the two greatest commandments, for each other as well.

SHALL OR SHALL NOT?
THE PROBLEM OF MORAL HIERARCHIES

One of the most complicated challenges in building a moral and political theory is organizing what appear to be competing goods. For example, how should we define the rights of the individual in relation to the well-being of the community? How do we support economic dynamism and wealth-producing free markets while protecting families from job losses and safeguarding the environment at the same time? How do we manage complex global issues in ways that uphold the agency of those most directly affected? These and numerous other ostensible "trade-offs" form the intricate web of ethical, legal, social, and political questions that constitute the set of problems any political philosophy will have to address. It can feel overwhelming. So where to begin?

The first point to highlight, which becomes more obvious the older you get, is that life is hard and finding a way to live together is even harder. One of the dangers of ideological thinking is that it seduces you into a reduction of reality that, upon sober reflection, is always too good to be true. Politicians who tell you that the oceans will cease to rise, that we will no longer be dependent on other nations, or that all poverty will disappear if they are elected are all trying to sell you something, and it isn't the truth. The reality is that finding just and durable solutions to immensely complex social problems is not something we should ever expect to be straightforward or painless.

Recognizing moral complexity, however, does not mean embracing moral ambiguity. One of the greatest strengths of Catholic social thought is its blend of theoretical clarity at the level of principles and practical agility at the level of applying those principles to the intricacies of human life. In a reversal from previous sections, I want to move forward by highlighting and explaining this blend of moral rigor and applied flexibility in the Catholic social thought tradition before showing how ideological models fail to live up to those standards.

First, however, we need some principles to work with, a set of criteria to compare the validity of competing sociopolitical theories. For the sake of argument, let's say that any theory worth its salt should be able to meet five fundamental criteria, each of which contains an internal tension. The theory should be able to:

1. recognize universal moral values while showing how those values can be applied to diverse times and places

2. recognize universal moral values while creating a space for the freedom of conscience to interpret and apply those values

3. recognize a framework of justice that is not reducible to the whim of a majority yet also enables individuals

to participate in the creation of the laws by which they
are governed

4. recognize a framework of justice that upholds the
moral unity of the human family while also recognizing
that individuals have both the freedom and responsibility
to give special care to those closest to them

5. recognize a framework for economic life that creates
the conditions for material prosperity while ensuring
that such prosperity does not come at the expense of
the most vulnerable or the integrity of the natural world

One of the golden threads that binds this set of principles,
especially principles one through four, is the need to build a
political theory on an objective foundation. Despite the pre-
dominance of moral relativism in the West, it remains the case
that no moral theory, including any political theory, can have
rational authority unless it is grounded in universal truth, as we
saw above. Secularism is allergic to these words, but the truth of
this statement remains self-evident: if we claim that all values
are relative—meaning none of them are objectively true—then we
are consequently accepting that every moral principle, whether
it be to care for the poor or to protect individual freedom or to
preserve the environment, is equally arbitrary. Saying "I don't
believe in universal truth but I do believe in environmentalism"
or "social justice" or "equal pay" is tantamount to saying "I am
a firm believer in things I do not believe to be true." To think in
this way is to embrace literal nonsense, canceling with my mouth
what I claim to believe in my mind. Principles one through four
thus stand athwart the incoherence of contemporary relativism,
affirming that if we don't have universal, objective moral values
to guide us forward, we have nothing at all.

At the same time, however, principles one through four also
recognize that human beings are diverse, both individually and

in the kinds of communities we form. At the anthropological level, universal truth must be apprehended and applied by each person living within her or his own circumstances. We are not interchangeable cogs within a mechanical moral universe. We are individuals who live in particular families, in particular places, within particular cultures. That particularity is profoundly morally important. For this reason, principles one through four also affirm that every political theory should conceive of universal values in ways that respect individuals' freedom of conscience, ability to participate in decision-making, and obligations to care for those nearest and dearest, not least because it is at the local level that many problems can be best diagnosed and most effectively addressed.

Principle five, in turn, recognizes the necessity for structuring the economy in a way that not only allows people to meet their physical needs but also engenders the conditions for the expansion of human ingenuity and the creation of wealth—wealth that can be used to fuel improvements in well-being like those we have seen in the past century, including a massive decrease in absolute poverty across the globe.[13] The same principle also recognizes, however, that economic growth can leave significant portions of the population behind and should never be an end in and of itself, as it can foment a consumerist mentality that hinders human development and the integrity of the natural world. The principle thus couches the morally justified call for economic stability and growth within an equally morally justified call for protection of the most vulnerable and the health of the environment.

13. The United Nations has recently observed, "There has been marked progress in reducing poverty over the past decades. According to the most recent estimates, in 2015, 10 per cent of the world's population lived at or below $1.90 a day. That's down from 16 per cent in 2010 and 36 per cent in 1990. This means that ending extreme poverty is within our reach." See "Ending Poverty," United Nations website, https://www.un.org/en/global-issues/ending-poverty#:~:text=There%20 has%20been%20marked%20progress,poverty%20is%20within%20our%20reach.

Of course, it is possible to take issue with any of these principles or all of them together. However, doing so would entail rejecting one or more of the following goods: universal morality, individual freedom of conscience, local autonomy, economic growth, and/or protecting the vulnerable and the environment. It's not clear that such a viewpoint would be morally—or politically—viable, at least in democratic contexts. So, at least for the sake of argument, let's assume that these principles do, indeed, serve as valid, if limited, criteria for evaluating a political theory. The next question, then, is how we can build a theory that meets these criteria.

The first step is to establish the right relationship between the political theory's "shalls" and "shall nots." We can call this the relationship between "negative prohibitions" and "positive injunctions." The reason this question lies at the foundation of every political theory is because all moral principles ultimately take only one of two forms—they either identify something we *should not do* (a prohibition) or something we *should do* (an injunction or obligation). At this point, I want to start introducing the substance of Catholic social thought itself because it serves as a paradigmatic example of how "shalls" and "shall nots" can—and, I will argue, should—be related to each other.

Given its affirmation of the unity of all truth, Catholicism recognizes that the truths of revelation in Scripture never contradict the truths we can apprehend by means of rational reflection. This is the case with moral truth as well. As such, we can turn to two familiar biblical passages, one from the Old Testament and one from the New Testament, to identify the Catholic conception of the relationship between the "shalls" and "shall nots." The first is Exodus 20, in which God first communicates the Ten Commandments to Moses. The ordering in Catholic tradition is:

1. I am the Lord your God . . . you shall have no other gods before me.

2. You shall not make wrongful use of the name of the Lord your God.

3. Remember the sabbath day, and keep it holy.

4. Honor your father and mother.

5. You shall not murder.

6. You shall not commit adultery.

7. You shall not steal.

8. You shall not bear false witness against your neighbor.

9. You shall not covet your neighbor's wife.

10. You shall not covet your neighbor's goods.

For our purposes, it is important to note that eight of the ten commandments—with the exceptions of "Remember the sabbath day, and keep it holy" and "Honor your father and mother"—take the form of negative prohibitions, meaning they explicitly and categorically forbid certain kinds of actions. Specifically, it is always and without exception wrong to engage in idolatry or misuse God's name, to kill an innocent human life, to have sexual relations outside of your marriage, to take what does not belong to you, to slander (and to lie more generally), to intentionally desire someone other than your spouse, and to intentionally desire that which belongs to someone else.

These prohibitions form the foundation of Catholic morality, a morality that recognizes moral absolutes—principles that must never be violated, no matter what purported "good" may result. Consequently, there is no freedom of conscience, and thus no room for debate, about whether or how to respect these principles because there is only one way not to do something—*not to do it*. If indeed an action is categorically prohibited, which is another way of saying that the action is intrinsically evil, then our minds are not free to come to a different conclusion, either about the morality of the principle itself or about the circumstances in which it would apply. Whatever additional principles Catholic morality broadly and Catholic social thought more particularly may contain, they cannot violate these prohibitions. "Shall not" always means "must not," no matter what.

Catholic morality, however, also contains injunctions or obligations in addition to prohibitions. Perhaps the clearest expression of these obligations comes in Matthew 25, when Jesus, discussing the Final Judgment, specifically enumerates the kinds of actions all humans, especially Christians, are called to perform. After identifying those who will be granted admission into eternal life, Jesus says:

> Then he will say to those at his left hand, "You that are ac-cursed, depart from me into the eternal fire prepared for the devil and his angels; for I was hungry and you gave me no food, I was thirsty and you gave me nothing to drink, I was a stranger and you did not welcome me, naked and you did not give me clothing, sick and in prison and you did not visit me." Then they also will answer, "Lord, when was it that we saw you hungry or thirsty or a stranger or naked or sick or in prison, and did not take care of you?" Then he will answer them, "Truly I tell you, just as you did not do it to one of the least of these, you did not do it to me." (Matt. 25:41–45)

In conflating the treatment of the "least" in society with the treatment of Jesus Christ himself, the same Lord who announced that he has come to fulfill and not abolish the Law (Matt. 5:17) leaves no ambiguity about the requirements of morality: We are called not only to refrain from certain prohibited actions but also to perform certain actions, those that, broadly, entail the care of the most vulnerable. Consequently, just as with the negative prohibitions, there is no freedom of conscience, and thus no debate, about whether we must obey these positive commands. We must. And Christ makes clear that the stakes could not be higher; refusing to care for the vulnerable, refusing to act on their behalf, is tantamount to refusing Jesus Christ himself and his offer of eternal life.

It is crucial to recognize, however, that even within these injunctions Catholic morality still recognizes expansive freedom of conscience—specifically, you have the liberty to consult and obey your conscience on how to live out the positive commandments in your life. To be sure, there is only one way to obey a negative prohibition—again, not to do it. And if we are indeed commanded to do something, there is also no choice about whether we obey. However, *there are numerous ways to obey*—numerous ways to feed the poor, to clothe the naked, and to give drink to the thirsty. This diversity of possibilities, a diversity of ways to pursue the same goods, generates a moral framework in which there can and should be authentic, good-willed debate about the most effective way to abide by Jesus' commands. There can be legitimate, even welcome, disagreement in this domain of morality and a legitimate plurality of approaches.

This is a mark of genius at the heart of Catholic morality and, more specifically, Catholic social thought. In recognizing both the existence of moral absolutes and the flexibility on how to apply those absolutes, it produces a theory that contains both the stability of universal moral objectivity and the suppleness required to interpret and apply that objectivity both at the level of individual conscience and at the level of diverse social, political, and environmental circumstances. What it means to care for the poor, for example, can and should look very different in a developing economy than it does within an advanced economy. Whether a particular welfare policy will harm rather than assist the vulnerable can be a question of serious debate, as can determining how to create conditions that produce the resources necessary to fund those programs in the first place. To put an

even finer point on it, the relationship between the "shalls" and
"shall nots" in Catholic morality allows for both the claim that
abortion is always wrong and should be categorically prohibited
and the responsibility to engage in good-willed conversation
about how to create a society in which mothers and fathers will
be less likely to consider abortion as an option. It is not one or
the other. It is both.

This both/and approach to morality synthesizes every principle in Catholic social thought, which, according to the moral
theologian Fr. William Byron, can ultimately be grouped into
ten ethical building blocks.[14] Let me conclude this section by
explaining each building block and then suggesting how together
they address the problem of competing goods and meet the five
criteria for a coherent sociopolitical theory outlined above.

The ten building blocks are:

1. Human Dignity: the principle that every human being
has inherent and irreducible value because every human
is made in the image and likeness of God

2. Human Life: the principle that, because of human
dignity, every person has a right to life from conception
until natural death

3. Human Equality: the principle that, because of equal
human dignity, each person must be treated with equal
moral regard independent of any unique personal characteristics he/she may possess or whatever utility he/she
may have for society

4. Association: the principle that, because human beings
are social beings, every person has the right to freely

---

14. Adapted from William J. Byron, "Framing the Principles of Catholic Social
Thought," *Journal of Catholic Education* 3, no. 1 (1999): 7–14.

associate with others, including (though not limited to) in religious and labor associations

5. Solidarity: the principle that all human beings are members of the same human family and that, therefore, to quote Martin Luther King Jr., injustice anywhere is a threat to justice everywhere

6. Participation: the principle that, because human beings live in unique specific communities, all people have the right to participate in the formation of the specific laws that govern them

7. Subsidiarity: the principle that, in light of the right to participation, political power should be relegated to those who are most directly responsible for the care of the community, starting with individuals and families

8. Stewardship: the principle that, in light of the goodness of creation, humans have an obligation to care for the integrity of the natural world

9. Preferential Option for the Poor: the principle that, recognizing that some members of the community are more susceptible to harm than others, all economic and social policies should be evaluated through the lens of how they might negatively affect the most vulnerable

10. The Common Good: the summative principle that all parts of society—individual, family, community, state, nation, and globe—should work to create the conditions for human flourishing, recognizing that justice is not a zero-sum game (meaning that the success of one group need not come at the expense of another if society is properly organized)

These constellations of principles, individually and taken together, show how Catholic social thought comprehensively addresses the problem of competing goods, with which we began this section. First, there are no "competing goods" from a Catholic point of view. Because there is one God who creates one human race, there is, consequently, one good that is the true good for all humanity. As such, the good for one person, family, community, state, or nation *cannot*, by definition, be in conflict with the authentic good of another person, family, community, state, or nation. This is the great synthesizing principle of the common good in Catholic social ethics: Although sin makes the realization of the perfect good impossible in human history, there is nothing that prevents us from continually aiming for a good that seeks the flourishing of all human beings, individually and communally.

Second, the ten building blocks, seen through the lens of the right relationship between moral prohibitions and moral obligations, identify a clear framework for how to construct a just moral hierarchy in society, one that *never* does anything to violate human dignity, human life, or equal regard and *always* acts to create the material and social conditions that are conducive to human flourishing and the pursuit of the common good (in a way that both respects local agency and individual conscience and protects the most vulnerable, including the most vulnerable of all—the unborn). To be sure, applying this framework to a particular society is complex, but at the very least, Catholic social ethics provides a sturdy and agile way to engage that complexity.

Finally, this framework also meets the five criteria identified earlier. Catholic social thought is built upon an objective and universal foundation and grounded in the authentic human good, which, in turn, is grounded in a doctrine of the source of all truth, God. At the same time, it upholds individual freedom of conscience, individual participation, and, more generally, applied flexibility in how each person and community decides to apply those values. Likewise, it recognizes both the need to engender vibrant economies and the need to protect the vulnerable and the environment.

So how, in the end, does this model stack up against the ideological alternatives? In short, very well. As we have seen in previous sections—and as we will explore in greater depth in part II of this book—one of the defining characteristics of an ideology is that it reduces moral reality in a way that forces individuals and communities to make a choice between authentic goods. Catholic social thought ultimately reveals the fallacy and futility of forcing such binary choices. For example, should we embrace moral universality or moral particularity? Respect individual rights (including the right to life) or the well-being of the community? Economic dynamism or care for the poor? Human solidarity or local autonomy? The good of one's nation or the good of the world? A healthy environment or a healthy GDP? Robust families or robust civic communities? To these and many other binary political questions, Catholic social thought offers a coherent and liberating answer: *choose all of them.*

VERBUM HOMINIS: THE PROBLEM OF FREE SPEECH

One of the greatest threats to freedom in our age is what we could call the "pathologizing of dissent." Rather than saying, "I think differently from you," or "Your position is false," or, even, "You are wrong," it is increasingly common to hear from those with whom you disagree that you suffer from a phobia or are motivated by "hate." These charges are equivalent to claiming that the person dissenting is mentally ill and/or morally repulsive. Think, for example, of the implication of being tagged as "homophobic" or "transphobic" (or both) for holding the utterly rational view that marriage is properly defined as a union between a biological male and a biological female and that males and females are not definitionally interchangeable. To have a "phobia" is to have an overwhelming fear that renders one incapable of thinking and acting reasonably. It is a form of mental illness. Thus, to call someone "homophobic" or "transphobic" is to say that they are mentally incapacitated and in need of therapy at best and medication and possibly institutionalization (or, perhaps better put, re-education) at worst.

The same goes for being called a "hater" for expressing an unauthorized point of view. Hate, at least in a secular context, primarily concerns the motivation of the speaker, so to call someone a "hater" is to say that she or he has the motivation to do harm, even to destroy, an individual or a group for no other reason than personal animus. In other words, it's to call someone evil. Being labeled this way, just as being labeled as having a phobia, effectively pushes the dissenting individual outside the bounds of rational discourse.

The motivation for this rhetorical ploy, which is overwhelmingly emerging from the political left (which we will explore in greater depth in the chapter on "progressivism/wokeism"), is as obvious as it is cunning: by marking people as mentally unfit and evil, this tactic eliminates the obligation to engage the content and rational validity of what they are saying. The thinking goes like this: There's just no reasoning with crazy people or evil people or, even more so, crazy evil people. Heck, you don't even have to tolerate them. The only viable option is to get them under control, to keep them from—and here's another word weapon in their arsenal—"harming" others with their speech. Combined with the postmodern assertion that there is no such thing as objective truth, this pathologizing of dissent creates the perfect storm for totalitarianism. Imagine all the people who can no longer disagree with the new orthodoxies because the very fact that they disagree is incontrovertible proof of their mangled minds and guilty consciences. The administrators of secular culture thus increasingly leave us with two options: either enthusiastically obey—no, celebrate—the prevailing cultural narrative or be swept under its unabated march toward progress. And, by the way, don't you dare think about trying to stay neutral, because, as the ski-masked chorus chants, "Silence is violence."

What can be done to turn this tide? Specific to our purposes, what can Catholic social thought contribute to a solution, to the re-legitimizing of dissent and the rebirth of moral argumentation? As I hope this book has shown this far—and as I hope this section will additionally demonstrate—*a lot*. Indeed, the Catholic social thought tradition contains within it the resources to justify a fundamental civil right to the freedom of speech. Thus, although Catholicism may not be known for it, the Church has every reason to advocate for the cause of free speech in society, both because free speech is a prerequisite for freedom of religion and, more broadly, because free speech lies at the heart of what it means to be human.

The first response to this claim very well may be, "Really?" Are you talking about the same Catholic Church that condemned Galileo and that has, in previous centuries, approved of the execution of heretics? Yes, I am. But two points on this. First, I do not mean this section to serve as a defense of actions taken by the institutional church in the past that violated rather than represented its moral teachings. The Church—understood as the members of the institutional Church and not the Mystical Body of Christ—is far from perfect and has often acted in ways that reflect the moral failings of its members and the culture of its period more than the truth of its principles. We need not hide from these failings. We should learn from them.

Second, it is important to qualify that Catholic social thought strongly supports a *civil* freedom of speech, which includes religious liberty protections and protections against viewpoint discrimination in public forums. The question of the regulation of speech in private forums is much more complex, as we see, for example, in contemporary debates about whether and to what extent social media companies should be free to police speech on their platforms while enjoying the legal protections of entities that do not regulate speech (like internet providers). In my interpretation of the Catholic defense of free speech, I in no way intend to support a position that could be used against the Church's freedom and responsibility to ensure that its clergy and lay employees faithfully communicate Catholic doctrine, which includes the right to dismiss those who willfully fail to do so. At the same time, however, I also defend an interpretation that is as expansive as possible, with the goal of creating a culture that allows and even encourages individuals to speak what they believe to be true without fear of reprisal, either from the state or from civil society.

With those provisos, where then does the Church's justification for a right to free speech lie in its social doctrines? The first feature of Catholic social thought to highlight is, as we have seen previously, its foundation in objective truth. One of the implications of such a foundation is that Catholic thought upholds not only moral realism but also ontological realism, meaning it recognizes that there are *true* definitions of things in the world. The significance of realism for the defense of free speech cannot be overstated. Without this foundation, without recognizing that words are—or at least should be—tied to fixed concepts, words can mean anything that those who have the power to manipulate them want them to mean.

Indeed, this is one of the central themes in the classic dystopian novel *1984*. The totalitarian Ministry of Truth in the book methodically unmoors words from any fixed meaning so it can use them to advance its control over society. So, for example, the Ministry's slogans are "War Is Peace," "Freedom Is Slavery," and "Ignorance Is Strength."[15] Such terms rightfully sound ridiculous to our ears, but how different are they from these phrases that have recently joined our lexicon: "Colorblindness Is Racism," "Men Are Women," "The Violence Is Mostly Peaceful," or "The

15. George Orwell, *1984* (New York: Penguin Classics, 1950), 26.

News Is Fake But Accurate"? Once again, it is only by upholding ontological realism and objective truth that such abuses of language can be both identified and condemned as violations of truth, both logically and substantively. That goes, too, for defending the meaning of freedom of speech—unless we fix the meaning of these words, the terms can be twisted to signify their exact opposite, which is seen, for example, in the claim that "free speech is a weapon against freedom."[16] In short, free speech, both as a concept and as a right, can only exist within a certain kind of linguistic and metaphysical context. Catholicism provides such a context.

Second, the principle of free speech appears in two complementary ways within Catholic social teaching itself, one as an instrumental good (meaning a good that serves a higher good) and the other as an intrinsic good (that is, as a good in and of itself). Let me begin by addressing free speech as an instrumental good.

The right to religious freedom and its moral twin, the freedom of conscience, has always been at the heart of Catholic teaching, but it emerged especially forcefully in Vatican II. *Dignitatis Humanae*, the Second Vatican Council's declaration on religious freedom, states, for example, "The right of the human person to religious freedom is to be recognized in the constitutional law whereby a society is governed and thus it is to become a civil right."[17] The document elaborates,

> Truth . . . is to be sought after in a manner proper to the dignity
> of the human person and his social nature. The inquiry is to
> be free, carried on with the aid of teaching or instruction,
> communication and dialogue, in the course of which men

16. See, for example, this article in the *New York Times* for a representative of this viewpoint: Adam Liptak, "How Conservatives Weaponized the First Amendment," *New York Times*, June 30, 2018, https://www.nytimes.com/2018/06/30/us/politics/first-amendment-conservatives-supreme-court.html.

17. Second Vatican Council, *Dignitatis Humanae* 2, December 7, 1965, vatican.va.

explain to one another the truth they have discovered, or think they have discovered, in order thus to assist one another in the quest for truth.[18]

Although the document does not discuss a right to free speech explicitly, it is clear from the context that such a right is presumed because there can be no religious freedom, no unhindered search for truth, without free speech. If we have a right to seek the truth, as the document states, then we also have the right both to hear others speaking and to speak freely ourselves as we come to our own understanding of truth. Indeed, the document confirms that the search for truth should be "immune from coercion on the part of individuals or of social groups or of any human power."[19] That's as clear as it gets. No one has the legitimate authority to prevent you from following the lights of your own conscience, which necessarily entails being able to say what you believe to be true. If there is a right to religious freedom, there is also a right to free speech.

To be sure, this interpretation of the meaning of religious freedom could generate some objections, both related to *Dignitatis Humanae* itself and more broadly to the conceptual relationship between freedom of religion and freedom of speech. Couldn't one say, for example, that the document is only recognizing the freedom to search for *the Catholic* understanding of truth and thereby surreptitiously imposing its view of reality on society through the Trojan Horse of religious liberty? Indeed, doesn't the same magisterial body hold the view that "error has no rights"?[20]

First, while the claim "Error has no rights" has long been an expression of magisterial teaching, the claim has more to do with

18. *Dignitatis Humanae* 3.
19. *Dignitatis Humanae* 2.
20. For an explanation of how to interpret the claim "error has no rights," see John Courtney Murray, "Religious Freedom," Georgetown University Library, https://www.library.georgetown.edu/woodstock/murray/1965ib.

the necessary conceptual relationship between the good and the true rather than serving as an argument against free speech. At a conceptual level, to have a "right" to something implies that that to which you have the right is "good." In turn, to say something is good necessarily implies that it is true; otherwise, we would be forced to say that there are good things that are also false things. Thus, to say that "error"—which is another way of saying "falsity"—"has no rights" is equivalent to saying that "there is no right to do that which is false," which, in a moral context, is equivalent to saying that "there is no right to do that which is bad." Thus, claiming "error has no rights" is merely a conceptual tautology; it does not have to lead to the conclusion that individuals do not have the freedom to say or do things that the Church deems to be wrong (that is, not in accordance with the truth).

Second, clarifying this point is precisely what *Dignitatis Humanae* does in restating the Church's perennial teaching that "man's response to God in faith must be free" and that "no one therefore is to be forced to embrace the Christian faith against his own will."[21] Pope Emeritus Benedict XVI has expressed the same point, saying that the "Church [only] grows by attraction."[22] In other words, in recognizing the freedom to pursue the truth, the Church is recognizing a right to follow one's conscience in discerning the nature of truth, whatever one's conscience determines that to be.

I hasten to add that that does not mean the Church believes that all personal truths are epistemically or morally equal, which would be a form of relativism. Rather, the Church's position is that all people have the right to pursue the truth in their own way, even if that means they are pursuing objective error. This right naturally transfers to the right to free speech as well—the

---

21. *Dignitatis Humanae* 10.

22. "Church grows by attraction, not proselytism, Pope says," Catholic News Agency, May 13, 2007, https://www.catholicnewsagency.com/news/church _grows_by_attraction_not_proselytism_pope_says.

Church's position is not that everyone's speech is true speech, but rather that they should be able to speak what they believe to be true even if it is objectively false. The corollary, of course, is that others would have the same right to identify the content of the speech as false and offer a better (truer) alternative. Free speech, in other words, cuts both ways—it allows for error and for the correction of error.

Another possible objection to linking religious freedom to freedom of speech is the question of why religious freedom *has* to take the form of public speech. Isn't it enough to say that individuals can say whatever they want in their private lives but should be limited when operating in the public sphere? First, *Dignitatis Humanae* explicitly rejects that the freedom of religion—and, consequently, the freedom of speech—should be limited to private spaces. It declares, for example, "The social nature of man . . . itself requires that he should give external expression to his internal acts of religion."[23] Seeking the truth, in other words, is an essentially private *and* public act, according to the Church; it is something that we do together, so constraining the search to some state-defined "private" domain of life would be to deny religious freedom itself, as well as the freedom of speech inherent within it.

There is a broader anthropological point here too, one which the famed psychologist and philosopher Jordan Peterson highlights in his own defense of free speech—and one I believe that the Church agrees with. In a now viral video with a BBC journalist who was assertively pressing Peterson on why he insisted that people should be able to speak freely even if some find it offensive, Peterson replied, "In order to be able to think, you need to risk being offensive."[24] His point is not that one should

23. *Dignitatis Humanae* 3.
24. Channel 4 News, "Jordan Peterson debate on the gender pay gap, campus protests and postmodernism," YouTube video, January 16, 2018, https://www .youtube.com/watch?v=aMcjxSThD54.

deliberately seek to be offensive. Rather, he is recognizing that there is a mutually dependent relationship between speaking and thinking whose integrity supersedes the moral obligation to not offend. For we do not merely speak what we know to be true—*we speak so that we can figure out what is true.*

As a professor, I see this dynamic relationship between speaking and thinking all the time. Students—and I count myself as a student—don't write papers simply to express what they believe about a topic. If they're taking the assignment seriously, they write papers to figure out what they believe about a topic. The implication of this connection between thought and speech is clear: if we are not able to speak freely—either out loud or on paper—we will not be able to think freely either. Likewise, if someone or some group can control our speech, including on the grounds of it being "offensive," then they can, in a decisive sense, control our thinking as well—a fact about human beings that every tyrant learns by heart.

In sum, and to repeat the original conclusion drawn from *Dignitatis Humanae*, there is no rational or moral way to sever a right to religious freedom from a right to free speech. If we have the former, we necessarily have the latter.

It is also important to recognize, however, that the freedom of speech has more than instrumental value in Catholic thought. Speaking freely is not only good because it enables freedom of religion. It is good in and of itself. We see the roots of this perspective on speech all the way back in the book of Genesis. In the narration of the creation story, God grants human beings a unique power over existence, a power that humans alone enjoy: the power of naming. In the second chapter of Genesis, we read:

> Then the Lord God said, "It is not good that the man should
> be alone; I will make him a helper as his partner." So out of
> the ground the Lord God formed every animal of the field and
> every bird of the air, and brought them to the man to see what

he would call them; and whatever the man called each living
creature, that was its name. (Gen. 2:18–19)

The biblical tradition is clear that God alone creates in an
absolute sense. However, we participate in that creation in the act
of naming. To be sure, we only have this power because God has
gifted it to us. But it is our power, and, in its use, we humanize
everything in existence. The power of speech is thus not merely
one human characteristic among others. It is at the heart of our
identity as humans; it is essential for both how we relate to God,
our Creator, and to creation itself. It is also at the heart of how we
relate to each other, which we see a few verses later. We hear the
first directly documented human words in biblical history as the
first man, Adam, recognizes the first woman, Eve. Adam speaks,

> This at last is bone of my bones and flesh of my flesh; this one
> shall be called Woman, for out of Man this one was taken.
> (Gen. 2:23)

It is speech, as we see in Genesis, that simultaneously differenti-
ates and unites human beings both in relation to existence and in
relation to each other. We are all individuals, none of us the same.
And we are all humans, all of us the same. The spoken word, the
naming, is the bridge we build, and that builds us, between this
diversity and unity.

For these reasons, speech is much more than an instrumental
good. It is at the same time the tool we use to understand the
world and our place in it and the expression of the same world
and our place in it. In short, when we speak, we don't just do. We
are. To limit the freedom of speech, therefore, is not only to stop
people from speaking. It is to stop them from being, to deprive
them of the fullness of their humanity. To come full circle, it is
to strip them of their dignity, which is precisely the reason that
the Second Vatican Council's title for its declaration on religious

freedom is *Dignitatis Humanae*—which, translated, means, "On the dignity of the human being."

In the end, this embrace of both the instrumental and intrinsic good of speech just might be Catholic social thought's most potent weapon against ideologies. The reason is because all ideologies, like different-shaped cookie cutters pressing themselves on the structure of reality, seek to constrict the scope of existence to fit within their particular narratives. Whatever doesn't fit the mold is useless at best and dangerous at worst and thus needs to be tossed away. Ideologies, in other words, are always tribal, not only politically but also epistemically—they build walls and pour moats around their incomplete packages of truth and prohibit thinking outside those boundaries. And the danger, of course, is that we get trapped within one of those boundaries, each of us stuck in a thought bubble, either listlessly stagnant or running around in frenetic circles. Either way, when you are trapped in a bubble, all you can hear is yourself, even if the words come through someone else's mouth. And that's just how the idealogues like it.

If there's one way to prevent this atomization and mental incarceration of humanity, or one way to escape it once it has been imposed, it is to allow people to speak freely. For once we are allowed to speak freely in an environment without coercion, we are finally allowed to think freely. And once we are allowed to think freely, we are free to believe freely. And once we are allowed to believe freely, we are free to give ourselves to the truth we have come to believe. In a fallen world, we should never expect that everyone will come to the same conclusion about what defines that truth. Yet, on this side of the eschaton, there is no better way to give each person a fighting chance to find the one true God, who alone can unite us, than to allow all people to think for themselves and speak their own minds. In this sense, all champions of free speech have a sure friend in Catholic social thought.

SYNTHESIZING AND EMBODYING CATHOLIC SOCIAL THOUGHT: THE EXAMPLE OF ST. JOHN PAUL II

One of the most powerful evangelical dimensions of Catholicism is its doctrine of the saints. The existence of saints—those whom the Church recognizes as being in heaven—enables those of us on this side of the veil to answer one of the toughest questions you can pose to a system of moral belief: "That may sound good in theory, but what does it look like in practice?"

Secular theories have a hard time answering this question honestly. What does a perfect Kantian, utilitarian, socialist, libertarian, or environmentalist look like? Can any one of these theories point to a concrete answer, someone who embodies the beliefs of the ethical system in such a way that little or no space exists between theory and practice? As a test, just read a bit of Marxism, for example, and compare it to Karl Marx the man, who, according to historian Paul Johnson, had a long-term live-in maid whom he never paid any wages (and with whom he fathered a child that he refused to recognize).[25] The least we can say, charitably, is there were some inconsistencies between Marx's personal life and his ideas about the exploitation of labor. And if Karl Marx can't be an ideal Marxist, who could?

To be sure, religions, especially Christianity, shouldn't get a pass on the authenticity test. Which Christian would be willing to say, at least out loud, that she or he is an ideal or even *good* representation of what it means to follow Christ? We should hope no one, not least because such a declaration would be a practical contradiction, like bragging about being humble. Yet that's precisely the beauty of sainthood in Catholicism—it is the Church that recognizes individuals as saints, not the saints themselves, and we do so not on human authority but through a process that confirms, through supernatural intervention in the form of demonstrable miracles, that the saints have "fought the

---

25. Paul Johnson, *Intellectuals* (New York: Harper Perennial, 1988), 78–79.

good fight . . . finished the race . . . [and] kept the faith" (2 Tim. 4:7). In other words, they have been saved, perfected in grace, for all eternity. As such, their lives offer an embodied, historical example of what it means to think, speak, and act like a true Christian, an authentic follower of Christ. It's not that they were perfect while on earth; they were, however, on the authentic path to perfection. Thus, the Catholic answer to "What does real Catholicism look like in practice?" is "Like all these holy people; take your pick!"

For the final section of this chapter, which concludes part I of the book, I will highlight the life and teachings of Pope St. John Paul II, who was born in 1920, became pope in 1978 and remained so until his death in 2005, and then was canonized on April 27, 2014. John Paul II is one of the Church's most vivid and comprehensive examples of its social thought in the flesh. He synthesizes the principles covered in this chapter, offers a model for how to live them, and provides a bridge to part II of the book, which explores how Catholic social thought can address specific secular political ideologies.

One of the pillars of John Paul II's sociopolitical thought was his rejection of ideological forms of thinking, all of which, he believed, imposed a false choice on human beings. In his 1991 encyclical *Centesimus Annus,* which was published to mark the one-hundred-year anniversary of the 1891 encyclical by Pope Leo XIII *Rerum Novarum*, he spoke these words about the relationship between human beings and the political and economic systems they construct:

> The individual today is often suffocated between two poles represented by the State and the marketplace. At times it seems as though he exists only as a producer and consumer of goods, or as an object of State administration. People lose sight of the fact that life in society has neither the market nor the State as

its final purpose, since life itself has a unique value which the
State and the market must serve.[26]

This passage captures Catholicism's fundamental rejection of
ideologies as false substitutes for authentic meaning and purpose
in life. "Market" and "State" here stand in for all political and
economic systems of thought. Whether it is the party, profits,
economic growth, economic equality, individual sovereignty, or,
more recently, the natural environment, living as if any of these
goods could serve as the *ultimate* human good is not only a lie,
ontologically and morally speaking, but also gets the relationship
between humans and the political and economic systems we
create precisely backward. We are not made to serve institutions.
They are made to serve us, to protect us and assist us in reaching
the fullness of our humanity—a fullness that cannot be reduced
to this or that temporal system because our true good exists
beyond all systems as such. As John Paul II puts it in the same
document,

> It is not possible to understand man on the basis of economics
> alone, nor to define him simply on the basis of class member-
> ship. Man is understood in a more complete way when he is
> situated within the sphere of culture through his language,
> history, and the position he takes towards the fundamental
> events of life, such as birth, love, work, and death. At the heart
> of every culture lies the attitude man takes to the greatest
> mystery: the mystery of God.[27]

This is not to say that all economic and political systems are
morally equal. In the same document, John Paul II unequivocally
defends private property, condemns socialism, and recognizes the

---

26. John Paul II, *Centesimus Annus* 49, encyclical letter, May 1, 1991, vatican.va.
27. *Centesimus Annus* 24.

limited but real power of the free market to do good. It is to say, though, that no economic or political system is a substitute for religion and for the worship of the one true God, who is present in the world but can never be reduced to anything in it. Without orienting ourselves to this mystery of the true God, every system of thought becomes a false religion constructing material idols to its artificial divinities.

John Paul II is adamant, however, that locating the true good of human beings in the mystery of God does not mean we must embrace moral ambiguity. Indeed, as he also states in *Centesimus Annus*:

> If there is no ultimate truth to guide and direct political activity, then ideas and convictions can easily be manipulated for reasons of power. As history demonstrates, a democracy without values easily turns into open or thinly disguised totalitarianism.[28]

In describing the truth as "ultimate" here, John Paul II is affirming that the right understanding and orientation of human life demands recognizing the existence of an objective moral order that is grounded in the source of all truth itself, God. The consequences of abandoning truth as an epistemic and moral foundation are devastating to humanity, a theme John Paul II discusses in depth in another encyclical, *Veritatis Splendor*. While noting freedom's authentic victories over Nazism and Communism in the twentieth century, he warns that freedom, without a grounding of truth, will create "an alliance between democracy and ethical relativism" that "would remove any sure moral reference point from political and social life, and on a deeper level make the acknowledgement of truth impossible."[29] In

28. *Centesimus Annus* 46.
29. John Paul II, *Veritatis Splendor* 101, encyclical letter, August 6, 1993, vatican.va.

other words, without recognizing and respecting objective truth as a necessary foundation for any moral and political system, it is impossible, both conceptually and in practice, to identify which systems are ethically superior to other systems, which, in turn, means that the only thing left to govern human life is raw coercive power—a state of affairs that Pope Benedict XVI, John Paul II's immediate successor, has described as "the dictatorship of relativism."

Now, it is one thing to recognize the necessity of truth from a formal perspective, meaning recognizing that we need truth as such. It is quite another to identify substantive truths. The latter is exponentially more difficult to do in a pluralistic world because it means making a commitment to a particular conception of the good, which means, in turn, rejecting alternative conceptions as false. It means taking a stand. John Paul II showed no hesitation in doing this either. He defended several universal principles against ethical pluralism, but two stand out in this context: (1) the truth that no human society should ever see itself as the perfect instantiation of the kingdom of God, and (2) the equal truth that all humans have an obligation to approximate the kingdom by building and defending what he called a "culture of life."

On the first point, John Paul II writes in *Centesimus Annus*,

> When people think they possess the secret of a perfect social organization which makes evil impossible, they also think that they can use any means, including violence and deceit, in order to bring that organization into being. Politics then becomes a "secular religion" which operates under the illusion of creating paradise in this world. But no political society— which possesses its own autonomy and laws—can ever be confused with the Kingdom of God. . . . It is for God alone to separate the subjects of the Kingdom from the subjects of the Evil One, and . . . this judgment will take place at the end of time. By presuming to anticipate judgment here and now,

man puts himself in the place of God and sets himself against the patience of God.[30]

John Paul II emphasizes here that it is both a theological and anthropological error to believe that any society is perfect or ever could be perfect. Utopianism is, therefore, always wrong, always a false way to understand and organize social reality.

At the same time, however, we can and should fight to progress toward the asymptotic ideal of the kingdom of God, which, for John Paul II, takes the form of building and defending a culture of life. At the heart of that culture is the protection of human dignity; and at the heart of protecting human dignity is protecting the right to life, which takes the form of a categorical prohibition against any law that would permit or enable the killing of innocent human beings. As John Paul II argues in another encyclical, *Evangelium Vitae*:

> It is impossible to further the common good without acknowledging and defending the right to life, upon which all the other inalienable rights of individuals are founded and from which they develop. A society lacks solid foundations when, on the one hand, it asserts values such as the dignity of the person, justice, and peace, but then, on the other hand, radically acts to the contrary by allowing or tolerating a variety of ways in which human life is devalued and violated, especially where it is weak or marginalized. Only respect for life can be the foundation and guarantee of the most precious and essential goods of society, such as democracy and peace.[31]

In locating human dignity and human life at the foundation of Catholic social thought, John Paul II identifies the paradigm that

30. *Centesimus Annus* 25.
31. John Paul II, *Evangelium Vitae* 101, encyclical letter, March 25, 1995, vatican. va.

must guide the construction of any hierarchy of social goods. Whatever else society does to create a just order for its members, it must always and without exception protect innocent human life, for the right to life is the necessary prerequisite for any other right. Period.

And yet, the culture of life, which is another way of saying the common good, is not merely a crystallization of prohibitions. It is a living, breathing culture of positive obligations, obligations we have to one another to create the kind of society in which human beings have the best shot at realizing their full potential. An essential dimension of such a society is the family, the first and most important social organization of every human being. As John Paul II writes in *Centesimus Annus*:

> The first and fundamental structure for "human ecology" is *the family*, in which man receives his first formative ideas about truth and goodness, and learns what it means to love and to be loved, and thus what it actually means to be a person. Here we mean the *family founded on marriage,* in which the mutual gift of self by husband and wife creates an environment in which children can be born and develop their potentialities, become aware of their dignity and prepare to face their unique and individual destiny.[32]

Upon this foundation of family, John Paul II teaches, we build communities that build neighborhoods that build counties and states and provinces and nations and regions and, ultimately, the international community. This is the common good in Catholic social thought—the idea that the right structuring of each level of society leads to a moral environment in which both the personal and communal dimensions of human life can flourish. As John Paul II affirms in *Evangelium Vitae*, "To be actively pro-life is to

---

32. *Centesimus Annus* 39.

contribute to the renewal of society through the promotion of the common good."[33]

Finally, throughout the intricacies of his expression of Catholic social thought, John Paul II recognizes that the implementation of justice and the pursuit of the common good must always include recognizing a right to the freedom of religion, which includes the freedom of speech. In a public letter to the Madrid Conference on European Security and Cooperation, John Paul II wrote:

> Freedom of conscience and of religion . . . is a primary and inalienable right of the human person; what is more, insofar as it touches the innermost sphere of the spirit, one can even say that it upholds the justification, deeply rooted in each individual, of all other liberties.[34]

In the same document, he additionally specifies that this right directly applies to being able to communicate one's views "inside as well as outside places of worship," which includes the use of "media of social communication ([like] press, radio, [and] television),"[35] and, we could certainly add for our time, the internet. In other words, it is clear that the freedom of religion, for John Paul II, necessarily includes within it the freedom of speech.

In the end, I cite all these instances of John Paul II's teaching not only to serve as evidence for the arguments in each section up to this point but to reaffirm that Catholic social thought is not just some free-floating theory. Rather, it is a living system of morality that has been applied throughout history, which we see paradigmatically in the papacy of John Paul II. Indeed, Catholic social thought doesn't just take place in history—it

33. *Evangelium Vitae* 101.

34. John Paul II, "Message of John Paul II on the Value and Content of Freedom of Conscience and of Religion" 5, November 14, 1980, vatican.va.

35. "Message of John Paul II" 4.

directs history. It turns tides that were once believed inexorable; it makes possible forms of justice and peace that were thought to have been impossible. To be sure, Catholic social thought rejects utopianism. But it also rejects pessimism and moral sclerosis with equal vehemence. We cannot be perfect. But we can be better, much better, and, again, we see that truth living in John Paul II.

The great biographer of John Paul II, George Weigel, quotes the renowned twentieth-century American Secretary of State Henry Kissinger, saying, "It would be difficult to imagine anyone having had a greater impact on the twentieth century than the Polish priest and bishop who . . . had described himself as a man called to Rome from a far country."[36] Historical counterfactuals cannot be proven, of course. But it certainly is hard to imagine the fall of Communism and the subsequent liberation of Eastern Europe without this Polish pope. It is hard to imagine that the Iron Curtain, as Winston Churchill famously described it, could have ever fallen were it not for this man of God fighting for the dignity and freedom of the human person. History thus rightfully judges John Paul II as belonging to the sparse but noble pantheon of great figures who fought injustice and won without shedding a drop of blood.

But we, the Church, also honor him as a saint, as a member of the Church Triumphant, which is a far greater honor than history can bestow. John Paul II embodies the spiritual and moral meaning of what it means to be Catholic. He shows us that being Catholic means knowing what is true and good and worth fighting for, speaking clearly in its defense. Equally important, he shows that being Catholic means having the guts to take action to build and defend a culture of life, doing what is right in season and out of season, in the glow of secular praise or, as is more often the case, under the sneer of its scorn. The truth is the truth is

---

36. George Weigel, *Witness to Hope: The Biography of Pope John Paul II* (New York: Harper Perennial, 2020), ix.

the truth is the truth throughout the ages—that's what it means to worship the one true God. And our job is to follow the truth, to fight for it, and to make way for it, wherever it may lead. As we do so, let us hear and heed one of the great anthems of John Paul II, words he spoke at the beginning of his papacy and lived out until the end: *Be not afraid.*

St. John Paul II, pray for us.

Catholic Social Thought and Contemporary Secular Ideologies

CHAPTER 5

Totality without Transcendence: The Anatomy of an Ideology

Part I sought to address two fundamental questions: (1) *How* do I assess and construct a political argument, and (2) *What* can I say to defend and advance the Catholic point of view in particular? Part II synthesizes these questions by illustrating how both the methodology of sound argumentation and the substance of Catholic social thought can constructively respond to secular political theories. Chapter 4 already touched on some of these theories in identifying and defending Catholic social thought's foundational principles. The following chapters will go into much more depth.

There are numerous theories we could engage. However, I focus on four in particular: utilitarianism, classical liberalism/ libertarianism, progressivism/wokeism, and non-theistic conservatism. While not exhaustive, these theories capture a good deal of the ideological diversity that dominates contemporary Western political culture, especially in the United States. Much of the politics of the "right" and the "left" can be charted entirely within them. Marxism stands out as a possible exception, especially given its distinct history and ongoing global influence through the People's Republic of China. However, I do not directly engage Marxism here because this book's focus is primarily on Western political cultures, and Marxism, at least currently, is not significantly influential in the West. Also, to the extent that it *is* influential, it has adopted the form of progressivism, which the book does directly address. In focusing on only these four ideologies, the goal is to provide a basic map of the ideological terrain that can serve as a foundation for more nuanced engagement in specific political contexts.

GRAVEN IMAGES

What is an "ideology"? I've already appealed to the term in the examination of the principles of Catholic social thought, highlighting that one of the characteristics that distinguishes Catholic political theory from all secular political theories is that the Catholic view is not an ideology. Here, in this introductory chapter to part II, I want to lay out in more depth exactly what it means to say that a political theory is or is not "ideological."

Pope St. John Paul II's critique of sociopolitical systems that deny or otherwise ignore humanity's relationship to the "mystery of God," which I cited in the previous chapter, gives us the first clue to what defines an ideology as an ideology—namely, that it provides a totalizing view of reality, including political reality, *without reference to the transcendent.* The *Catechism of the Catholic Church,* promulgated by John Paul II, develops this point in greater detail. It states,

> Every institution is inspired, at least implicitly, by a vision of man and his destiny, from which it derives the point of reference for its judgment, its hierarchy of values, its line of conduct. *Most societies have formed their institutions in the recognition of a certain preeminence of man over things.* Only the divinely revealed religion has clearly recognized man's origin and destiny in God, the Creator and Redeemer. The Church invites political authorities to measure their judgments and decisions against this inspired truth about God and man: Societies not recognizing this vision or rejecting it in the name of their independence from God are brought to seek their

criteria and goal in themselves or to borrow them from some ideology. Since they do not admit that one can defend an objective criterion of good and evil, *they arrogate to themselves an explicit or implicit totalitarian power over man and his destiny*, as history shows.[1]

The rest of this chapter unpacks and critically evaluates the insight that ideologies, notwithstanding their substantial differences, are, as the *Catechism* puts it, united in asserting "a certain preeminence of man over things." In other words, ideologies ground their vision of both what is good and how to achieve that good in something other than God and, as such, relegate all power to govern human life into human hands alone.

Expressed in more formal terms, an ideology is a comprehensive worldview that seeks to *describe* the sum of reality and to *prescribe* a systematic moral and political response to reality so described. As such, ideologies aim for descriptive and normative *totality*—they not only tell you what the world and everything in it is but want to make sure you understand how it all should be as well. It is crucial to add that ideologies establish their totalizing worldviews in one of two ways: they either deny the existence of God altogether (or argue that God's existence has no bearing on morality and politics) or erase the ontological distinction between God and existence by affirming that God's presence is or can be fully manifest in a particular moral and political regime (as we see in theocratic forms of government, for example).

Secular ideologies in particular—which are the focus here—possess three additional characteristics. First, all secular ideologies are forms of idolatry, locating the highest human good as existing within the temporal order rather than in the transcendent. Second, all secular ideologies impose unnecessary mutual exclusivities, insisting that we must make zero-sum

---

1. *Catechism of the Catholic Church* 2244 (emphasis added).

choices between goods (for example, having to choose equality over freedom) when, in fact, we can coherently unite them under the banner of "both/and." And third, all secular ideologies either fail to recognize the full depth, perversity, and persistence of human sin or deny the renewing possibilities of authentic moral progress. Let me explain each feature in more detail.

First, idolatry. At first blush, describing secular ideologies as "idolatrous" may sound like an odd approach for engaging in critique. Isn't idolatry only about "religious stuff"? Doesn't it mean the worshiping of objects, like representations of Baal or Santa Muerte? What does that have to do with morality, politics, and the social order? In the specific sense, "worshiping" can indeed include acts we typically associate with religiosity, like praying, kneeling, offering sacrifices, giving praise, etc. However, there is a broader definition of "worship" as well: "To worship," in its most expansive sense, means *to live for*, to give one's whole life to, to love above all else. This is the sense of "worship" at play when speaking about ideologies. Remember, one of the fundamental characteristics of an ideology is that it seeks to establish a descriptive and prescriptive totality within a purely temporal horizon. By definition, then, if you are living according to an ideology, you are living for a good that is neither grounded in nor oriented toward the transcendent. Functionally speaking, that's the same as worshiping an idol—you are organizing your life according to something that is contingent, temporary, and finite. You might as well be prostrating before a graven chunk of stone.

Think, for example, of communist ideology. Its highest good is the establishment and maintenance of the classless society. That's an idol. Or, on the other side of the spectrum, think of libertarianism; at the heart of libertarian ideology is the belief in the absolute sovereignty of the individual in all affairs in life, only limited by the sovereignty of other individuals. To be a libertarian, then, is to make oneself and one's own conception of reality and morality the highest good. That's an idol too. Fascism, in turn, makes an idol of the nation and, usually, its charismatic leader. In a recent mutation of fascism, different strands of identitarianism render race, ethnic group, sexual orientation, or culture into an idol. The secular green movement practices a more old-school idolatry by fashioning the planet itself as the object of worship. The secular humanist movement shifts the idolatrous focus back to the "progress" of humanity but then dissolves into an internecine battle between classical liberals and utilitarians on the meaning of "progress." In short, there are lots of kinds of ideologies; however, whatever flavor you choose, all of them are ultimately made of the same raw material, a fundamental belief that the purpose of human life is to conform yourself to a reality whose source and summit is in space and time.[2]

But again, why call this idolatry? Couldn't, for example, a libertarian and a communist—bitter ideological enemies—unite in saying they don't worship anything? That worshiping is only something religious people do and that they are *not* religious? (Or, even if they are religious, that their politics and their religion have nothing to do with each other?)

This brings us back to the definition of worship and to the recognition that "worshiping" is as much a part of human life as breathing. *Everybody*, no matter what they believe, must worship something. The logic behind this claim, drawing on St. Thomas Aquinas' examination of the meaning of happiness in the *Summa theologiae*, goes like this: All human beings always act for a goal every time they act voluntarily; in other words, what motivates everything we do on purpose is the attainment of some good

2. It is important to add that not all ideologies are atheistic or agnostic. Theocracies are also forms of idolatry, though they make the obverse error of secular ideologies: instead of seeking to turn something in the world into God, they seek to turn God into something in the world. This is what we see, for example, in the terrorist organization ISIS's attempt to establish a universal Islamic caliphate that erases all substantive differences between worshiping God and being loyal to a political regime. In both secular and theological ideologies, the transcendent is ossified into some expression of temporal totality. The focus of this book, however, is on the nature of and constructive response to secular ideologies in particular.

that we have in mind. Without that good, purposeful action is unintelligible and impossible. For example, a student goes to class because he wants participation points—that's the reason he gets up in the morning, gets dressed, swings on his backpack, and gets on the bus. However, as Aquinas notes, every small goal we have, like getting participation points, is subservient to a higher, more inclusive goal—so, for example, the student wants participation points not because he values the points in and of themselves but because he wants a good grade in the class. But, of course, the chain of motivational reasoning doesn't stop there. The good grade is not desired for itself but for the sake of attaining a high GPA, which, in turn, is not desired for itself but for the sake of becoming valedictorian, which, in turn, is not desired for itself but for the sake of getting into a good college, which is in service of gaining admittance into a top graduate school, which is in service of getting a high-paying job, which is in service of being able to maintain a comfortable lifestyle for him and his family, which is in service of . . . what exactly?

This hypothetical chain of reasoning reveals that whatever we do, we can ultimately trace the reason for it to one dominant goal that both explains every other action we have taken along the way and why we chose one goal over another when they conflicted (for example, choosing to work more hours rather than spending more time with your family). That highest goal, Aquinas argues—the goal in which all our desires finally seek to come to rest or, put differently, a condition that we desire *for its own sake*—is what we call "happiness," and every human being, he observes, lives for that.[3]

Yet even if this observation about human nature is true, what does it have to do with "worshiping"? Two things. First, another way of saying that we all have a highest goal in life is to say that

---

3. The material in the previous paragraphs has been adapted from Lecture 1 of my Word on Fire Institute course *Re-enchanting the Secular*.

we all ultimately give our life to one thing and one thing alone, at least at any given time. The reason is because we cannot, in a literal sense, concurrently pursue two conflicting goals. As noted above, for example, we cannot both work more hours and spend more free time with our family; we cannot both eat whatever we want and be maximally healthy; we cannot both be famous and enjoy the benefits of anonymity; we cannot both seek power at all costs and act morally without exception. One of these objects of desire will have to lose out to the other at any given time when they come into conflict. Moreover, which of the conflicting options we ultimately choose—say, again, electing to work more hours rather than spending time with our children—will tell us not only what we value more in life but, when we trace our desires all the way to their final object, what we value *the most*. It will tell us, that is, what we live for, which is another way of saying what we worship.

Second, all of us, no matter what specific definition of final happiness we pursue, can ultimately choose only one of two alternatives: We either live for something in the world, for something in space and time—something material, contingent, changeable, and subject to inevitable death and decay, which we could call a "god"—or we live for that which transcends the world and everything in it, that which transcends space and time, a reality that is immaterial, non-contingent, changeless, and eternally alive, which we could, in the language of Aquinas, call "Being itself," or more colloquially, "God." Both logically and metaphysically, it's either one or the other. Either everything we do and every goal we have finds its source and summit in something here—our own life, our family, our political party, our nation, the love of pleasure, etc.—or everything we do finds its source and summit in that which includes temporal reality but also transcends it. Whether a person identifies as "religious" or not, those are the only two options. We cannot not choose, and we must choose one or the other. We either worship a god, or we worship God.

To define secular ideologies as forms of idolatry, therefore, is to recognize that they locate the human good and the means to achieve the good exclusively within a temporal framework. As such, they produce systems of value in which something in the world—either in the form of a temporal object (e.g., the planet) or something of human creation (e.g., the classless society, an ethnic group, a state of mental and physical pleasure)—serves as the purpose of the ideologue's life. I will develop this point in greater detail in a subsequent chapter, but this characteristic applies to classical liberal and libertarian forms of political thought as well. In their affirmation that all human beings have the right to define "the good" however they choose according to any criteria they choose so long as they respect the rights of others to do the same, liberalism and libertarianism recognize, by default, that there is no ultimate objective good, no objective human happiness. Consequently, they see the good as a subjective human creation—that is, an idol. In sum, by rejecting a theistic grounding and final goal for their (competing) systems of value, secular ideologies may fiercely disagree about which temporal good to bow down to, which god to offer their lives to, but they all agree on one thing: whatever shape the final purpose of human life and human society takes, its basic ingredients are nothing more than earth, water, fire, air, and a dash of human fancy.

FALSE CHOICES

To be sure, describing ideologies as idolatrous, even if accurate, may not carry much critical bite nowadays, especially for a culture that is increasingly distant from belief in God and for whom the charge of "idolatry" holds little motivational punch. However, recognizing ideologies as idols highlights two additional implications that may have more traction with the secular mind. The first is that, because of their rejection of a theistic foundation, secular ideologies necessarily portray human social and political life as a competition between winners and losers. Conversely, one of the greatest moral and political implications of embracing monotheism—the belief that there is one God who created and sustains all existence—is that there is only one authentic good, because God cannot be in opposition to himself. Therefore, anything that is authentically good for human beings cannot be in competition with anything else that is authentically good. For example, if human freedom and human equality are both good, both willed by God as part of human nature, then there is no reason to see them in opposition. The same is true of individual well-being and social well-being, private property and public goods, a healthy economy and care for the poor, etc. If all these are truly good under a monotheistic vision of reality, then, at least theoretically, we shouldn't have to choose among them.

Secular ideologies, however, are always zero-sum games. What one group sees as good will inevitably end up being what another group sees as evil; what one group sees as supporting individualism will, for another group, be seen as undermining society; what one group sees as good for business, another will see as hurting the poor; what one group sees as respecting the integrity of the environment, another will see as killing economic opportunity. In short, ideologies always end up imposing false mutual exclusivities. They force us to choose sides between goods when in fact there is a coherent way to integrate them into an overarching framework that Catholic social thought calls "the common good." The ideological alternative to the common good is at best an unending game of king of the hill—in which being a winner necessarily implies the existence of a loser—and at worst, as the political philosopher Thomas Hobbes put it, "a war of all against all."

Yet why *must* secular ideologies impose false mutual exclusivities? Can't they find some way around them, some way to identify common ground so that authentic goods don't have to compete? The explanation ties directly back to the rejection of theism as a conceptual foundation.

The debate about God's existence is often framed as if it were a conceptually and practically distinguishable question from all other questions we might debate. So, for example, a hypothetical society might share some relatively common values—say, a common history, common cultural practices, common language, etc.—yet be in disagreement about whether there is ultimate or transcendent truth, including moral truth. Upon those common values, those in the society might say that they have sufficient common ground to unite the society as "a society" and to give moral grounding to its civic institutions. In other words, they might say that, while interesting in an academic sense, the question of God is ultimately irrelevant to the question of sociopolitical foundations because those foundations can be coherently established independently of the question of God.

This compromise can temporarily work in practice. However, it contains a fundamental flaw in reasoning that will sooner or later lead to an existential fissure in society. If there is no God, then there is no comprehensive unity to reality and thus no common truth or common values that can serve as the basis for social unity. That is, if the statement "God exists" is ultimately false, then the implications of that falsity course through every dimension of reality, including political reality. If there is no God, then all agreements, all consensuses among different groups of people, are arbitrary; they are only accidents of history that can be unmade as quickly as they are made. Every political claim that any group can make—e.g., "All people have a right to vote" or "The powerful should be allowed to rule without the interference of the weak" or "Only people of a certain skin color should be allowed to sit in the front of the bus," or "All human beings have inherent dignity and must be respected"—are equally random, equally nonsensical, equally subject to infinite contestation. The fact that some people happen to agree on them in some societies at some times in history is just that—a "fact" that *happens* to be the case. But what about the people who disagree with what these people happen to agree on? Well, they're just as "right" as the others—the racial supremacists, the liberationists, the traditionalists, the progressives, the individualists, the socialists, the greens, the jihadists, the secessionists, the unionists—*all* of these groups, with all of their competing values, are just as right and just as wrong as every other group.

In short, with no objective foundation to locate the source of possible agreement, people only agree until they don't—and when they don't, there is no resource to settle the dispute beyond sheer coercive power. In this sense, then, the question of God is not academic; it is the most important political question any society can ask and seek to answer. Either denying the existence of God or sidestepping the question of God in the name of "consensus" is akin to inviting people to play soccer, football, wrestling, golf, badminton, baseball, sport hunting, cricket, gladiatorial combat, beer pong, and bocce ball on the same field at the same time with no rules and no referees; here and there you might see some order (temporarily), but zoom out and it's a mess with no hope of a solution beyond "May the most powerful group win."

The reason, therefore, that secular ideologies impose false mutual exclusivities is because they lack the metaphysical conditions to locate and justify moral unity. They reduce humanity to competing tribes, some of which prefer freedom, some of which prefer equality, some of which prefer stability, and some of which prefer dynamism, yet *all of whom* believe that their preferences cannot be universalized into objective truth because they reject the condition for the possibility of objective truth existing in the first place. Thus, they force us to choose between things that, properly understood, we should not have to choose between. That is one of the most important implications of monotheism for politics: If it is true that there is one God, then it is also true that there is one good, including the human good. And if it is true that there is one good for human beings, then every individual thing that is authentically good for human beings will not be in competition, just as, for example, healthy relationships between parents and children, wife and husband, and friend and friend contain diverse goods that can be enjoyed without pitting one against the other.[4] The condition for that unity, however, is affirming the existence of one God, which is what all secular ideologies, either explicitly or implicitly, refuse to do.

TOO HOT, TOO COLD

Relatedly and finally, secular ideologies embrace visions of human nature that are simultaneously both too high and too low. Put in theological terms, they make one of two errors: they either downplay (or completely ignore) the depth, persistence, and perversity of human sin, including sin's power to creep into "humanitarian" moral and political goals, or, conversely, see human beings as so fallen and society as so degenerate that they become blind to the real possibility of moral progress. Communism, for example, holds a utopianly positive view of humanity, believing in the perfectibility of human beings achieved by the vanguard leading us to the promised land of the classless society. This gullible anthropology is paradigmatically captured in John Lennon's juvenile anthem "Imagine," in which "no God above us" and "no hell below us" ushers in world peace and prosperity. (Tens of millions of corpses later, the Communist experience turned out rather differently from what Lennon imagined.) Libertarians, on the other extreme, tend to look at their fellow human beings as engaged in an unending conspiracy to stab them in the back and take everything they own while, for good measure, plotting to make them kneel before a jumbotron flashing hypnotic images of dear leader. As such, communities, especially civic communities,

---

4. Think, for example, of God's invitation—indeed, command!—to Adam and Eve in the Garden of Eden to freely eat the fruit of *all* the trees, except one: the tree of the knowledge of good and evil. The goods in creation are thus not uniform in nature; they are profoundly diverse, and God invites us to partake of all of them—but one. See Genesis 2:16–17.

are seen as grave threats to freedom rather than opportunities to flourish. The difficulty with these diametrically opposite depictions of humanity is that both have elements of truth to them. Human beings certainly can be peaceable and cooperative, and they can also be conniving and cruel. So what's the solution? Can't we just split the difference, adding the angel with the devil and dividing by two?

No, and the reason points back to the absence of God in secular ideologies. They lack a comprehensive metaphysics that can coherently account for both the objective, unqualified goodness of humanity and its freedom to violate that goodness. Thus, they cannot explain how humans can be both fundamentally good and capable of tremendous evil; how social action can lead both to tyranny and to liberation; how groups can justifiably see each other as enemies yet still recognize the possibility of authentic reconciliation. In short, without the Christian doctrines of the goodness of creation *and* original sin *and* the possibility of redemption through grace, ideologies must choose mutually exclusive sides at the anthropological level—defining human beings as either primarily good or primarily evil—and then construct their moral and political visions accordingly. The consequence is that we once again get cornered into a false choice, a choice between a deadly naïve optimism and an equally deadly sclerotic pessimism about human nature and the possibilities of moral progress.

The alternative to all of this, as the book has been arguing from its first pages, is the Catholic social thought tradition. In the following chapters, we'll see how the tradition responds to specific secular ideologies. Each chapter will identify the distinctive form of idolatry practiced by the secular alternative, offer a brief intellectual history of the ideology's development, explain the ideology's fundamental features using the Thinking in Circles map from chapter 3, and identify how Catholic social thought can fix the ideology's deficiencies.

Let's turn now to our first idol in the political pantheon: the god of pleasure, otherwise known as utilitarianism.

CHAPTER **6**

The God of Pleasure: Utilitarianism

"The greatest good for the greatest number." On the surface, this anthem of utilitarianism sounds like a reasonable, even inspired solution to the problem of governance. How should we organize society, especially considering the vast differences among individual goals and preferences? The very complexity of the problem seems to point to only one solution: set up a system that benefits most people most of the time by giving them what they want most—physical and mental gratification. Society becomes a pleasure party and (mostly) everyone is invited. Who could argue with that?

Those abandoned outside the party's gates might, but that gets us ahead of ourselves. What defines "pleasure" in the first place, for example? What is its content and by what standard is "more" or "less" of it calculated? And who's doing the calculating, by the way? Moreover, by "the greatest number," do we mean 99% of society or 51% of society? And, within that society, which would be a better scenario: 51% of people receiving 99 "units" of pleasure each? Or 99% of people receiving 51 "units" of pleasure each?

There are, indeed, many questions about the meaning of "utilitarianism," or, as it is also often called, "consequentialism." However, as with every political theory, the first step is to identify its fundamental presuppositions about reality, human nature, and especially human knowledge. To do so, it is helpful to turn again to the thought of the Enlightenment philosopher David Hume, who, if not the father of utilitarianism (that title might go to the classical Greek philosopher Epicurus), is at least one of its most historically influential proponents.

MAPPING DAVID HUME

To grasp the significance of Hume's thought, both in itself and in how it relates to utilitarianism, it's helpful to keep the Thinking in Circles map in mind from chapter 3. Here it is again:

To locate the conceptual root of Humean utilitarianism (and, in fact, all forms of utilitarianism), the best place to look is not within the circle of morality, applied morality, or even politics. Rather, the focus should be on its epistemology—what the theory says about the nature of human knowledge. Recall from chapter 4 that David Hume ends his book *An Enquiry Concerning Human Understanding* by declaring:

> If we take in our hand any [book]; of divinity or school meta-physics, for instance; let us ask, does it contain any abstract reasoning concerning quantity or number? No. Does it contain any experimental reasoning concerning matter of fact and existence? No. Commit it then to the flames: for it can contain nothing but sophistry and illusion.[1]

Appreciating the meaning of Hume's claim about knowledge (and his belief about which books he thinks should be "committed to the flames") requires digging deeper into his philosophy. Indeed, we cannot grasp why Hume would eventually embrace utilitarianism without first understanding his metaphysical, or, better put, *anti-metaphysical* project more broadly. Hume's primary target is, as he puts it, "divinity or school metaphysics." The definition of "metaphysics" traces its roots back to classical Greek philosophy, especially Aristotelian philosophy. "Meta" is Greek for "before" or "beyond," and "physics" comes from the Greek word for "nature." Doing metaphysics thus means seeking to understand what is "beyond nature," the causal and substantive structure of reality as such. It means developing a rational "theory of everything" that can account for the unity and diversity, change and stability, and generality and particularity of existence as a whole. As the Thinking in Circles map illustrates, the only thing "greater" than metaphysics ("ontology" in the map) is God; as such, metaphysical inquiry includes asking and answering questions about not only "reality" but also human nature, human knowledge, human morality, and even politics. In short, Hume

---

1. David Hume, *An Enquiry Concerning Human Understanding* (London: J.B. Bebbington, 1861), 120.

is not tinkering with the outer margins of philosophy here—he's going after *everything*.

The history of metaphysics is as old and diverse as the history of philosophy itself, but by the time Hume was writing, metaphysics had become closely associated with two primary schools of thought: Scholasticism, which is related to the thirteenth-century philosophical theology of St. Thomas Aquinas, and Cartesianism, based on the seventeenth-century philosophy of René Descartes. Although Scholasticism and Cartesianism both do metaphysics, they do so in very different ways. Scholasticism generally reasons *from* a metaphysical doctrine of God's existence *to* truths about human beings (and everything else), while, oppositely, Cartesian metaphysics reasons *to* the truth about God (and everything else) *from* metaphysical doctrines about human beings. (Descartes is the philosopher who famously wrote "I think, therefore I am" in his 1637 *Discourse on Method*.)

One of the features that unites Scholastic and Cartesian metaphysics is that both affirm that the human mind is capable of recognizing rational necessity in the world, meaning that we are capable of tapping into both the ontological and moral structures of reality and the source of those structures, God. Though invisible to our physical senses, Scholasticism and Cartesianism argue that this rational structure to reality must "be out there," must be ontologically real, in order for everything else in reality to exist the way that it does.

A contemporary form of this thinking is evident in what the Christian apologist William Lane Craig has called the Kalam Cosmological Argument for God's existence. The argument takes this form:

Premise 1: All things that begin to exist have a cause.

Premise 2: The universe began to exist.

Conclusion: Therefore, the universe has a cause.[2]

Without delving into the complexity of the argument, the basic insight here is that, in order to explain the nature of the universe as we perceive it, we must recognize that the universe could not have caused itself and therefore must have been caused by an intelligent force metaphysically "outside" of itself. Put differently, the argument seeks to demonstrate that it is rationally impossible for the universe to exist without affirming the existence of God. It is important to highlight here that this is not only a metaphysical claim about the nature and cause of existence but also an *epistemological* claim about the nature of the human mind, namely that it is capable of apprehending metaphysical truth.

This, in brief, is exactly the kind of thinking that Hume sought to consign to the flames. Although he does not engage the Kalam Cosmological Argument in particular, any attempt to provide "rational proof" for God's existence and, by extension, the existence of a metaphysical order to reality is, for Hume, a fool's errand. The reason is because he believes that the human mind is incapable of apprehending a rationally necessary relationship between cause and effect.

The argument Hume lays out leading to this conclusion is complex, but this is the gist of it: Just because we experience events in the world in a certain way—for example, we experience that every time we drop a pen it falls to the floor—does not, in fact, mean that there is a rationally necessary connection between "letting go of a pen" and "the pen falling to the floor." As strange as it may sound, for Hume there would be no violation of rationality if after a million tries under the same circumstances, the pen were to suddenly float upward rather than fall downward. In fact, Hume's claim is even more radical than that: Associating a rational connection between a sequence of events, like letting go

2. William Lane Craig's version of the Kalam Cosmological Argument can be found on his apologetics website, Reasonable Faith. See reasonablefaith.org.

of a pen and it falling to the floor, is just as rational as saying that a man scratching his nose in Anaheim can be the cause of rain in Buenos Aires. That comparison may sound absurd on the face, but Hume's point is that the more you epistemically dig into any sequence of events, the deeper and deeper into the causal chain you get, the more you realize that you do not in fact see any true "cause" of anything. All you see, rather, is your impression of one thing happening after another.

Using the pen example again, if you were to increasingly zoom in on the causal sequence of events, you'd see that there is much more going on than fingers opening and then a pen falling to the floor. In addition to the external force of gravity, there is also, internally, an electrical impulse sent from the brain to the finger muscles, the generation of the electrical impulse by chemicals interacting, the atomic activity of each chemical individually and in relation to the others, the subatomic activity of each atom within each chemical, and so on. The point is that at no moment along this chain of events do we see a singular cause leading to a singular effect. Rather, like a cartoonist stringing together otherwise discrete, disconnected images to create an animation, all we see is our impressions of causality—not causality itself.

Of course, Hume did not have access to this kind of empirical knowledge in the 1700s; he used billiard balls rather than neurobiology to illustrate his reasoning. However, the conclusion remains the same. For Hume, we never see an actual, distinct cause to anything that we observe, and therefore we cannot claim that there is any rational connection between any series of events in existence. There is—and this gets to the very heart of Hume's critique—no rational reason to believe that the future will or should resemble the past or that we should expect certain causes always to have certain effects.

But how does this conclusion about the lack of a causal relationship between events relate to Hume's criticism of metaphysics more broadly? In brief, all metaphysics, notwithstanding their differences, employ some form of causal reasoning in order to reach their respective conclusions; all, like in the Kalam argument, use some formulation of "this must happen/exist" in order for "that to happen/exist." If Hume is right that all such statements are absurd because no human mind can apprehend a rationally necessary relationship between any events—and I want to stress here that the Church thinks Hume is decidedly wrong about this—then the whole conceptual rug gets pulled out from doing any form of metaphysical inquiry. Consequently, no one can say with any rational authority that there is an invisible but real causal structure to reality, including that a single unique, transcendent cause (God) created and sustains all that is and gives meaning and moral direction to human life. For Hume, we are blind, rationally speaking, to the true nature of reality, including moral reality (e.g., a "natural law"). Reason can tell us nothing about how things are or how they should be.

DAMAGE CONTROL

To be sure, Hume understood that this conclusion had revolutionary implications. Some implications, like (in his mind) undermining Church doctrines, he welcomed. Others, like jettisoning all forms of knowledge in the embrace of a radical skepticism, he did not. Indeed, he wanted to avoid the charge of advocating for an eighteenth-century form of Pyrrhonism, a philosophy based on the ancient Greek skeptic who had to be physically restrained from walking through fires or throwing himself off cliffs because he doubted their (and his own) existence. Hume thus seeks to navigate between jettisoning all metaphysical inquiry on the one hand and adopting philosophical know-nothingism on the other by embracing an epistemology he calls "mitigated skepticism." In a nutshell, mitigated skepticism holds that while abstract reasoning cannot tell us anything apodictically true about God, the world, human nature, or morality, *our senses* (sight, touch, hearing, smelling, and tasting) can still give us rationally valid information so long as we submit them to what he calls "experimental reasoning" (what we would call "science").

To come full circle, then, when Hume states that "experimental reasoning concerning matter of fact and existence" stands as an exception to his general call to consign metaphysics "to the flames," he means that empirical, scientific inquiry is *the only source of knowledge that can be trusted*.[3] For Hume, if you are trying to know something that cannot be squeezed into the epistemic parameters of a scientific experiment, you are chasing phantoms. Such a search will only contain, in his words, "sophistry" (false, deceptive reasoning) and "illusion." To translate Hume's overarching point into contemporary language: Only scientific knowledge is valid knowledge. Everything else is, at best, fodder for a book-hungry blaze. Hume's legacy thus places him among the most influential philosophers in intellectual history and bestows on him the dubious honor of being the first open advocate for scientism.

EMPIRICISM AND ITS CONSEQUENCES

Given this intellectual background, we now have a datapoint to plot on the Thinking in Circles map. At the epistemological level (the level asking, "What can we know and how can we know it?"), we can now write in, "Human beings can only know that which their senses reveal to them and which experimental reasoning

---

3. It is important to note that Hume also carves out an exception for "abstract reasoning concerning quantity and number"—what we might call "logic" and "math." These, too, are valid sources of knowledge for Hume, since they contain truths that are logically impossible to deny (for example, that a circle cannot be a circle and a square at the same time in the same way). However, Hume emphasizes that these logical truths are truths about *ideas*, or what he calls "the relations of ideas," and *not* about the world or anything in it. For example, we can calculate the square root of negative one and come up with an imaginary number that concords with mathematical rationality; however, this "proof" remains in the world of ideas and the world of ideas alone. The world itself, for Hume, remains unknowable in a metaphysical sense—we can't know where it came from, how it came into being (in an absolute sense), who made it (if it was made at all), and certainly not what it is "for." All we can know is that it is there and detectable by our senses alone.

confirms." Let's run that statement through the map's conceptual logic: If, with Hume, we accept that we can only accept sensory knowledge as true, what, consequently, must also be true? More specifically, what does such a claim presuppose at the level of anthropology, ontology, and theology (moving outward)? And what does it imply about the nature of morality, applied morality, and eventually politics (moving inward)?

First, moving outward in the circle, we would have to conclude that all that we can know about human nature, nature itself, and the existence of God would have to be empirical—that is, it would have to be accessible to our senses. That, in turn, would mean that we could not affirm the existence of an immaterial soul in human beings at the anthropological level (which is another way of saying humans are just made out of "stuff" like everything else), we could not affirm the existence of any immaterial law in nature like a natural moral law (which is another way of saying there are no universally objective truths, including moral truths, accessible to human reason), and we could not affirm the existence of God, who, by definition, is immaterial and thus not accessible to our senses. This is all another way of recognizing that God and the metaphysical and moral implications of God's existence play no role in Hume's thought.

The question of whether Hume was an atheist is a topic that some philosophers like to debate in their free time. Hume himself was coy on the question, though many of his contemporary philosophical opponents made that charge against him, which, at the time, was an explosive claim to make.[4] Part of the challenge of reaching a conclusion on that question is that the epistemology Hume embraces basically makes the question of God's existence moot. If human beings cannot know anything in existence that is non-material, then it doesn't matter in both a metaphysical and

---

4. For a full discussion on Hume's relationship to "religion" see C.M. Lorkowski, "David Hume: Religion," Internet Encyclopedia of Philosophy, https://iep.utm.edu/hume-rel/.

moral sense whether or not God exists. In other words, whatever Hume's private beliefs were, he establishes a system of thought in which the embrace of functional atheism—acting as if God does not exist—is unavoidable.[5] In this sense, then, though there may be an intellectual distinction between saying "God does not exist" and "We cannot know if God exists," the difference between the two is nonexistent in a practical sense—either way, God cannot provide any rational guidance for how humans should act.

This implication of Hume's thought is especially tangible as we move "inward" in the circle from epistemology to morality and applied morality. Indeed, it is precisely in this movement from the epistemological to the moral that we see the birth of utilitarianism, which Hume lays out in his subsequent book, *An Enquiry Concerning the Principles of Morals*. Hume's argument here, like in the previous text, is complex, but it can be summarized by highlighting this basic sequence in his chain of reasoning:

- Sensory data from sense experience is the only thing human beings can know about the world.

- The only sensory data we have about morality comes from examining human sentiments, or feelings.

- There is a common observable element to all human feelings called "benevolence," which is a natural (meaning, it is empirically observable in human nature) feeling that derives pleasure from seeking other people's well-being, even independently of one's own self-interest.

- "Benevolence" is universally (in an empirical sense) praised among human beings and, therefore, is deemed by humans to be universally (in an empirical sense) good.

5. It is possible that Humeism could allow for a purely fideistic form of religion (one in which rationality plays no role at all); however, religion in this case would be relegated entirely to the realm of private experience and, as such, could not provide any common guidance to human beings.

- Good action, therefore, is action that is benevolent in nature—that is, action that is useful for preserving and advancing the well-being of humanity.

- Therefore, all action should be evaluated by the criterion of the consequence that the action has on the well-being of humanity; good action is action that benefits humanity's well-being, and bad action is action that harms humanity's well-being.

The standard of "usefulness" or "utility" thus emerges, for Hume, as the preeminent moral principle that should guide all other principles, including the definition and application of "justice." As Hume writes,

> The necessity of justice to the support of society as whole is the *sole* foundation of that virtue; and since no moral excellence is more highly esteemed, we may conclude that this *circumstance of usefulness* has, in general, the strongest energy and most entire command over our sentiments.[6]

Or as Hume also writes, summarizing his conception of morality,

> We must be acquainted with the nature and situation of man, must reject appearances which may be false . . . and must search for these rules which are, on the whole, *useful and beneficial*.[7]

It is important to stress that human reason, for Hume, has no capacity and therefore no authority to determine the content of what is "useful" and "beneficial" as it relates to human well-being.

---

6. David Hume, *An Enquiry Concerning the Principles of Morals* ed, J.B. Schneewind (Indianapolis: Hackett Publishing Company, 1983), 34 (author's emphasis).

7. Hume, *An Enquiry Concerning the Principles of Morals*, 28 (author's emphasis).

That content exists exclusively within sentiment, particularly the sentiment of "benevolence," which Hume believes is empirically observable. Thus, the only role Hume can assign moral reason is to be an adjuvant "helper" to the sentiments by identifying the best means of increasing benevolence as the sentiments define it. In other words, reason can say nothing about the definition of the good, but it *can* say something about how to pursue that good more efficiently. To use a nautical analogy, Captain Feeling sets the destination for morality, and First Officer Reason obediently determines the best course to get there without asking any questions about the meaning or purpose of the journey.

Completing the inward movement on the map, we can now see how Hume's epistemology leads to his embrace of utilitarianism. Given that all that we can know is in the senses, and the only moral thing our senses tell us is that we have good feelings for others, then "good feelings for others" and "the advancement of good feelings for others" can be the only foundation for morality, including the meaning of "justice." The fundamental political question that rests upon this moral foundation thus takes the following form: How can we advance the most well-being for the greatest number of people? Or, in other words, how do we attain the greatest good for the greatest number? Seeking to accomplish that goal, for Hume and utilitarianism more broadly, is not just the best but the *only* thing an individual and society can do from a moral perspective. The rejection of metaphysics and the consequent limits of empiricism leave no other option. If we only accept what our senses tell us, and the only moral thing we can extract from our senses is that humans have a capacity to help other humans feel good (a.k.a. "benevolence"), then those are the only ingredients we have to work with to make our moral and political cake.

Yet why, in this calculus, must it be limited to "the greatest number"? Why not aim to increase good feelings and decrease bad feelings for everyone? In addition to there being logistical problems in increasing everyone's well-being, the majoritarian morality of utilitarianism is espoused because it is a direct consequence of its empirical foundations, to wit: *The human senses cannot make universal observations.* Even with advanced technical instruments, it remains the case that we cannot "see" everywhere and all the time. Strictly speaking, then, empirical epistemologies cannot say anything is universal. Thus, when Hume states that benevolence is "universal" in human nature, he only means that it is widespread—that you tend to see it in most people in most places. By the logic of his empiricist position, he cannot mean that all humans in all times without exception have "benevolent" feelings. Indeed, even one exception to that observation—an exception that would be easy to find historically (or, perhaps, even in one's own heart)—would violate the observation's putative universality. The upshot is that utilitarianism can only speak in generalities. Hence, the greatest good for the greatest number—not for everyone.

QUANTIFYING THE GOOD: JEREMY BENTHAM'S UTILITARIAN FORMULA

Hume's theory raises many questions. For example, even if we grant that humans have an empirically observable feeling of "benevolence" toward others, why, morally speaking, should we act on that feeling as opposed to acting on the also empirically observable feeling of schadenfreude (taking pleasure in another's misfortune)? Also, what defines "good feelings toward others" in the first place? There is a danger of falling into a vicious circularity: If "good feelings for others" is that which we define as "benevolence," and "benevolence" is that which we define as "having good feelings for others," where do we get our standard of "goodness" from in the first place? (This points back to empiricism's more general problem of having to "pre-define" that which it seeks to "discover" discussed in chapter 4; we will return to it again soon.) Moreover, how would we calculate such goodness in a way that enables us to measure the consequences of our actions on the goodness of society as a whole? And who is "society" anyway? Your club soccer team? Your cul-de-sac? Your city? Your state? Your nation? All humanity? If the latter, are *future* humans included in these calculations?

These questions already point to the Catholic critique of utilitarianism. But first, it's important to get a few more utilitarian thinkers on the table, especially since, though all utilitarians embrace Hume's epistemology, Hume is often not associated with contemporary forms of utilitarianism. For many, the true father is the Englishman Jeremy Bentham (1748–1832), who is known for his pithy expressions of both the content and consequences of utilitarian calculation and for expanding the scope of those calculations to include the suffering of non-human animals.

Bentham writes in his 1789 text *An Introduction to the Principles of Morals and Legislation*:

> Nature has placed mankind under the governance of two sovereign masters, *pain and pleasure.* It is for them alone to point out what we ought to do, as well as to determine what we shall do. On the one hand the standard of right and wrong, on the other the chain of causes and effects, are fastened to their throne.[8]

In these lines, Bentham concretizes Hume's gauzy musing about "benevolence" and "utility" into language that he thinks everyone can immediately relate to: pleasure and pain. Indeed, all moral terms, Bentham believes, can be reduced into meaning "pleasurable" and "painful," including "happiness," which for him simply means a state of individual or social affairs in which pain has been minimized and pleasure has been maximized. Accordingly,

---

8. Jeremy Bentham, *An Introduction to the Principles of Morals and Legislation*, 1.1 (Oxford: Clarendon, 1879), 1.

pleasure and pain become the sole criteria for adjudicating both individual and social action; actions that have the consequence of increasing the sum total of pleasure and decreasing the sum total of pain are good—that is, *useful*—and should be done; actions that, oppositely, decrease the sum total pleasure and increase the sum total pain are bad—*useless*—and should be avoided. As Bentham writes,

> By the principle of utility is meant that principle which approves or disapproves of every action whatsoever, according to the tendency which it appears to have to augment or diminish the happiness of the part whose interest is in question: or, what is the same thing in other words, to promote or oppose happiness.[9]

Upon this foundation, Bentham devises a formula to calculate the relative quantities of pleasure vs. pain as they pertain to the possible consequences of individual or group actions. For individuals, Bentham advises calculating the intensity, duration, certainty/uncertainty, proximity/remoteness, and likelihood of producing more or less pleasure and pain. This formula would predict, for instance, that while consuming a colossal portion of hot wings accompanied by jalapeño-bedizened nachos may initially provide intense pleasure, the duration of that pleasure will likely be short-lived and followed by an even more intense and longer-lasting pain. That's a superficial example, but, for Bentham, the logic it contains applies to every choice we make in life: whether to get married (and to whom), whether to have children (and how many), what career to pursue (and whether to work longer hours), what car to drive, where to live, etc. For every decision, big or small, the moral task is to add up all the possible positive consequences of each possible action in the near and long

9. Bentham 1.2, 2.

term and all the possible negative consequences of each possible action in the near and long term, calculate whether there are ultimately more pluses or minuses, and then choose accordingly.

This method also applies to morally adjudicating society's actions when one additional variable is added to the formula: the number of people the consequences of any action will affect positively or negatively. Bentham calls this variable "extent." Combining the variables into one comprehensive calculation, therefore, the goal of any law or social policy should be to maximize pleasure across as many variables as possible (maximizing intensity, duration, certainty, proximity, etc.) for as many people as possible while minimizing pain across the same variables. In other words: Seek the greatest good for the greatest number.

It is important to add that Bentham, consistent with his view that pleasure and pain constitute the only foundation of morality—and consistent with the broader epistemic presupposition that only physical objects can be known—extends the circle of moral concern beyond human beings to any form of sentient life, that is, any being that can feel pleasure and pain. As he famously concludes his treatise, after averring that an adult horse is "beyond comparison more rational" than a human infant, "The [relevant moral] question is not, Can they reason? Nor can they *talk?* But, Can they *suffer?*"[10] With these words, Bentham openly tells utilitarianism's dirty secret: Not only are some human beings worth less than other human beings—some human beings are worth less than *animals*—which is to say, worth nothing at all. Hume's "benevolence" has taken a dark, if entirely predictable, turn.

10. Bentham 17.1, 311n.

OF PIGS AND MEN: JOHN STUART MILL'S
REDEFINITION OF "PLEASURE"

There are a few more pieces to the utilitarian puzzle to complete before turning to the Catholic response. Jeremy Bentham's account, while detailed in its description of how to calculate pleasure and pain, remains ambiguous on the specific definitions of pleasure and pain themselves. The problem is that, though the terms may seem to point to a universal, easily comprehensible experience—we've all had pleasurable and painful sensations— those experiences can be difficult to define, categorize, and rank upon closer examination. This is especially the case when we include "mental pleasure" into the mix of possibilities. As we see in the example of an athlete pushing his body to become the best player on the team to the detriment of his health, or of a guitar player practicing until her fingers bleed to produce the most perfect melody possible, mental pleasures might exceed physical pleasures and may even cause intense and prolonged physical pain in the process. From a social perspective, mental pleasures also introduce additional complexity into utilitarian calculations. For example, is it ever morally justified to distribute public funds to arts programs when medical and nutritional programs still need support?

The English philosopher John Stuart Mill (1806–1873) sought to address these questions. Although perhaps not widely recognized as such because of his advocacy for individual liberty and free speech (more on that below), Mill was a firm supporter of utilitarianism. He recognized, however, that the doctrine, as it emerged from Jeremy Bentham, still needed refinement precisely on the question of how to define pleasure and pain. Thus, in his 1861 book *Utilitarianism*, Mill added an additional variable to Bentham's formula for calculating the consequences of individual and social action: quality vs. quantity. He writes,

It is quite compatible with the principle of utility to recognize the fact, that some *kinds* of pleasure are more desirable and more valuable than others. It would be absurd that while, in estimating all other things, quality is considered as well as quantity, the estimation of pleasures should be supposed to depend on quantity alone.[11]

Mill thus advocates for distinguishing between what he calls lower and higher human faculties. Lower faculties pertain to the pleasure of the body (e.g., eating, drinking, resting, sexual activity, etc.), while higher faculties pertain to the pleasure of the mind (e.g., listening to music, reading great literature, viewing timeless art, etc.). Mill's justification for making this distinction is, unsurprisingly, empirical in nature (though it is perhaps more accurate to call it anecdotal). He writes, "It is an unquestionable fact that those who are equally acquainted with, and equally capable of appreciating and enjoying both, do give a most marked preference to the manner of existence which employs the higher faculties."[12] Sharpening the highbrow sentiment in this observation, Mill goes on to aver,

It is better to be a human being dissatisfied than a pig satisfied; better to be Socrates dissatisfied than a fool satisfied. And if the fool, or the pig, is of a different opinion, it is because they only know their own side of the question. The other party to the comparison knows both sides.[13]

In other words, "real" human beings know that that the pleasures of the mind are superior to the pleasures of the body; those who don't know this truth are "fools" to Mill and, echoing Bentham's blurring of the lines between humanity and animals, functionally

11. John Stuart Mill, *Utilitarianism* (Boston: Willard Small, 1899), 18.
12. Mill, 19.
13. Mill, 21–22.

the same as pigs. Consequently, the "greatest good for the greatest number" means the greatest good *for the right kind of people.*

Mill's contribution to utilitarianism is important not only for historical reasons but also because his redefinition of pleasure points to a fundamental question within utilitarian thought, especially as it relates to governing society: In calculating the greatest good for the greatest number, do we determine the definition of "good" by surveying the greatest number? Or, in line with Mill, do we only survey those who have the right definition of the good—for example, those who know that there is a moral difference between indulging in "higher" and "lower" pleasures? Politically speaking, how we answer this question has enormous consequences. The low-brow utilitarianism of Jeremy Bentham could potentially justify a system in which most people get to determine how most people live; the highbrow utilitarianism of Mill, on the other hand, could potentially justify a system in which a few people (those who are not "fools") determine how most people live. In the balance lies not only political power but the power to define what it means to be truly human and worthy of moral concern.

RAISING A FIST AGAINST "SPECIESISM"

This definitional question—essentially, "What is the form of pleasure and pain that deserves the most moral consideration?"—is also apparent in contemporary forms of utilitarianism, many of which harken back to the more corporeal definitions of pleasure seen in Jeremy Bentham. For example, one of the most renowned utilitarian philosophers today, the Australian Peter Singer, has retrieved Bentham's focus on "sentience" as the locus of moral concern and in so doing openly called for the *de*valuing of human life.

One of Singer's most controversial arguments is that preferring human well-being over animal well-being amounts to what he calls "speciesism." As the neologism suggests, speciesism means the prejudicial and thus unjust treatment of one class of beings (humans) over another class of beings (non-humans). He writes in his appropriately titled collection of essays *Unsanctifying Human Life*, for example, "Can it be right to make great efforts to save the life of a mongoloid human infant when the mother does not want the infant to live, and at the same time can it not be wrong to kill, slowly and painfully, a number of monkeys?"[14] Based on a strict empirical analysis—remember, empiricism is the *only* standard of knowledge that utilitarianism accepts as valid—Singer's claim here is that there is no observable reason why humans should give moral preference to the child with Down syndrome rather than to the healthy monkey. As he bluntly states, "The doctrine of the sanctity of human life, as it is normally understood, has at its core a discrimination on the basis of species and nothing else."[15]

This form of discrimination—caring for the pain and suffering of our own species only because it is *our* species—is analogous, in Singer's view, to racial discrimination and thus should be morally condemned on grounds of arbitrariness. What makes the distinction arbitrary is that the definition of a human being—again, from an empirical perspective—includes the recognition of capacities that (a) do not belong to human beings alone and (b) are not present in all beings we might call "human." Singer's argument on this front can be summarized by being broken down into two pieces, one seeking to show that *not* all humans are in fact moral humans (meaning worthy of moral concern), the other seeking to show that some non-human animals *are* in fact moral humans:

---

14. Peter Singer, *Unsanctifying Human Life*, ed. Helga Kuhse (Malden, MA: Blackwell, 2002), 219.

15. Singer, 220.

Argument #1:

Being a human means having capacities such as self-awareness, purposeful action, communication, etc.

There are beings whom we call "human" who do not possess these capacities and do not have the hope of either acquiring or reacquiring them (e.g., a severely disabled infant, a man in a coma, an elderly person near death, etc.).

Therefore, those who do not possess these capacities and do not have the hope of either acquiring or reacquiring them (e.g., a severely disabled infant, a man in a coma, an elderly person near death, etc.) are not, in fact, human.

Argument #2:

Being a human means having capacities such as self-awareness, purposeful action, communication, etc.

Some animals have capacities such as self-awareness, purposeful action, communication, etc.

Therefore, some animals are human.

For Singer, juxtaposing these arguments reveals the rampant speciesism in contemporary moral thinking. We show great moral concern for humans who do not have the capacities we typically associate with being human, while we show much less (or even no) concern for non-human animals who do have human capacities. This, for Singer, is arbitrary discrimination and ultimately explains why he thinks it unjust to save the life of an unwanted "mongoloid human infant" while also performing medical experiments on healthy monkeys—who, for him, are much more human (in a moral sense) than the disabled child.

As shocking as it may sound, the next step in Singer's reasoning is entirely consistent with the utilitarian parameters he has established. If we must test our medicines and other health products to ensure their safety, why not test them on disabled human infants rather than healthy monkeys? Indeed, such an action would be not only more ethical (since the monkeys are "more human" in a moral sense than the disabled babies) but more efficient and more effective, because, unlike the monkeys, we (the healthy, non-disabled) are a perfect genetic match with the disabled babies. As Singer writes,

> Since many drugs affect different species in unpredictably different ways, we would probably achieve our goal sooner by testing the drug on the retarded member of our own species than on the monkey; this would mean that we would have to use fewer subjects for our experiment and so inflict less suffering all told.[16]

This last line here—"and so inflict less suffering all told"—cuts directly to the heart of Singer's utilitarian conception of morality and the principles he supports for governing society. Since we can only define things according to empirically observable criteria, the only thing we see that we all have in common—"we" meaning any sentient being that shows evidence of feeling pleasure and pain—is that (a) we can suffer and (b) we don't want to suffer. Based on this observation, the attempt to circumscribe a line around "humanity" for special moral concern is contrary to empirical reasoning.

Thus, the only way to rectify this moral irrationality is to stop defining humans as special and start treating all beings who can suffer as worthy of equal moral regard, both in our individual actions and in the actions of societies as a whole. In this wider,

16. Singer, 221.

more inclusive framework of moral concern, the way in which we make decisions is to determine which actions will lead to the greatest pleasure—or, at least, the least suffering—for *all* sentient beings. The result is that many non-human beings will be plucked from the sea of moral irrelevance and lifted to the platform of moral concern. Conversely, many human beings will be cast off the moral platform of concern into the sea of moral irrelevance. Singer concludes,

> We have to change our attitudes in both directions. We have to bring non-humans within the sphere of our moral concern and cease to treat them purely as means to our ends. At the same time, once we realize that the fact that severely and irreparably retarded infants are members of the species *Homo sapiens* is not in itself relevant to how we should treat them, we should be ready to consider current practices which cause suffering to all concerned and benefit nobody.[17]

Some might object to this proposal by arguing that even the severely disabled still have human souls that confer equal dignity on them independently of their diminished capacities, to which Singer has this to say:

> [Beliefs in the sanctity of human life] are not insights of self-evident moral truths, but the historically conditioned product of doctrines about immortality, original sin, and damnation which hardly anyone now accepts; doctrines so obnoxious, in fact, that if anyone did accept them, we should be inclined to discount any other views he held.[18]

17. Singer, 225.
18. Singer, 230.

For Singer, "religious people," or anyone who believes in the existence of immaterial souls, are analogous to John Stuart Mill's "fools" and can therefore be summarily ignored if not ridiculed. Thus, in addition to a reaffirmation of utilitarianism's embrace of pleasure and pain as the only relevant moral consideration, we see again in Singer's thought the tendency toward elitism; "the greatest good for the greatest number," as it turns out, ends up meaning "the greatest good for the greatest number as *the right-thinking people define it.*"

MORE THAN A THEORY OF FEELING

Although its content often sounds academic, utilitarianism is not some rarefied theory that seldom finds its way outside of a university lecture hall. It permeates contemporary secular society. It is especially and unsurprisingly present in health care and public health policy debates, which came sharply into view during the 2020–2022 pandemic. For example, in an article entitled "When Will the Pandemic Cure Be Worse than the Disease," Peter Singer and another academic named Michael Plant argue,

> Health isn't all that matters. What we really need to do is compare the impact different policies have on our overall wellbeing. To do that, we think it's best to measure wellbeing by using individuals' reports of how happy and how satisfied with their lives they are. . . . Doing this means we can, in a principled way, weigh up otherwise hard-to-compare considerations when deciding how to respond to COVID-19—or to any other systemic risk.[19]

19. Peter Singer and Michael Plant, "When Will the Pandemic Cure Be Worse Than the Disease?" Project Syndicate, April 6, 2020, https://www.project -syndicate.org/commentary/when-will-lockdowns-be-worse-than-covid19-by -peter-singer-and-michael-plant-2020-04.

Notwithstanding the crucial question of whether economic lockdowns were in fact necessary to prevent the spread of COVID—or even whether they were efficacious at all—the principle Singer and Plant point to as the moral adjudicator in determining how to respond to the virus is utilitarian in nature: to determine public policy, don't look at individuals, but rather at the aggregate "wellbeing" of a society defined by how most people feel about their lives. This subjective reporting of well-being is what provides the empirical, measurable data for normative decision-making. As they write, "A problem with the current conversations about whether we should strangle the economy to save lives is that we cannot directly compare 'lives saved' against 'lost GDP.' We need to put them into some common unit."[20] Consequently, those policies that will have the effect of producing a net increase of units of well-being across society (or a collection of societies) are good and should be pursued, and those policies that will lead to a net reduction in units of well-being are bad and should be avoided. Note, crucially, that the authors clearly imply that making such calculations will entail the creation of both winners (those whose units of well-being are favored by the majority) and losers (those whose units are disfavored by the majority). In other words, some individuals' well-being will matter more than other individuals' well-being. That is utilitarian thinking in action.

Such thinking is also prevalent among many "pro-choice" advocates in the abortion debate. Consider, for example, these words offered by the celebrity Michelle Williams—who was pregnant at the time—during her acceptance of the Golden Globe award for best actress:

20. Singer and Plant, "When Will the Pandemic Cure Be Worse Than the Disease?".

As women and as girls, things can happen to our bodies that are not our choice. I've tried my best to live a life of my own making, and not just a series of events that happened to me. . . . And I wouldn't have been able to do this without employing a woman's right to choose. To choose when to have my children and with whom. . . . Women, 18 to 118, when it is time to vote, please do so in your own self-interest. It's what men have been doing for years.[21]

Williams' claim here is that it is not only morally permissible but morally good to sacrifice the life of one's unborn child for the greater good of career advancement in certain circumstances. The fact that she is pregnant while she makes this claim also indicates that, in line with utilitarian thinking, the calculus of pleasure/pain can change over time; sometimes there is more pain and less pleasure in bringing a baby to full term (which would justify terminating the baby) and sometimes there is more pleasure and less pain in the same action (which would justify letting the baby live). The action itself—and the pleasure/pain of the unborn child—do not have intrinsic moral goodness but rather depend upon the effects they will have on the mother's sense of well-being, including her career prospects.

As the enthusiastic applause Williams received after making her televised declaration (one in which she also referenced "God") indicates, this way of (de)valuing human life is common, even mainstream, in contemporary Western culture. Translated from a personal decision into a general social policy, the argument is that, when considering the relative value of the life of the unborn, we should consider whether the presence of unwanted children will be a net benefit to society. Indeed, sometimes the calculation

21. Li Cohen, "Michelle Williams advocates for abortion rights in Golden Globes acceptance speech," CBS News, January 6, 2020, https://www.cbsnews .com/news/golden-globes-michelle-williams-advocates-for-womens-rights-in -golden-globes-speech/.

of the value of life is reduced literally to dollars and cents, as, for example, we see in this argument made by a chief counsel at the Center for Reproductive Rights[22] against abortion restrictions:

> When we think about the money that is being spent litigating unconstitutional abortion restrictions, that money could absolutely be better spent supporting people in these states through Medicaid expansion, child care support, family leave, extended post-partum Medicaid coverage, Title X funding.[23]

In other words, public money would be better spent—"better" meaning leading to more desirable social outcomes—if we were to allocate it to the people whose lives really matter: (born) children, (born) families, and (born) poor mothers. This is a raw utilitarian calculation in which, once again, we see an "expert" making the determination of whose interests are more valuable than others.

Another "expert" named Diana Greene Foster, who also advocates for unrestricted abortion access, makes the utilitarian reasoning in the pro-choice platform even more evident. Speaking to the *Los Angeles Times* in an article titled "When a woman who wants an abortion can't get it, the children she already has suffer the consequences," the University of California demographer summarizes her empirical investigation, stating, "The research here is clear. Restricting abortion access doesn't just harm women. It harms their children as well."[24] To be clear,

22. It is important to note that casting the abortion debate as one over "reproductive rights" is a rhetorical red herring since, by definition, abortion is only a moral question *after* reproduction has already taken place.

23. Kylie Cheung, "The cost of the GOP's war against abortion is adding up—and taxpayers are footing the bill," Salon, July 22, 2021, https://www.salon.com/2021/07/22/the-cost-of-the-gops-war-against-abortion-is-adding-up-and-taxpayers-are-footing-the-bill/.

24. Deborah Netburn, "When a woman wants an abortion but can't get it, the children she already has suffer the consequences," *Los Angeles Times*, October 30, 2018, https://www.latimes.com/science/sciencenow/la-sci-sn-abortion-denied-children-20181030-story.html.

this statement—which, again, is widely representative of many who identify as pro-choice—asserts that mothers not killing their children harms their children. To avoid this being an outright Orwellian contradiction, the presupposition here must be that some children's lives (those who are born) are categorically more valuable than other children's lives (the unborn). In calculating the right social policy, the lives of the former matter enough to catch the attention of the *Los Angeles Times*; the lives of the latter are equivalent to the value of medical waste. That, too, is utilitarian thinking in action.

Utilitarianism is deeply embedded in many other contemporary issues, including policies regarding welfare, the environment, defense, farming and food supply, transportation, international aid, and trade, among others. Yet whatever the complexities that inhere in these diverse topics, utilitarianism has one formula to unite them all. Step 1: Reduce the relevant variables to some form of a pleasure vs. pain calculus. Step 2: Make predictions about how the consequences of different actions and policies will likely affect the relative sum of pleasure vs. pain in society. Step 3: Choose the action or policy that will most likely increase aggregate pleasure and decrease aggregate pain—and, as a precondition to all these steps, make sure you have the "right-thinking people" both defining the variables and crunching the numbers (i.e., be sure there are no fools or religious folk corrupting the data). Whether practicing "act utilitarianism" (looking at the aggregate consequences of actions) or "rule utilitarianism" (looking at the aggregate consequences of laws and policies), this is the recipe for governing society. To be sure, predicting the future is always laced with ambiguity, but one utilitarian outcome is as predictable as a casino's likelihood to turn a profit: the utilitarian house ultimately belongs to those whose interests constitute the majority and who have the power to ensure their interests count the most—and the house always wins.

THE CATHOLIC RESPONSE

This implication alone already indicates why Catholic social thought rejects utilitarianism, but it's important to note that there are three features of the theory that Catholics can agree with. First, Catholic social thought recognizes the moral legitimacy of employing consequence-informed reasoning (that is, making moral adjudications based upon the predicted consequences of an action or policy) so long as such reasoning does not lead to a violation of a negative moral prohibition (e.g., intentionally killing an innocent human being) or the preclusion of acting on a positive moral injunction (e.g., failing to feed those who cannot feed themselves). For example, Catholic social thought will always reject the thinking inhering in the abortion examples above—namely, that it is morally licit to exterminate one life in order to advance the "wellbeing" of another's life.[25] However, it would be morally acceptable, even morally advisable, to employ consequence-informed thinking to, for example, decide how to allocate limited financial resources to fund emergency pregnancy clinics. Asking the question, "Where is it most likely that we will be able to help the most mothers and save the most children's lives?" is premised on consequence-informed reasoning—pro-lifers, in this example, are looking at different possible scenarios and weighing different possible outcomes with the goal of maximizing the desired impact of a limited resource. There is nothing morally wrong with thinking and acting like this, again, provided

---

25. The principle underlying this belief is that all lives have equal dignity, no matter what "stage" they are in. However, Catholic teaching recognizes that when, for example, two lives are in danger, it is morally licit, if absolutely necessary, to save one life even if that means the loss of another life. This is the case in ectopic pregnancies, for example. The Church allows for the removal of the fallopian tube to save the mother's life, even though the unintended, if unavoidable, consequence is that the operation ends with the death of the developing child. Even in these terribly difficult circumstances, however, the intended goal is *never* to kill one life in order to save another. It is, rather, to do everything possible to save both lives while recognizing that, in some circumstances, that is impossible, at least by today's technological standards.

that one of the potential scenarios does not entail committing an immoral act to bring about the desired outcome. Precisely because Catholic social thought recognizes that there are often multiple morally licit means to achieve the same good end, basing decisions on the possible consequences of action, both individually and socially, is perfectly reasonable within limits.

This points to a broader point of partial agreement between Catholic social thought and utilitarianism: the necessity of empirical information to make applied moral judgments. A careful distinction is again necessary. As I'll explain below, Catholic social thought cannot *derive* moral principles empirically (indeed, it is rationally impossible to do so); however, empirical information is frequently necessary to *apply* moral principles. For example, it is impossible to derive the moral injunction "care for the vulnerable" by using empirical observation or "science" alone. However, determining *how* to care for the vulnerable greatly depends upon observation. One derivative principle from "care for the vulnerable," for example, is to "care for children"; caring for children entails, among other things, providing proper nutrition, protecting them from toxic materials like lead paint, and working with their unique learning styles to realize their full intellectual potential. Consequently, the knowledge we gain from the sciences about the nutritional values of food and its effect on growing bodies, the dangers of specific chemicals to proper development, and how learning environments affect the functioning of the young brain is essential for effectively applying the moral principle "care for children." In this sense, Catholic social thought has no quarrel with empirical observation and scientific reasoning in the service of morality. In fact, it positively embraces it as a necessary (though insufficient) condition for doing what we are supposed to do, both individually and socially.

Finally, Catholic social thought also partially agrees with one of the anthropological presuppositions in utilitarianism. Put in philosophical language, it is the recognition that reason alone is not practical, or, as Aristotle puts it, "reason alone moves nothing." Colloquially, this means that merely knowing something is morally right, merely possessing the correct moral knowledge, does not provide sufficient motivation to act on that knowledge. David Hume, for all the faults in his moral theory, gets this right about human nature. One of the reasons he locates morality in the sentiments is because he believes that human beings must desire the good in order to act on its behalf. We must, in other words, want to do the right thing, not merely know that we should do it.

On this point, Catholic social thought is in significant agreement. Unlike theories of morality that locate both the justification and the motivation for moral action in reason alone (we'll see such a theory in the next chapter), Catholic social thought recognizes that human desires and the human will, in conjunction with reason, serve an essential function in properly apprehending what is good and having the sufficient motivation to act in accordance with it. Indeed, this anthropological feature of Catholic thought helps explain why it embraces virtue theory. The goal of the moral life is not only to do the right thing at the right time but to become the kind of person who desires and enjoys doing the right thing at the right time. In short, both Catholic social thought and utilitarianism understand that acting morally necessarily entails engaging the heart in addition to the head.

There are, then, some areas of consensus that can provide the grounds for constructive conversation between Catholics and those who espouse some form of utilitarianism. However, as this chapter has long been suggesting, there are profound areas of disagreement as well. To categorize and analyze the differences, recall chapter 4's discussion of the five fundamental problems Catholic social thought addresses and chapter 5's discussion of the problematic characteristics of an "ideology." Summarized, they are:

- the problem of truth

- the problem of perfection

- the problem of human dignity

- the problem of moral hierarchies

- the problem of free speech

- the problem of idolatry (which includes the problem of false mutual exclusivities and the problem of too high / too low human nature)

Let's take each in turn—and keep the Thinking in Circles map in mind as we move forward.

THE PROBLEM OF TRUTH

To put it bluntly, utilitarianism has a problem telling the truth. In a literal sense, it is unable to speak with epistemic authority because it lacks the methodological capacity to identify both ontological truth (truth about the nature of the world) and moral truth (truth about the nature of good and evil). It lacks this capacity for two reasons. First, as we will see in the next chapter, there is no such thing as a "pure" empirical experience. The world and everything in it are not just "out there" for the grasping by our senses. Rather, our senses detect information in the world and our minds interpret that information. This, it is crucial to note, happens before or at least at the same time as the empirical experience of the world itself. Think of our sense of vision, for example. We have long known that the human eye does not "see" in the sense of grasping objects out in the world; rather, it detects different frequencies of light bouncing off external objects and passes on that information to the optical nerve that ties directly into the brain, where the light is translated into a coherent image. What's more, the physical structure of the eye bends the entering light in such a way that the image it produces is "upside down" until the brain flips it right side up. In a literal sense, then, we are never actually "seeing the world" with our sight; we are, rather, seeing an image generated by our brain in relationship with light and matter. And so, too, with all our other senses: taste, touch, sound, smell—none give us the world, per se, but rather an interpretation of the world.

What does this Anatomy 101 factoid have to do with utilitarianism? Recall that utilitarianism is constructed entirely on an empirical epistemology. Thus, if we can show that this epistemology has fundamental rational flaws, then, by extension, the moral theory that emerges from it will have fundamental rational flaws as well. One of the flaws in pure empiricism is that even a superficial analysis of the way our senses work reveals that empiricism is not self-sufficient; it depends upon non-empirical structures of knowledge—that is, ways of knowing prior to any knowledge of the external world, what is also often called "a priori" knowledge. More specifically, having a sense experience depends on a pre-existing interpretive mental framework that can translate data from the world into meaningful information (light into images, vibrations into sounds, chemicals into taste, force into touch, etc.). Without the pre-existence of this framework, sense data cannot even accurately be defined as "data"—that is, bits of unified, intelligible information. Rather, it is merely a cacophony of undifferentiated, refracted, bouncing, buzzing stuff. In this sense, empiricism cannot engage in empirical observation without a pre-made, a priori knowledge pack already in place.

Yet why couldn't we respond by claiming that the senses get that interpretive framework from the outside world? That is, we could grant that empiricism needs a mental interpretive framework yet maintain that empiricism can provide itself that framework by means of observation. This "solution" to the problem of empiricism's lack of an epistemic foundation, however, only plunges us into a vicious epistemic circle. On the one hand, we would be claiming that in order to have meaningful sensory experiences, the senses would need to go out into the world to identify and appropriate the necessary "mental equipment" to produce meaningful sensory experiences. On the other hand, we would be implying that that mental equipment is actually already in place before the search even begins (otherwise, how would the senses be able to identify the necessary mental equipment they need in the first place?).

This circularity explains why Hume's "mitigated skepticism" cannot offer a way out of the quandary either. Mitigated skepticism says that we will test our senses using what? Our senses. As discussed in chapter 2, that is like saying we will use the scientific method in order to determine whether the scientific method is valid. It is another epistemic circle. Thus, empiricism ultimately has two justificatory options: it must either admit that it depends upon a non-empirical epistemic foundation in order to function, in which case it ceases to be pure empiricism, or admit that what it says about the world and everything in it is completely arbitrary and has no rational authority whatsoever.

Indeed, this issue with pure empiricism points to an even deeper problem in Hume's epistemology, which, again, serves as the foundation for utilitarianism. Hume argues, on the one hand, that the human mind has no capacity to perceive an actual relationship between cause and effect. The implication of this claim is that all cause and effect in the world we think we perceive is, in fact, illusory and arbitrary—it has no basis in reason. On the other hand, Hume qualifies this radical conclusion by claiming that some causal relationships in the world—namely, those that have been established by employing the technique of "mitigated skepticism" (a.k.a. the scientific method)—are, in fact, "real" in some way, or at least real enough to have rational justification for believing in them. What this ultimately amounts to is Hume declaring, "All cause-and-effect relationships in the world are arbitrary, but some are less arbitrary than others."

The problem is that this is grammatical, logical, and metaphysical nonsense. Because arbitrariness does not come in degrees, it is either the case that all cause-and-effect relationships in the world are arbitrary (Hume's first conclusion) or that not all cause-and-effect relationships in the world are arbitrary (Hume's second conclusion). It is impossible to have it both ways. Indeed, Hume's position brings to mind the famous line in George Orwell's *Animal Farm* in which the authoritarian pigs announce to the other animals, "All animals are equal, but some are more equal than others." For Hume, all cause-and-effect relationships are arbitrary (like those in metaphysical inquiry), but some cause-and-effect relationships are less arbitrary than others (like those discovered by Hume and his fellow mitigated skeptics).

Again, this may sound like fussy philosophical nit-picking, but remember that utilitarianism is based exclusively on an empirical epistemology. If that epistemology cannot account for any rational cause-and-effect relationships in the world (again, Hume's first conclusion), then that completely undermines the foundations of utilitarian morality; namely, that we can use consequences—that is, effects of causes—to determine what constitutes right and wrong action. If there is no epistemic basis for believing that any consequences of actions are any more rationally valid than any other, then the whole utilitarian system of moral reasoning collapses. In short, utilitarianism either has to admit that it has no rational basis to make any claim about anything at all, including morality, or admit that it needs a non-empirical epistemology in order to operate, in which case it would be violating its own fundamental presupposition.

It gets even worse. Let's say, for example, setting aside the critiques above, that it were possible to extract morality from empirical observation alone. How would we go about doing so? Hume's answer, and the answer that all utilitarians give, is that we identify and isolate a characteristic or group of characteristics in human nature and then ask, "What actions should we perform in order to increase the aggregate prevalence of that characteristic or group of characteristics?" Thus, Hume appeals to the sentiment of "benevolence," Bentham to "physical pleasure," J.S. Mill to "mental pleasure," and Peter Singer to "wellbeing." The goal for each of these thinkers is to increase benevolence/(mental) pleasure/wellbeing across the population and decrease antipathy/ (mental) pain/suffering across the same population.

Yet two questions jump out. First, how can we know what these terms refer to definitionally from a purely empirical perspective? Equally important, how can we know that they designate something good? This problem with the definition of moral terms goes all the way back to Socrates' question in the dialogue *Meno* about whether it is possible to identify a definition of morality ("virtue," in his language) using empirical observation alone. The problem, Socrates recognizes, is this: When setting out to find what is good, we either already know the definition of good (in which case, when we say we are looking for morality out in the world, all we are doing is seeking to confirm knowledge we already possess) or we do not know the definition of good (in which case, no matter how hard we look, we will never be able to discover that which we seek because we have no idea what it is). In other words, we either have an a priori definition of morality or no definition of morality at all, because, as we also saw above, it is impossible to observe that which you have not pre-defined.

This philosophical dilemma, called the Meno paradox, points to the problem of the utilitarian definition of the good. The same definitional conundrum applies to pleasure, pain, suffering, and wellbeing. Either utilitarians already have an a priori, non-empirical definition of these terms so that they can know what they are observing when they see it in human nature (which, again, would undercut the empirical foundations of utilitarianism) or they don't have a non-empirical definition of these terms, in which case they have no justified reason for calling anything in the world pleasure, pain, etc. They are merely inventing the meanings, in which case their definitions have no rational basis. In other words, at the epistemic level, utilitarianism is either non-empirical (and thus not utilitarianism) or empirical but completely arbitrary.

But, again, let's set even this objection aside and say (contrary to reason) that utilitarianism can give an exclusively empirical account for the definition of its key moral terms. The next question would be "Why is pleasure better than pain?" or even "Why should we seek to avoid suffering?" It is crucial to recognize here that utilitarianism is not merely seeking to be descriptive in nature. It seeks to be prescriptive as well. It is not only saying "Humans tend to like pleasure" but "Humans should pursue pleasure" and, more broadly, "Humans should construct society in such a way that maximizes pleasure." Utilitarianism, in short, is full of "oughts"; it clearly wants to tell us what the right and wrong thing to do is and that we should do the right thing and should not do the wrong thing.

Now, on its face, that's not surprising. Indeed, that's what a moral theory is supposed to do—guide action. The problem is that it is not clear how utilitarianism has any authority to guide actions or issue moral commands precisely because it claims to be an exclusively empirical theory. To understand why this is a problem, it is important to note that every moral theory, no matter what its specific content, must be capable of not only identifying what constitutes "good" actions but also how it is possible to violate or contradict what is good—in other words, how it is possible to act "badly." The issue is that utilitarianism has no mechanism for identifying what constitutes a contradiction of the good, even if we assume that it can coherently define the good in the first place.

An example helps explain why. Say that an anthropologist with a background in evolutionary biology is studying a society of 1,000 people seeking to determine what their moral values are. Of that 1,000 people, the anthropologist observes that over 900 of them (90%) seem to be peaceable and agreeable, meaning they are willing to sacrifice their individual interests, at least to a limited degree, for the good of the whole community. However, the anthropologist also observes that about 100 people in the group (10%) are not only unwilling to sacrifice their interests for the good of the whole but actively seek to manipulate other members of the population in order to get what they want. Indeed, 10 of those 100 (1%) are willing to not only use manipulation to get what they want but employ force to kill, maim, and otherwise physically intimidate the 900 peaceable folks with the goal of establishing a ruling structure in which few benefit at the cost of the many. On the surface, this hypothetical society would seem to serve as evidence in favor of utilitarianism's underlying premise that the way to determine what is good and what is bad is to survey human behavior. In this case, 90% of the population is one way (peaceful and cooperative) and only 10% of the population is another way (violent and uncooperative). Doesn't that mean there is a moral justification for setting society up in a way to prevent the 10% of the population from imposing its will on 90% of the population?

Yes—but not if you are a utilitarian. The problem is that making the moral claim "It is wrong for 10% of the population to impose its will on 90% of the population" is founded on the implicit moral principle that "the majority should not be dominated by the minority." However, we see violations of that principle in human nature—and nature more broadly—all the time. This deviation from "majority rule" in terms of actual human behavior points directly to the issue. The fact that some humans are peaceable and some humans are violent tells us nothing from an empirical perspective about which option is morally superior. It just tells us that more people tend to do one thing rather than another. Yet there are massive exceptions to this rule (think of the 1994 genocide in Rwanda, for example, in which the majority population of Hutus turned out to be vastly more violent than the minority community of Tutsis—to the tune of over 800,000 murders in 100 days[26]). Thus, the "rule" itself is not really a rule, in the sense that it is not connected to any kind of rational necessity. It's just an observation, one with, again, innumerable exceptions. As such, when minorities act against majorities, or majorities act against minorities, no rational rule has been broken; a pattern has merely been disrupted.

To be sure, a utilitarian, especially one influenced by evolutionary biology, could reply by saying, "Being peaceable and agreeable is morally better because humans value the creation of communities in which violence is less common because it gives them a better chance to survive and get their genes into the next generation." However, the moral problem remains the same: empiricism has no rational mechanism to declare "Being alive and staying alive is preferable to not being alive" or "Those who act aggressively are acting immorally." Again, all empiricism can do is observe—and what we observe, when looking at human nature as a whole, is that some people do everything possible to take advantage of others to advance their own self-interest, some people make great sacrifices to help others with no expectation for repayment, and many, many people drift between these extremes depending on numerous internal and external individual, social, and environmental factors. The same goes for pleasure and pain—perhaps most people seek pleasure most of the time, but what honest observer of human nature would deny that sometimes we like the pain and even seek it for its own sake? All of this is "human behavior," and none of it by itself can tell us what we *should* do. It only tells us what we *do* do.

In sum, for utilitarianism to gaze upon the jumbled mass of human comportment and select "pleasure seeking" as the feature upon which it will construct its entire system of morality (and, by

---

26. There remains debate about the precise number of people slaughtered in the Rwandan massacre; however, for a reasoned estimate, see, for example, "Rwanda genocide: 100 days of slaughter," BBC News, April 4, 2019, https://www .bbc.com/news/world-africa-26875506.

extension, politics) is logically akin to choosing a moral theory by having ten blindfolded people thrust their hands into a barrel of multicolored marbles, each one representing a different form of human behavior. Of the ten, four choose green marbles, two choose blue, two choose black, and one chooses white. After looking at each other, the four green marble-holders declare, "Green is not only the majority color but also the only correct color to possess; therefore, the rest of you will have to do what we say." In other words, utilitarianism is not only unjust to those who end up in the minority but rationally warrantless for *everyone*.

The Catholic view of truth as it relates to morality and human nature is fundamentally different. At the foundation of the Catholic conception of natural law lies a recognition that created reality, what we could refer to as the natural world, is structured by an invisible but real objective order, including a moral order.[27] St. Thomas Aquinas describes the relationship between the natural and supernatural realities this way: God, who is the eternal law, creates a universe that is ontologically different from God yet governed by God both in the act of creation itself and in its ongoing ordering and existence. As Aquinas, quoting St. Augustine, memorably puts it in his *Summa theologiae*, "If the ruling power of God were withdrawn from his creatures, their natures would at once cease, and all nature would at once collapse."[28] In other words, it is only because God *is* that nature is and continues to be. This relationship between God and nature is important to recognize for many reasons, but, for our purposes, this is what matters most: Grounding natural law in the eternal law allows human beings to identify actions that are in accordance with natural law and actions that contradict natural law.

27. Parts of this section have been adapted from the lecture "The Law Is a Form of Grace," from my Word on Fire Institute course "Re-enchanting the Secular."

28. Thomas Aquinas, *Summa theologiae* 1.104.1.

The possibility of contradiction is very important here. God is, according to Aquinas, the only being who must be; God cannot not be because God is God, a point Aquinas also expresses by arguing that God's essence (what God is) and God's existence (that God is) are, unlike everything God created, one and the same. God, in other words, does not change and does not become. God is. This divine metaphysical necessity is crucial for understanding how and why natural law can have both epistemic stability and moral authority. Within this framework, in which the natural law is derived from the eternal law, we can say that the natural law is and is good because God is and is good. We are consequently able to establish our definition of evil—namely, that which contradicts the natural law. Note that contradiction is only a possibility because (a) there is a fixed, rational standard establishing moral truth and (b) human beings have the free will to act in accordance with that fixed standard or not. In this sense, violating the natural law is not only going against God's commands (though it is that) but analogous to calling a "1" a "0" or a "married person" a "bachelor." That is, sinning and doing evil is a rational contradiction.

In the Humean version of nature at the heart of utilitarianism, however, there is no God, and that changes everything. If you remove God from the order of nature, you remove metaphysical necessity; and if you remove metaphysical necessity, you remove the possibility of contradiction; and if you remove the standard for contradiction, you remove a fixed, objective standard for determining the true content of right and wrong. In contrast, by affirming God's existence and nature in the way St. Thomas Aquinas does, we can solve the problem of rational necessity and objectivity as a precondition for moral authority, and we can solve the Meno paradox (the natural law inheres in human beings by nature, and so does not need to be "discovered" out in the world), the problem of objective definitions (if God is real then creation is intelligible and thus knowable by human reason), and the missing link between cause and effect (if God exists and is the creator of the world, then causal relationship are real, not arbitrary). In other words, the Catholic conception of truth fills the holes in utilitarian epistemology while still upholding both the possibility of and need for empirical observation in moral reasoning. Consequently, and most importantly, it prevents those who have the most power—the lucky, we might say—from being able to dictate to everyone else, "Do as we say because we are stronger than you."

THE PROBLEM OF PERFECTION

Utilitarian ideology has influenced two of the most important novels in modern English literature, Aldous Huxley's *Brave New World* and George Orwell's *1984*. In both books, the authors portray a future in which totalitarian government has seized control of almost every aspect of individual and social life in the name of "Community, Identity, and Stability"[29] in the World State of *Brave New World* and the four government ministries of "Truth," "Peace," "Love," and "Plenty," which constitute "Big Brother," in *1984*. It is not incidental that these literary critiques of utopianism target the principles underlying utilitarianism. Whatever "benefits" we might be able to attribute to planning society according to "the greatest good for the greatest number," utilitarianism, by design, has no limiting principle that serves as a buffer against government encroachment in the name of creating an ever-more "perfect" society. Indeed, it lacks two limiting principles in particular: limits on the meaning of language and limits on the definition of humanity and the human good.

First, precisely because of its rejection of metaphysical truth, the meaning of words from a utilitarian perspective is as malleable as those who control the language want it to be. We have already seen the difficulty that empiricism has with defining key terms

29. Aldous Huxley, *Brave New World* (New York: Perennial Classics, 1998), 3.

like "pleasure," "suffering," "wellbeing," and even "empiricism" itself because those definitions must be determined a priori before they can be empirically detected "out in the world." Beyond this definitional problem, the moral core of utilitarianism—the greatest good for the greatest number—also positively authorizes those who oversee society to alter the meaning of language and even logic so long as they make the case that doing so will lead to an aggregate increase of pleasure. We see in *Brave New World*, for example, that the character of Mustapha Mond, the authoritarian who oversees the World State, prevents the populace from having access to "pre-World State" history, literature, art, and even science. Mond tells the protagonist John the Savage, "[Our society] hasn't been good for truth, of course. But it's been very good for happiness. One can't have something for nothing. Happiness has got to be paid for."[30] Happiness, Mond makes clear, can and should be in direct opposition to the truth if defining it that way will increase the overall levels of satisfaction. That may sound absurd—how could a society knowingly embrace a false definition of happiness?—yet that is, as Huxley brilliantly points out, within the logical possibilities of utilitarian ideology.

George Orwell picks up the same theme in *1984* when he attributes these three slogans to the Party (Big Brother) that administers society: "War Is Peace," "Freedom Is Slavery," and "Ignorance Is Strength."[31] Moreover, the novel's protagonist, Winston, works at The Ministry of Truth, and his job is to destroy previous versions of history and rewrite them according to the Party's narrative. In other words, the purpose of the Ministry of Truth is to generate lies. To be sure, all this constitutes a logical contradiction; however, because of utilitarianism's moral logic, anything—including a violation of logic itself—can be authorized in the name of advancing social well-being. Indeed, if the

---

30. Huxley, 238.
31. George Orwell, *1984* (New York: Signet Classics, 1961), 4.

consequences of altering the structure of reasoning, the events of history, and the meaning of words themselves can be deemed to generate more benefits than costs for the population, then utilitarianism not only authorizes such garbling of the truth but commands it be done. As such, utilitarianism offers a carte blanche to those who hold power to manipulate language in any way they see fit for the "good" of society.

Second, utilitarianism places no limits on the definition of "human being" or "the human good." If modifying human nature can be deemed to advance net well-being, then utilitarianism once again not only authorizes but enjoins such alteration. For this reason, *Brave New World*'s society is built upon a state-produced caste system of genetically customized humans, with Epsilons at the thick base of the social pyramid engineered to do slavish manual labor and, moving upward in the pyramid, Deltas, Gammas, Betas, and Alphas produced to do ever more manually and intellectually complex work. *1984*, in turn, shows the extent to which the utilitarian state will go to alter the human body and mind through psychological and physical torture to enforce individual conformity to government ideology. For example, Winston and his love interest, Julia, are brutalized by state authorities until Winston breaks down and confesses that he loves Big Brother more than he loves her. Whether it is the shattering of the nuclear family, the manipulation of romantic relationships, or the very altering of human biology itself, the point is that utilitarian ideology has no internal mechanism to limit the boundless modification of human nature because it authorizes the state to do anything in the name of the "greater good." In this sense, utilitarianism is a paradigmatic example of a utopian model from chapter 4's discussion of models of political perfection. Yet given its free rein over language and human nature, it should come as no surprise that such "utopias" can be depicted as nightmarishly dystopian.

In contrast, Catholic social thought categorically rejects the premises that either language or human nature is malleable. As such, it recognizes real definitions of concepts like "pleasure," "pain," "well-being," and "happiness" and a real definition of what it means to be human. These definitions form the first line of defense: Whatever goal government (or those who hold power broadly) seeks to pursue, it cannot ("cannot" in the sense of "it would be a violation of truth to do so") redefine terms to advance a political agenda. Moreover, contra utilitarianism, Catholic social thought recognizes a fixed human nature, which provides the grounds for defining the authentic human good, and thus a moral and political standard for society to pursue, and the existence of sin, which recognizes the limits of what humans can accomplish by their own efforts. Finally, Catholic social thought's conception of the common good defines the individual good in relation to the social good in such a way that the two should never be defined as opposed. Any social movement that would be willing "to break some eggs to make an omelet," as the Soviet tyrant Stalin (apocryphally) said of his plans to drag Russia into a new era of peace and prosperity, would thus be immoral. For Catholics, no human being can ever be sacrificed for the good of the whole. More broadly, Catholicism recognizes that any attempt to create a heaven on earth, as the twentieth century terrifyingly confirmed, is a sure recipe for unleashing hell.

THE PROBLEM OF HUMAN DIGNITY

Peter Singer's *Unsanctifying Human Life* says everything you need to know about the utilitarian conception of dignity—namely, that the worth of any individual depends upon whether and to what degree she or he contributes to a net positive or net negative of aggregate social well-being. Singer is not a radical utilitarian outlier in holding this position. He is simply being consistent with the principles of utilitarianism and their grounding in empiricism and, consequently, atheistic materialism. His advocacy for the killing of "irreparably retarded infants" only sounds shocking if you believe that human life has intrinsic dignity rooted in a reality that is not reducible to a random agglomeration of particles. But if you reject that premise, then why not take Singer's position on "damaged" human life? Indeed, why not go even further to argue that any life, whether "damaged" or not, is subject to the same cost-benefit analysis?

For example, does a society really want to have large numbers of "unwanted" children around, especially with their higher tendencies to engage in antisocial behavior and the fact that they'd be using up resources that could otherwise go to the "wanted"? Perhaps exterminating chubby, cooing babies is too much even for the most diehard utilitarian to stomach, but what if, maybe, we could do the cleansing at the point of entry—that is, right at birth or just after? Some newborns, after all, are not very pleasant to look at, especially just after they've exited the birth canal, and, technically—if we're going to follow "pro-choice" biology and logic all the way—the child is still part of the mother's body until the cutting of the umbilical cord. As a bonus, think of all the money we would also save on feeding future prisoners.

Sound dystopianly horrific? You (fortunately) haven't spent enough time reading the musings of utilitarian medical "ethicists"—a.k.a. the "experts." Indeed, one infamous academic article entitled "After-birth abortion," by Alberto Giubilini and Francesca Minerva of the University of Melbourne, offers this abstract of their argument:

> Abortion is largely accepted even for reasons that do not have anything to do with the fetus' health. By showing that (1) both fetuses and newborns do not have the same moral status as actual persons, (2) the fact that both are potential persons is morally irrelevant and (3) adoption is not always in the best interest of actual people, the authors argue that what we call 'after-birth abortion' (killing a newborn) should be permissible

in all the cases where abortion is, including cases where the newborn is not disabled.[32]

The designation here between "fetus" and "actual persons"—which we will pick up again next chapter—cuts to the heart of utilitarian thinking. It's not only the case that the minority can justifiably be sacrificed for the majority; the definition of what defines the minority is entirely within the purview of the majority, those who have the most power. Again, as disturbing as it may sound, there is nothing inconsistent with utilitarianism justifying "after-birth abortion" (once quaintly known as "infanticide") so long as it can make the case that disposing of these "not actual people" serves the majority of the interests of the "actual people" in society. And how do you know which people are the actual ones? Consult the experts at the University of Melbourne. They manage the spreadsheet.

The Catholic view categorically rejects this formulation of the value of human life, both methodologically and substantively. Methodologically, as argued previously, the empirical foundation of utilitarianism means that it cannot coherently attribute value to anything at all, including human beings. It also cannot coherently identify any fixed principle in humanity or human nature that could justify a durable conception of moral equality because, again, empiricism cannot "see" moral equality and therefore cannot make any appeal to it. Thus, making an empirical moral distinction between different kinds of human beings and their relative values (e.g., "actual" vs. "non-actual" people) has no rational justification.

In contrast, while Catholic thought can and does incorporate empirical forms of knowing into its understanding of human nature and human dignity by, for example, relying on science

---

32. Alberto Giubilini and Francesca Minerva, "After-birth abortion: why should the baby live?" *Journal of Medical Ethics* 39, no. 5 (2013): 261–263, https://jme.bmj.com/content/medethics/39/5/261.full.pdf.

to tell us how to preserve and advance human health, it does not found its conception of worth on empiricism. Rather, it deduces the equal dignity of human beings from the metaphysical existence of God—who both transcends material reality and is embedded within it as a causal principle—and draws on God's revelation in Scripture that all human beings, without exception, are made in the image and likeness of God. This also explains why Catholic thought rejects any attempt to calculate some lives as morally more important than others. That is not to say it doesn't recognize any morally relevant inequalities among human beings, including inequalities of virtue and merit. It only means that, unlike utilitarianism, Catholicism recognizes and unwaveringly upholds a floor of moral equality beneath which no human being can fall—not even those about whom society is tempted to say, "We would be better without you." As Pope St. John Paul II puts it in the papal encyclical *Evangelium Vitae*, "Not even a murderer loses his personal dignity, and God himself pledges to guarantee this."[33]

Thus, for Catholics, no human being has the right to treat any other human being as anything less than a full moral equal. With utilitarianism, there are always exceptions, and, if you are lucky enough to make it past the white-coated birth censors, know that, if you live long enough, you'll eventually outlive your utility and become one of them.

THE PROBLEM OF MORAL HIERARCHIES

Utilitarianism, recall, has two problems with its dominant principle. The first is that it identifies "pleasure" (or, conversely, "the reduction of suffering") as its highest good yet cannot rationally account for what should specifically define pleasure or why it should constitute the highest moral principle (or even a moral

---

33. John Paul II, *Evangelium Vitae* 9, encyclical letter, March 25, 1995, vatican. va.

principle at all). The second problem, a consequence of the first, is that utilitarianism delivers both the definition and application of its foundational principle into the hands of those who have the power to impose their definition on others. Because it lacks any rationally objective moral content, the only alternative is for someone or some group to make that content up—and it should come as no surprise that those someones will conjure definitions that comfortably place themselves among the "greatest number" whose "greatest good" is the top political priority.

The practical consequence of these errors is that utilitarianism forces us to make zero-sum choices between authentic goods—e.g., individual liberty vs. social cohesion, human dignity vs. human welfare, economic efficiency vs. worker well-being. Since it has no objectively stable means of either defining different forms of the good or adjudicating one in relationship to another, utilitarianism will inescapably impose a king-of-the-hill, winner-takes-all principle of justice in society. Again, keep in mind that every potential principle of justice we might think of—e.g., voting rights, free speech (more on this below), free movement throughout a country, private property, even having and raising your own children—is subject to a utilitarian calculation that, in turn, is subject to the whims of those who make those calculations. If the expert class determines that you speaking your mind or choosing where your kids are educated or owning a home contributes to less aggregate pleasure, then those "rights" can (and will) be abrogated in a heartbeat—which is another way of saying that rights do not and cannot exist within a utilitarian paradigm.

Indeed, Jeremy Bentham famously wrote the following about the existence of objective individual rights:

> That which has no existence cannot be destroyed—that which cannot be destroyed cannot require anything to preserve it from destruction. Natural rights is simple nonsense: natural and imprescriptible rights, rhetorical nonsense—*nonsense upon*

stilts. But this rhetorical nonsense ends in the old strain of mischievous nonsense for immediately a list of these pretended natural rights is given, and those are so expressed as to present to view legal rights.[34]

Bentham's claim here is that affirming the existence of rights that exist objectively (independently of any political community) is sheer nonsense. To make the additional claim that, based upon the existence of these objective rights, there are also specific rights—like to freedom of religion, or to own a firearm, or to travel domestically without identification—is what he calls "nonsense on stilts." There are, in other words, no such thing as rights from a utilitarian perspective.

And why should there be? To affirm the existence of an objective right is to say that there are actions that are categorically prohibited, things that must never be done to others (and to oneself) no matter what putative "benefit" they may have to society. That is precisely what utilitarianism rejects—all actions are potentially permissible, including the violation of "rights," if those actions contribute to the greatest good for the greatest number (which, it is crucial to emphasize, is an ever-moving target insofar as what constitutes the greatest good and how that good can be achieved changes as the society's whims change). The only principle of justice within utilitarianism, therefore, is this: "In all things, perform those actions that will lead to the net increase of pleasure in society and do not perform those actions that will lead to the net decrease of pleasure in society—no matter what." This principle does not and cannot organize society around a properly ordered hierarchy of distinct human goods because it only, in the end, recognizes one human good as mattering: net

34. Jeremy Bentham, *Anarchical Fallacies*, 1776, https://h2o.law.harvard.edu /text_blocks/28863 (emphasis added).

social pleasure (not your pleasure but "our" pleasure, defined, of course, by those with the power to do so).

In contrast, because Catholic thought rejects the conceptual moral foundations of utilitarianism, it also rejects its practical conclusions with regard to the question of both the existence of rights and how society should be justly organized. The following chapter will analyze the Catholic conception of rights in more depth, but suffice it to say here that Catholicism disagrees that rights are "nonsense," whether on stilts or not. Indeed, although the use of the language of "rights" is a relatively recent development, the foundations for the existence of objective rights lie at the core of Catholic moral theology and have from the very beginning. The result is that Catholic social thought, contra utilitarianism, imposes a strict limiting principle on all actions no matter what "good" consequences they may have for society. Whatever society seeks to do, it cannot ("cannot" in the sense that it would be an objective violation of justice to do so) violate an individual's rights.

So, for example, even if killing one child would mean that ten children would be able to have more access to resources, Catholicism says no. Even if euthanizing comatose patients who have no scientifically grounded hope of recovery would free up money for more disease-fighting research, Catholicism says no. And even if aborting just one child to harvest her organs would mean the creation of a vaccine that saves hundreds of thousands, even millions, Catholicism says no. These nos correspond with the "thou shall not" dimension of Catholic morality, the recognition that some actions are categorically prohibited, no matter what the consequences.[35] This does not mean that there are no grounds

35. It is also important to note that the "consequences" the experts predict are oftentimes wrong, sometimes so wrong as to be upside down. For example, several decades ago, there was strong scientific consensus that the global population would soon reach a level in which mouths to feed would far exceed the supply of food. There were numerous calls for governments to encourage (or coerce, as we saw in China) their populations to restrict the number of children born in each family

for nuance in dealing with complex moral issues—for example, Catholic moral theology permits the removal of the fallopian tube in an ectopic pregnancy on the grounds that such action is necessary to save the life of the mother (the intention is not to kill the unborn child). It only means that all the deliberation about moral complexity takes place within a horizon of firm limits, limits that no one is ever permitted to cross.

Recall, however, that Catholic social thought also upholds the existence of positive moral injunctions, the "thou shalls" of morality. There are many things that we should not do. There are more things that we should do. There are, that is, many goods to pursue in life, not only individually but socially—as a community, and as a state and nation. Some of these goods can appear to be at odds with each other. However, without downplaying both the theoretical and practical difficulty of harmonizing what appear to be disparate goods, the Catholic conception of the "common good" provides both a conceptual and applied framework for organizing individuals, families, neighborhoods, towns, cities, regions, nations, and countries in ways that allow for the possibility of both defining and pursuing the good without producing objective losers. By "objective losers," I mean individuals and groups who must sacrifice an objectively valid good in order for someone else or some other group to enjoy that good (for example, one group having to give up their right to free speech so that others can have it or one group working for unjust wages so that other people can earn just wages). The common-good tradition upholds that, if all levels of society are functioning as they should be, no one should be forced to suffer unjustly for the good of another. (As a matter of charity, people can freely choose to sacrifice if they believe it

by using birth control and even abortion. Today, however, many regions in the word are in steep demographic *decline*, and the world is fatter than ever—so fat, in many regions, that life-expectancy is beginning to fall due to obesity-related problems. (See, for example, Joseph Chamie, "America's unhealthy lifestyles," The Hill, June 22, 2021, https://thehill.com/opinion/finance/559501-americas -unhealthy-lifestyles.) The experts got this one wrong.

will benefit others; the point is that the government should not coerce them to do so as a consequence of having embraced a false ideology.)

It is crucial to remember here that Catholicism completely rejects utopianism. There will therefore be innumerable instances of suffering in the world, much of it caused by the action and inaction of oneself and other people, and no society, no matter how justly organized, will be able to eradicate it. Indeed, Jesus Christ recognizes, "You always have the poor with you" (Matt. 26:11); there will thus be no heaven on earth this side of the eschaton, and the belief that there can be is dangerous folly. The Catholic social thought tradition's conception of the common good does not say that justice for all people is possible to achieve—it says that it is possible to define. As such, the common good provides a paradigm for adjudicating among all the different authentic human goods among all levels of social organization, and it makes at least theoretically possible principles of justice in which, in the language of St. Thomas Aquinas, each person gets his/her due from every other person and from every relevant social and civic institution.[36]

In the end, the utilitarian conception of justice is, as noted before, like a crapshoot in which the house always wins. The Catholic conception, on the other hand, is like an immensely complex yet still solvable puzzle that requires both individual initiative and social cooperation to put together. All the pieces for the creation of a maximally just society are there, ready to be assembled. Whether we have the good will and virtue to do the necessary work to make it happen—that's another question.

---

36. St. Thomas Aquinas' conception of justice is richly complex and includes both "commutative" and "distributive" forms of justice, but he succinctly defines the *virtue* of justice as a "habit whereby man renders to each one his due by a constant and perpetual will" (*Summa theologiae* 1-2.58.1).

THE PROBLEM OF FREE SPEECH

When many people think of "free speech," one of the first names that comes to mind is John Stuart Mill and his classic 1859 treatise *On Liberty*. In the text, Mill famously defends individuality, the free and open exchange of ideas, the toleration of dissent, and the maximizing of freedom in society. He is one of the most influential political philosophers in the Western intellectual tradition, and some of his words have entered the pantheon of so-called common wisdom. Indeed, though he is a utilitarian (a point to which I will soon return), his broad defense of freedom and individuality often makes him sound as if here were a classical liberal, which, as we will see in the next chapter, is diametrically opposed to utilitarianism. Mill writes, "The only freedom which deserves the name is that of pursuing our own good in our own way, so long as we do not attempt to deprive others of theirs or impede their efforts to obtain it."[37] Within such freedom, he maintains, also inheres a freedom of expression, even if such expression is considered "immoral" by society: "There ought to exist the fullest liberty of professing and discussing, as a matter of ethical conviction, any doctrine, however immoral it may be considered."[38] Indeed, permitting a diversity of opinion is necessary for individuals to seek what Mill often refers to as "the truth." As he memorably observes, "He who knows only his side of the case knows little of that."[39] Through the back-and-forth of examining competing positions, Mill believes, individuals will eventually discard false ideas about the nature of reality, humanity, and the good and move closer and closer to the truth:

> If the lists [of books one can read] are kept open, we may hope
> that, if there be a better truth, it will be found when the human

37. John Stuart Mill, *On Liberty* (London: Walter Scott, 1901), 23, gutenberg
.org.

38. Mill, 29n.

39. Mill, 67.

mind is capable of receiving it; and in the meantime we may rely on having attained such approach to the truth as is possible in our day. This is the amount of certainty attainable by a fallible being, and this is the sole way of attaining it.[40]

Freedom of speech? The robust exchange of ideas? A productive blend of intellectual curiosity and intellectual humility? Respecting others' pursuit of the truth as you seek yours? *What's not to love?* It is certainly understandable why J.S. Mill has earned his place in the hearts of the lovers of liberty. But remember: he's a utilitarian, which means there is a condition attached to his embrace of individual freedom in general and free speech in particular. In the same treatise, Mill writes,

> That mankind are not infallible; that their truths, for the most part, are only half-truths; that unity of opinion, unless resulting from the fullest and freest comparison of opposite opinions, is not desirable, and diversity not an evil, but a good, until mankind are much more capable than at present of recognising [sic] all sides of the truth, are principles applicable to men's modes of action, not less than to their opinions.[41]

At first blush, this passage seems to be a reaffirmation of the good of individual liberty, including of thought, expression, and action. But Mill sneaks in a contingency: "until mankind are much more capable than at present of recognizing all sides of the truth." This "until" changes everything. Mill is not a defender of individual freedom and free speech per se; rather, he is a defender of individual freedom and free speech as a tool to achieve a greater social goal. In other words, Mill, as a utilitarian, has instrumentalized

40. Mill, 39.
41. Mill, 105.

individual rights and in so doing already identified the final goal that will trigger their demise.

What is that goal? Unsurprisingly, Mill calls it "utility." The precise definition is difficult to pin down in the text, but Mill gives a clue when he writes, "I regard utility as the ultimate appeal on all ethical questions; but it must be utility in the largest sense, grounded on the permanent interest of man as a progressive being."[42] Mapping this definition of utility onto Mill's broader discussion of the "interests of man" in *Utilitarianism*, it becomes clear that the condition Mill imposes on all individual freedoms is whether they ultimately contribute to the growth of aggregate pleasure in society, especially mental pleasure. By his own logic, then, if any of the freedoms he otherwise defends, including the freedom of speech, were to act against progress toward greater mental pleasure, then the right would instantly cease to be a right—which means it's not a right at all. Indeed, Mill says as much when he writes, the "diversity of opinion [is] advantageous, and will continue to [be] so until mankind shall have entered a stage of intellectual advancement which at present seems at an incalculable distance."[43]

Relying on a Millian principle of freedom to safeguard your rights is thus like signing a marriage license with an expiration date on it—it may be good while it lasts, and the expiration may be far in the future, but, by design, the relationship's going to end. To be sure, Mill deserves credit for being honest up front. Like a future philanderer cooing to his new conquest, he is simply disclosing to his freedom-loving fans, "You know I won't be here forever, baby, but, until my true love Lady Utility arrives, I am totally into you." This is what the utilitarian embrace of free speech sounds like. It can certainly feel seductively convincing in the moment. But don't be surprised when you hear the door

42. Mill, 19.
43. Mill, 84.

shut and find your copy of the Bill of Rights missing when you wake up in the morning.

In contrast, Catholicism does not place an expiration date or conceptual poison-pill mechanism that cancels its support for individual rights, including the right to free speech, once a particular social goal has been attained. Rights can certainly serve an instrumental function insofar as they can lead to a more just, peaceful, and prosperous society. However, the justification for those rights is not instrumental. It is, rather, objective, grounded in the dignity of every individual human being. As such, the right to free speech, just like every other right, is not a favor that society bestows upon its members so long as they advance social welfare; it is a right that every society must respect if it wishes to call itself authentically just.

AMORAL MAN PROSTRATED BEFORE
THE ALTAR OF PLEASURE

John Stuart Mill's admission that it is the continual march toward ever greater utility that serves as the overarching moral purpose of individual and communal human life once again lays bare utilitarianism's true nature. Despite the highbrow sneering against religion that we see in the thought of Peter Singer—which is representative of David Hume, Jeremy Bentham, and Mill alike—utilitarianism has not done away with religion. It has merely created its own. It has emptied the Eucharist from the tabernacle and replaced it with mental and physical stimulants; the community of saints has been fired and replaced by an expert class of scientists and accountants; and behind the veil is not the transcendent God who fills the deepest yearning of the human heart but an imminently temporal idol who, with a frozen half-smile cracked in both satisfaction and disgust, commands human obedience upon pain of being banished from the majority. Utilitarians have not abandoned the act of worshiping, in other words; they've chosen to worship something in this world, something physical, finite, and, I hasten to add, chillingly fragile and ephemeral: the reduction of suffering and the augmenting of pleasure. This is the only "good" it can point to in existence. With all the wisdom and compassion of a dollar store "Get well" card, the best response it can provide to the question "What's it all for and what am I supposed to do in life?" is "Feel better!"

Yet in addition to its problems with defining good and bad physical and mental feelings—an unavoidable problem because empiricism cannot make normative moral distinctions—utilitarianism cannot even tell you why you should want to feel better in the first place or why you should care how others feel. The utilitarian might scoff, "You want to feel better because you like to feel better and you want others to feel better too." Yeah, maybe—and maybe not. Sure, a lot of people often like feeling better and seeing others feeling better. But a lot of people also delight in causing themselves and others pain, not just in weird ways (though there is plenty of that in the shadows), but in everyday, ordinary ways, ways so pedestrian that we accept them as just a normal part of life—ways like eating too much, injecting heroin into your veins, treating your children like unwanted burdens, conniving to ruin a good person's reputation, lying to yourself that you can quit at any time, having sex with strangers as if they were animated flesh pots, seeking opportunities to feel like a victim, complaining incessantly, cheating, stealing, being incompetent at work, stewing in a depression even after you've seen a way out, and, generally, letting things fall apart around you when even a modest amount of care and attention would prevent their destruction. People—we—do all that, as well. Our pleasure is our pain sometimes. Or is it, our pain is sometimes our pleasure?

It can be hard to tell.

Whatever the answer, utilitarianism ultimately can't give it to you because it can't tell you what is good or bad or right or wrong. Thus, in the end, for this ideology to perch itself above the vast landscape of humanity and declare, "You must seek the greatest good for the greatest number," is as rationally authoritative as if it were commanding (with the voice of emasculated, ersatz Moses in a silk robe), "You must prostrate yourselves before this impressive-looking hunk of shimmering stone (that I've carved myself)." Yes, utilitarianism thinks that it has liberated humans from religion. But all it has done is replace it with a cult of pleasure, one that will welcome you and caress you and feed your every desire—until the temple priests no longer find your presence gratifying and decide you'd be more useful as an object of sacrifice.

CHAPTER 7

The God of My Self: Classical Liberalism and Libertarianism

"You do you, I'll do me." These words, so ubiquitous in the secular West that they have achieved the status of common sense, constitute the heart and soul of classical liberalism and libertarianism. Just as with "The greatest good for the greatest number," the appeal feels enticingly obvious: What better way to organize society than to declare that everyone gets to do *whatever* they want *however* they want as long as they don't interfere with others' endeavors to do the same and secure full consent anytime the satisfaction of their desires requires another's participation? It is an individualist's paradise: In the wonderful world of the autonomous self, the human person is not only like a liberated stone carver who gets to create whatever she/he/[pronoun of choice] desires with her/his/[possessive pronoun of choice] life; each person is also the hammer, the chisel, the raw stone, even the very quarry itself! The heteronomous books of old say that we are made in the image and likeness of God. The new books, the modern books, finally free us from this oppressive "God" and declare: "You are made in the image and likeness of YOU."

Yes, it sounds good—so good, in fact, that it's hard to imagine anyone objecting except for Talibanesque fanatics who are dead set on imposing their views on others. If there's one thing we've learned from history, isn't it that individuals should be free to do whatever they want so long as they leave everyone else alone? In harmony with Jon Bon Jovi, shouldn't we all be able to proclaim, "It's *my* life"? Can't we at least agree on *that*?

CHOOSING A PARADIGM OF CHOICE

Like every political theory, classical liberalism and libertarianism are not free-floating concepts. They have a history and philosophical genealogy, one that traces its primary roots back to a man who never ventured further than ten miles from his birthplace and didn't produce a scholarly work that anyone cared about until he was well into his fifties: the German philosopher Immanuel Kant (1724–1804).[1] Before examining the Kantian foundations of both liberalism and libertarianism, it is important to explain why this chapter focuses on Kant in particular. At their ideological core, both classical liberalism and libertarianism uphold the existence of not only individual liberty but also, consequently, the value of "consent" as it applies to social interactions. In the Western political tradition, freedom and consent are at the heart of not only Kantianism but also the great "social contract" theories, notably those of Englishman Thomas Hobbes (1588–1679), Hobbes's fellow Englishman John Locke (1632–1704), and the Swiss/French political theorist Jean-Jacques Rousseau (1712–1778). Each of these influential thinkers argued that consent is foundational both to justice among individuals and justice between the individual and the political order. In this sense, broadly speaking, each could thus also be considered a source of contemporary classical liberalism and libertarianism.

However, Kant represents something unique in this pantheon. Unlike Hobbes, Locke, and Rousseau, Kant establishes a philosophical system that is entirely independent of "nature" (including both human nature and natural law), and, in so doing, opens a new space in moral and political theory: he appeals to

---

1. For an excellent intellectual biography of Immanuel Kant, see Michael Rohlf, "Immanuel Kant," Stanford Encyclopedia of Philosophy, July 28, 2020, https://plato.stanford.edu/entries/kant/.

universal reason and universally binding moral laws without relying on classical metaphysics or empirical arguments. It is this philosophical move that opens the door to the kinds of moral and political claims we see in contemporary classical liberalism and libertarianism, including, as noted at the outset, "You do you, I'll do me," but also, as we'll see, "My outside matches my inside," "I am the creator of my own happiness," and "I am the only one who can tell myself what to do," among others. For various metaphysical and anthropological reasons, these kinds of statements would not make sense in the Hobbesian, Lockean, and Rousseauean strands of individual liberty and social contract theory.[2] Thus, while the social contract theorists have certainly influenced classical liberalism and libertarianism, it is ultimately Kant's thought that holds the most responsibility (or blame) for their interpretation of individual rights as "uninhibited personal choice" in the political and cultural realm.

Two more introductory comments are important. First, the conflation of "libertarianism" with "classical liberalism" is only temporary; they are, in fact, not only different but rival political theories. We will look at the differences more below. However, notwithstanding their quarrels, both embrace a conception of "autonomy" at their justificatory cores and thus fall within the Kantian tradition of moral reasoning. Second, while Kant's thought does indeed give birth to classical liberalism and libertarianism, were he alive today, he would likely be dismayed at how contemporary secularism has employed his conception of "autonomy" to justify almost all consensual activity, including suicide, which Kant firmly rejected. Yet as we'll see below, the

2. While Thomas Hobbes, John Locke, and Jean-Jacques Rousseau fundamentally disagree on the definition and moral purpose of "nature," including human nature, they do agree that there is such a thing as an objective nature in existence that human beings have rational access to, which, in turn, allows nature to provide moral guidance for human action. In this sense, these three natural law contract theorists stand united in opposition to Immanuel Kant, who will reject *any* rational capacity for the human mind to know and follow natural law.

contemporary appeal to autonomy to justify actions that Kant would contest are not abuses of Kant's ideas but rather perfectly logical implications of his thought that he simply could never have imagined given the culture in which he lived. Indeed, one of the lessons of Kantian autonomy as it relates to classical liberalism and libertarianism could be expressed aphoristically: What is made permissible in theory will find a way to become real in practice.

I DID IT MY WAY: IMMANUEL KANT AND THE ORIGINS OF AUTONOMY

As in the previous chapter, let's turn to the Thinking in Circles map as a guide for moving forward:

In many ways, Kant's philosophy begins precisely where David Hume's ends—squarely within the epistemological question of how it is possible to know anything with rational authority. Indeed, in one of the most famous lines in Western intellectual history, Kant thanks Hume for setting him on the path to the truth, a path he would not have discovered were it not for Hume's arguments against metaphysics. He writes in the introduction to his 1783 work *Prolegomena to Any Future Metaphysics*, "I openly confess that my remembering David Hume was the very thing which many years ago first interrupted my dogmatic slumber and gave my investigations in the field of speculative philosophy a quite new direction."[3] The slumber from which Kant was awakened was his belief—which he eventually jettisoned—that it is possible to use classical metaphysics to rationally demonstrate the existence of God and, by extension, the true nature of reality (the theological and ontological rungs of the Thinking in Circles map). However, this awakening to the limits of metaphysics did not lead Kant to embrace Humean empiricism. Rather, in direct opposition to the epistemology underlying Hume's arguments, Kant developed a new metaphysics, one that denied human reason the capacity to speak authoritatively either about God or existence—a conclusion that Hume agreed with—while retaining the existence and authority of rational necessity itself, including on moral matters, something Hume completely denied.

SETTING THE TABLE

Kant's "new metaphysics" forms one of the most complex, nuanced, and intricate theories in the history of ideas. He formulated his philosophical project by seeking to provide a systematic response to three interrelated questions: (1) What can we know? (2) What should we do? and (3) What can we hope for? Three of Kant's greatest works generally correspond with each of these questions: (1) *Critique of Pure Reason* (What can we know?), (2)

---

3. Immanuel Kant, *Prolegomena to Any Future Metaphysics*, trans. James W. Ellington (Indianapolis, Cambridge: Hackett Publishing Company, 1977), 5.

Critique of Practical Reason (What should we do?), and (3) *Religion Within the Limits of Reason Alone* (What can we hope for?). For the purpose of understanding Kant's moral theory and how it establishes the conceptual foundations for classical liberalism and libertarianism, we'll focus on the first two questions, which will also take us into another watershed Kantian text, *Groundwork of the Metaphysics of Morals.*

Before plumbing the depths of Kant's thought, it's important to pause and reaffirm why a detour like this is important. Can't we just get to the political stuff already? This sentiment is understandable. At the same time, the inclination to stay out of the basement of political philosophy, where it is dark and difficult to navigate, and to stick with the pressing, practical questions is one of the major reasons there remains so much political confusion and tumult. As the Thinking in Circles map seeks to illustrate, the realm of politics depends upon not only a theory of morality but, more deeply, a theory of knowledge, humanity, existence, and ultimate existence. So, for example, when a utilitarian is arguing with a libertarian about public policy—say, whether healthcare should be government funded—the surface of the debate may make it seem like they are arguing about the state's involvement in healthcare. However, the real source of disagreement lies far below (or above, depending on how you conceptualize it) in the realm of moral knowledge, human nature, and even nature itself (e.g., whether rights objectively exist). For this reason, we have no alternative but to take a deep dive into the theoretical foundations of each school of thought. It is impossible to critically assess different political ideologies—and to see how Catholic social thought can provide a more rational alternative—without understanding why they disagree with each other.

A PHILOSOPHY OF LIMITS

As noted above, Kant's first move in establishing "Kantian metaphysics" is to agree with Hume that classical metaphysics—both in the scholastic form (demonstrating God's existence and then deducing the nature of reality) and the Cartesian form (demonstrating the existence of a rational mind and then demonstrating the existence of God and the nature of reality)—escapes the bounds of human reason. In other words, reason, for Kant, contains sharp epistemic limits that prevent it from making any rationally authoritative metaphysical claim about either God or anything "out in the world."

One of the most well-known instances of this position against metaphysical inquiry takes place in Kant's rejection of what is commonly called the ontological argument. With roots in the thought of the great medieval theologian St. Anselm of Canterbury (1033–1109), the ontological argument seeks to proceed from the idea of God to the necessary existence of God (it is important to note that this is *not* one of the arguments that the later theologian, St. Thomas Aquinas, endorsed to demonstrate God's existence). The contemporary Christian philosopher and apologist William Lane Craig provides this helpful summary of St. Anselm's reasoning:

> God is, by definition, the greatest conceivable being. Now, what would the greatest conceivable being be like? Well, he would be omnipotent, he would be omniscient, he would be all-good, and he would be necessary in his existence—he would exist in all possible worlds. Now, if such a being is possible, that means that a being like that exists in some possible world. But you see, if a being of that nature exists in even one possible world, then it exists in all of them, because that's part of what it means to be the greatest conceivable being. But if it exists in all of them, then it exists in the actual world. Therefore, God exists.[4]

---

4. William Lane Craig, "What is the Ontological Argument?" Reasonable Faith, https://www.reasonablefaith.org/videos/interviews-panels/what-is-the-ontological-argument-bobby-conway.

Kant's "great awakening" led to his rejection of not only this particular metaphysical argument for God's existence but *all* metaphysical arguments. Summarizing why he believes such arguments fail, he writes in his *Critique of Pure Reason*,

> If I now take the subject (God) together with all its predicates (among which also omnipotence belongs) and say "God is" or "there is a God" then I provide no new predicate to the concept of God but rather only [assert] the subject on its own with all its predicates, and indeed the object in reference to my concept. Both must contain precisely the same (predicates) and hence nothing further can come additively to the concept, which expresses merely the possibility. And this for the very reason that I think its object as absolutely given (through the expression, "it is"). And so the actual contains nothing more than the mere possible. One hundred actual dollars do not contain the least bit more than one hundred possible dollars.[5]

Kant's point here is that the statement "God is" cannot serve as a coherent foundation for an argument that seeks to demonstrate the metaphysical truth of the claim "God's exists." The reason is because, he argues, nothing can be added to the idea of God (i.e., what he analogously refers to as the "the possible one hundred dollars") by adding the predicate—that is, the modifier—"God is" (what, analogously, he refers to as "the actual one hundred dollars"). In other words, the ontological argument, for Kant, is like claiming that the amount of an actual one hundred dollars could be more than the amount of a potential hundred dollars simply by adding the word "is"; yet saying "one hundred dollars is" instead of "one hundred dollars could be" does not make the one hundred dollars "bigger," whether in potentiality or actuality.

---

5. Immanuel Kant, *Critique of Pure Reason*, trans. Philip McPherson Rudisill, 3.4, 10.4–10.8, https://kantwesley.com/Kant/CritiqueOfPureReason.pdf.

So, too, for Kant, with the ontological argument: God's potential being cannot be metaphysically increased to God's *actual* being simply by adding the words "God is." The argument, for him, thus fails. It and all similar metaphysical arguments, he ultimately concludes, can tell us nothing about God's existence, nature, or relationship to the world.

It is important to stress that Kant is not claiming that God doesn't exist. Rather, his position is that reason cannot know whether or not God exists—not in the sense that "reason just hasn't been able to figure it out yet, but someday it might," but rather that reason has structural limits that the human mind cannot transcend. It lacks the capacity to arrive at objective truths about any external reality, including God's existence, God's relation to existence, and the nature of existence itself. Every attempt to transcend these limits, for Kant, ultimately ends in encountering an epistemic abyss across which reason cannot see or, even less, jump. Arguments that deny this limitation are at best foolish and at worst engaged in sophistry.

The consequences of this epistemic conclusion for Kant's understanding of reality cannot be overstated. Given, he believes, that reason has no access to the existence of a being that necessarily exists (a being that cannot not exist by definition—that is, God), it follows that reason cannot deduce the existence of any rationally fixed, objective objects or relationships in the world that have their origin in God, including causal relationships. If there is no metaphysical necessity at the top, in other words, there cannot be any metaphysical necessity anywhere below. Thus, in agreement with Hume, Kant believes that humans have no rational authority to say anything like "The natural world is governed by laws of nature" or "Human beings have an immaterial soul" or even "Humans have a divinely ordained telos (goal)." All these claims entail a recognition of a causal relationship among objects in the world, some form of making the claim that "this is the way *this* is *because* of the nature of *that*." Yet if we cannot rationally know that God exists, we cannot know that God exists as the creator of all that is; and if we cannot know that God is the creator of all that is, we can't know the true causal structure of anything in existence.

Vitally, as we'll see in more detail below, these rational limits apply to moral knowledge as well. To say, for example, that we cannot know what normative human nature is (because we cannot know the objective nature of *anything*), we consequently cannot say what any human "purpose" or "reason for existence" might be. Likewise, insofar as morality based on human nature is defined by conforming to an objective standard, it contains, by definition, a future orientation. In saying that morality is defined by being virtuous, for example, and that virtue means becoming the kind of person who is courageous, honest, charitable, etc., what we are saying is that the actualization of the principle of morality in practice takes a relationship between potentiality and actuality. This relationship, in turn, implies a causal structure to morality, meaning that "if I do this" then, because of the structure of reality and human nature, "I will be like this." However, because Kant rejects the possibility of identifying any cause-and-effect relationships in the external world, no form of morality founded on a cause and effect, or, more precisely, no morality founded on the possibility of realizing a potential in human nature by living according to a natural law, can have any rational validity.

We'll return to this dimension of Kant's thought soon, but first it is important to finish explaining the complex way in which Kant's thought relates to Hume's. At this point, it may seem that Kant and Hume entirely agree with each other, insofar as both believe that metaphysical analysis is rationally impossible and thus rationally unwarranted. On the other hand, we just saw that Kant rejects virtue theory (seeking to conform to a normative standard in human nature) as a foundation for morality, which directly contradicts Hume's argument from "benevolence." Two questions emerge: (1) Why does Kant partially agree with Hume and partially disagree with him if they both reject metaphysics? and (2) If not from human nature, where does Kant get his morality?

The short answer to both questions is "Kantian metaphysics," a new kind of metaphysics, but first we need to return to the epistemic rung in the Thinking in Circles map. As with Hume, the substance of Kant's entire understanding of reality, including moral reality, is determined by his epistemology. Recall that Hume's conclusion that the only form of rationally valid knowledge is that which we receive via the senses through the process of "mitigated skepticism" means that, moving outward from the epistemic circle, human nature (anthropology) and nature (ontology) can only be defined in physical, empirical terms (thus no soul, no immaterial natural law, no God), and, moving inward, morality, applied morality, and politics can also only be defined in empirical terms (thus the observable sentiment of "benevolence" as the foundation for Hume's conception of "utility"). Similarly, Kant's epistemology also determines the content—or, better put, the lack of content—in every other realm in the Thinking in Circles map.

For example, given that Kant, like Hume, believes reason cannot know anything about God's existence and its metaphysical implications, he concludes that there is nothing we can say about the nature of God or human nature. Theology, ontology, and anthropology are thus substantively *empty* for Kant. That does not mean he thinks that nothing exists "out there"; indeed, he thinks something must exist, or reason itself would not exist. Rather, his position is that, whatever does exist in the realm outside the mind, we have no rational means to access it and no way to know whether what our senses tell us corresponds with what actually is.

Kant calls this chasm between the real and our perception of the real the difference between "noumena" and "phenomena." Phenomena are how we experience the world—that is, what our senses tell us about the nature of physical existence (e.g., that it has shape, color, texture, changes over time, etc.). Noumena, on the other hand, are how things actually are in and of themselves, both individually and collectively. And this, for Kant, is the most important takeaway in understanding the relationship between the two: With the exception of the human free will, which is a rationally necessary postulate of practical reason (I'll soon explain what that means), there is *no* connection between the realm of noumena and the realm of phenomena. Kant believes that they both exist; however, they are like two train rails with no wooden cross beam, running infinitely into the horizon without ever touching or growing closer to each other.

At this point, it may again seem like Kant is adopting Hume's position that we cannot discern any form of metaphysical necessity in existence. Doesn't that mean that he must therefore adopt a Humean form of empiricism as the only alternative? No, and this is where things get interesting. Kant certainly agrees with Hume that we cannot perceive rational necessity in existence; however—and this is the fundamental difference that generates his new form of metaphysics—*we can perceive rational necessity in the mind*, or, more specifically, in the operation of reason itself and how it interacts with the world.

To understand Kant's move here, we first need to grasp how Kantian philosophy represents a form of *transcendentalism* in philosophy. Transcendentalism is related to the concept of "the transcendent" but also has key differences. "The transcendent" usually refers to a reality that exists metaphysically beyond and before the physical, material realm. The most common use of the term is to describe God or the divine, though it can also refer to metaphysically lesser beings as well ("lesser" in the sense that they are immaterial yet still contingent upon God for their existence, like angels). The transcendent, in other words, usually describes the substantive content of being itself (God) or a related immaterial reality. "Transcenden*tal*," on the other hand, typically refers not to the content of something transcendent or even transcendence itself, but rather to the *conditions for the possibility of the knowledge of the transcendent*. In other words, the transcendent typically refers to being, while transcendental typically refers to the conditions to know being.

On the surface, this can seem like an obscure distinction without a difference. But think of it this way, drawing on an analogy inspired by Platonic thought: We could say, for example, that seeing the sun directly, up close and without a filter, would be impossible to do. Indeed, imagine staring directly at the sun from a very close distance; you wouldn't see anything at all. You would be blinded not only to the sun's existence but to the existence of everything else as well. Now, however, imagine turning around away from the sun and toward that upon which the sun shines. To be sure, you still wouldn't be seeing the sun. However, you would be *seeing* something—that is, you would no longer be blind.

From this new standpoint, the fundamental question at stake has now shifted. Having accepted that you cannot see the unfiltered sun itself, you now ask, "How is it possible to see anything at all?" or, put more philosophically, "What is the condition for the possibility of vision itself?" Thanks to modern biology and physics, the answer to this question is now easier to grasp: Our eyes do not "see" objects in and of themselves but rather capture the light that reflects off of them. We also know that light operates according to fixed rules or patterns that correspond with, or at least are detectable by, similar rules or patterns in our minds. Moreover, we can say that without this light, the objects in the world outside of our mind would be invisible to us. We thus find ourselves in a peculiar epistemic position: On the one hand, we cannot see (that is, directly perceive) the source of light itself; on the other hand, we need light in order to see anything at all. Light, then, serves as the bridge between the sun and the perception of the external world. We cannot have direct, unfiltered knowledge of either end of this bridge (the sun on one hand, un-illumined objects on the other), but *we can know the bridge itself*. Indeed, we cannot *not* know the bridge because that bridge is necessarily present in every act of knowing.

This admittedly limited analogy describes the relationship between the "the transcendent" and the "transcendental." To say that the sun is real and that we can know it is real would be using the language of the transcendent; to say that we must presuppose the sun's existence in order to explain sight itself, even though we cannot see the sun directly, would be using the language of the transcenden*tal*. And here's where all this returns us to Kant. The "sun" for Kant would be God and God's true relationship to the world. The "light," on the other hand, would be "the bridge" in the form of the light of reason, that which is necessary to be able to perceive anything at all. In these terms, Kant rejects the possibility of speaking about the transcendent (i.e., the "sun") because he thinks that the true nature of reality, including ultimate reality in the form of God, escapes the capacity of human reason. Likewise, he rejects the possibility of being able to speak about the true nature of external objects in the world in and of themselves. However, he affirms the possibility of speaking about the transcendental—that is, "the light" that bridges the sun and the external world—because, he believes, the light is the condition for the possibility of being able to see itself. In short, we cannot see the sun, and we cannot see the external world, but we can—indeed, cannot not—see the light in our own minds that connects to the two. We can know reason itself; indeed, it is the only thing that we can know.

It is for this reason that Kant's new epistemology has been called a "Copernican revolution" in philosophy. The mathematician, astronomer, and faithful Catholic Nicolaus Copernicus (1473-1543) is famous for, among other great intellectual feats, first discovering that the sun—not the earth—was the center of the solar system and thus that which all other planets revolved around. Analogously, Kant is believed to be the first philosopher to argue that human reason itself—and not "nature" or "God" (though Kant never argued against the existence of God)—is the source of all truth (light). This insight fundamentally shifted the source of gravity in philosophy, causing a reorientation away from classical metaphysics to an examination of reason and the condition for the possibility of knowing itself.

This move from examining the object of knowledge to the act of knowing—or, drawing on the previous analogy, moving from the object of sight to the act of seeing—is one of Kant's greatest contributions to the history of ideas. Indeed, it is precisely this shift that explains how Kant both rejects classical metaphysics while concurrently rejecting Humean empiricism. Kant's "third way" is to argue that, while we cannot know reality (that is, noumena) we *can* know the way that human reason perceives reality. Indeed, upon examination of human reason itself (reason examining reason), we can determine that reason is structured by universal rational laws that not only provide an epistemically stable understanding of the realm of the external world (that is, phenomena) but also, crucial for our purposes, provide an a priori rationally necessary justificatory grounds for identifying universal moral laws.

Kant divides the rational principles that structure the mind's understanding of reality and morality into theoretical and practical principles respectively. Theoretical principles structure our understanding of the world (i.e., what is). Practical principles, in turn, structure our understanding of how to act (i.e., what *ought* to be). The four theoretical rational principles Kant identifies are quantity, quality, relation, and modality. Each of these categories also contains three sub-categories. The description and epistemic function of each category and sub-category is complex,[6] but there are two important takeaways for our purposes.

6. For an excellent discussion of Kant's a priori rational categories and how they relate to other epistemic categories in different philosophical schools, see Amie Thomasson, "Categories," Stanford Encyclopedia of Philosophy, November 22, 2022, https://plato.stanford.edu/entries/categories/.

First, by identifying the rational categories that structure human understanding, Kant re-establishes a rational grounding for believing in cause and effect, which, recall, Hume's philosophy had sought to demolish. Kant does not maintain that cause and effect exists "out there" in the world; however, he does believe that the mind necessarily imposes the existence of cause and effect as a rational, transcendental principle of understanding that makes perception of the world possible. Second, all the categories together provide for Kant, and the Kantian philosophical tradition, the fundamental justification for rejecting both idealism (the belief that the world and everything in it is merely a creation of the human mind) and absolute skepticism (the belief that we cannot know anything at all). In this sense, Kant's new metaphysics does indeed serve as a compromise position between classical metaphysics, which has confidence in reason's ability to know God and the nature of reality, and Humean empiricism, which constricts the horizon of knowledge to sensory stimuli alone. As Kant famously writes in the *Critique of Pure Reason*, "Thoughts without content are empty, intuitions without concepts are blind."[7] Translated into more colloquial language, we could say, "We cannot have thoughts without having experiences of the world, and we cannot have experience of the world without perceiving it through our mind's fixed rational lenses."

GETTING PRACTICAL

But what does any of this have to do with morality and politics? We're finally at a point when we can begin to identify the substance of Kant's moral theory—and the first step in doing so is highlighting that Kant's moral theory deliberately lacks substance. As we'll see, the principles that structure practical reasoning—that is, reasoning about how to act—will take the

7. Immanuel Kant, *Critique of Pure Reason*, trans. Paul Guyer and Allen W. Wood (Cambridge: Cambridge University Press, 1998), 50.

form of placing restraints on action. Outside of those restraints, Kantian morality has nothing to say about what humans should do. In other words, the most accurate question to ask of Kantian morality is not "What is good and what is evil?" but rather "What is permitted and what is not permitted?" As long as your actions don't violate one of the few "unpermitted" prohibitions, you can do whatever you desire.

But we need to back up again. Kant may believe he has solved the problem of knowledge in his new metaphysics, but a fresh conundrum emerges as our focus shifts from the nature of reality to the nature of morality: Can Kant coherently uphold the existence of human freedom? To be sure, the question of free will is an important anthropological issue. However, it takes on additional significance when asked in relation to morality, because if humans are not free, then morality is moot. Morality's fundamental purpose is to guide human action by identifying principles that tell us "Don't do this" or "Do do that"; if humans have no freedom to obey these principles—if, for example, we are merely chemically composed automatons that blindly react to environmental stimuli—then telling people to be good is tantamount to commanding rocks to behave. If, on the other hand, we say that humans *do* have freedom, then, minimally, we have at least established a conceptual floor that can support the existence of morality even if we have not yet specified what the content of that morality is. The whole question of morality, in short, depends upon how we first answer the question of free will.

This, however, puts Kant in a pickle. If it is true that humans must have free will in order to act morally (or immorally), then we would have to say that humans are free or that freedom exists in human nature. Yet Kant's epistemology disqualifies him from making any such claim. If we call freedom an instance of phenomena, meaning we experience it in the world but can't be sure if it's really there in the way we experience it, we are saying, "It is impossible to know if the freedom we experience actually exists."

On the other hand, if we call freedom an instance of noumena, we are saying, in Kantian epistemological terms, that "freedom is something that we cannot know because it falls outside the limits of our rationality." Thus, whether we choose to define freedom as a phenomenon or noumenon, it seems Kantian epistemology must lead to the conclusion "Free will might exist, but we cannot know anything about it," which is functionally equivalent to saying "Free will does not exist." However, making this claim would, in turn, mean that Kant cannot have any moral theory, because morality presupposes the existence of free will. Wouldn't attempting to extract morality from Kant's thought thus be rationally akin to squeezing blood from a stone or, perhaps more logically apt, trying to square a circle?

Not exactly. Kant, if it's not evident yet, was a very smart man. He knew his theory of morality had to address this objection to be coherent. His solution, which he develops in his treatise *Groundwork of the Metaphysics of Morals*, takes this very Kantian-sounding form: human freedom does not exist in human nature, but rather as a necessary postulate of practical reason. Kant maintains his belief that we cannot prove the existence of free will in the noumenal realm because we cannot know anything about noumena. However, for the very same reason—that is, the fact that we cannot know anything about noumena—he argues we cannot deny the existence of free will either. This move, in turn, allows him to say that it is at least rationally possible for free will to exist, which allows him to say that, though we cannot know that freedom exists, we nevertheless can still postulate its existence because human beings necessarily affirm the existence of freedom any time we think, "What should I do?" For Kant, formulating this question necessarily implies the belief that thinking about different possible courses of action could make a difference in how one acts; that belief, in turn, necessarily implies that one believes oneself to be free. So insofar as we are all asking the question, "What should I do?" we are all postulating the existence of free will.

Now, we could go in one of two directions here. We could reply to Kant, "No, it's false that human beings ever ask themselves the question 'What should I do?'", in which case we could sever the connection he makes between free will's existence and free will as a rational postulate. Yet this is a challenging position to defend, especially because anyone arguing this way would have to deny that he/she ever thought, "What should I do?" On the other hand, we could agree with Kant and affirm that it is, indeed, the case that we must presuppose the existence of free will in order to make sense of the statement "What should I do?" This position seems much more reasonable. Yet wouldn't recognizing free will in this way still be a violation of the hard line he draws between phenomena and noumena?

Kant's response is nestled within his claim that we can postulate—not know—that free will exists. To "postulate" does not mean to affirm as true; it means to presume as true. That, for Kant, is sufficient for his purposes, because when we are talking about free will we are not talking about human nature, which would, indeed, be in the unknowable realm of noumena. Rather, we are talking about human action and, in particular, about how deliberation on human action presupposes, as a postulate, the existence of a free will to act differently based on one's deliberations. In other words, if you deliberate about actions you cannot *not* postulate the existence of free will because it would be a contradiction to do so, akin, for example, to saying out loud, "It is impossible for me to speak." Just as the act of speaking necessarily implies the capacity to speak, the act of deliberation necessarily implies the belief that your deliberations make a difference for action, or, in other words, that you are free.

This can seem like an especially arcane point in an already arcane philosophy, but its importance is difficult to overstate. What Kant believes he has accomplished in establishing the rational validity of necessarily postulating the existence of free will in relation to action is a rational foundation for morality overall, meaning a foundation that can identify which kinds of actions contradict morality and which kinds of actions are *in accord* with morality. In other words, Kant believes he has established the foundations for rational necessity. Compare this to David Hume's theory. Recall that one of the problems with empirical forms of rationality is that they can merely describe different kinds of behavior; they have no rational mechanism for prescribing what individuals or communities should or shouldn't do because they have no standard of comparison that can identify possible contradictions. The fact that most people don't kill other human beings descriptively does not mean that it is irrational or contradictory when someone does kill another person. It just means there is a deviation from a numerical norm. In contrast, what Kant will eventually argue is that acting as if human beings did not have free will is a contradiction because it violates the necessary postulating of the existence of free will in all deliberation about action—and everyone deliberates about action. Thus, unlike Hume, Kant has established a rational mechanism for saying, "These kinds of actions are right" (permissible), and "These kinds of actions are wrong" (impermissible).

THE CATEGORICAL IMPERATIVES: KANT'S "THOU SHALL NOT . . ."

Kant then moves in the *Groundwork of the Metaphysics of Morals* from defending the postulated existence of free will to identifying what it would mean to act contrary to free will and, therefore, to be engaged in self-contradiction (or, in other words, to be acting immorally). He ultimately gives the name "categorical imperatives" to the rational principles that govern morality. Kant explains the meaning of categorical imperatives by comparing them to what he calls "hypothetical imperatives." Both imperatives relate to deliberation about action; however, only one kind of imperative—the categorical kind—can serve as a universal moral principle.

In the Kantian and colloquial sense, an "imperative" simply means "a command," with the implicit addition that the imperative is authoritative. Yet we should already pause and ask why Kant would appeal to commands at all. The very concept seems to be connected to religious forms of morality, such as the Ten Commandments in the Old Testament, and Kant's new metaphysics explicitly rejects the possibility of appealing to God's existence as a source of moral knowledge. What's more, in another watershed text, *Religion within the Limits of Reason Alone*, Kant argues that all authentic religion can be reduced to acting morally, and both knowing the nature of morality and acting in accordance with it can in no way depend explicitly or implicitly on knowledge about God's existence. And yet Kant maintains not only that moral commands govern all human action but also that every human being has an absolute duty to obey those commands.

The distinction between "categorical" and "hypothetical" helps explain why Kant thinks he can make this claim without appealing to religion. As the name suggests, a hypothetical imperative means a conditional command, a command that depends on another variable. A cynical yet commonplace example would be the imperative, "Tell the truth unless you believe you can get away with lying." The imperative in this command is to "tell the truth"; the condition is "not getting caught." Someone acting according to this imperative would thus be truthful unless she or he believes there is a sufficiently low likelihood of getting caught in a lie, in which case the imperative would switch from "Tell the truth (because you think you would get caught lying)" to "Tell a lie (because you think you can get away with not telling the truth)." The same could be said of the imperative not to steal; from the perspective of a hypothetical imperative, you should not take others' belongings unless you think you could do so without getting caught. More comprehensively, the theory of utilitarianism is one massive example of hypothetical morality; it subjugates all moral imperatives—e.g., tell the truth, follow the speed limit, pay your taxes, do not kill innocent people—to the condition that obeying the imperative will advance the greatest good for the greatest number. If, upon examination, following a given imperative would act against this final goal, then, by the logic of utilitarianism and hypothetical imperatives more broadly, you would be permitted, indeed, obligated not to obey the imperative.

Kant believes that hypothetical imperatives are not "moral" at all but rather purely prudential in nature. "Prudential" in this context means reasoning only about means and not about ends (the Catholic virtue of prudence is something entirely different). In this sense, morality based on hypothetical imperatives only tells you what to do in order to attain your goal without saying anything about the morality of the goal itself. Given that there is, from Kant's point of view, an incalculable number of goals any person or community could potentially have, there would, consequently, be no universal morality; it would all depend on the different goals that different people desire to attain. Moreover, given the mutability of desires, changing one's goals would also change one's morality (for example, if I changed my goal from "Being liked by as many people as possible" to "Being feared by as many people as possible," the actions I believe are right and wrong would considerably change). Morality based on hypothetical (which is to say, conditional) imperatives is thus merely a form of moral relativism in disguise.

It is for this reason that Kant insists that morality must be based on *categorical* imperatives. Categorical, as opposed to hypothetical, imperatives are unconditional commands, meaning commands whose moral authority remains intact no matter what goal an individual or group may be pursuing. In this sense, categorical imperatives are both rationally objective and universal; they cannot be reduced to any group or individual desire or preference.[8] It is important to note that these universal prohibitions—which Kant also couches in the language of "duty"—already distinguish Kantian morality from utilitarian morality, which, as we saw above, Kant would deny as being moral at all. Unlike utilitarianism, which, by definition, makes the moral adjudication of all actions conditional on whether they advance aggregate utility, Kantian morality is unconditional. It is based on the commands of reason, and the only reason anyone should act in accordance with the commands of reason is because reason commands it. What you desire, what goals you have, what causes you believe in, even the kind of person you want to become are all irrelevant to the moral enterprise. Your only motivation and reason for moral action is to do your duty—no matter what the consequences.[9] For Kant, we are thus not receiving commands from God about how to act. We are receiving commands from reason itself, commands that, precisely because they originate in human reason, have the authority to guide human action.

8. As we'll see below, one example of a categorical imperative from a Kantian point of view would be a prohibition against murder. Another would be a prohibition against slavery or any other form of physical coercion, unless necessary for self-defense (in which case one is acting in accordance with the duty to protect one's own life and not with the goal of harming the other). By identifying these imperatives as "categorical," Kant is claiming "it is never justified to kill an innocent human being" and "it is never justified to enslave a human being."

9. Put this way, even before we explain the specific content of Kant's categorical imperatives, we can already see how Kantian thought could undergird political values like "individual liberty" and "individual rights." It is fair to say that Kant does indeed champion these values. However, it is crucial to understand why. The reason is not because he believes in the political "cause" of individual freedom per se; it is, rather, because his "new metaphysics," as outlined above, prohibits him from basing his moral system on anything but doing one's duty. Recall that Kant's insistence that we cannot know "the world" means, among many other things, that we cannot base morality on the existence of an objective moral order in the world, like we see, for example, in natural law moralities. Saying that "the good" is defined by acting in accordance with an objective moral order and that "the bad" is defined by acting in contradiction to an objective moral order is, for Kant, a non-starter; "objective moral orders" belong to the world of noumena and therefore cannot be known or appealed to as guides for human conduct. This point will be especially important to keep in mind when we later ask of Kantian morality, "What am I supposed to do with my life?" As we'll see, Kant would reply, "That question has nothing to do with morality."

Yet we still need to identify what defines the content of the categorical imperatives. We know, at this point, that Kant believes we can rationally postulate the existence of a free will *and* that the only principle that could possibly regulate the exercise of that free will would have to be a categorical, rather than hypothetical, imperative for the imperative to be moral. The next question, then, is this: What, specifically, does the categorical imperative command? Or, put more informally: What tells us what we are allowed to do and not allowed to do?

Kant identifies three expressions of the categorical imperative in *Groundwork of the Metaphysics of Morals* that he believes mutually imply each other (meaning, if you believe one to be true you must rationally believe all of them to be true). They are:

> 1. Act only in accordance with that maxim through which you can at the same time will that it become a universal law.[10]

> 2. Act so that you use humanity, as much as in your own person as in the person of every other, always at the same time as end and never merely as means.[11]

> 3. From [the two principles] follows the third practical principle of the will, as the supreme condition of its harmony with universal practical reason, the idea *of the will of every rational being as a will giving universal law.*[12]

Decoding the language Kant employs to describe the imperatives is characteristically complex. Although it loses some philosophical nuance, here are the three categorical imperatives translated into more common language with some additional content from Kant's arguments added:

10. Immanuel Kant, *Grounding of the Metaphysics of Morals*, trans. Allen Wood (New Haven, CT: Yale University Press, 2002), 37.
11. Kant, 46.
12. Kant, 49.

1. Only act in such a way that the *reason for your action* (that is, the "maxim") can be universalized without contradiction.

2. Given that every person can act according to universalizable maxims, never act in a way that treats another person (what Kant refers to as "humanity"), including yourself, as if they were incapable of formulating universalizable maxims—that is, as if they lacked the capacity to act according to reason. Doing so would be to treat them as a "means," that is, merely as a resource to satisfy your own desires, and not as an "end," that is, as a person who is free to formulate and act according to rational maxims.

3. Given that persons can (and morally should) universalize their reasons for action and treat all other persons as capable of doing the same, we therefore ought to conclude that every person is capable of being *self-legislating*, meaning having and acting according to a free will that provides its own universal rational law. In other words, every person is "autonomous" (Greek for a "law unto oneself"). No person therefore ought to be subject to laws that violate their autonomy; or, put differently, every action that violates a person's autonomy, whether from an individual or from a group, is immoral.

Kant uses the example of promise-keeping to illustrate the meaning of the first expression of the categorical imperative, but we can also use it to illustrate the second and third expressions as well. Imagine a person who says to himself, "I will make promises but have no intention of keeping them." In addition to serving as an example of a hypothetical rather than categorical imperative, this maxim—that is, this reason for action (making false promises to reap the benefits of making promises without having to pay the cost of keeping them)—is, for Kant, an example of a violation of the first categorical imperative. The reason is that if we were to universalize the maxim "Make promises that you have no intention of keeping," then the whole concept of "promise" would dissolve. The very definition of promise implies an intention to keep it, but if no one were to have the intention of keeping a promise, then there would be no such thing as a concept of "promise" in the first place. In other words, it is a self-refuting rational contradiction and thus a violation of the nature of the postulated free will to say, "I will make promises that I do not intend to keep." To be clear, Kant is not arguing that breaking a promise is wrong because it can lead to bad consequences (although that is undoubtedly the case); remember, consequences have to do with phenomena and therefore can play no role in Kantian morality. Rather, it is wrong because making a promise you do not intend to keep is rationally equivalent to saying, "I will act as a married bachelor"—it is a self-contradiction.

As a violation of the first imperative, making false promises would also be a violation of the second imperative as well. Why? Because to make a false promise to someone—that is, to lie to them—is to treat them merely as a means to something you want, like in the case of a cheating husband lying to a late-night bar conquest that the ring he forgot to take off his finger is in memory of his beloved wife, who, in fact, is very much alive two thousand miles away caring for a feverish child. In telling the lie, the man, colloquially speaking, is just *using* the tipsy woman, treating her as a tool for gratification rather than as an autonomous person. So, too, for Kant, in every instance of lying, which is why he identifies all forms of lying as a violation of the categorical imperative (meaning it is always immoral to do so).

Closely related, the problem with false promises, and lies more generally, is not only that they treat this particular person as a means to an end but that they represent a general affront to the principle of autonomy itself. They contradict the universal rational truth that all persons are self-legislating and thus should never be treated as if they were controlled by external powers, which is what happens when they are lied to. To treat one person as an end in and of herself or himself rationally requires treating all people as ends in themselves, which is nothing less than recognizing that they have (postulated) rational free wills that are self-legislating. Obversely, treating one person as a means rather than an end is, rationally speaking, to treat all people as means rather than ends. In short, Kant is upholding (though from a completely different philosophical standpoint) a principle similar to Martin Luther King Jr.'s famous declaration, "Injustice anywhere is a threat to justice everywhere."[13]

SIGN HERE

How, then, do followers of Kantian morality ensure that they are treating others as ends rather than means and thus not exploiting them? Although Kant does not explicitly develop the idea in the *Groundwork of the Metaphysics of Morals*, the overall structure of his argument provides a clear answer. In addition to never acting in ways that clearly violate individual autonomy—which not only includes lying but also all other forms of direct coercion (killing, assaulting, kidnapping, etc.) and indirect coercion (blackmailing, cheating, manipulating, etc.)—respecting others' autonomy requires asking for and receiving their full, free, and informed permission any time the attainment of your goals requires another's assistance. In other words, consent is king. To be sure, unlike contemporary applications of Kant's theory in classical liberalism and libertarianism (more on this below), there are, for Kant, some things that one must never consent to, including some self-directed actions. The preeminent example of such a prohibition is Kant's insistence that suicide is immoral

---

13. The line comes from Martin Luther King Jr.'s 1963 "Letter from a Birmingham Jail."

because it consists of instrumentalizing one's own life (treating oneself as a means) rather than upholding the rational truth that, precisely because one has a free, self-legislating will, one has irreducible dignity that the act of suicide contradicts. Given the nature of the categorical imperatives, selling oneself into slavery or accepting the services of someone who wishes to sell himself into slavery would also be prohibited. Such actions form the outer parameters of possible moral conduct in Kantian morality, the few but clear hard lines that must never be crossed whether or not one consents to them.

However—and this cuts to the heart of how Kantian morality serves as the foundation for libertarianism and classical liberalism—within those parameters every person is unqualifiedly free to do whatever they want, however they want, with whomever they want, so long as they secure consent along the way. Indeed, it is even more than that: in addition to doing whatever one wants within the limits of consent, every person can also invent their own conception of truth, including truth about God, reality, and the purpose of existence. This relativizing of truth occurs because there is no mechanism in Kantian thought to identify one answer as better or truer than another; every statement about reality, about noumena, is equally arational because the human mind has no capacity to discern truth outside the narrow epistemic confines explained above. This means, to put it bluntly, that it is equally "rational" to believe in classical monotheism as it is to believe in a polytheistic temporal pantheon of feline divinities that oversee the cosmos with benevolence and compassion (a "religion" that a former neighbor of mine sincerely claimed to believe in). In short, religious and metaphysical questions that pertain to the structure of reality are a matter of sheer preference and empty speculation within a Kantian paradigm.

The same goes for discussions about what defines the human good. Outside the a priori epistemic categories that rationally structure the human perception of reality, the rational postulating

of the free will, and the identification of the universal categorical imperatives that govern that will, every statement about
"goodness" is equally preferential in nature. Thus, claiming that
"it is good for human beings to get married and have children"
is, from a Kantian perspective, equally reasonable to claiming
that "it is good for human beings to spend their lives alone, in
the dark, playing video games with Cheeto-stained fingers." The
categorical imperatives are grounded in rationality. Everything
else is merely taste, and, Kant would have to conclude, *de gustibus
non est disputandum* (there is no arguing about taste).

RESPECT INDIVIDUAL RIGHTS!
(BUT DON'T CALL THEM "GOOD")

It is for this reason that the language of good and evil does not
fit within a Kantian moral paradigm. Rather, as noted earlier,
the moral dichotomy forms along the lines of permissible versus
impermissible, which, applied in the political realm, typically
takes the form of individual rights versus a violation of individual
rights. The distinction can appear academic, but saying that an
action is "good" in a moral theory typically means that it conforms with some conception of what is ultimately good—that
is, to some final goal that defines total goodness. This is the
case with Catholic morality, which we'll see below, but it also
applies to utilitarianism as well. Good actions, from a utilitarian
perspective, are those that conform with aggregate social welfare,
and bad actions are those that decrease aggregate welfare. Even
though Catholicism disagrees with this definition of the final
goal of human action, it does agree that the right way to define
and adjudicate morality is in reference to a final goal.

Kantianism, however, rejects the possibility of knowing any
such goal, which it would define as residing in the unknowable
realm of noumena. Indeed, for Kant, the only thing that can be
good is a "good will," which he defines as a will that acts according
to the dictates of reason alone. This "good" is not a good that

exists "out there" in the world or even in human nature; it is only in the will, which itself is a postulate of practical reason, not an object that practical reason itself can directly grasp. Consequently, the Kantian moral tradition typically speaks in terms of "rights," specifically understood as boundaries that correspond with the rational dictates of the categorical imperative. Every individual may do whatever she or he wants without limitation so long as her/his actions do not violate the rights of others (that is, as long as the actions do not violate their autonomy).

At this point, Kant's ruminations about the a priori structure of practical reason are likely starting to sound more familiar to contemporary secular ears. While, as we'll see, the Catholic social thought tradition also defends the objective existence of individual rights, it remains the case that, culturally and politically speaking, the contemporary understanding of both the derivation of individual rights (autonomy) and the purpose of individual rights (empowering individuals to do whatever they want so long as they do not violate the rights of others) has its roots in Kantianism. In other words, thank (or curse) Kant the next time you hear someone say "You do you, I'll do me" as if it were the most obvious thing in the world.

TWO STREAMS OUT OF THE RESERVOIR
As I noted earlier, however, it's not fair either to Kant or to his legacy to lay the entire contemporary conception of individual rights at his feet. In ways Kant likely would not have been able to predict, his philosophy became the foundation for twin schools of political thought, each of which has become massively influential. And as is the case with all schools of thought, they are wont to drift from their founders' original vision.

Such is the case with classical liberalism and libertarianism. We're now at the point where we can understand how both political philosophies have their roots in Kantianism and how and why they represent substantially different points of view, notwithstanding their common origin. To recognize this similarity and difference, keep in mind the following question as we move forward: Does the categorical imperative require individuals only to refrain from violating others' rights, or does it additionally require performing positive actions on behalf of others as well? The answer will illuminate the fault line between classical liberalism and libertarianism. Moving forward, I turn to two representatives of each Kantian offshoot: John Rawls, who represents classical liberalism, and Robert Nozick, who represents libertarianism.

John Rawls: Classical Liberalism[14]

The late Harvard philosopher John Rawls (1921–2002) is one of the most renowned political theorists of the twentieth century. His book *A Theory of Justice* is widely considered to be the paradigmatic expression of classical liberalism, a reputation Rawls cemented by writing a follow-up book entitled *Political Liberalism*. Academics, public intellectuals, politicians, and armchair philosophers alike still read Rawls as a source of insight.

Rawls builds his political theory atop an explicitly Kantian platform. He declares at the beginning of *A Theory of Justice*, for example,

> Each person possesses an inviolability founded on justice that even the welfare of society as a whole cannot override. For this

---

14. I have been using the term "classical liberalism" in this chapter to distinguish liberalism as we see it in the Kantian tradition from "liberalism" in the sense of being "politically progressive." Unlike "liberals/progressives," classical liberals uphold individual rights like private property, free speech, and freedom of religion and generally support some view of a free-market economy. "Liberals," in contrast, usually emphasize communal rather than individual rights (and thus do not believe in absolute individual rights) and see the "rights" of private property, free speech, and even religion as subjugated to the good of "progress," meaning that rights can be modified or even jettisoned if progress requires it. In this sense, liberals could be defined either as utilitarian in philosophy or as adherents to the progressive/woke ideology we will examine in the next chapter.

reason justice denies that the loss of freedom for some is made right by a greater good shared by others. It does not allow that the sacrifices imposed on a few are outweighed by the larger sum of advantages enjoyed by many.[15]

This foundational claim distinguishes Rawls' conception of justice from utilitarianism and reveals his adoption of the Kantian view of individual dignity, the centrality of individual freedom, and the moral bindingness of the categorical imperatives—namely, that there is never justification for overriding an individual's freedom in the name of pursuing a "greater good." It is important to emphasize, however, that Rawls is operating within the Kantian *moral* framework because he has adopted the Kantian *epistemic* framework as well—namely, that human rationality cannot identify an objective good either in human nature or nature itself (i.e., a natural law) and therefore cannot appeal to a metaphysical "good" to justify morality, including the principles of justice. For example, in distinguishing what he calls "the good" from "rights," Rawls argues, "Each person is free to plan his life as he pleases (so long as his intentions are consistent with the principles of justice)."[16] In other words, everyone gets to do whatever they want with their lives—to define and pursue "the good" however they desire—so long as they stay within the bounds of justice. This is a Kantian vision of the purpose of the political order—namely, to protect individual rights while freeing individuals to do whatever they want within the confines of respecting others' rights to do the same.

Yet what is "justice" for Rawls more specifically? At its core, and unsurprisingly given its Kantian roots, it hinges on consent, or what Rawls also refers to as a "social contract." Rawls believes that rational deliberation will logically lead individuals to consent

15. John Rawls, *A Theory of Justice* (Cambridge, MA: Harvard University Press, 1999), 3.
16. Rawls, 392.

to the following two core principles of justice, which, combined, constitute what he calls "justice as fairness":

1. Each person is to have an equal right to the most extensive scheme of equal basic liberties compatible with a scheme of liberties for others.

2. Social and economic inequalities are to be arranged so that they are both (a) reasonably expected to be to everyone's advantage and (b) attached to positions and offices open to all.[17]

In other words—and Rawls devotes much of his expansive book to teasing out the meaning of each one of these concepts—what is "just" is to give individuals as much freedom as possible with two attendant conditions: (1) individual freedom should not be construed in a way that limits other individuals' freedom, and (2) the inequalities that inevitably result from the exercise of freedom (some people earning more money than others, or going to better schools, or having bigger homes, etc.) must, in turn, be socially managed so that those inequalities benefit society as a whole (e.g., paying brain surgeons more to incentivize enough people to become brain surgeons) and are open to all (e.g., there should be no structural obstacles that prevent a poor child from becoming a brain surgeon should he/she have the requisite talent and desire to do so). In short, Rawls is calling for a society that equally champions both individual liberty and equality of opportunity.

Yet why, one might ask (and, as we'll see below, Robert Nozick *does* ask), would free individuals consent to sacrifice some of their freedom to the state in the name of equality of opportunity? More to the point, why would such a choice be rational, in the sense that choosing otherwise would constitute a contradiction and be morally wrong? Rawls' answer comes in the form of what he calls

17. Rawls, 53.

the "original position." Imagine, he argues, that you are behind what he describes as a "veil of ignorance" with regard to the basic structure of your individual life narrative: You do not know if you will have excellent prenatal care while in the womb or if you will be absorbing your birth mother's methamphetamine; you do not know if you will end up in a rich family or a poor family, grow up in a good school district or a dismal school district, will be driven to school in an SUV or have to walk past gangs; if you will have many physical and/or mental talents or will have to battle against a disability; if you will have parents who drop you off at college with a new laptop, phone, and credit card or parents who require your care while you are still young because they are addicted, sick, or even just cruel and have no desire to help you. Behind the veil of ignorance in the original position, in other words, you don't know how fortunate or how unfortunate you will be in life. You just know that some people are very fortunate and some people are very unfortunate and that you could be in either one of those extremes or fall somewhere in the fat part of the bell curve.

If this is where you are standing when you ask the question, "What is the nature of justice and a just society?" Rawls believes that you will come up with the same two principles of justice that he has: maximal freedom and equality of opportunity. Behind the veil of ignorance, the most rational choice is to hedge your bets against the possibility of ending up on the wrong side of the tracks, and thus it is rational to support the social distribution of resources to mitigate inequality. Yet, according to Rawls, you also recognize that it is rational to allow for *some* inequality because that inequality can produce a safer, healthier, more prosperous society for everyone—including you. At the same time, returning to the first principle of justice, you believe it is rational to be as free as possible to define and live according to your own conception of the good life. It is important to emphasize that these principles of justice, for Rawls, do not coerce you to give over your freedoms to create a just society; rather, you willingly choose to sacrifice some of your freedom because, on rational grounds, you perceive it to be in your best interest. The sacrosanct principles of autonomy and consent thus remain firmly intact, even as you give the government the coercive power to tax and redistribute your earnings to others (or, alternatively, to tax others' earnings and redistribute them to you).

This transfer of individual sovereignty and limited but substantial deference to state authority, particularly in matters of social welfare, is what Rawls calls "justice as fairness." Yet, even in summary form, we can see that all Rawls has done (which is not to belittle his intellectual achievement) is embrace a Kantian epistemological and moral platform and, atop that platform, construct a layer of universalized self-interest in order to justify adding positive categorical imperatives (e.g., pay taxes to fund social programs) in addition to negative categorical imperatives (e.g., do not violate others' autonomy). This combination of negative rights (which protect individual autonomy) and positive social obligations (which seek to establish some form of equality of opportunity) defines the basic nature and purpose of classical liberalism. It is one of the major political streams that flows out of the Kantian reservoir.

Robert Nozick: Libertarianism

Yet there is another stream as well, one which runs in a considerably different direction, even if it originates from the same source. Another Harvard philosopher named Robert Nozick (1938–2002) argues that John Rawls' liberalism radically misconstrues the meaning of individual liberty. Although also influenced by the social contract theory of Enlightenment philosopher John Locke, Nozick, like Rawls, founds his political framework on the Kantian conception of individual autonomy and individual rights construed as categorical (absolute) prohibitions on violating others' autonomy. Indeed, Nozick translates Kant's categorical imperative into what he calls "side constraints" on action. He writes in *Anarchy, State, and Utopia*, for example,

> What is the rationale for placing the nonviolation of [individual] rights as a side constraint upon action instead of including it solely as a goal of one's actions? Side constraints upon action reflect the underlying Kantian principle that individuals are ends and not merely means; they may not be sacrificed or used for the achieving of other ends without their consent. Individuals are inviolable.[18]

This key passage in Nozick's text establishes his connection with the Kantian tradition of individual rights and the moral necessity of securing consent to "use" someone to obtain a goal. Likewise, and unsurprisingly, it reveals substantial overlap with Rawls' first principle of justice: "Each person is to have an equal right to the most extensive scheme of equal basic liberties compatible with a scheme of liberties for others." Nozick also overlaps with Rawls in believing in the idea of "the priority of the right over the good," meaning that individuals are free to define the good however they like so long as their pursuit of it does not violate the rights of others. Indeed, in a rousing crescendo at the end of the book that aptly summarizes Nozick's thesis, he writes,

> The minimal state treats us as inviolate individuals, who may not be used in certain ways by others as means or tools or instruments or resources; it treats us as persons having individual rights with the dignity this constitutes. Treating us with respect by respecting our rights, it allows us, individually or with whom we choose, to choose our life and to realize our ends and our conception of ourselves, insofar as we can, aided

---

18. Robert Nozick, *Anarchy, State, and Utopia* (New York: Basic Books, 1974), 30–31.

by the voluntary cooperation of other individuals possessing the same dignity. How *dare* any state or group of individuals do more. Or less.[19]

For Nozick, the *only* purpose of the political order is to ensure that every person is as free as possible—defined as uninhibited by others' actions—to pursue his/her own vision of the good. Indeed, "respecting others" has entirely negative content; it means not interfering with their autonomous choices so long as those choices are not interfering with yours. To be sure, if you'd like other people to participate in your self-defined life project, you are certainly free to request their "voluntary cooperation," which includes paying for their services. However, that choice, like nearly every other choice, solely depends on their autonomous consent. And for those who ask for others' assistance but find no one willing to help? Too bad. Respecting individual autonomy, for Nozick, requires nothing less. Or more.

This description of Nozick's thought helps explain how he parts way with Rawls, notwithstanding their shared Kantian foundations. Nozick accepts Rawls' first principle of justice and the belief that individuals are free to construct their own vision of the good. However, he fundamentally disagrees with Rawls' second principle, the principle that seeks to establish equality of opportunity in society by the distribution of goods. In fact, Nozick argues that a proper interpretation of the first principle of justice *prohibits* the existence of the second; if it is truly the case that individuals have the freedom that both Rawls and Nozick say they do, then there is no rational justification for ever obligating individuals, especially in the form of law, to give to others that which rightly belongs to them. As Nozick puts it, "Whether or not people's natural assets are arbitrary from a moral point of

19. Nozick, 333–334.

view, they are entitled to them, and to what flows from them."[20] Consequently, it would be unjust, from Nozick's perspective, to create a society that has authority to redistribute individuals' resources.

What, then, distinguishes Nozick's political proposal from outright anarchy, which views all forms of government as unjust? The answer is in the book's title: *Anarchy, State, Utopia*. Embracing Rawls' first principle of justice but rejecting his second, the only categorical imperative that all individuals must abide by is the principle of non-aggression—that is, not physically harming other individuals unless necessitated by self-defense. Nozick recognizes, however, that merely refraining from harming each other leaves individuals unable to meet their needs and fulfill their desires. In a move similar to Rawls', Nozick thus creates his own hypothetical "original position," which he calls (like social contract theorists Hobbes, Locke, and Rousseau before him) a "state of nature." In the state of nature, all individuals are radically independent of any organized government; as such, they are free from all laws, except for the law of non-aggression, which is written into our rational nature. However, all individuals also suffer from considerable inconveniences, which make them vulnerable to the vicissitudes of nature (e.g., not being able to store enough food for the winter). Nozick calls living in the state of nature "anarchy" for this reason—individuals are free from central authority but also miserable. He thus reasons that all people in this radically free but precarious position would make the rational choice *to consent* to forming public institutions that help provide common protection and oversee the exchange of goods, ensuring, for example, that individuals abide by the consensual contracts they enter into, like paying their bills on time. Nozick calls this social development—which marks the individual's consensual exit from the state of nature—the "state." Nozick then argues that, left to

20. Nozick, 226.

their own autonomous self-governance, different states would end up excelling over other states in providing greater security, efficiency, opportunity, and prosperity. Since all individuals are free to enter the state, they have the right to exit the state as well, and, in turn, to request entrance into another state that they deem more attuned to their interests. Nozick calls this social arrangement—large clusters of independent societies vying to attract the most talented and productive individuals—"utopia." It is "utopian" because it constitutes the best state of affairs possible for individuals operating within a framework of near absolute individual sovereignty. Like a well-functioning free market economy, the competition among states—all equally respecting individual autonomy but offering different forms of social, economic, and political organization—will, in Nozick's view, produce the best possible outcome for the greatest number of people without violating anyone's individual rights along the way. As Nozick writes,

> Utopia is a framework for utopias, a place where people are at liberty to join together voluntarily to pursue and attempt to realize their own vision of the good life in the ideal community but where no one can *impose* his own utopian vision upon others.[21]

In other words, "You [plural] do you, we'll do us—and we all promise to leave each other alone (or else)." It is, in short, libertarian paradise.

FRENEMIES FOREVER

Rawls and Nozick do not represent the only origins of classical liberalism and libertarianism, nor does their thought capture all the ideological permutations of the two theories within

21. Nozick, 312.

contemporary politics. However, like a tree with a common root system whose branches eventually grow far apart, comparing their thought provides a framework for understanding their similarities and differences both in relation to each other and in relation to competing political ideologies outside the Kantian tradition.

First, as offspring of Kant's new metaphysics, both classical liberalism and libertarianism fundamentally agree on the following:

- All individuals have rights that protect them from being used, against their consent, for any social goal. This right includes, foundationally, a right against aggression either from other individuals or from the government.

- All individuals are autonomous agents who should be able to define and pursue their respective conception of the good unmolested by others, including the government, so long as their pursuit of the good does not unduly interfere with other autonomous agents pursuing their own conceptions of the good.

- It is epistemically and rationally impossible to make distinctions among different individuals' conceptions of the good; therefore, the government should be "viewpoint neutral" and merely procedural in nature, meaning that its purpose should be to protect and enforce individual rights—*not* to pursue a common vision of the good.

While Kant may not have expressed the political implications of the categorical imperative in these terms, the moral core of both classical liberalism and libertarianism rests upon the general epistemic and moral conclusions in Kant's thought. Put differently, the primary reason classical liberalism and libertarianism get along *at all* is because they share a common philosophical father.

Yet as any family knows, sometimes the sharpest debates occur between those who are most closely related. Rawls and Nozick reveal this division in the Kantian household. On the Rawlsian side, classical liberalism makes the case that individuals have a rationally grounded duty to create societies that minimize inequalities by redistributing wealth and opportunity. On the Nozickean side, libertarianism maintains that the very philosophical foundations of individualism categorically prohibit a centralized, government-imposed redistribution of wealth and opportunity; consequently, seeking to create such a society would be a violation of the individual rights that otherwise morally justify the existence of government in the first place. Libertarianism maintains that individuals can elect to redistribute their own wealth and opportunity, and it has no moral qualms with those who choose to do so. However, they stand against coerced redistribution in the form, for example, of redistributive taxes that go beyond the minimal state function of protecting individual liberty.

One common way to summarize these similarities and differences takes this form:

Classical liberals are socially liberal and economically liberal

vs.

Libertarians are socially liberal and economically conservative

Being "socially liberal" in this comparison means maximizing individual liberty to do whatever individuals want with their lives limited only by the principles of non-aggression and consent. Liberals and libertarians agree on this. While what it means to be "economically liberal" vs. "economically conservative" has more definitional variability, the basic disagreement, which we also see in Rawls and Nozick, is over the role the state can justifiably play in redistributing wealth and opportunity. Liberals believe that the state has an expansive, morally justified role in such redistribution, while libertarians believe that the state has a minimal or even non-existent role in such redistribution (some libertarians argue, for example, that it is a violation of individual rights to force people to pay for common civic protection in the form of police, fire, and other emergency services).

LAW OF THE LAND

It's ultimately not clear how this family feud could ever reach a resolution. Despite their basic agreement on individual rights, classical liberals and libertarians fundamentally disagree on the validity of Rawls' second principle of justice and will thus continually be at odds over how to structure and govern society, especially regarding economic questions. Yet while the economic back-and-forth between the two camps will likely carry on indefinitely, their shared consensus on the impossibility of defining an objective, rational good that applies to all people, coupled with their belief that it is always morally unjust to impose a definition of the good on others, has been incredibly influential in Western secular societies. In fact, in many ways it has become the *dominant* consensus, both culturally and politically (though we will examine in the next chapter how classical liberalism and libertarianism are now losing ground to another ideology that rejects individual rights in favor of "group rights" based on identity).

One of the most palpable pieces of evidence in support of this conclusion appears in a line from Supreme Court Justice Anthony Kennedy's majority opinion in the 1992 case *Planned Parenthood v. Casey*. The ruling upheld the court's previous decision in *Roe v. Wade* that concluded that states cannot interfere with a woman's decision to receive an abortion. In defending the majority's ruling in favor of the plaintiff, Planned Parenthood, Kennedy wrote,

> [Personal decisions] involving the most intimate and personal choices a person may make in a lifetime, choices central to personal dignity and autonomy, are central to the liberty protected by the Fourteenth Amendment. *At the heart of liberty is the right to define one's own concept of existence, of meaning, of the universe, and of the mystery of human life.* Beliefs about these matters could not define the attributes of personhood were they formed under compulsion of the State.[22]

I will address the question of how classical liberalism and libertarianism handle the issue of human dignity below. Yet what is important to highlight here is that Kennedy is making the claim, from the standpoint of a jurist, that the definition of human life ("personhood" in his language) is, like the nature of the universe and the "mystery" of human life itself, *completely within the realm of "autonomy."* In making this argument, Kennedy, on behalf of the Supreme Court, is adopting the same Kantian epistemology and morality at the foundation of both classical liberalism and libertarianism—namely, that claims about existence per se, including about what defines a human life and human purpose, are by their very nature outside the scope of human reason and thus sheerly a matter of autonomous preference. The court, Kennedy maintains, thus cannot speak about such matters, not only because they are extra-judicial and fall outside the scope of Constitutional jurisprudence, but because they belong to the realm of personal belief. There is no right answer and no wrong answer because there is *no answer* at all, at least from a rational perspective. This is not, it is important to note, a form of pure subjectivism in which Kennedy is claiming that there is no truth per se; rather, Kennedy is averring that autonomy is true and must be legally respected, and, indeed, that it is the only thing that is

---

22. *Planned Parenthood v. Casey,* 505 U.S. 833 (1992), https://supreme.justia.com/cases/federal/us/505/833/case.pdf (emphasis added).

true and thus the only thing that must be respected. Everything else belongs to the domain of personal liberty.[23]

Kennedy employs similar reasoning in the majority opinion for the landmark 2015 *Obergefell v. Hodges* case, which legalized homosexual marriage throughout the United States, overturning the remaining state laws that defined marriage as being between one biological man and one biological woman. In the majority opinion, Kennedy writes, "A first premise of the Court's relevant precedents is that the right to personal choice regarding marriage is inherent in the concept of individual autonomy."[24] Here, Kennedy is stating that the principle of autonomy applies to *whether* to get married, which, of course, is something that Catholic social thought would robustly agree with; however, he is also asserting that autonomy is the defining principle in determining the *meaning* of marriage itself. Given this claim, the logic leading to the majority's conclusion is evident: If humans have definitional autonomy, then individuals should be able to define marriage however they like—for example, as between a man and a woman, a man and a man, or a woman and a woman. (Curiously, Kennedy and the court majority remained silent on why this same principle does not also guarantee a right to polygamous marriage and even marriage among biological siblings and between parents and

---

23. It is important to stress how different this understanding of reality is from that which is both implicit and explicit in the founding documents of the United States, especially the Declaration of Independence, which recognizes the existence of God and an objective natural law: "When in the Course of human events, it becomes necessary for one people to dissolve the political bands which have connected them with another, and to assume among the powers of the earth, the separate and equal station to which the *Laws of Nature and of Nature's God* entitle them, a decent respect to the opinions of mankind requires that they should declare the causes which impel them to the separation. We hold these truths to be self-evident, that all men are created equal, that they are endowed by their Creator with certain unalienable Rights, that among these are Life, Liberty and the pursuit of Happiness" (https://www.archives.gov/founding-docs/declaration-transcript, emphasis added). In other words, the foundation of American democracy and jurisprudence is not autonomy—it is natural law.

24. *Obergefell v. Hodges*, 576 U.S. 644 (2015), https://www.supremecourt.gov /opinions/14pdf/14-556_3204.pdf.

children; I'll return to that question below.) As Kennedy writes, echoing his words in *Planned Parenthood v. Casey*, "Same-sex couples, too, may aspire to the transcendent purposes of marriage and seek fulfillment in its highest meaning."[25] Once again, we see that the substantive meanings of "transcendence," "purpose," "fulfillment," and "highest meaning" are left to the autonomous prerogative of individuals. Everyone (except, for the moment, those who wish to practice bigamy and incest) can define marriage however they wish so long as they respect the rights of others to do the same.[26]

Staying on the judicial track, these precedents, and the reasoning underpinning them, have unsurprisingly also led the court to recognize the autonomy to define "male" and "female." In the 2019 case *Bostock v. Clayton County of GA*, for example, the majority ruled that workplaces cannot discriminate on the basis of sex—a principle that Catholic social thought would agree with—but also that *the individual has the power to determine which sex he or she wants to identify as in the workplace*. If, for example, like in one of the cases the court eventually ruled on in *Bostock*, a business has a dress code for biological males and biological females and a biological male decides to start "identifying" as a biological female and dressing accordingly, it is an act of discrimination on the basis of sex to either compel the male to dress like the other males at work or fire him if he refuses to do so. Writing for the majority, Justice Gorsuch provides this example of the

---

25. *Obergefell v. Hodges*.

26. While this ruling was supposed to protect the religious freedom of those who continue to believe that marriage should be defined as a union between one man and one woman, LGTBQI+ advocates, some holding government power, have repeatedly sued businesses that refuse to participate in gay wedding ceremonies or transgender transition celebrations on religious and free speech grounds in the years following the ruling. Perhaps the most persecuted target has been the Masterpiece Cakeshop and its Christian owner, Jack Phillips. See, for example, Colleen Slevin, "Christian Baker Sued Again for Refusing to Bake a Cake," *Christianity Today*, March 24, 2021, https://www.christianitytoday.com/news/2021/march/colorado-christian-baker-jack-phillips-sued-lgbt-cake-court.html.

legal reasoning behind the decision as it pertains to people who identify as transgender:

> Or take an employer who fires a transgender person who was identified as a male at birth but who now identifies as a female. If the employer retains an otherwise identical employee who was identified as female at birth, the employer intentionally penalizes a person identified as male at birth for traits or actions that it tolerates in an employee identified as female at birth. Again, the individual employee's sex plays an unmistakable and impermissible role in the discharge decision.[27]

Note here the anthropological, even metaphysical presupposition underlying this reasoning: Discriminating against a woman only because she is a woman is legally tantamount to discriminating against a man who says he is a woman. That can only be true, legally speaking, if "woman" means the same thing in both instances of discrimination—and *that* can only be true, in turn, if the definition of "woman" is not fixed to biological reality but rather to the individual's autonomous self-determination. In other words, Gorsuch's reasoning presupposes that the content of the nature of the physical world, including the content of the nature of human beings' physical bodies, is sheerly a matter of personal autonomous preference. So long as the formal rational standard stays the same—in this case, the illegality of discriminating on sex alone—the substantive meaning of "sex" is left to the individual's discretion.

Setting aside the broader implications of the epistemology underlying this legal reasoning at the highest level of the US courts (one wonders whether an eighteen-year-old who is cited for underage drinking can now claim "age discrimination" because he

---

27. *Bostock v. Clayton County*, 590 U.S. (2020), https://www.supremecourt.gov/opinions/19pdf/17-1618_hfci.pdf.

identifies as a twenty-one-year-old), these representative rulings illustrate just how deeply the Kantian metaphysics at the heart of classical liberalism and libertarianism have permeated secular morality and culture. Autonomy is not only king in jurisprudence; it is often *the* deciding moral principle in every other area of civic and private life as well.

Yes, though Kant may be rolling in his proverbial grave seeing what classical liberalism and libertarianism have done with his once morally pristine rational imperatives generated by the postulated autonomous free will, he can at least take solace in knowing that his thought continues to be profoundly influential.

REDUCTIO AD ABSURDUM: THE STORY OF ARMIN MEIWES (READER DISCRETION ADVISED)

Before turning to the Catholic response, the first reaction, even from Catholic readers, may be, "What's wrong with granting people as much autonomy as possible? Why wouldn't we want to do that?" As I'll explain below, Catholic social thought robustly defends expansive individual liberty, including the liberty to follow one's own conscience and write one's own personal life story (within limits). Indeed, I will argue that Catholicism provides a stronger, more durable foundation for individual liberty than either classical liberalism or libertarianism. However, as a first salvo in challenging these twin political ideologies, let me tell the story of a man named Armin Meiwes. I'm not including this account to shock readers into emotional revulsion to classical liberalism and libertarianism. I include it because it provides a concrete example of what such thinking can logically and practically lead to. As noted at the chapter's outset, what is made possible in theory will always find a way to become real in practice.

Armin Meiwes was a soft-spoken computer repair technician from Rotenburg, Germany, who had never committed a crime in his life. He is now known as "The Rotenburg Cannibal" and

"Der Metzgermeister," German for "the master butcher."[28] At some point in his youth, Meiwes developed a strong desire to eat human flesh. In 2001, at the age of 40, he said he could no longer suppress the urge and so posted an "advertisement" on a website devoted to cannibalism stating that he wished to kill and eat a human, preferably, in his words, a "young, well-built man." To his surprise, Meiwes received a response from a forty-three-year-old man who shared that he wanted to end his own life and fancied the idea of being eaten after his death. The two men agreed to meet at Meiwes' apartment where the victim permitted Meiwes to kill, dismember, and eat him. It is likely that Meiwes' actions would have never been discovered had someone not contacted police when he posted *a new* advertisement seeking another "volunteer." Upon receiving the tip, law enforcement entered Meiwes' apartment, discovered the remnants of his first victim, and placed him under arrest for the act he had committed.

Now, I say "act" instead of "crime" here—and, using the logic of autonomy, I shouldn't be using the word "victim" but, rather, something like "consensual partner"—because it turned out that Meiwes' case was exceptionally difficult to prosecute under German law. Part of the trouble that prosecutors had in making their case was due to the fact that Meiwes had video-recorded proof that his partner/victim had *consented* to every act that Meiweis committed, including the killing and cannibalizing. "Murder" is the crime of killing someone who does not want to be killed. "Assault" is physically harming someone who does

---

28. The case of Armin Meiwes has been widely covered by the European press. Here is a short journalistic account of the details of what he did and why he did it: Roisin O'Connor, "Armin Meiwes: Interview with a Cannibal documentary sheds new light on one of Germany's most infamous murderers," The Independent, February 9, 2016, https://www.independent.co.uk/news/world/europe/armin -meiwes-interview-cannibal-documentary-sheds-new-light-one-germany-s -most-infamous-murderers-a6863201.html. Here is another journalistic account that emphasizes the *consensual* nature of the act: Luke Harding, "Victim of canni- bal agreed to be eaten," The Guardian, December 3, 2003, https://www.theguardian .com/world/2003/dec/04/germany.lukeharding.

not want to be harmed. Thus, what charge applies to someone who assaults and kills a person who unequivocally requests it? Notwithstanding these procedural and philosophical challenges, German prosecutors did, indeed, end up charging Meiwes with a crime in 2004. The charge was "manslaughter," which typically describes cases in which someone *unintentionally* kills another person while committing another negligent or criminal act, like a death due to driving drunk. Perhaps because of this legal non sequitur, and because German law does not prohibit double jeopardy (being tried twice for the same crime), prosecutors later retried and successfully convicted Meiwes on murder charges. He is currently serving a life sentence.

The first response to this story, besides shock and nauseous abhorrence, may be to say something like, "This man is clearly mentally ill and, for that reason, his case should not be used as evidence in an argument against the supremacy of individual autonomy either in civil law or common culture." Perhaps, indeed, Meiwes is mentally ill, though he seemed quite in control of his actions and the reasons for them both during and after the horrific act. Yet, as the trouble German prosecutors had in legally demonstrating that Meiwes had committed a *crime* indicates, his case invites broader questions about the implications of adopting "autonomy" as the preeminent principle of justice and morality. The German courts were eventually able to get a murder, as opposed to manslaughter, charge to stick because they determined that Meiwes had killed motivated by "sexual gratification." However, that does not change the fact—a fact that Meiwes had documented on camera—that *the victim had explicitly consented to everything Meiwes had done.* "Sexual gratification" has to do with interior motivations and goals that individuals want to accomplish, but remember: "goals" have no moral value for classical liberalism and libertarianism. They fall into the realm of amoral (neither moral nor immoral) personal autonomy. Indeed, the only relevant moral consideration of a "goal" for both classical liberalism and libertarianism is if its pursuit violates another's autonomy. It is for that reason that "consent" is the preeminent mechanism for guiding action. It's the only surefire way you can determine whether pursuing your goal is "permissible" or "impermissible." Yet that's precisely the issue here: Meiwes had his victim's full, knowing, and explicit consent every step of the way. In other words, Meiwes did not violate his partner's autonomy; indeed, one could make the case that he *respected* his autonomy by carrying out his explicit wishes.

Think of it this way. Fewer than ten years after Meiwes' retrial and murder conviction, Germany legalized the practice of euthanasia, legally permitting individuals to assist in killing other individuals who desired to die and had freely consented to receive assistance in ending their own lives. The 2015 law, however, limited the practice only to those who had "altruistic motives," meaning it was illegal to charge the recipients of euthanasia for receiving death-delivering services. After years of pushback from pro-euthanasia groups who argued that the 2015 law was too restrictive, the German courts issued a new ruling in 2020 that removed the "altruistic" conditions, thus opening the door for businesses to kill willing German citizens for a fee. This, the court ruled, was necessary because individuals clearly have the autonomy to end their own lives in the way they wish. As the lead judge of the panel, Andreas Voßkuhle, explained, "The [2015] rule is not compatible with the basic law and thus void. . . . [The right to die] includes the freedom to take one's life and to rely on the voluntary help of another person."[29] In other words, it doesn't matter what *motive* one might have in assisting another to die;

29. See, for example, Christopher F. Schuetze, "German Court Overturns Ban on Assisted Suicide," *New York Times*, February 26, 2020, https://www.nytimes.com/2020/02/26/world/europe/germany-assisted-suicide.html. It is important to note, again, that Kant was explicitly against suicide and believed it to be a violation of the categorical imperative. However, subsequent interpretations of Kantian autonomy have removed all moral and legal obstacles to taking one's own life and, indeed, helping another to take his or hers.

all that matters morally and legally is that individuals have the right to die and other individuals have the right to help them if they want to. Justice calls for no less.

Well now. One wonders whether Mr. Meiwes would be free today had he waited a little longer to carry out his fantasy. That may sound flippant given the gruesomeness of his crime, but that's precisely the point: even the word "gruesome" has no objective content from the perspective of classical liberalism and libertarianism. The *only* thing that is ultimately prohibited is violating another's autonomy. By the logic of their own position, *everything else is permitted*. That's not to say that classical liberalism and libertarianism endorse cannibalism and consensual homicide. But they certainly aren't *against* them either. How could they be? It's just a preference like every other preference.

As disturbing as these words may sound, it is not only the case that the conception of autonomy at the heart of classical liberalism and libertarianism *could* justify these actions. They already are in many cases. There may be the understandable impulse to reply, "But it is *unnatural* to sever your own healthy genitals, breast tissue, and even spinal cord," "It is *unnatural* for adult men to act as if they were woman in public libraries in front of children," "It is *unnatural* for individuals to have intercourse with robots," "It is *unnatural* to want to end your own life and certainly *unnatural* to want to help others end theirs," etc. Yet these objections ultimately point back to the Kantian core of classical liberalism and libertarianism: there is no such thing as a rational category of "the natural." There is only the naked human will, which is permitted to do whatever it wants to the raw, amoral materials of the physical world—including our own bodies—so long as all the parties consent. To be sure, Kant may never have been able to imagine that he would be a source of inspiration for performing and even less celebrating these kinds of actions. But he was writing in a time and place that generally embraced Christian theism and all its moral and political implications.

That cultural context has dramatically changed in the West, pushing the meaning of "morally permissible" to an infinitely absurd horizon. And so once again we see: what is made possible in theory will find a way to become real in practice.

THE CATHOLIC RESPONSE

The Catholic social thought tradition stands unequivocally against this interpretation of "autonomy," but it is important to make some preliminary clarifications before explaining why. First, while natural law clearly prohibits the actions above (and more), it does not necessarily endorse making all of them *illegal*. To be sure, the Church believes that some acts, like abortion, should be criminalized, meaning there should be legal sanctions against them. (And since pro-choice advocates frequently bring this up as a scare tactic, criminalizing abortion does *not* mean jailing women who seek or procure abortions; the penalties would be only against those, frequently men, who perform the procedure.) Yet other violations of natural law would not necessarily fit into the "legal prohibition" category. For example, while trimming the flesh of your outer ears in an attempt to look like a "demon"[30] is an objectively grave violation of bodily integrity, it's not clear that the social thought tradition would seek to make such an act "illegal." Indeed, the tradition has long recognized the principle that though all illegal acts should be defined as immoral, not all immoral acts should be defined as illegal. Without a doubt, protecting human life and human dignity requires making some acts punishable by law; yet Catholic morality seeks to safeguard and advance the individual and common good primarily by means of persuasion, not coercion. As St. Thomas Aquinas put it in the thirteenth century,

---

30. See, for example, Pablo Leite Garcia, "'The sinister attracted me': Brazilian tattoo artist morphs into devil look-alike," Reuters, August 20, 2021, https://www.reuters.com/lifestyle/the-sinister-attracted-me-brazilian-tattoo-artist-morphs-into-devil-look-alike-2021-08-20/.

A human law is laid down for a multitude, the majority of whom consists of men not perfect in virtue. And therefore not all the vices from which the virtuous abstain are prohibited by human law, but only those graver excesses from which it is possible for the majority of the multitude to abstain, and especially those excesses which are to the hurt of other men, without the prohibition of which human society could not be maintained, as murder, theft, and the like.[31]

This point is especially important from an evangelization perspective. One of the most prominent myths circulating in secular culture is that "religious people" seek to *coerce* individuals to act morally. That is certainly not the case for Catholic social thought.

It is also important to note that there is substantial overlap between classical liberalism, libertarianism, and the Catholic social thought tradition on both the existence of individual rights and the belief that there is never any justification to deny an individual's rights in the name of a "greater" social good. Another way of expressing this agreement is that Catholicism, like both classical liberalism and libertarianism, upholds the existence of moral absolutes; there are some things that must never be done, no matter what the consequences for society. In this sense, Catholicism, classical liberalism, and libertarianism stand arm-in-arm united against utilitarianism.

Third, Catholicism also finds common ground with classical liberalism's claim that justice entails addressing issues of equality of opportunity. Note here that the support is for the principle of equality of opportunity, not equality of outcome. Equality of outcome tends to describe communist, socialist, and, as we'll see in the following chapter, progressive/ "woke" ideologies. In contrast, the Catholic social thought tradition has unambiguously

31. Thomas Aquinas, *Summa theologiae* 1-2.96.2.

and repeatedly argued that there is a natural law right to private property and that both communism and socialism are contrary to the natural law and the will of God.[32] At the same time, however, Catholicism upholds the moral legitimacy of "distributive justice" within the broader umbrella of "justice." For example, in his treatment of the virtue of justice, St. Thomas Aquinas describes distributive justice in the following way:

> In distributive justice something is given to a private individual, in so far as what belongs to the whole is due to the part, and in a quantity that is proportionate to the importance of the position of that part in respect of the whole. Consequently in distributive justice a person receives all the more of the common goods, according as he holds a more prominent position in the community.[33]

This principle can morally justify some people being paid higher wages than others, which corresponds with Rawls' principle that some inequalities in the distribution of goods are morally justified. Yet the same principle can also justify the creation of policies that distribute goods and opportunities to ensure individuals are able to support themselves and their families, which is necessary to maintain and advance the common good. Indeed, the mid-twentieth-century Thomistic scholar Fr. John Ryan used this line of reasoning to support the argument that the natural law justifies a living wage for all workers. For example, Fr. Ryan wrote in his book *A Living Wage*:

> The remuneration of the laborer is the most important single question in any scheme of social reform. . . . The industrial

32. See, for example, *Quod Apostolici Muneris* (On Socialism) and *Rerum Novarum* (On Capital and Labor) by Pope Leo XIII (vatican.va). Both unequivocally recognize a natural law-grounded right to private property.

33. Thomas Aquinas, *Summa theologiae* 2-2.61.1.

> question in so far as it relates to the less prosperous classes, is a question of wages almost entirely. If the working people have sufficient income, they will be able themselves to meet many of the problems for which reformers are trying to find remedies.[34]

In other words, redistributive policies that support workers' capacities to support themselves and those for whom they are responsible are justified by Catholic social thought and seen as an effective means to address social inequalities and the problems that emanate from them. In making this observation, it is crucial to stress that the precise content of distributive justice is primarily a matter of prudential judgment that needs to be worked out through a transparent and deliberative democratic process. What is important to recognize in this context is that the Catholic social thought tradition generally agrees with the Rawlsian insight that the distribution of goods and opportunity is a question of justice in addition to being a question of charity. In this sense, Catholicism finds itself at odds with libertarianism, which tends to reject the moral validity of distributive justice altogether.

At the same time, however, Catholicism does find common ground with libertarianism on the question of how to delegate civil power in society. Similar to libertarian thought, Catholic social thought recognizes the principle of subsidiarity, which holds that political power should be as localized as possible. While the tradition also affirms the principle of solidarity—which recognizes, to paraphrase Martin Luther King Jr., that injustice anywhere should be a concern for those who love justice every-where—its insistence on subsidiarity in the form of empowering individuals and communities to govern themselves serves as a stalwart limiting principle against unwarranted centralized control. In this sense, Catholic social thought stands at odds

---

34. John Ryan, *A Living Wage*, quoted in Harlan Beckley, *Passion for Justice: Retrieving the Legacies of Walter Rauschenbusch, John Ryan, and Reinhold Niebuhr* (Louisville, KY: Westminster / John Knox Press, 1992), 174.

with the excesses of unchecked classical liberalism on economic and other policy matters.

Indeed, all in all, Catholic social thought has much more in common with classical liberalism and libertarianism than it does with utilitarianism. Forced to choose between the two—between an ideology that denies moral absolutes and individual rights and an ideology that defends them—Catholicism would ally with classical liberalism and libertarianism over utilitarianism any day. Moreover, tyrants and autocrats don't tend to like classical liberals and libertarians, which is another mark in their favor.

Yet as the analysis up to this point has already suggested, the Catholic social thought tradition may be able to befriend classical liberals and libertarians, but a marriage is neither possible nor advisable. The differences are ultimately irreconcilable. As with previous chapters, let's examine those differences in the following areas, keeping in mind, as always, the Thinking in Circles map to understand the origin and character of those differences:

- the problem of truth

- the problem of perfection

- the problem of human dignity

- the problem of moral hierarchies

- the problem of free speech

- the problem of idolatry (which includes the problem of false mutual exclusivities and the problem of too high / too low views of human nature)

THE PROBLEM OF TRUTH

Unlike utilitarianism, classical liberalism and libertarianism don't have a problem telling the truth, or at least the partial truth. Their Kantian foundation not only equips them to defend individual rights but provides the epistemic resources to do so. While philosophers will continue to question Kant's epistemology and the categorical imperatives he derives from it, it is at least plausible to conclude that Kant has built a framework that can coherently account for rational necessity in morality (meaning he has identified principles that cannot be denied except on pain of self-contradiction) and, consequently, has provided the rational grounds for determining what would and would not contradict moral truth. For example, treating other people as if they were merely a means to fulfill one's desires while knowing that they have a self-legislating rational free will identifies a real moral contradiction; such a person is violating the incontrovertible truth, accessible to all rational minds, that all individuals with rational free wills are equally autonomous and thus have equal value. Recall that being able to identify principles that can be contradicted—which is another way of saying identifying rationally true principles—is a sine qua non of any moral theory. Utilitarianism fails that basic test. The Kantian legacies of classical liberalism and libertarianism pass it. Their insistence on a rationally defensible foundation to morality makes them especially fruitful dialogue partners and, as noted above, potential allies within the political sphere.

Nevertheless, the Catholic social thought tradition reveals three interrelated errors in classical liberalism, libertarianism, and their Kantian heritage related to the problem of truth. Both ideologies: (1) are substantively empty, meaning that they have no mechanism to instruct either individuals or societies on what moral goods to pursue (this is usually touted as one of the "benefits" of classical liberalism and libertarianism, but it contains the seeds of the ideologies' own destruction); (2) wrongly assume that Kant has the final word on the rational validity of classical metaphysics (that is, reasoning about the existence of God and objective natural moral norms); and (3) fail to adequately account for the problem of moral motivation, meaning they cannot explain why individuals and communities ought to respect the very individual rights they uphold. Let's address each problem in turn.

First, classical liberalism and libertarianism may be able to coherently generate rationally valid moral commands, but those commands have no substantive content because they cannot identify any good that an individual or society should seek to pursue. To be sure, both ideologies can speak coherently about what individuals shouldn't do—for example, not assaulting others, not stealing from others, not preventing others from speaking or practicing their religion (more on that below). However, they lack the rational resources to be able to say anything about what individuals *should* do. The reason is because to identify a good—whether that good is an object (e.g., food, water, shelter) or a goal (e.g., the reduction of poverty)—is to identify something that exists "out there" in the world. Yet recall that claiming the rational capacity to know anything "out there" is verboten in the Kantian universe because what's truly "out there" is in the realm of noumena and the only rational connection we have to noumena is the postulated free will. By definition, then, saying that "I/we/they" *should* do something is to make a claim that is at best sheerly preferential and at worst completely arbitrary. In other words, it is intellectually dishonest for any Kantian to say that any object or goal out in the world is good and should thus be pursued.

What, however, about John Rawls' attempt to link Kantianism to distributive justice? Isn't he seeking to incorporate a conception of objective goods into a Kantian epistemic paradigm? Indeed, he is. In fact, Rawls gives those goods a name: "primary goods." Primary goods are the necessary goods that any individual needs to pursue any goal at all. So, for example, if someone does not have access to clean water, sufficient nutrition, or basic education, they will not be able to exercise their autonomy to live as they choose. Recall that for Rawls, as a Kantian, individuals should be able to do whatever they want with their lives so long as they respect the rights of others to do the same. The primary goods, for him, are thus the things and opportunities that are necessary to be able to make these kinds of preferential, individual choices. In the starkest possible terms, if there is a dearth of primary goods then individuals will not be able to make any autonomous choices because they will be dead. Rawls wants to avoid this scenario in constructing a just society (Nozick is less concerned). It is an understandable, even laudable goal.

Yet a Kantian paradigm of justice cannot coherently distinguish such a goal from a sentiment—a feeling, a whim, a personal desire, nothing more than one preference among so many other preferences. Indeed, there's a dual problem with Rawls' proposal. The first is that calling goods "primary goods" still does not fix the fact that, as goods, they belong squarely in the noumenal realm and therefore cannot be spoken about rationally or, even less, identified as a goal to pursue. Second, Rawls, as many critics have noted, violates the bright Kantian line between phenomena and noumena by smuggling a description of normative human nature into his conception of the "original position" and its "veil of ignorance," both of which ostensibly justify the moral validity of primary goods. Recall that his position is that all human beings would make the rational choice to adopt both the first and second principles of justice (i.e., maximal freedom and managing inequality so that it benefits everyone in society) because, in the original position, they would not know where they would be born and raised in the socioeconomic hierarchy. Yet this description of human nature is not only highly debatable (one could make the argument that many would rather gamble behind the veil of ignorance, calculating that, though the likelihood of ending up on Skid Row might be higher, they could also get lucky and end up richer in a more unequal society); the bigger issue is that Kantian epistemology prohibits making *any* claims about human nature at all. This critique also applies to Robert Nozick's position that free human beings, in a state of nature, would rationally choose to form societies to mitigate the material inconveniences of living alone. Indeed, Kantian epistemology disqualifies all talk about "states of nature," even hypothetical ones used to justify the foundation of a normative social and civil order. All nature is purely noumenal and therefore beyond the scope of reason.

So why don't classical liberalism and libertarianism just drop their affiliation with Kant and get on with their respective political causes? The answer is because abandoning Kant pulls out the entire epistemic and moral foundation from both ideologies. The only reason that classical liberalism and libertarianism can avoid the nihilistic Scylla of moral relativism on one side and the incoherent Charybdis of empiricism-based utilitarianism on the other[35] is because they ground objective morality in the exercise of human reason itself. Rejecting the hard Kantian distinction between phenomena and noumena by saying that we can in fact talk about nature, including natural law, with rational validity would be doing classical metaphysics—identifying a rationally necessary structure to reality and deducing moral norms from that reality. Yet that is precisely what Kant and the Kantian moral tradition rejects. There's no splitting the difference on this one. If you're a Kantian, you don't get to talk about human nature. Likewise, if you want to talk about human nature, you and Kant are ultimately going to have to part ways. In short, classical liberalism and libertarianism are conceptually married to Kant. A divorce would not only be messy but would render both ideologies without a foundation.

Yet, setting the nature objection aside, let's say that it *is* possible to make a coherent Kantian case for Rawls' second principle of justice, or the idea that all individuals have a rational duty to

---

35. The fourth alternative, which classical liberalism and libertarianism also reject, would be to ground objective morality in nature, as the Catholic social thought tradition does.

ensure that society provides primary goods for its members.[36] Would this solve the problem of classical liberalism only being able to rationally justify negative rights (rights to be protected from harm by others)?[37] Would Rawlsian liberals be able to say that their philosophy does in fact provide an answer to the question, "What good or goods should society pursue?" Perhaps in a limited sense, yes. A Rawlsian liberal could say something like, "In addition to protecting everyone's negative rights, classical liberalism seeks to create a society in which everyone has access to the opportunities and primary goods that are necessary for them to be able to pursue their own preferential vision of the good life." That sounds like a goal, a noble goal even.

But it's deceptive. Saying that society should ensure that everyone has basic opportunities and goods to be able to pursue whatever goals they want is equivalent to saying that the purpose of society is to enable individuals to do whatever they want to do. But that still leaves unanswered this all-important question: "What should individuals *want* to do?" Classical liberals (and libertarians) proudly proclaim, "We let the individuals decide what they want to do!" which conforms to the Kantian view that desires are amoral—they are neither good nor bad in and of themselves. The reality, however, is that this view of individual autonomy, even coupled with some form of distributive justice, makes the specific substantive character of any civil society completely arbitrary.

Think, for example, of a Rawlsian society that decides, by consensual vote, that it will spend public money to provide equal opportunity for its citizens to undergo voluntary sterilization procedures—and engage in a massive marketing campaign to

---

36. The classical liberal philosopher Alan Gewirth seeks to make such an argument in his book *Reason and Morality*. I will discuss Gewirth on the question of human dignity below.

37. Libertarianism, rejecting the moral validity of distributive justice on principle, would not find this to be a problem.

encourage the use of this free service—in order to "save the planet." On the surface, this may sound irrational—why would a society want to legislate its own demise by financially encouraging its citizens to stop having children? Yet if this objection comes to mind, you're not thinking like a Kantian liberal. To be sure, the good of humans choosing to form families and raise children fits squarely within the realm of natural law—but remember, there are no natural laws to classical liberals. Consequently, a society that chooses to interpret "equality of opportunity" as providing free public sterilization is just as "moral" (which is to say "amoral"—neither good nor bad, just a preference) as a society that interprets "equality of opportunity" as using public resources to support the creation and stability of healthy child-bearing families. Likewise, a Rawlsian society that, on grounds of equal opportunity, votes to fund a public-school curriculum that teaches that "boys" and "girls" are interchangeable terms and that even identifying as "human" is a question of individual choice would be just as "rational" as a society that chooses to teach its young people standard human biology. Why? Because the interpretation of "nature" is sheerly a matter of preference from a Kantian perspective, and so any society can choose to define nature in any way it wants without any limiting principle. The same goes for a society that would pay to encourage as many of its citizens as possible to voluntarily take Xanax and spend their days inside virtual reality machines in order to reduce crime and free up jobs for those who have more talent. There would be nothing "wrong" about a Rawlsian society seeking to do this—and nothing "right" about it either. All that would matter is respecting consent and ensuring that everyone gets their share of primary goods along the way.

The overriding point is this: classical liberalism and libertarianism may tell themselves that they have created a political paradigm that safeguards individual rights, yet all they have accomplished in practice is abandoning individuals to the *a*rational (neither rational nor irrational) whims of the majority. However the majority chooses to define "the good" for society is by definition what is in fact good. No dissenter can say, "But isn't subsidizing voluntary state dependency a bad thing for people?" There is no "bad"—only "permitted" and "not permitted." No one can say, "But wouldn't it be unnatural to create a culture in which people are incentivized to live alone and not have children?" There is no "nature"—only "permitted" and "not permitted." No one can say, "Wouldn't it be detrimental to children's proper development to teach them that sex is purely a social construction?" There is no "proper development"—only "permitted" or "not permitted," and, besides, since children are not yet fully autonomous they do not, properly speaking, have full rights anyway, and so society can choose to do whatever it wants with them until they reach the age of full consent (whenever society determines that might be).

There is, in short, no common moral culture possible in a classical liberal/libertarian paradigm because there is no basis for a common morality beyond "Don't violate others' rights" and perhaps "Make sure everyone has enough of what they need in order to do what they want with their lives." Within those parameters, anything is permitted, which is another way of saying that classical liberalism and libertarianism have no rational basis for specifying what good individuals or societies should pursue. The "good" of social self-preservation is just as good, just as rational, as the good of social self-extinction. (And if you think no society would voluntarily choose to destroy itself, may I suggest spending more time browsing Twitter?). In short, anything, everything, and nothing are all equally good from a Kantian political framework, which means that classical liberalism and libertarianism cannot say anything true about the good and can't even lie about it either. Silence is the only coherent option.

The second issue classical liberalism and libertarianism have with telling the truth is that they presuppose that Kantianism has had the final word on the rational validity of doing metaphysics. Although this is not the forum for a systematic metaphysical response to Kantian epistemology, it is crucial to note that classical metaphysics—again, by which I mean the search for objective and ultimate truth in existence, including the existence of God—is not, in fact, dead. Indeed, there has been a great revival of metaphysics in the past decades, spearheaded by Christian philosophers like Edward Feser, Peter Kreeft, Fr. Robert J. Spitzer, and William Lane Craig. There has also been a proliferation of online Christian apologetical resources that draw deeply on metaphysical analysis; these include the vast content of Bishop Robert Barron's Word on Fire Catholic Ministries and the Word on Fire Institute, and other related sites like Catholic Answers, the Thomistic Institute, the Lumen Christi Institute, the Magis Center, and Strange Notions. It is certainly fair to say that Kantian epistemology has dominated the philosophical, moral, and, to a significant degree, political spheres both inside and outside universities in both the United States and Europe for many decades. However, the ongoing strength and duration of that philosophical reign is far from inevitable and, indeed, appears to be coming to an end (though not only because of a resurgence of Christian philosophy—progressivism/"wokeism" is also bringing down Kantianism, as we'll see in the next chapter).

On the surface, this return to classical metaphysical inquiry may seem to be of interest only to academics. Yet its moral and political importance both for Catholic social ethics and the debate about politics more broadly is difficult to overstate. The whole rational infrastructure of the Catholic social thought tradition is built upon the natural law, and the natural law, in turn, is built upon classical metaphysical analysis. If, as Catholicism maintains, we can indeed rationally confirm God's existence both in and of himself and as the Creator of all that is, then we can, from that foundational truth, deduce other derivative objective truths about existence itself, including both anthropological and moral truths about human nature. This provides Catholicism a rational means to identify not only what is "permitted" and "not permitted" but also, more substantively, what is "in accordance with nature" and "in violation of nature."

Thus, while classical liberalism and libertarianism must be silent about human beings consenting to kill themselves, the Catholic social thought tradition can say coherently that it is irrational to seek to end your own life. While classical liberalism and libertarianism must be silent on individuals who would seek to have surgery to sever their own healthy reproductive organs, Catholicism can say that mutilating yourself is contrary to human nature (doing the same thing to *children* is a horrific moral evil). While classical liberalism and libertarianism will be, at best, agnostic about including pornographic material in high school libraries, Catholicism can say that grooming youth for sexual activity is harmful to their moral and social development. More broadly, while classical liberals and libertarians must shrug their shoulders as their societies are literally dying off because too few people are having children, Catholicism can say that it is good for men and women to get married and form families and that we should do everything possible to support that.

These moral claims do not emerge out of thin air; they emerge from the Catholic social thought tradition's natural law framework, which, in conjunction with God's revelation in Scripture, emerges from its rational analysis of God's existence, nature, and relationship with creation. To sum up using the Thinking in Circles map: Whereas Kantian liberalism and libertarianism deactivate the anthropological, ontological, and theological spheres of inquiry, evacuating them of any rational content, the metaphysics underpinning Catholic social thought not only reactivates these realms but in so doing brings them to bear directly on moral and political questions. Consequently, Catholicism can offer a comprehensive, systematic, integrated, and rational vision of the purpose of human life, the purpose of society, and the purpose of government. As the *Catechism of the Catholic Church* affirms, for example,

> Every human community needs an authority to govern it. The foundation of such authority lies in human nature. It is necessary for the unity of the state. Its role is to ensure as far as possible the common good of society.[38]

And,

> Authority does not derive its moral legitimacy from itself. It must not behave in a despotic manner, but must act for the common good as a "moral force based on freedom and a sense of responsibility": "A human law has the character of law to the extent that it accords with right reason, and thus derives from the eternal law. Insofar as it falls short of right reason it is said to be an unjust law, and thus has not so much the nature of law as a kind of violence."[39]

If there is one God, there is one truth, and if there is one truth, there is one true human good, and if there is one true human good, then just civil laws identify not only what we shouldn't do to violate that good but what we *should* do to instantiate, support, and advance it as well. This provides a much broader, deeper, and more coherent moral foundation for deliberations about the specific nature of civil laws than anything that classical liberalism and libertarianism can offer.

The third problem with classical liberalism and libertarianism has to do with the motivation to tell the truth and to act in accordance with the truth. Recall from the previous chapter that one of the areas in which utilitarianism and Catholic social

---

38. Thomas Aquinas, quoted in *Catechism of the Catholic Church* 1898.
39. CCC 1902.

thought overlap is in the recognition that moral motivation requires more than moving the mind; it requires moving the *will* as well, which David Hume, notwithstanding his other errors, rightfully recognized in his conception of virtue theory grounded in the sentiment of benevolence. Kantianism, on the other hand, divorces morality not only from the specific sentiment of benevolence but from anything that we could broadly associate with desire as it relates to moving the human will. Reason, for Kant, is the only thing that can move the will, because his epistemology rules out desires or sentiments having any moral content, both because they are part of the body and because they are goal oriented, which means that their true nature is noumenal and thus unknowable. To boil this understanding of moral motivation down to its most basic expression, Kant is arguing this: knowing something to be true provides the necessary and sufficient motivation to act on behalf of the truth.

This account of moral motivation overlooks the complexity of human anthropology and human psychology. As Aristotle (whom we'll also examine—and critique—in the penultimate chapter) famously observes in his *Nicomachean Ethics*:

> The origin of action . . . is choice, and that of choice is desire and reasoning with a view to an end. This is why choice cannot exist either without reason and intellect or without a moral state; for good action and its opposite cannot exist without a combination of intellect and character. Intellect itself, however, moves nothing, but only intellect which aims at an end and is practical.[40]

Aristotle's point here—which the Catholic social thought tradition agrees with—is that properly formed desire in the form of good character is necessary not only to act in accordance with a

---

40. Aristotle, *Nicomachean Ethics*, 6.2.

moral truth that the intellect has identified but also to apprehend that moral truth properly in the first place. A man in the grips of lust, for example, is not going to properly grasp the full dignity of the woman whom he desires and therefore will likely not act morally; someone who is overtaken by ambition will not see the effect that working too many hours has on her family and therefore will likely act in a way that harms her household; in an extreme case, someone addicted to drugs or alcohol will see everyone merely as a means to get drunk or high. Thus, it is not enough merely to know what is morally good in order to do the good; one must have rightly formed desires.

Kantian morality cannot address these anthropological and social dimensions of good action because it insists these realms of life are within the domain of noumena and therefore outside rational analysis. Why does this lacuna in Kant's thought matter politically? Because not being able to talk about anthropology means that all discussions about politics must omit any rational discussion about good character, virtue, noble desires, or even creating a civil environment that encourages civility, kindness, and compassion. The only "virtue-sounding" word in the Kantian lexicon is "respect," and all respect means is not violating others' autonomy. Any appeal to other values is sheer individual preference and can have no more moral weight than the claim "Sandals should not be worn with socks." To summarize, the political ideologies that emerge from the Kantian legacies cannot foster an environment that assists people in becoming good. Good is in the eye of the beholder—and every Kantian eye beholds a different conception of the good, all of them equally arbitrary.

THE PROBLEM OF PERFECTION

To their credit, classical liberalism and libertarianism do not typically engage in utopian fantasies. Given their recognition of inalienable individual rights, they have a built-in utopia blocker in the form of prohibiting society from justifying "means-to-end" moral and political thinking. Unlike utilitarians, they are not interested in cracking any eggs to make any omelets (though they also won't object, indeed can't object, if any eggs would like to crack themselves).

Likewise, both ideologies have objective metrics to determine whether a society is getting better or worse (recall the graphs of different models of perfection from chapter 4). For classical liberalism, the standard of progress (the y-axis) would be both maximizing individual freedom and ensuring equal access to primary goods and opportunities; for libertarianism, it would only be maximizing individual freedom. Either way, both ideologies, again, to their credit, avoid not only the utopian model of perfection but also the other extreme—the pessimist model that denies that any kind of shared moral progress is possible in society. It is also important to note that classical liberalism and libertarianism avoid the nihilistic model as well because of their roots in Kantian rationality. In a formal sense, then, it is fair to say that both ideologies, similar to Catholic social thought, embrace the asymptotic model of perfection: Authentic progress is possible, but no society can ever fully attain perfection and thus should never seek to do so. The attempt would inevitably violate individual rights.

Where the Catholic conception of social progress differs from the classical liberal/libertarian model is that Catholic thought affirms a comprehensive vision of the common good for its standard of perfection, while classical liberalism and libertarianism can only appeal to, minimally, individual rights or, maximally, individual rights plus primary goods. For the reasons outlined above, limiting the definition of progress in this way fails to capture the multifaceted anthropological dimensions of human existence and the human good. Classical liberalism and libertarianism tell individuals to define the good however they desire; yet, at the same time, by virtue of the logic of their position, they also tell them that all their desires are equally arbitrary because all desires per se, and the goals that they seek, are arational.

This viewpoint has massive implications for how individuals understand the meaning and purpose of their own lives. As noted before, classical liberalism and libertarianism cannot say anything about whether it would be better for an individual to become an accomplished doctor or an accomplished bong hitter—all they can counsel is "It's your choice." Yet the social implications are just as important to highlight: beyond increasing the protection of individual rights and, possibly, access to basic goods, society can potentially take any shape at all. As argued in the previous section, "perfection" is an almost completely blank canvas for classical liberals and libertarians and whatever vision of the good they decide to paint there. Whether it is one that encourages family formation or discourages family formation, encourages self-reliance or encourages state-reliance, values children (who, by definition, are not autonomous) or disvalues children, it is as good or as bad as any other. All that matters is that it is chosen.

The Catholic view of the common good, in contrast, includes the protection of individual rights and the provision of access to the basic goods necessary for living a fully human life (which, again, does not necessarily mean that the state should directly provide these goods). However, precisely because the common good is grounded in natural law and human nature, its conception of what defines a just, well-ordered, flourishing society is much more robust. For example, here are some of the questions that would be a matter of rational political concern for a Catholic yet only a matter of arbitrary preference for a classical liberal or a libertarian:

- Is society encouraging and supporting its members to become independent adults who marry, stay married, have children, raise their children, and do everything possible to create stable households?

- Is society encouraging and supporting its members to realize their full moral potential (becoming the best people they can possibly be)?

- Is society encouraging and supporting its members to realize their full intellectual potential (becoming as knowledgeable and capable of critical thinking as they can possibly be)?

- Is society encouraging and supporting its members not only to refrain from causing others harm but also to seek to advance their positive good?

- Is society encouraging and supporting its members to cultivate a spirit of discovery and respect for longstanding ideas and themes in science, art, literature, philosophy, and religion?

These and many related questions emerge from the Catholic conception of the common good because the common good seeks the flourishing (that is, the full realization) of the human person and society in relation to each other. This is not to say that the common good necessarily calls for spending taxpayer money on the study of great poetry or that there should be a law that punishes people if they do not act virtuously. It only means that these topics are of political concern for Catholic social thought because the political order is integrated with and in service of the total human good—not, as is the case with classical liberalism and libertarianism, entirely independent of that good.

THE PROBLEM OF HUMAN DIGNITY

Both libertarians and classical liberals, grounded in the Kantian moral tradition, uphold the objective existence of human dignity. As Kant argues, it is the autonomous free will that gives humanity its irrevocable value. This recognition and championing of dignity is certainly to the ideologies' credit. However, their conception of human worth also has two grave defects: (1) it is not universal, meaning it does not and cannot apply to all beings whom we would otherwise describe as human, and (2) it is morally invulnerable to external harm and therefore cannot coherently justify the individual rights classical liberalism and libertarianism otherwise seek to defend.

First, despite claiming the mantle of defending human dignity and human worth, the Kantian conception of autonomy that grounds the existence of dignity and worth does not apply to all humans. Although pinpointing the exact nature of the "autonomous will" is complex in Kant because it is a postulated noumenon, one basic way to describe it is to use the language of "capacity." The free will is not only something people have but also something people use or exercise. Indeed, the categorical imperative necessarily presumes that individuals are in fact acting freely; were there no free actions there would be no need for imperatives to guide those actions.

Why is this a problem for a universal conception of human dignity? Because not everyone is capable of free action. Expressed more generally, if human dignity is based upon a capacity, and capacities are unequal or otherwise nonexistent in some humans, then some humans will either have no dignity or have less dignity than those who have fully autonomous rational wills. There is, of course, the question of babies in the womb, which I'll address below. But consider babies outside the womb. They are certainly human, but they are not autonomous. Indeed, "autonomy" as the Kantian tradition interprets it (being able to make free choices absent any heteronomous coercion) does not even apply to toddlers and young children generally. US law identifies the "age of consent" and "adulthood" as eighteen years; perhaps some individuals have fully developed autonomous capacities before that (or perhaps not—indeed, perhaps even most eighteen-year-olds don't have them). Yet whatever the right age of autonomy might be, it is not the moment of conception, which means, by

Kantian logic, that there are many human beings in the world at any given moment who have no dignity, or at least not full dignity. Consequently, these human beings are worth less than others. We can also ask similar questions about individuals with mental disabilities, those in comas, the elderly, and even all of us when we are asleep. In each of these cases, the autonomous will is diminished if not completely dormant. That would mean that the dignity of these individuals is diminished or at least temporarily suspended until dawn. Moreover, even if we were to substitute "potential for autonomy" for "autonomy" as the criterion that confers dignity on individuals, we may be able to save the sleepers from transient worthlessness,[41] but the mentally handicapped and all others who do not appear to have any potential to be or become fully autonomous will remain as second, third, and even no-class members of the human species.

It is this gap between autonomy and humanity that explains why some classical liberals and libertarians use the language of "personal dignity" rather than "human dignity." Personal dignity means the worth of those who are full persons, those who have the full use of their autonomous capacities. It is also for this reason that most—though it is important to note, not all[42]—classical liberals and libertarians have no trouble in supporting the "right," as they call it, to have an abortion. As non-autonomous, the children in wombs are not persons and therefore do not enjoy the same moral protections as fully autonomous individuals. It is therefore simply a matter of choice what is done to the child in utero; the preference to allow the child to live and continue

---

41. Although classical liberal and libertarian pro-choice advocates are often loathe to admit it, saying that the "potential for autonomy" confers dignity actually bolsters the arguments in support of outlawing abortion—for what else is a child in utero but a *potentiality* that is growing toward her/his full biological and moral personhood?

42. See, for example, Charles C.W. Cooke, "The Secular Case against Abortion," *National Review*, November 11, 2021, https://www.nationalreview.com/magazine/2021/11/29/the-secular-case-against-abortion/.

growing or the preference to kill the child before (or during) his or her exit from the birth canal is just that—a preference, akin, morally speaking, to the choice to receive liposuction or plastic surgery, especially when the child is in the earliest stages of development.

The late University of Chicago philosopher Alan Gewirth (1912–2004), who was one of the most influential proponents of the Kantian and Rawlsian moral tradition, lays out the logic of rights as they relate to autonomy (or "agency," as he calls it) this way:

> The justifying criterion for having . . . the generic rights is that one is a prospective agent who has purposes he wants to fulfill. When someone is less than a full-fledged prospective agent who has purposes he wants to fulfill, his generic rights are proportional to the degree to which he approaches having the generic abilities constitutive of such agency and the reason for this proportionality is found in the relation between having the rights and having the generic abilities required for acting with a view to purpose-fulfillment. The fetus, of course, lacks the abilities, except in a remotely potential form. In addition, it also lacks any purposes of even the most rudimentary sort, because of its lack of any physically separate existence and of even an initial acquisition of memories. Hence its generic rights, by comparison with the rights of its mother, are minimal.[43]

Setting aside the antiquated prenatal biology in Gewirth's argument (e.g., prenatal babies do, indeed, have some form of memory[44]) and his odd definition of "physically separate existence" (the unborn have *entirely separate* DNA and body structures from

---

43. Alan Gewirth, *Reason and Morality* (Chicago: University of Chicago Press, 1978), 142.

44. Janet L. Hopson, "Fetal Psychology," *Psychology Today*, September 1, 1998, https://www.psychologytoday.com/us/articles/199809/fetal-psychology.

their mother from the moment of conception), this passage aptly captures the dominant classical liberal and libertarian thinking on the relationship between autonomy/agency, dignity, and rights: because the baby in utero has no agency, she therefore has no (or very little) value, no rights. However, if we were to apply this criterion consistently across all human beings, we would have to recognize that many born individuals also fall into the categories of diminished (or no) agency and, consequently, diminished (or no) value. It is rare to find a classical liberal or libertarian who admits this. Yet for a system of thought that rightfully champions universalizing rational maxims, it's an unavoidable implication. If dignity is founded on a capacity, it's not only the unborn who will be worth nothing or next to nothing. For example, take a tour of the nearest nursing home and look at its residents, slumped in the corridors and babbling in their beds, with classical liberal and libertarian eyes. The once bright line between classical liberalism/libertarianism and utilitarianism, between the good guys (defenders of liberty) and the bad guys (majoritarian tyrants), fades pretty quickly. Once you've justified, on principle, tossing individuals off the boat of moral concern, does it really matter what the principle is?

The second problem with the liberal/libertarian conception of dignity is that, despite linking the existence of dignity to the existence of rights (i.e., persons have rights *because* they have dignity), their Kantian underpinnings ultimately render rights morally moot. Rationally speaking, for a right to be a right at least two conditions must hold: (1) there must be some justification for the right's existence, and (2) there must be some need or purpose for the right to fulfill. Kantianism seems to meet the first criterion in the form of its defense of the autonomous rational will, which is the ground of its conception of dignity; because (some) humans have this dignity, they therefore have the moral claim on others not to attack or otherwise undermine their dignity, which, in turn, justifies the existence of rights both conceptually and legally.

Yet the fact that Kantianism grounds rights in the autonomous will, which is a noumenon and not part of the physical phenomenal world, means that Kant has located the will—and therefore the dignity that it generates—beyond the reach of anything in the world. In other words, Kantianism ultimately defines dignity as invulnerable to harm; because phenomena (the world as it is perceived) and noumena (the way things actually are) do not intersect, nothing in the realm of phenomena can "get into" the realm of noumena, which, again, means that nothing in the world can harm or otherwise affect the source of human dignity.

It therefore appears to be the case that the second condition for a right to exist—that it meets some need or purpose (e.g., "protection")—does not and cannot hold in the Kantian conception of dignity. If the purpose of rights is to protect vulnerable human dignity, yet dignity is defined in a way that renders it invulnerable to harm, then rights have no purpose. They are merely window dressing on the autonomous will. Whatever may affect the use of freedom in the world, the source of the freedom itself will, by definition, remain unscathed by the world and everything in it. Thus, though classical liberalism's and libertarianism's embrace of dignity and rights is preferable to utilitarianism's rejection of both, these two ideologies can ultimately explain neither how human dignity applies to all human beings without exception nor why Kantian humanity needs rights in the first place.

The Catholic conception of human dignity fixes both problems. First, Catholicism founds its understanding of human dignity on the ontological and anthropological fact that human beings are made in the "image and likeness of God" (Gen. 1:27). This definition has many moral implications, but the first is that human dignity can consequently be described as both universal (applying to all human beings without exception) and equal (applying to all human beings in equivalent kind and degree) without contradiction or ambiguity. Whatever capacities—including the capacity to act freely—any human being may or may not have, this baseline dignity remains the same both across the human family and within the individual arc of each person's life, from conception to natural death. As bizarre as it may sound to some secular ears (classical liberals, libertarians, and utilitarians alike), the full moral truth is that the embryo in the womb, the man lying in a coma hooked to a feeding tube, the severely autistic woman who cannot speak, and the CEO of a multinational corporation are all worth the same and deserve identical moral regard. There are no exceptions, no need to calculate relative agency and render a judgment on the proportional worth of each. All humans are valuable. All lives matter equally. It is a moral fact grounded both in creation and the Author of creation.

But if this is true, isn't the Catholic conception of dignity also subject to the critique that it has defined human worth as invulnerable and therefore morally moot? If dignity inheres in human beings by nature, how could we say that it needs protection in the form of recognizing and respecting individual rights? Recall that the underlying epistemology of the Catholic social thought tradition does not have the same limitations as Kantian epistemology. Kant cannot talk about the world. Catholicism can. Why? Because it affirms that human rationality is capable of discerning metaphysical truth. What this means for human dignity is that the Catholic social thought tradition can affirm both that human dignity is grounded in human nature defined as "the image and likeness of God" *and* that that same dignity takes the form of a potential to be realized, like an acorn growing into an oak tree.

For example, Pope St. John Paul II captures this dynamic dimension of dignity in his encyclical *Evangelium Vitae*, writing, "The dignity of this life is linked not only to its beginning, to the fact that it comes from God, but also to its final end, to its destiny of fellowship with God in knowledge and love of him."[45] God freely gives us the gift of our dignity, yet it is our responsibility, individually and collectively, to bring the potential of that gift to fruition by freely acting in accordance with God's purposes, with the goal of growing in fellowship with God and ultimately abiding in his presence eternally. Setting aside the important theological dimensions of this claim, its implications for the meaning of human dignity are clear: as an ontological gift *and* a potential to be realized, dignity is acutely vulnerable to one's own actions and the actions of others. Individuals who, for example, are victims of human trafficking or gang violence or domestic abuse or torture or unjust incarceration can be harmed in the sense of damaging their capacity to realize their full moral potential as human beings by acting in accordance with God's purposes.

In sum, this authentic vulnerability in the Catholic conception of human dignity illuminates the necessity for protection. The core dignity grounded in the image and likeness of God can never be stripped or sullied; it is, indeed, outside the reach of the world. Yet the realization of that dignity is acutely vulnerable to the world. Catholicism thus answers not only how and why human beings have universal and equal human dignity but also why we have and need rights to protect and foster that dignity.

THE PROBLEM OF MORAL HIERARCHIES

Classical liberalism and libertarianism, despite their differences on questions of distributive justice, agree on the existence of "negative rights," or rights that protect individuals from the actions of other individuals, groups, and even the government itself. ("Positive rights," in contrast, typically refer to individuals having a right to receive something from another individual, group, or the government; a child's right to public education

45. John Paul II, *Evangelium Vitae* 38, encyclical letter, March 25, 1995, vatican. va.

would be an example.) As noted, the Kantian moral foundation does provide a foundation for negative rights—even if it renders those rights moot by defining dignity in a way that makes it impervious to harm. Yet setting aside this conceptual confusion about the relationship between rights and dignity, it remains accurate to say that classical liberalism, libertarianism, and the Catholic social thought tradition are in general agreement on the existence and moral bindingness of negative rights, or the "Thou shall nots" of morality, both individually and civically.

The primary fault line between classical liberalism, libertarianism, and the Catholic social thought tradition thus primarily pertains to the "Thou shalls" of morality—that is, what individuals and societies ought to do in addition to what they ought not to do. As argued above, Catholicism's natural law foundation provides it numerous resources to identify and justify positive goods that individuals and societies have reason to pursue—goods like the support of families, the cultivation of virtue, the expansion of intellectual discovery, etc. Consequently, Catholic social thought can explain how society can have an overarching goal or purpose that is also inclusive of each person's authentic individual good. This goal or purpose takes the name of "the common good." Classical liberalism and libertarianism, on the other hand, can only justify talking about the good of society in terms of defending individuals' rights to pursue their own arational conception of the good (classical liberalism and libertarianism) and perhaps also having access to primary goods to do so (classical liberalism alone). In this sense, these ideologies are only procedural in nature, meaning that they only seek to ensure that the mechanisms for individuals to do what they want are in place and properly functioning. They thus possess no moral hierarchy and no means to discern what goods are in service of what other goods (e.g., the good of economic prosperity being a good in service of the greater good of people becoming full flourishing persons). We therefore see once again how different

Catholicism's vision of the nature and purpose of society and the state is from the visions of classical liberalism and libertarianism.

It is crucial to emphasize, however, that Catholicism, though rejecting the idolatry of choice in classical liberalism and libertarianism, recognizes limited yet nevertheless still expansive freedom for each society to determine how best to govern itself, pursuing the good in a way that is consonant with its own best collective judgment. Recall from chapter 4's discussion of the relationship between the "Thou shall nots" and the "Thou shalls" that while there is only one way to act in accordance with an authentic "Thou shall not"—*not to do it*—there are potentially numerous ways to act in accordance with a "Thou shall," ways that may or may not include formal government involvement. For example, let's say—as Catholic social thought, based on natural law, affirms—that there is a moral duty to educate the young. Providing public schooling may be one of the ways to fulfill that duty. Yet private schooling, homeschooling, or even "pods" of homeschoolers working together could be another morally acceptable, even morally superior, option depending on circumstances. The same thinking applies to the moral duty to ensure that families do not go hungry, thirsty, or without adequate shelter and medical care. To recognize this moral duty, from a Catholic perspective, does not necessarily entail the government providing these services directly. Again, based on the virtue of prudence, every society must deliberate and reach a consensus on how to fulfill its moral duties in a way that takes into account the numerous economic, sociopolitical, and even cultural variables that define its particular circumstances in the particular moment. There is, in short, extensive room within the Catholic social thought tradition for democratic deliberation on questions of moral imperatives as they pertain to the common good.

This moral flexibility applies to individuals as well. One secular critique of religion in general and Catholicism in particular is that it imposes morally uniform rules on its adherents at the expense of individuality. Yet this criticism is a red herring. What matters about any set of rules is not whether they are rules but whether the rules are *true*—that is, whether they conform to reality properly defined. Unless those who are tut-tutting religious rules are anarchists, their beef is not with the rule-ness of the rules but rather with their source. Moreover, to say that being an individual implies following no rules whatsoever is not only nihilistic but also precludes authentic individuality, because individuals who seek to live according to no rules would have no distinctive pattern to their characters and personalities that would define them as distinct, unified persons. Indeed, they would be indiscernible from someone suffering from a severe personality disorder.

To be sure, Catholicism has its good share of moral "rigidity" (though I prefer the word "consistency") in its embrace of moral absolutes. Yet it also, to use a contemporary bon mot, celebrates diversity. Anyone who doubts this should take a quick look at the pantheon of Catholic saints. They are, indeed, morally uniform in respecting Catholicism's categorical moral prohibitions; they are also morally uniform in doing everything possible (and more) to advance the positive good of their communities. Deep and consistent prayer and a love for the Church and the sacraments also unites them. Yet their personalities, charisms, talents, ways of communicating, means of accomplishing their goals, and styles of life vastly differ. Compare, for example, St. Thomas Aquinas, who rarely did anything but think and write, to St. Teresa of Kolkata, who, when she was not praying, was out in the streets or in one of her missionary houses tending to the sick and dying, scrubbing bathrooms, meeting with visitors, or raising money for the poor. Compare the mystical St. Catherine of Siena to the eminently down-to-earth St. John Henry Newman. Compare the public charisma of St. John Paul II to the humble serenity of St. Thérèse of Lisieux, who produced some of the best theology in the history of the Church behind her Carmelite community's secluding walls.

This multiplicity of forms of life—all of them Catholic—should put to bed any claim that Catholicism imposes uniformity on its believers. Much the opposite, it makes authentic individuality possible by providing a fixed starting point, a definitive end point, and clear rules for moving forward (and getting back on track when you get lost) and then inviting each of us to blaze our own path.

In short, Catholicism teaches that if you want to be an authentic individual, you don't make up your own rules. You follow the rules in your own way.

THE PROBLEM OF FREE SPEECH

Another feather in the classical liberal and libertarian cap is its reliable defense of the right to free speech, which includes the free practice of religion. The support for this right is a logical implication of the ideologies' embrace of autonomy as the preeminent moral principle governing both individual and civic life—the idea that people should be free to do whatever they want so long as their actions do not violate the autonomy of others. Sticks and stones, as it were, would be a violation of this autonomy, but words are just words. Thus, excluding those concerning direct, literal, and immediate calls to engage in physical violence,[46] classical liberalism and libertarianism tend to reject all government restrictions on freedom of speech.

There has been a growing movement in recent years by self-identified "progressives," however, to equate certain kinds of speech with violence. Lisa Feldman Barrett, a professor of psychology at Northeastern University, for example, provides a paradigmatic example of the logic behind the claim that speech

---

46. In the 1969 *Brandenburg v. Ohio* case, the United States Supreme Court ruled that for speech to count as "incitement"—and thus not be protected by the First Amendment—it would have to be "directed to inciting imminent lawless action and is likely to produce such action" (*Brandenburg v. Ohio*, 395 U.S. 444 [1969], https://supreme.justia.com/cases/federal/us/395/444/).

equals violence in a recent *New York Times* opinion piece. She argues, "If words can cause stress, and if prolonged stress can cause physical harm, then it seems that speech—at least certain types of speech—can be a form of violence."[47] As most who are sympathetic to this position do, Barrett goes on to assert that she is not advocating against free speech per se and indeed welcomes "open conversations and vigorous debate about controversial or offensive topics." Yet, she concludes, "We must also halt speech that bullies and torments. From the perspective of our brain cells, the latter is literally a form of violence."[48] Barrett leaves the definition of "we" and "must" and "halt" suspiciously ambiguous in the op-ed, but the die has been cast in this new front in the culture war: if violence is criminal and some speech can count as violence, then some speech can count as criminal. And we all know what society is supposed to do with criminals.

Again, to their credit, classical liberals and libertarians typically reject equating speech with violence, and they can thank their Kantian principles for that. The only form of action that can affect the integrity of the autonomous free will (setting aside the question of whether the autonomous free will is vulnerable to any form of harm) would have to entail coercion of some sort, some physical force from the realm of the phenomena that violates the autonomous free will by acting against it in some unjust way. Hearing speech that one does not like, even hearing speech that one finds disturbing, does not and cannot meet this criterion of coercion. Why? Because one is usually free not to listen to the upsetting speech by, for example, walking away. Moreover, there is a subjective dimension to the interpretation of the speech that, from a classical liberal/libertarian perspective, cannot be rationally assessed and regulated.

---

47. Lisa Feldman Barrett, "When Is Speech Violence?" *New York Times*, July 14, 2017, https://www.nytimes.com/2017/07/14/opinion/sunday/when-is-speech-violence.html.
48. Barrett.

Indeed, that is the missing premise in Barrett's *New York Times* article. Even if we accept that speech can affect the physical integrity of brain cells, the "attack" speech can make on the body, unlike physically assaulting someone, passes through a psychological filter that is at least partially dependent on the ideas one holds. For example, someone who passionately believes that "sex and gender are social constructs" and that "men can have uteruses and menstruate" and that "women can impregnate other women or other men" may be greatly distressed, even to the point of psychological trauma, if they hear the words "Biological women and biological men are not definitionally interchangeable." Likewise, perhaps some physiological, empirically observable change occurs in the bodies of passionate pro-choice advocates when they hear the words "Abortion kills an innocent child." Maybe these words do, indeed, cause them a kind of physical distress, just as hearing someone say that women should "celebrate" or "shout" their abortions makes me experience a wave of nauseous disbelief that raises my blood pressure and accelerates my heart.

But so what? In any of these cases, the fact that words have a negative influence on the body of the person who hears them says *nothing* about the truth content of the words themselves and cannot be blamed, certainly not in a legal sense, on the person who says them. Indeed, whether or not someone reacts badly to words does not mean that that response is justified. Should, for example, parents feel morally culpable if, when they tell their overtired two year old it's time for bed, he collapses and histrionically convulses so violently that he bangs his head against the floor, which causes an eruption of sincere tears? (The answer is no—parents shouldn't feel guilty, even if they feel bad about what happened). Should a woman feel guilty for breaking up with an abusive boyfriend who, in response, tears out a chunk of his own hair? (The answer is no—the woman should not feel guilty, even if she feels bad about the guy having such a negative emotional reaction.) In short, speech is not the same, either morally or causally, as physically harming someone. Classical liberalism and libertarianism understand this difference and stick to their guns. Thank God.

That is not to say, however, that the classical liberal/libertarian view of free speech is sufficient. It's not. The reason is because while these ideologies can justify and defend a right to free speech per se, they render the content of all speech arational and morally empty. Recall that both ideologies affirm that all definitions of "the good" are sheerly a matter of personal preference. If that's true, there's no rational mechanism to distinguish among competing moral points of view. Consequently, the classical liberal/libertarian society is one in which individuals are free to speak their minds but unable to say why their viewpoints are better than any other viewpoint. With the exception of speech specifically about individual rights and (possibly) primary goods, all ideas about what society should and should not do or what goals society should or should not pursue or what laws should or should not be passed are equally arbitrary because there is no shared rational standard by which to evaluate them.

Thus, from a liberal/libertarian perspective, one person publicly affirming, "I believe it would be good to create a government-funded civics program that teaches our young people how their government works," has no rational advantage over another person publicly declaring, "I think it would be good to create a government-funded online gaming program so our young people can learn how to spend more time on their phones and tablets." These are, indeed, two different visions of what is good for young people and for society, but how, from a classical liberal/libertarian perspective, can we know which one is better? The point is we can't, at least not rationally, since no one can appeal to a common conception of what is good for young people and society. In short, classical liberals and libertarians exercising their right to free speech are not, ultimately, speaking at all. They're merely emoting. Consequently, no one can understand or evaluate what anyone else is saying except if, by blind luck, you happen to share the same arational point of view as the speaker.

Recognizing this limitation is important for two reasons. First, it once again reveals why and how classical liberal/libertarian societies will invariably drift in the direction of majoritarian whim. Since there is no rationally objective common good, the only "good" that such a society will pursue is the good that most people happen to want at any given time. Second—and more pertinent to the problem of free speech—classical liberalism/ libertarianism has no mechanism for morally adjudicating between different kinds of speech. Distinguishing between "good speech" and "bad speech" would require appealing to some rational standard of the good, which is exactly what these ideologies deny. Thus, while they would recognize the right of someone to publicly say something like "All Catholics are bigoted, superstitious Neanderthals who should be shunned by society because of their backward attitudes and poisonous influence on children," they would not be able to say that this is an example of bad speech, even if it should remain permissible by law. That goes for any form of speech that does not directly and imminently entail a physically violent act. Speech is speech, is speech, is speech, is speech—all of it preferential and thus neutral from a moral perspective, including slurs. To be sure, many, perhaps almost all, classical liberals and libertarians would say that they don't agree with such statements; yet that disagreement would hold the same moral weight as saying you don't agree that chicken and waffles should be on the same plate and under the same syrup. Like all substantively moral matters, it would just be a personal opinion, a preference, a taste.

The Catholic social thought tradition provides an alternative. Like classical liberalism and libertarianism, it upholds the inalienable right to free speech. Likewise, it recognizes that it is crucial to distinguish between subjective and objective definitions of "harm" as it applies to the effects speech can have on individuals. Truth always trumps feelings. Yet, in contrast to classical liberalism and libertarianism, Catholicism recognizes that upholding the right to the freedom of speech does not rationally entail that all speech is morally neutral. Catholics can coherently claim both "You have a right to say terribly offensive and hateful things" and "But it is *bad* for you to say them because you are saying things that are false—and I can make an argument to show you why that is the case." Goodness and badness are not merely a matter of preferential opinion from a Catholic point of view. As such, the Catholic social thought tradition condemns, on the one hand, the hyperventilating charge of "bigotry" made against ideas one simply doesn't like while, on the other hand, providing a stable conceptual foundation for being able to identify actual cases of bigotry—that is, instances of *objectively false* disparaging statements about a person or group. In short, Catholicism restores the category of truth to morality and to the (public) expression of moral points of view. Without such truth, there is no falsity. And if there is no falsity, then everyone is someone else's bigot.

MIRROR, MIRROR

In the end, classical liberalism and libertarianism sell themselves as liberating humanity to pursue its own definition of the good, yet, in the same act of liberation, also proclaim that every definition of the good is equally arbitrary. What is ultimate truth? Anything you want it to be! (Just as long as you don't call it "true.") What is the purpose of life? Anything you want it to be! (Just as long as you don't think that it's rational.) What is the nature of a just, well-ordered society? Beyond making sure no one kills or robs each other and, perhaps, is not desperately poor, anything you want it to be! (Just be sure you don't call it "good"). In short, the flip side of near absolute liberty is unmitigated narcissism, both individually and socially. Since nothing anybody says or does makes any more sense or any less sense than anything someone else says or does, each society can be no more than a community of solipsists, each member believing that his or her way of life and understanding of reality is the best and that no one—literally, no one—can say it is mistaken or wrong. As such, classical liberals and libertarians may still be mortal, but they are transformed into epistemic and moral gods, each creating the world in his or her own image and likeness.

With such a delusively high anthropology, such an artificially optimistic estimation of what we are capable of, it should thus come as no surprise that the towers of Babel we erect across the socioeconomic landscape not only fail to take us to the heavens but come tumbling back down upon us. Humans freed from all objective conceptions of good and evil can certainly construct stunningly creative, wealth-generating economies and technological marvels worthy of the gods themselves, but we employ those same powers to manufacture interactive online pornography, customizable android sex bots, trans fats, nuclear bombs, the "like" button, and personalized suicide pods. We raise ourselves up by our bootstraps only to tie a noose around our individual and communal necks. "Who am I to judge?" you say. Nobody, of course. Both of us, all of us, nobodies. In the name of individuality, classical liberalism and libertarianism have pressed us into one morally indistinguishable writhing heap of nobodies, all of us manipulating each other (because persuasion is rationally impossible) for the consent to step on each other's backs and climb ever higher to a baseless and peak-less summit of our own fancy.

As with utilitarianism, libertarianism and classical liberalism have thus not freed humanity from orienting our lives to a final good. They have not solved the problem of worship. All they've done, in the end, is removed the tabernacle and replaced it with a mirror. Multiplied across a population, the societies that emerge from this self-idolatry will conform themselves to whatever the majority of people think they desire in any given period of history. Kant's dream to free humanity from external, heteronomous sources of control may be well-intentioned, but its practical application leads not to liberty but to the worst form of slavery—being bound to our own emotive whims that, because they lie outside the sobering and stabilizing reach of reason, will end up eating us alive individually and collectively.

CHAPTER 8

The God of My Tribe: Progressivism (a.k.a. "Wokeism")

Imagine possessing the power to advance your political goals simply by incanting a spell-like litany of endlessly-ambiguous terms that supply immediate and unquestionable moral supremacy over your ideological rivals—words like "anti-racism," "intersectionality," "homo-" and/or "transphobia," "(white) privilege," "misgendering," "patriarchy," "triggering," "diversity," "equity," and "inclusion." Imagine being able to assert that mere disagreement with your self-defined "community's" political position is itself proof of your critic's intellectual confusion and moral corruption. Imagine society granting you the authority to proclaim that your self-described "lived experience" can trump all contrary evidence and that the declaration "This is *our* truth" is sufficient to supply you with fawning media coverage, lavish corporate sponsorship, and even civil legislation to protect and advance your political aims. Imagine a world with no objective rationality below and only a utopian intersectional sky above, a world in which winning an argument is as simple as silencing your opponents, and silencing your opponents is as simple as calling them dirty names. Imagine, best of all, being able to use every economic, political, and social benefit of "the system" while openly calling for "the system's" dismantling. Yes, that's right—heads you win, tails everyone else loses. If group dominance is the name of the game, who would turn down those odds?

PROGRESS VS. PROGRESSIVISM

To understand what defines progressive ideology, it is vital to understand what makes it so attractive. There are two answers, one already not-so-subtly suggested in the opening—namely, gaining sociopolitical power for one's identity group. It is important to emphasize, however, that there is a non-cynical reason progressive ideology can be attractive as well. For all of its faults, which this chapter will catalog and analyze, progressivism can also appeal to those who have a sincere concern to address social injustice, which could be broadly defined as systemic discrimination that targets groups solely on the basis of one or more morally irrelevant, usually immutable characteristics, like sex, skin color, or ethnicity. Denying women the right to vote on the grounds of being women or denying black individuals the right to full participation in society because of their skin color are two obvious historical examples of social injustice. In the chapter's latter sections, I will highlight how Catholic social thought not only takes the problem of social injustice seriously but contains the intellectual and moral resources to take it more seriously and be more effective in addressing it than the ideological alternatives, including progressivism.

It is examining progressivism's conception of power, however, that most effectively reveals its intellectual foundations and moral logic. Indeed, it is fair to say that power—acquiring, expanding, and maintaining it—is the one thing that unites the ideology's otherwise wildly disparate, even contradictory strands. I'll be using the term "progressivism" as a catch-all to describe the ideology but will also make the case that the contemporary term "wokeism" or "being woke" falls into the same category.

THINKING IN CIRCLES?

In previous chapters, I've introduced the Thinking in Circles map at this point to explain the respective ideology's ontological, anthropological, epistemological, and ethical foundations.

Progressivism requires temporarily bracketing the map because it, uniquely among the other ideologies in this book, has no single philosophical foundation. Indeed, progressivism is the Frankenstein of political ideologies. It is comprised of bits and pieces of scavenged parts from other political theories, including obscure academic ones that were once safely contained behind university walls. This bricolage of ideas, however, has now amassed into an unwieldy intellectual monstrosity, broken out of the ivory tower and is currently stomping, highly motivated but aggressively disoriented, through every institution in society, swallowing those whose power it can absorb (like well-meaning but naïve social justice advocates) while seeking to crush those who oppose it.

Below is a description of the ideological components that constitute progressivism. Though not exhaustive, it provides a basic picture of how progressivism both appropriates and distorts different political theories before yoking these distortions into the service of a particular group's political interests.

Classical Liberalism and Libertarianism

This piece of the progressive ideological corpus may be the most surprising of the bunch. Given that the ideology champions group identity as the highest good, radically individualistic classical liberalism and libertarianism would seem to be natural ideological foes. And indeed they are, at least in terms of their political goals. For example, YouTube political commentator Dave Rubin claims that it was progressivism's groupthink that ultimately led him to abandon the ideology and convert to classical liberalism and libertarianism.[1] As will become more apparent as we move

---

1. Rubin speaks frequently about the problems with progressive-wokeism in his shows, but for one example of him specifically explaining the reason for his "conversion," see The Daily Signal, "Dave Rubin on Why He Became a Conservative and His Fight Against Wokeism," YouTube video, June 11, 2021, https://www.youtube.com/watch?v=utv4yDYFZX4.

through progressivism's ideological ingredients, Rubin is right on this point: progressivism does indeed paradigmatically represent groupthink. However, it employs a distinctively Kantian tool to do so—namely, the total rejection of classical metaphysics, which precludes the possibility of anyone being able to claim that anything "out in the world" is objectively, truly good. Consequently, anyone can describe reality and everything in it—including the nature of the human being, the nature of the good society, even the nature of nature—any way they want to without any rational restrictions. The good, in short, is a sheer invention of the individual human will.

Progressivism takes this Kantian insight, that the good has no rationally objective content, and fills the definitional vacuum not with the individual will but with the will of the group. "My" definition of the good becomes "our" definition of the good; "My truth" becomes "Our truth"; "You can't judge me" becomes "You can't judge us." Although classical liberalism and libertarianism may balk at this socialization of autonomy, they cannot, on principle, make a cogent argument against it. If it's true that any individual can define the good however he or she wants to, then there's no reason a group cannot do the same. In this sense, the individualism of classical liberalism/libertarianism and the communalism of progressivism may be ideological enemies above the table, but their ankles are epistemically and morally cuffed beneath. Indeed, Dave Rubin himself observes, in a conversation with Bishop Robert Barron and Word on Fire Institute Senior Director Jared Zimmerer, that, taken to its logical end point, classical liberalism/libertarianism will lead to progressivism.[2] He's right about this, too, though the realization does not appear

---

2. Bishop Robert Barron, "Has Liberalism Failed? – Bishop Barron Presents: A Conversation Featuring Dave Rubin," YouTube video, November 2, 2020, https://www.youtube.com/watch?v=tctSwn04VR8. Rubin says, "At the end of liberalism, you kind of end up with wokeism" (4:45).

to have made him reconsider his ideological commitment to classical liberalism/libertarianism.

Another outcome of this unhappy marriage between classical liberalism/libertarianism and progressivism is that the former paves the way for the latter to commandeer the meaning of language. Think, for example, of the common progressive claim that being "colorblind" is being racist. Logically speaking, these two terms seem to be both contradictory and mutually exclusive. If you are treating someone equally regardless of their skin color, then you are not being racist; conversely, if you are racist, it means that you treat someone differently because of the color of their skin. Indeed, it is precisely these definitions of the terms that are operative in Martin Luther King Jr.'s famous call for all people to be judged by the content of their character and not the color of their skin. Skin color should be irrelevant to moral judgment. Believing and acting otherwise—that is, *not* being colorblind in how we morally assess individuals or groups—is actually racist.

Yet it has become a matter of dogma for progressivism that, contrary to the original meaning of the word, colorblindness is itself racist.[3] Conversely, treating people differently solely based on the color of their skin (what used to be called "racism") is actually not racist, or, in the new parlance, it is "anti-racist." In other words, for progressive ideology, in order to avoid being racist you are morally obligated to see and treat people differently based

3. See, for example, Monnica T. Williams, "Colorblind Ideology Is a Form of Racism," *Psychology Today*, December 27, 2011, https://www.psychologytoday.com/us/blog/culturally-speaking/201112/colorblind-ideology-is-form-racism. The author argues that saying "Color is not morally important" blinds people to recognizing the ways in which people of color have suffered injustice. This, however, is a category error. What morally matters is the injustice, not the pigmentation of the skin of the person who experienced injustice. And claiming that skin color is the cause of the injustice and that is why it matters morally would appear to lead to the principle, "It is wrong to treat people differently based on the color of their skin," which is exactly what the author seems to be arguing against. This kind of contradiction is emblematic of the lack of consistency in progressive-wokeist thinking. This section means to highlight how classical liberalism/libertarianism has contributed to making that inconsistency possible, even if unintentionally so.

upon their racial differences. This may sound like a mind-aching contradiction. However, it is a linguistic ploy that has been made possible by classical liberal/libertarian epistemology. Since "race" is something that belongs to the world and not to the exercise of rationality itself, its "true" definition—and the way that definition should function in a comprehensive vision of the good—is entirely dependent on the individual's desires. All progressivism has done is substitute "individual's desires" with "group's desires," and, presto chango, it established the conceptual grounds for being able to claim with a straight face that colorblindness is racism.

The linguistic consequences of classical liberalism/libertarianism are perhaps even more apparent in the progressive adoption of the dogma that "men" can be "women" and that "women" can be "men" (or any other of the 56 gender identities that Facebook once officially recognized[4]). Recall, again, that their underlying Kantian epistemology prohibits making any objective truth claims about anything out in the world. That includes not only race but also biological sex. Both are characteristics of human bodies, which are things that exist in the world, and the definition of the nature and purpose of anything in the world is left entirely within the domain of the autonomous human will. Thus, a man saying he is a woman is just as "rational" from this perspective as a man saying he is a man. Both statements refer to preferences, not to objective truth. Progressivism appropriates this epistemic belief and multiplies it across groups to create communities that claim the prerogative to define gender identity however they choose and, concurrently, claim that *no one*, especially no one outside their "community," can rationally contest their choice.

4. Peter Weber, "Facebook offers users 56 new gender options: Here's what they mean," *The Week*, January 8, 2015, https://theweek.com/articles/450873/facebook-offers-users-56-new-gender-options-heres-what-mean. Facebook now currently offers three gender options: "male," "female," and "custom." The "custom" option speaks to the fact that progressivism/wokeism has now pushed the boundaries of possible genders so far that they are endless; gender is whatever you want it to be, without restriction.

If a "man" can be a "woman," then it necessarily follows that "men" can be "women." It is, from this perspective, irrational to deny the "truth" of this claim, which means the only reason that someone would disagree with the identity claims of others would be sheer personal animus against them. Disagreeing with an identity group's claims thus gets redefined as a form of bigotry.

It is important to highlight that there is no limiting principle to this socialization of autonomous self-definition once it gets into progressive hands. All sorts of "communities" can and will pop up on the sociopolitical landscape, each one of them with an equally valid claim to recognition. There is, of course, the LGBTQIA+ community (which is comprised of sub-communities whose identities often contradict and conflict with each other, as we see in the ongoing battle over female identity and sexuality between men who identify as women and women attracted to other women[5]). But there are also communities of people who identify as dogs, people who identify as aliens, and people who identify as inanimate objects. The logic of progressivism says that all these communities have equal rational standing in society—that is, we must respect all of their "truths"—and classical liberalism and libertarianism cannot disagree.

To be sure, classical liberalism/libertarianism and progressivism still have massive differences between them. The former is committed to the defense of individual rights, especially from groups that would seek to usurp them. The latter is committed to advancing the good of their identity group as they define it, which, in contrast, can and does entail gaining social and political power at the expense of individual rights. In this very important sense, classical liberalism/libertarianism and progressivism stand directly and irreconcilably opposed. However, notwithstanding

5. See Julie Compton, "'Pro-lesbian' or 'trans-exclusionary'? Old animosities boil into public view," NBC News, January 14, 2019, https://www.nbcnews.com/feature/nbc-out/pro-lesbian-or-trans-exclusionary-old-animosities-boil-public-view-n958456.

their different political visions, they come, at least partially, from the same ideological family.

Utilitarianism

However, the progressive family is a mixed family, so mixed—so inclusive!—that it contains connections to not only classical liberalism and libertarianism but also their ideological foe, utilitarianism. There are two features of utilitarianism that progressivism appropriates: (1) a consequentialist emphasis on securing the good of the group even if it must sacrifice individual group members to do so, and (2) a conceptualization of "virtue" that takes the form of public demonstrations of morality intended to communicate that group members and allies are the "right kind of people" with the "right kind of feelings"—a performance commonly called "virtue signaling."

To understand these utilitarian elements within progressivism, it is important, first, to specify its conception of "community." In order to define a community as a community, progressivism typically appeals to some observable and shared characteristic that also has cultural and political potency. The most dominant examples are race, ethnicity, gender / gender identity, and sexual orientation (assuming members of the last category share their attractions publicly). Yet there are a couple of caveats to this. First, these categories, and the criteria for membership, are not definitionally fixed in progressive ideology and do not include all possible permutations of sub-identities within each category. For example, as we saw above, "sexual orientation" can mean different things according to different subgroups within the LGBTQIA+ community, like when a person who identifies as "trans" also claims to be sexually oriented to those of the same biological sex. The "+" in the community's name also serves as a titular admission to the fact that it has no limit to possible identities that could fit within the "community" (though in an Orwellian some-identities-are-more-equal-than-others move, note that only a few get to enjoy their own designated letter). The community, in short, can constantly redefine itself. This definitional mutability and instability is a product of progressivism's socialized autonomy discussed above—definitions of "community" do not come from any rationally objective standard but, rather, from the will of the identity group itself.

However progressivism settles the definitional question of communal identity, it is also important to note (and this is the second caveat) that it sees some identities as having more moral and political importance than others. There are numerous kinds of ethnicities, for example, but only a handful have any political currency in contemporary progressive politics in the United States. For example, we do not hear much about the "Argentine community" or "Costa Rican community" (progressivism would likely group them under the "Latino/Hispanic" or "Latinx" category,[6] despite the fact that there are tremendous cultural and linguistic differences among peoples from Mexico, Central America, and South America), or about the "Taiwanese community" or "Vietnamese community" (progressivism would likely group these individuals under the "Asian" category despite, again, the profound cultural and linguistic differences among different people from Asia). One reason for this discrepancy could

---

6. "Latinx" is a neologism meant to strip Spanish of its masculine/feminine gendered structure (adjectives and nouns that end in an "o" in Spanish are typically masculine while those that end with an "a" are feminine). When practically applied, it also dissolves the capacity for the language to communicate male/female binary identities (e.g., a man saying, "I am (a) Latino," or a woman saying, "I am (a) Latina"). It is part of the broader LGBTQIA+ ideology's efforts to excise all binary male/female distinctions from the social and political order. It is important to note that the Latino community in the United States overwhelmingly rejects this linguistic change and what it communicates about the lack of sexual differentiation. For example, a recent Pew Research Poll found that just 3% of Latinos choose to use the term "Latinx" (Luis Noe-Bustamante, Lauren Mora, and Mark Hugo Lopez, "About One-in-Four U.S. Hispanics Have Heard of Latinx, but Just 3% Use It," Pew Research Center, August 11, 2020, https://www.pewresearch.org/hispanic/2020/08/11/about-one-in-four-u-s-hispanics-have-heard-of-latinx-but-just-3-use-it/). Progressives have a name for the practice of an elite group of people seeking to alter the culture of others: "cultural imperialism." Pot, meet kettle.

be the size of the respective communities, meaning that smaller ethnic communities understandably get less political attention than larger ones. However, that principle does not hold up across the broader scope of politically relevant identities in progressive ideology. For example, according to the UCLA School of Law Williams Institute, only 1.4 million people in the United States identify as "trans," about 0.4 % of the population of the United States in 2020.[7] Alternatively, Pew Research estimates that 2.4% of the US population is Jewish, representing 7.5 million people.[8] In other words, there are six times more Jews in the United States than people who say they are trans. Yet progressive ideology pays little to no attention to the political interests of the Jewish community (indeed, it often displays outright hostility[9]), while the trans movement often occupies center stage.

We also cannot account for the different treatment when we factor in the variable of vulnerability to discrimination or harm—which usually plays a central role in organizing progressive identity group hierarchies—since Jews and people who identify as trans are both victims of hate crimes. According to 2019 FBI statistics, for example, there were 1,032 hate crimes against Jews in the United States compared with 227 hate crimes against people

7. Andrew R. Flores, Jody L. Herman, Gary J. Gates, and Taylor N.T. Brown, "How Many Adults Identify as Transgender in the United States?" UCLA School of Law Williams Institute website, June 2016, https://williamsinstitute.law.ucla .edu/wp-content/uploads/Trans-Adults-US-Aug-2016.pdf. I recognize that being "trans" is typically not considered to fall into the category of ethnicity. The point here is that progressivism is inconsistent in the criteria it generates and applies to create its moral and political hierarchies among its favored identity groups.

8. "Jewish Americans in 2020," Pew Research Center, May 11, 2021, https:// www.pewforum.org/2021/05/11/the-size-of-the-u-s-jewish-population/.

9. See, for example, this op-ed in the *Pittsburgh Post-Gazette*, which captures the general sense in which progressive politics in the United States has been inimical to the Jewish community in the United States: Bari Weiss, "Bari Weiss: Stop being shocked at bigotry," *Pittsburgh Post-Gazette*, October 21, 2020, https://www.post-gazette.com/opinion/Op-Ed/2020/10/22/Bari-Weiss -Stop-being-shocked-at-bigotry-Jewish-AOC-Alexandria-Ocasio-Cortez-Jews /stories/202010220023.

who identify as trans.[10] Calculated in terms of total hate crimes committed, Jews far exceed people who identify as trans. To be sure, when adjusted for relative population size, people who identify as trans are moderately more likely to be the victim of a hate crime than Jews; however, the broader point is that hate crimes are a problem for both groups, yet progressive ideology tends to view hate crimes against people who identify as trans as of much greater moral and political concern than hate crimes against Jews.[11] Thus, despite the fact that progressivism locates its entire moral and political center of gravity in group identities, it does not hold that all identities are created equal, even when we factor in vulnerability.

That said, let's say that progressivism did regard all identity groups as morally equal. Even if that were the case, progressivism still does not view all group members as deserving of equal moral regard *within* their respective group. Rather, in utilitarian fashion, its operating principle is to seek the greatest good for the greatest number of the identity group, which can, if necessary, exclude the good of individuals within the same group.

Perhaps the most conspicuous examples of this dimension of progressivism appear in racial politics. In a recent recall election in the state of California, for example, black attorney, author, political pundit, and widely listened to radio talk show host Larry Elder challenged the white governor of California, Gavin Newsom, who, in addition to serving as governor, owns a winery in the Napa Valley. Larry Elder grew up in a poor neighborhood. Gavin Newsom did not. Larry Elder experienced overt racial discrimination during his life, including during his campaign (a white woman in a gorilla mask threw an egg at Elder while he was walking in public). Gavin Newsom did not. Gavin Newsom

10. "2019 Hate Crime Statistics: Victims," FBI website, https://ucr.fbi.gov /hate-crime/2019/topic-pages/victims.

11. See, for example, Melissa Block and Jerome Socolovsky, "Antisemitism Spikes, And Many Jews Wonder: Where Are Our Allies?" NPR, June 7, 2021, https://www.npr.org/2021/06/07/1003411933/antisemitism-spikes-and-many-jews -wonder-where-are-our-allies.

had the support of most of the (white) business elite in California and throughout the United States. Larry Elder did not. Using progressive logic, this match-up should have been a no-brainer—a marginalized black man from South Central Los Angeles versus a privileged white man from an elite fourth-generation San Francisco family? Could the right way for progressives to vote in this election be any clearer?

Something interesting happened on the way to the ballot box, however. Progressives did not only attack Larry Elder on ideological grounds. They attacked him on racial grounds. For example, a black female columnist for the *Los Angeles Times* wrote a piece titled "Larry Elder Is the Black Face of White Supremacy."[12] Consider the meaning of this title: it is directly implying that Larry Elder is either a bad person because he supports white supremacy (though he is black) or so dumb and incapable of formulating his own point of view that he can be manipulated to embrace positions that go directly against his self-interest as a black man. In other words, Larry Elder is either a self-hating villain or a moron—*not* a competent individual who, weighing different political ideologies, has reached his own reasoned conclusion. This article did not appear in some anonymous blog in the hinterlands of the internet. It was in the *Los Angeles Times*. The widely read political site Politico also ran a piece, written by another black woman, arguing that Larry Elder was harming black people.[13]

This tendency to attack members of racial groups that do not toe the progressive ideological line has certainly not been limited to Elder. Other nationally recognized African Americans who have been disparaged for their views on race include intellectual

12. Erika D. Smith, "Column: Larry Elder is the Black face of white supremacy," *Los Angeles Times*, August 20, 2021, https://www.latimes.com/california/story/2021-08-20/recall-candidate-larry-elder-is-a-threat-to-black-californians.

13. Erin Aubry Kaplan, "Opinion: The Off-Mic Moment That Changed My View of Larry Elder," *Politico*, September 9, 2021, https://www.politico.com/news/magazine/2021/09/09/larry-elder-debate-radio-california-republican-510563.

and author Thomas Sowell, political commentator Candace Owens, sports journalist Jason Whitlock, Supreme Court Justice Clarence Thomas, former Secretary of State Condoleezza Rice, and politicians Tim Scott, Winsome Sears, Allen West, and Ben Carson, among many others. What unites these and many other instances is that progressive racial politics includes these individuals as belonging to the "black community" only until they say or do something with which the "community" disagrees, at which point they are jettisoned in the name of the community. This willingness to sacrifice members of the group is typical of the utilitarian calculation of "aggregate well-being." All progressivism does is remove "aggregate" from society as a whole and apply it to the group as a whole. And voilà: you get an unquestionably highly accomplished black man being demeaned as a "white supremacist" because he challenges progressive racial politics and thereby threatens the identity group's political goals.[14]

The second feature of utilitarianism detectable in progressivism is the construal of morality in terms of a feelings-based "virtue." Recall that utilitarianism, because of its rejection of rationally necessary moral principles, locates the foundation of morality in the sentiments. As we'll see in the subsequent section,

14. This casting off of inconvenient representatives from an identity group when they undermine the group's political power has also taken place in the "Me Too" movement. One of the movement's mantras is "Believe all women," which activists employed to attempt to derail the nomination of Supreme Court Justice Brett Kavanaugh, nominated by then President Donald Trump, on the grounds that he had sexually assaulted a woman at a party while in high school. A thorough Congressional investigation, however, determined that there was no credible evidence such an event ever happened. Yet many "Me Too" activists maintained that Justice Kavanaugh should be disqualified from serving nevertheless, claiming that they "believed" his accuser. During the 2020 presidential election, on the other hand, then Democratic/Progressive candidate Joe Biden was also accused of sexual assault, with, unlike in Kavanaugh's case, some corroborating evidence supporting the allegation. With only a few exceptions, however, the "Me Too" movement refused to support Biden's female accuser—that is, they refused to "believe all women." See, for example, Catherine Cherkasky, "'Believe all women'? Now that Reade has accused Joe Biden of sexual assault, never mind," *USA Today*, April 29, 2020, https://www.usatoday.com/story/opinion/2020/04/29/joe-biden-tara-reade-sexual-assault-allegation-me-too-column/3040158001/.

progressivism, like utilitarianism, also rejects the existence of rationally necessary moral principles (though, unlike utilitarianism, it rejects empiricism as well). Through a process of elimination, there is, therefore, only one source left to generate moral principles: feelings. However, whereas utilitarian philosopher David Hume identifies universal benevolence as the feeling that defines morality and consequently the supreme human virtue, progressivism, in its signature appropriate-and-mutate style, embraces the feeling of *particularistic* benevolence. Likewise, whereas Hume defined virtue as performing actions that serve the good of humanity, progressive politics defines virtue as performing actions that serve the good of a particular group. To be good thus means demonstrating, to yourself and to others, that you have the right kinds of feelings for the right kinds of groups.

This public display—indeed, *performance*—of sentimental morality lies at the heart of "virtue-signaling." To virtue-signal is to make a public display of solidarity with an identity group by, for example, putting a black square on your Instagram profile, wearing a knitted pink hat putatively in the shape of female genitals, serving LGBTQIA+-positive rainbow Oreo cookies at a children's party, or putting a protective talisman-like sign in your front yard advertising your household's progressive values. Making these public displays does not produce any concrete improvements for anyone, but it does demonstrate that you are either a member of or an ally to a politically favored identity group and, as such, are one of the "good people." This may sound far from Hume's insistence that morality entails virtue and virtue entails benevolence, but progressivism agrees with Hume (and utilitarianism more broadly) that the foundation of morality and politics lies not in the head but in the heart. As a bonus to its political aims, progressivism can consequently accuse its detractors not of having the wrong ideas, but rather of having a bad heart (that is, having the wrong kind of feelings)—or, better yet, being "full of hate."

Postmodernism

Postmodernism is famously difficult to define because postmodernism rejects the existence of objectively true definitions. It is a body of beliefs that rejects the existence of true beliefs. It is a system of thought that rejects the existence of all systems. In short, postmodernism is thoroughly self-refuting. However, if there is one thing that contemporary politics in the US and beyond has taught us, unapologetic incoherence in no way precludes a way of thinking from becoming massively influential. Such is the case with postmodernism, a once obscure academic theory[15] that progressivism has fed off, altered, and made politically mainstream.

To understand postmodernism we can, in the spirit of postmodernism, begin with a linguistic analysis. Postmodernism supersedes modernism, the "post" meaning coming after. But what, then, does modernism mean? Philosophers can spend their whole careers burrowing into the nuances within and relationships between intellectual movements because they are, indeed, complex. However, modernism tends to refer to the thought of the Enlightenment, which, in turn, is composed of three main strands: (1) the deistic classical metaphysics of thinkers like Voltaire, Gottfried Leibniz, and Thomas Jefferson, (2) the non-metaphysical rationalism of thinkers like Immanuel Kant, and (3) the non-metaphysical empiricism of thinkers like David Hume. These three schools of thought profoundly disagree with each other on the question of the nature of existence, including human existence. Yet all agree that human reason has the capacity to provide rationally true answers to those questions.

---

15. Like most academic theories, postmodernism is internally complex and, as such, challenging to define as one unified whole (especially since postmodernism typically rejects the existence of "unified wholes" both definitionally and ontologically). For an excellent summary of the different elements of postmodernism and its relation to similar theories (e.g., "post-structuralism"), see Gary Aylesworth, "Postmodernism," Stanford Encyclopedia of Philosophy, February 5, 2015, https://plato.stanford.edu/entries/postmodernism/.

Indeed, that is what primarily unites them as "Enlightenment" philosophies—they affirm both the existence of universal human reason and the independence of that reason from any kind of biblical conception of God.

This is where the "post" enters the history of ideas, stage left. For all the differences among postmodern theorists, one characteristic that unites them is their categorical rejection of the Enlightenment belief that human reason can provide any objectively true insight into the nature of existence and human existence, including the nature of human reason itself. While the intellectual genealogy leading to this position is multifaceted, it passes through a turn to the study of human language and how, according to postmodernists, "language," and especially the content of language, is not an inherent and universally shared characteristic of humanity but rather a socially constructed phenomenon that is generated by those in the linguistic community who hold the most power over others. You can probably already see a postmodern origin-story syllogism forming here (even though postmodernism rejects the validity of syllogisms). It goes something like this:

> Premise 1: Rationality is the product of human language.
>
> Premise 2: Human language is a social construction.
>
> Conclusion: Therefore, rationality is the product of a social construction.

Another way of stating this conclusion is to say that rationality is arbitrary. It contains no true objective content and is ultimately only what the powerful say it is. There is no such thing as "truth," only "power." That is postmodernism in a nutshell: the only thing that really exists in any domain of human existence is power.

How and why progressive ideology takes a fancy to postmodernism is likely already becoming apparent, but there are a few more implications to tease out before directly making the connection. First, if it is true that there is no truth, then it is consequently true that there is no moral truth in particular; there is no objective difference between good and bad and right and wrong. Second, given that language is a social rather than individual construction, and control of the language is the ultimate foundation of power, postmodernism has a keen interest not just in power per se but in group power. Third, if it is true that the only thing that is "real" is group power, then everything in human existence—the human individual, the human family, the economy, entertainment, sports, etc.—becomes politicized because the only purpose anything in human life has is gaining or maintaining group power. Fourth, since there is no shared universal rationality that exists beneath or around groups competing for power, the only way to settle a dispute among groups is by exercising dominant power over your group's competitors. To be sure, this does not mean that all disputes must be settled by physical violence; all things considered, it would be better for a group to beat other groups by, for example, getting them to destroy themselves by fomenting internecine strife. That limits if not prevents your own group's casualties while weakening your competitors. Yet since there is no objective good, physical violence to dominate another group is not morally prohibited. Fifth and related, if there is no common rationality among groups, then the only way groups can ally with each other is by (a) offering other groups something they want or (b) identifying a shared enemy that both groups desire to topple because of its perceived dominance. (We will see how this takes the form of "intersectionality" in progressivism below.) Sixth, and finally, any attempt to criticize the actions of one group by another group can be immediately defused by the claim that "This is *our* truth" or "This is *our* lived experience." Since "truth" and "experience" are entirely socially constructed concepts in postmodernism, any group's statement about the nature of reality, morality, politics, etc. cannot be rationally contested by any other group. Whatever a group says is, by definition, true—simply because they say it.

Progressivism adopts all these tenets of postmodern thinking while, as we have seen with other ideologies, rendering them more politically potent. Remember that postmodernism holds that morality is a social construction, which means that any group that claims its vision of morality is "right" should be met, by all other groups, not only with skepticism but with outright denial: no group can be right because no group can be wrong. It's all a wash for postmodernism. Progressive ideology embraces this moral relativism; however, it concurrently adopts a moralistic imperiousness toward all competing political viewpoints, rejecting its critics not only as intellectually mistaken but also, frequently, as corrupt if not depraved. Progressive ideology's mutation of postmodernism, in other words, produces a strange combination of moral nihilism on the one hand (the belief that there are no universal objective moral truths) with chauvinistic moral certainty, on the other hand—the belief that their point of view is intellectually and morally superior to others simply because it is *their* point of view.

This oxymoronic form of thinking permeates contemporary culture in the United States and much of the West. However, one recent instantiation is particularly notable becomes it comes from a US government–funded institution dedicated to educating the American public: the Smithsonian Museum of African American History and Culture. In the summer of 2020, the museum published an infographic titled "Aspects and Assumptions of White Culture and Whiteness in the United States." According to the infographic—which, again, was produced by one of the most influential educational institutions in the world—"whiteness"

> refers to the ways white people and their traditions, attitudes and ways of life have been normalized over time and are now considered standard practices in the United States. And

since white people still hold most of the institutional power in America, we have all internalized some aspects of white culture—including people of color.[16]

Begging the question of how a skin color can intrinsically determine culture (analogously, we could say that height intrinsically determines personality or age intrinsically determines sociability), the document goes on to specify numerous features of "whiteness," including:

- Self-reliance

- Independence & autonomy highly valued + rewarded

- The nuclear family—father, mother, 2.3 children is the ideal social unit

- Wife is homemaker and subordinate to husband

- Objective, rational linear thinking

- Cause and effect relationships

- Hard work is key to success

- No tolerance for deviation from single god concept

- Plan for future

- Progress is always best[17]

First, note here that, according to the Smithsonian, being white means that you are a patriarchal tyrant and religious bigot. (Negative blanket generalizations of racial groups like this used to rightly be considered as "racist.") Yet the statements most relevant

16. Marina Watts, "In Smithsonian Race Guidelines, Rational Thinking and Hard Work Are White Values," *Newsweek*, July 17, 2020, https://www.newsweek.com/smithsonian-race-guidelines-rational-thinking-hard-work-are-white-values-1518333.
17. Watts.

to showing how progressivism appropriates and politicizes post-modernism are that "whiteness" entails engaging in "objective, rational linear" thinking and upholding the belief in "cause and effect relationships." To claim that objective rational thinking and the recognition of cause-and-effect relationships is not universal to all human beings—that it only belongs to a particular group (whites)—is equivalent to claiming that there is no such thing as universally objective human rationality. This assertion confirms the first principle of postmodernism: objective, universal truth does not exist because "truth" is socially constructed. That is precisely what the Smithsonian document is implying in its description of rationality pertaining specifically to whiteness (it also entails the conclusion that non-white people are not rational or capable of rationality, which sounds . . . racist).

However, there is another claim smuggled in here between the lines. If someone says, "I believe that there *is* such a thing as universally objective rationality," then that person, according to the document's logic, is not only mistaken but actually engaged in the act of embracing "whiteness" over and against all other racial groups. In other words, disagreeing with the document on rational grounds makes you a racist in general and a white supremacist in particular.

This is the deviously clever sleight of hand progressivism plays with its use of postmodernism. On the one hand, it denies the existence of objective truth altogether, and on the other hand, it asserts that mere disagreement with that position is a severe moral defect. That leaves the befuddled observer of this ideological ploy with two options: either submit to what the identity group is saying, shut up, and obey or go ahead and use "supremacist rationality" to disagree with the identity group and thereby prove that you are in fact guilty of everything they are accusing you of. In short, thanks to the modified intellectual contributions of postmodernism, progressivism has the rhetorical tools to proclaim, "Heads we win, tails you lose." This feature of progressive ideology makes it exceedingly attractive to those who have a taste for wanting to get other people to do what they say merely because they are saying it—people otherwise known as bullies and tyrants.

Postcolonialism

If classical liberalism/libertarianism, utilitarianism, and post-modernism compose the fragmented head of the progressive ideological Frankenstein, postcolonial theory constitutes its raging heart. Postcolonial theory, like postmodern theory, first emerged within an academic context. Its general scope of inquiry is the examination of how Western nations, including the United States, not only physically colonized other regions of the world through the use of coercion and violence but also, more subtly, "created" the colonized subject. As with postmodernism, the field of postcolonial studies is vast and contains diverse intellectual strands. Yet one name lies at the heart of the theory's substance and spirit: Frantz Fanon (1925–1961).

Fanon was a French West Indian psychiatrist and political theorist who wrote extensively about colonial oppression, especially in the French colony of Algeria in northern Africa before its independence in 1962. Fanon's writings are multifarious, yet they appear to endorse overt physical violence in the name of liberation. For example, he writes at the beginning of his watershed text *The Wretched of the Earth*, "National liberation, national reawakening, restoration of the nation to the people or Commonwealth, whatever the name used, whatever the latest expression, decolonization is always a violent event."[18] It is important to keep this theme of violence in mind when examining postcolonial theory. The reason is because, though not all postcolonial theorists endorse violence, the theory's tacit and

---

18. Frantz Fanon, *The Wretched of the Earth*, trans. Richard Philcox (New York: Grove Press, 1963), 1.

sometimes explicit support of violence in the name of liberation fundamentally distinguishes postcolonialism from other forms of liberative politics, like those we see in the writings of Gandhi or Martin Luther King Jr., who, though also struggling against oppression, categorically rejected violence as a means to freedom. Fanon does not fall into that camp. He is not a pacifist. Indeed, perhaps the most unsettling words of the book come not from Fanon but from the French existentialist philosopher Jean-Paul Sartre, who writes in the book's preface,

> We have all taken advantage of [the colonized], they have nothing to prove, they won't give anyone preferential treatment. A single duty, a single objective: drive out colonialism by every means. . . . [Those who call for non-violence] would do well to read Fanon; he shows perfectly that this irrepressible violence [of the colonized] is neither a storm in a teacup nor the reemergence of savage instincts nor even a consequence of resentment: it is man reconstructing himself. . . . The colonized are cured of colonial neurosis by driving the colonist out by force. . . . Killing a European is killing two birds with one stone, eliminating in one go oppressor and oppressed.[19]

In other words, the Fanonian flavor of postcolonialism is seasoned with the belief that the only way to peace in the face of oppression is through violent revolution. In this sense, then, the argument that Fanon makes is not aimed to persuade the colonizers of their wrongdoing or to assemble a moral case for freedom (again, in contradistinction to Gandhi and Martin Luther King Jr.). It is rather a rallying cry to the colonized to unite and war against their oppressors.

Taken by itself, this willingness to engage in violence in the name of anti-colonial freedom should sound neither foreign nor

---

19. Jean-Paul Sartre, "Preface," in Fanon, *The Wretched of the Earth*, lv.

immoral, especially to an American audience that grounds its political identity in a war of independence from colonial rule. Yet, as is already evident in Sartre's framing of the struggle for liberation, the most morally significant dimension of Fanon's thought, particularly as it relates to progressive ideology, is how it defines the nature of the oppressors and the nature of the oppressed.

For example, to say Fanon's view of humanity is Manichaean—divided, morally and ontologically, into good and evil—is not to impose an extrinsic interpretive framework on his writing. It is to employ the very same category he uses to describe the relationship between the colonizer and the colonized. He writes,

> The colonial world is a Manichaean world. . . . As if to illustrate the totalitarian nature of colonial exploitation, the colonist turns the colonized into a kind of quintessence of evil. Colonized society is not merely portrayed as a society without values. The colonist is not content with stating that the colonized world has lost its values or worse never possessed any. The "native" is declared impervious to ethics, representing not only the absence of values but also the negation of values. He is, dare we say it, the enemy of values. In other words, absolute evil.[20]

This is a summation of Fanon's rejection of both the colonial world and the colonist: the fundamental problem is that *they*, the colonizers, define *us*, the colonized, as evil incarnate. The fitting response, however, is not to proclaim a common humanity and seek to break down the wall between oppressor and oppressed. It is, rather, to reverse the Manichaean polarity, to flip the terms, to make the bad guys the good guys and the good guys the bad

20. Fanon, 6.

guys, which, in turn, morally justifies the oppressors' (the new bad guys) complete physical annihilation. As Fanon writes,

> To blow the colonial world to smithereens is henceforth a clear image within the grasp and imagination of every colonized subject. To dislocate the colonial world does not mean that once the borders have been eliminated there will be a right of way between the two sectors. To destroy the colonial world mean[s] nothing less than demolishing the colonist's sector, burying it deep within the earth or banishing it from the territory.[21]

It is crucial to highlight that, in this struggle for liberation—which Fanon clearly frames not as a battle of ideas but as the physical eradication of colonizers from a geographic territory—there is, consistent with Manichaean philosophy, no middle ground, no room for dissenting voices, indeed, no room for mercy. You are one of us or one of them; and if you are not with us, you are against us:

> The collective struggle presupposes collective responsibility from the rank and file and a collegial responsibility at the top. Yes, everyone must be involved in the struggle for the sake of the common salvation. There are no clean hands, no innocent bystanders. We are all in the process of dirtying our hands in the quagmire of our soil and the terrifying void of our minds. Any bystander is a coward or a traitor.[22]

The use of religious language here is revealing—not only about how Fanon perceives the postcolonial enemy, the oppressors, but also how he views himself and his fellow revolutionaries: to wit,

21. Fanon, xx.
22. Fanon, 140.

Fanon and his acolytes see the colonized as objects of salvation and themselves as their redeemers. This may sound hyperbolic, but Fanon does not shy away from establishing himself and his fellow "African politicians," as he refers to them, as they who must remake the colonized into their own image and likeness and thereby "humanize" them. He writes,

> Our greatest task is to constantly understand what is happening in our own countries. We must not cultivate the spirit of the exceptional or look for the hero, another form of leader. We must elevate the people, expand their minds, equip them, differentiate them, and humanize them.[23]

Elsewhere, Fanon claims that the de-colonial project is no less than "creating a new man" that, moreover, is a product of the new "nation," which is a product of intellectuals like Frantz Fanon: "When the nation in its totality is set in motion, the new man is not an a posteriori creation of this nation, but coexists with it, matures with it, and triumphs with it."[24] The (de)colonized, in other words, are not individuals. They are a (de)humanized mass, one that is either oppressed by the colonizers or liberated by the de-colonizers. Either way, the masses are never to be thought of as independently thinking individuals who are capable of coming to their own conclusions using their own inherent rational capacities. It is evil that the oppressed belong to the colonizers, says Fanonian postcolonial theory—let us free them by fashioning them into a new people, a new nation, that will be gloriously led by us (me). In other words, with a hat tip to the classic rock band The Who, we could summarize postcolonialism in relation to the colonialized subjects it seeks to save: meet the new boss, *same as the old boss.*

23. Fanon, 137.
24. Fanon, 233.

As with the previous theories, progressive ideology adopts the major moral and epistemological tenets of postcolonial theory while once again applying its signature modifications to make the ideology more politically potent. In this case, progressivism makes two alterations to postcolonialism: (1) while it preserves the Manichaean distinction between them (evil) and us (good), it generalizes the historically specific conflict between "the colonizers" and "the colonized" into the ongoing conflict between "the oppressors" and "the oppressed"; and (2) while it preserves the belief that there is an enlightened class of liberators that uniquely holds the true knowledge about the nature of oppression and the way to overcome it, it redefines the criteria for enlightenment from being a university-educated intellectual, like Frantz Fanon, to simply having the right kind of self-proclaimed "lived experience."

These two progressive modifications of postcolonial theory are palpable in the contemporary Black Lives Matter movement or, as it is frequently referred to, "BLM." It is vital to emphasize that I am analyzing and critiquing the political action organization "Black Lives Matter" in this section, not the substance of the words "Black lives matter." Indeed, having to make a disclaimer like this—clarifying that, like all Catholics and people of good will, I unequivocally support the substance of the statement "Black lives matter"—has been one of the cunningly clever tools that BLM, the advocacy group, has employed to shield itself from criticism: for those inclined by fear, self-interest, and/or cynicism, the charge can be made—and, indeed, has repeatedly been made—that critiquing BLM is tantamount to critiquing the statement "Black lives matter," which would imply that the critic is a racist and, therefore, can be denounced and removed from mainstream society as a moral pariah. This strategy is one of the bluntest yet most destructive in BLM's arsenal. Unfortunately, it's effective, or at least it has been. Yet it remains the case that it is a lie—it is, indeed, possible to champion the equal dignity of all black individuals while criticizing the organization "Black Lives Matter" as a progressive appropriation of postcolonialism, which is exactly what this section intends to do.

The Black Lives Matter movement is largely decentralized both in the United States and globally, mostly operating on a localized franchise model. However, it maintains a central organizational website that states the movement's aims (which once included to "disrupt the Western-prescribed nuclear family structure"[25]), keeps tabs on relevant issues in the news (always covered from a racial angle), highlights opportunities to support the movement, and sells official Black Lives Matter™ merchandise. Under "About BLM," the site offers this description of its mission and purpose:

> We are expansive. We are a collective of liberators who believe in an inclusive and spacious movement. We also believe that in order to win and bring as many people with us along the way, we must move beyond the narrow nationalism that is all too prevalent in Black communities. We must ensure we are building a movement that brings all of us to the front. . . . We affirm our humanity, our contributions to this society, and our resilience in the face of deadly oppression.[26]

This statement captures how contemporary progressive identity politics expands the postcolonial "colonizer" vs. "colonized" dichotomy into a broader, indeed global, "oppressor" vs. "oppressed" dichotomy. Moreover, the oppressors are no longer specific nations and their policies; rather, for BLM, the catch-all oppressor is "white supremacy" and those who enable it. As the

25. See, for example, Joseph A. Wulfsohn, "Black Lives Matter removes 'What We Believe' website page calling to 'disrupt . . . nuclear family structure'," Fox News, September 21, 2020, https://www.foxnews.com/media/black -lives-matter-disrupt-nuclear-family-website.

26. "About BLM," Black Lives Matter website, https://blacklivesmatter.com /about/.

mission statement says, this is not a national issue but rather an international, borderless struggle for liberation. In other words, BLM globalizes postcolonialism.

Yet what is the precise meaning of white supremacy, and where is it located specifically? Despite a concrete history of actual white supremacists in the United States (like the Ku Klux Clan) and a legacy of laws that explicitly discriminated against black people (like forcing them to sit on the back of the bus, attend different schools, and even drink from different water fountains), it is not easy to get a concrete answer to this question from the Black Lives Matter movement. The reason is because BLM has also adopted and modified the postcolonial insistence that epistemic authority belongs to the oppressed identity group and the oppressed identity group alone. Consequently, Black Lives Matter endows itself with the authority to define racism however it chooses—and that definition can shape-shift according to the group's political goals.

A recent case helpfully crystallizes this form of thinking in action. In the winter of 2020, a black actor named Jussie Smollett claimed that he was the victim of a hate crime. He reported to the police and an exceptionally credulous press—which made his story quickly go viral—that two white men wearing red "Make America Great Again" hats jumped him in the middle of a frigid night on the streets of Chicago, beat him up, poured bleach over his head, and then placed a noose around his neck while shouting "This is MAGA country." Despite the fantastical nature of his story, support from numerous celebrities and politicians immediately poured in, including from then-presidential candidates Joe Biden and Kamala Harris (who later became president and vice president respectively). However, the Chicago police conducted a full investigation and not only found no evidence to support Smollett's claims but also discovered that he had orchestrated the attack himself. Despite the Cook County prosecutor initially dropping the charges, the police were eventually able to get a new prosecutor to indict Smollett for filing a false police report, among other related counts. A full trial followed during which the prosecution argued that Smollett had hired two Nigerian brothers to stage the attack with the hopes that it would be filmed by a nearby camera and become a national news story. Smollett was eventually found guilty by a jury of five of the six counts filed against him and eventually spent some time in jail.[27]

Given the incredible nature of the claims and the availability of evidence undermining the veracity of Smollett's story, it was probable from the moment this news first broke that the "attack by white supremacists" did not occur. The trial process proved this initial conclusion beyond any reasonable doubt. Yet this is what the Black Lives Matter website has written about the trial and its outcome, a statement that also calls for the abolition of police:

> [This] is not about a trial or a verdict decided in a white supremacist charade, it's about how we treat our community when corrupt systems are working to devalue their lives. In an abolitionist society, this trial would not be taking place, and our communities would not have to fight and suffer to prove our worth. Instead, we find ourselves, once again, being forced to put our lives and our value in the hands of judges and juries operating in a system that is designed to oppress us, while continuing to face a corrupt and violent police department, which has proven time and again to have no respect for our lives. . . . In our commitment to abolition, we can never believe police, especially the Chicago Police Department (CPD) over Jussie Smollett, a Black man who has been courageously present, visible, and vocal in the struggle for Black freedom.[28]

27. Rasha Ali, "Jussie Smollett found guilty of 5 counts of staging racist, anti-gay attack in Chicago, lying to police," *USA Today*, December 9, 2021, https://www.usatoday.com/story/entertainment/2021/12/09/jussie-smollett-guilty-verdict-orchestrating-attack/8838114002/.

28. "Statement Regarding the Ongoing Trial of Jussie Smollett," Black Lives Matter website, https://blacklivesmatter.com/statement-regarding-the-ongoing-trial-of-jussie-smollett/.

The statement does not provide any evidence for its claim that the trial was defined by white supremacy. It does not provide any evidence that the police investigation was corrupt. It does not provide any evidence for how the system is "designed to oppress us." Instead, it makes the sheer assertion that "we can never believe the police over Jussie Smollett." In other words, we believe what we believe because we believe it and that is the only explanation you will get.

This is a paradigmatic example of the "lived experience" epistemology that defines both BLM and progressive ideology more generally. In a fusion of postmodernism (there is no objective truth and thus no objectively true description of events) and postcolonialism (true knowledge is limited to the oppressed and their self-proclaimed representatives), progressivism destroys the possibility of objective truth with one hand and reconstitutes it in the image and likeness of an identity group's "experiences" with the other. This is, of course, self-contradictory; it is incoherent to deny the existence of objective truth out of one side of your mouth while claiming that one's experiences are true (and should have universal moral authority) out of the other. However, progressivism views the maxims "Try to be coherent" or "Try not to contradict yourself," recall from the previous section, as particularist ("white") forms of thinking that cannot and should not be applied to all groups. All that matters morally and politically is what the representative of the identity group says the group experiences; and the only standard of truth that can be applied to evaluate those experiences is the experiences themselves. It is an impossibly closed, self-justifying epistemic circle whose authority is impervious to anyone deemed outside the identity group—and as we saw above, the identity group has full authority over who is in and who is outside that group.

Thus, a student claiming she was the victim of racism because a janitor asked her why she was in a restricted area of campus is, by definition, a victim of racism, despite a 35-page report that finds zero evidence of discrimination.[29] A teenage boy waiting for a bus after attending a pro-life rally in Washington, DC, can become the viral face of white privilege and white supremacy merely by standing still as a Native American man, without any provocation, approaches and bangs a drum close to his face.[30] Numerous members of a college lacrosse team can be accused of rape, publicly denounced by their own university, and persecuted by a corrupt local prosecutor despite there being easily accessible and completely exonerating evidence nearly from the moment the accusations were first made.[31] These events, all of which became national news stories in the United States, only had the traction they did because they were seen through the epistemic lens of progressive identitarian politics: If a member of a favored identity group says something is true, it must be true no matter what the facts are. Indeed, for progressivism there is no such thing as a category of objective facts. It is all experience all the time.

To be sure, none of this means that there are not in fact real hate crimes motivated by real prejudice. All of them should be thoroughly investigated and prosecuted to the full extent of the law if the evidence supports the accusation. Yet that's precisely the problem with progressive identitarian epistemology—even asking for evidence is interpreted as a form of racism (or homophobia, or transphobia, etc.). Indeed, this is one of the basic premises underlying the concept of "white fragility." Robin DiAngelo, the white female author of a book entitled *White Fragility: Why It's So Hard for White People to Talk about Racism*—which has sold hundreds of thousands of copies—argues that white people who either deny

29. Jackie Salo, "Probe finds Smith College student was not victim of racism for 'eating while black,'" *New York Post*, February 25, 2021, https://nypost.com /2021/02/25/smith-college-student-was-not-victim-of-racism-probe-finds/.

30. Chauncey DeVega, "White victimology, white privilege and the Covington Catholic rules of race," *Salon*, January 25, 2019, https://www.salon.com/2019/01/25 /white-victimology-white-privilege-and-the-covington-catholic-rules-of-race/.

31. Ashe Schow, "Ten years after Duke Lacrosse rape hoax, media has learned nothing," Washington Examiner, March 14, 2016, https://www.washingtonexaminer .com/ten-years-after-duke-lacrosse-rape-hoax-media-has-learned-nothing.

they are racist or ask for evidence showing their racism are, in these very acts, proving that they are indeed racist. She writes,

> Habitus maintains our social comfort and helps us regain it when those around us do not act in familiar and acceptable ways. . . . Thus, white fragility is a state in which even a minimum amount of racial stress in the habitus becomes intolerable, triggering a range of defensive moves.[32]

"Habitus," for DiAngelo, means the status quo for white people (a.k.a. not casually being accused of racism or of supporting a system of white supremacy). Responding to these accusations with statements like "No, I do not believe I am a racist" or "No, I do not believe that I am perpetuating systemic racism" or "No, I don't believe that being 'colorblind' is an idea that advances white supremacy" counts, from DiAngelo's point of view, as a defensive move that confirms your "white fragility"—which means that you are simply unwilling to recognize how racist you actually are. In other words, if you have pale skin and you deny that you are perpetuating systemic racism, the only reason you could possibly be doing so is because you are in denial—not because you have thought carefully about the proposition and find it to be false. DiAngelo thus offers her white readers two options: either (a) unquestionably accept everything that I am saying about you and thereby admit that you are in fact racist or (b) critically question what I am saying (that is, "become defensive") and thereby demonstrate that you are in fact racist. It is precisely in this Catch-22 that we see the progressive epistemic and moral pattern repeated once again: Heads I win, tails you lose.

Setting aside the fact that DiAngelo has come under fire from many black individuals who find her to be, in the words of the

---

32. Robin DiAngelo, *White Fragility: Why It's So Hard for People to Talk about Racism* (Boston: Beacon Press, 2018), 103.

prominent black academic John McWhorter, "a well-intentioned but tragically misguided pastor [who teaches] how to be racist in a whole new way,"[33] the most important takeaway is to recognize how her ideas capture the progressive impulse, adapted from post-colonialism, to bestow "true" moral knowledge only on those who have the right kinds of "experience." Now, in DiAngelo's case, she is a white woman and so cannot plausibly claim that she has the experiences of people of color (though that hasn't stopped others from trying);[34] her relevant lived experience, however, the token that purchases her moral authority on racial issues, is her work as a "diversity trainer" for businesses and organizations, teaching their white employees how to stop being racist, a job that has awakened her to just how big the problem is—so big, in fact, that it is everywhere all the time. As she writes, "As African American scholar and filmmaker Omowale Akintunde says: 'Racism is a systemic, societal, institutional, omnipresent, and epistemologically embedded phenomenon that pervades every vestige of our reality.'"[35] DiAngelo can see this omnipresent evil. And to anyone with pale skin who agrees with her, she says: congratulations for admitting you're an open racist who perpetuates a system of white supremacy. But if you happen to see things differently, if you happen to have an alternative view of the current nature of and solution to the problem of racial discrimination, DiAngelo offers this gentle advice: buy my book and take my course now before anyone begins suspecting that you don't believe that you, personally, are perpetuating white supremacy—which, according

33. John McWhorter, "The Dehumanizing Condescension of *White Fragility*," *The Atlantic*, July 15, 2020, https://www.theatlantic.com/ideas/archive/2020/07/dehumanizing-condescension-white-fragility/614146/.

34. A white woman named Rachel Dolezal became a national news story when it was discovered that she had been publicly identifying as a black woman and had even served as the president of a local chapter of the NAACP. See Kirk Johnson, "Rachel Dolezal, in Center of Storm, Is Defiant: 'I Identify as Black,'" *New York Times*, June 16, 2015, https://www.nytimes.com/2015/06/17/us/rachel-dolezal-nbc-today-show.html.

35. DiAngelo, *White Fragility*, 72.

to the experts, is the most racist thing of all. Trust in your own reason and moral integrity at your own peril.

This dimension of progressive ideology, possessing a distinctive set of morally authoritative experiences or recognizing others' morally authoritative experiences (a.k.a., "being an ally"), also helps explain the relationship between progressivism and, in contemporary parlance, "being woke." Although the term has a complex history and contested contemporary uses, it captures a basic disposition to morality and politics that has its roots in the progressive adaptation of postcolonial epistemology. As we see from both the Black Lives Matter website and the writings of Robin DiAngelo, being "woke" does not merely mean "paying attention"; rather, it means seeing things from the perspective of those who have deemed themselves to be morally authoritative on questions of morality and politics—and not asking any questions. For example, those who look at everything from the premise that, as DiAngelo has asserted, "racism is the foundation to the society we are in"[36] are "awake"; they see things the right way—namely, that everything around you is racist except the people who are telling you that everything around you is racist. Conversely, those who do not see things this way are morally and politically asleep and therefore blind to the true nature of moral and political reality. Again, this may sound like a contradiction; if there is no such thing as universally objective moral truth, then how could one identity group's description of morality be seen as any more authoritative than any other description? But if you are thinking those thoughts, that just means you're not woke enough. In sum, to be woke means to stop asking questions like "What is actually going on here?" or "Is anything I'm being told actually true?" and to start asking questions like "What's the most efficient way to get what we (from the perspective of the identity group) or

36. Ari Shapiro, "'There Is No Neutral': 'Nice White People' Can Still Be Complicit in a Racist Society," NPR, June 9, 2020, https://www.npr.org/2020/06/09/873375416 /there-is-no-neutral-nice-white-people-can-still-be-complicit-in-a-racist-society.

they (from the perspective of an 'ally') want?" In other words, being woke means anesthetizing your inner critically thinking philosopher while supplying your inner political strategist with a steady stream of morally sanctifying, self-justifying Red Bull. You'll never rest again.

SUMMARIZING THE GREAT AWOKENING: NOISY INCOHERENCE IN THE SERVICE OF GROUP POWER

This is not an exhaustive list of the ideologies that progressivism has appropriated. There is no limiting principle to Mx. Frankenstein's ambling across the ideological landscape and gobbling up of anything that will make progressive politics more powerful. A complete list of all the ideological scraps pressed in progressivism would also include Marxism, sundry forms of socialism, the sociopolitical theory of Jean-Jacques Rousseau, Jacobinism, Romanticism, a potpourri of "critical theories" (e.g., critical race theory, queer theory, feminist theory), and a dash of Nietzschean will-to-power nihilism for good measure. Indeed, seeking to provide a comprehensive summary of progressivism is like trying to get a hundred unruly children to look in the same way and keep their eyes open long enough to take a decent picture. Good luck.

With that disclaimer in place, however, here is my hazarding of such a summary.[37] Progressive ideology is defined by the following features.

Experientially Based Epistemologies: Progressive ideology tends to derive its ideas from the self-reported "lived experiences" of individuals the theory deems to be representative of a politically favored group. Often, the ideology will assert that "rational objectivity" and "epistemic universality" (the belief that all human beings can potentially apprehend and assent to a shared truth)

---

37. Some of this section comes from material adapted from my chapter "Wokeness and Social Justice," in *The New Apologetics*, ed. Matthew Nelson (Park Ridge, IL: Word on Fire Institute, 2022), 238–242.

are social constructs employed to oppress the groups for whom progressivism is advocating. This epistemology is evident in the claim "We are speaking our truth." The ideology also often holds that any dissenting members of an identity group—for example, a person of color who disagrees with some or all tenets of critical race theory—are not "real" or "authentic" representatives because they have adopted "the oppressor's" point of view. Moreover, since experience cannot be falsified (there is no way to ascertain whether an experience is true or not using experience alone), those outside the identity groups have no rational mechanism to challenge the ideology's epistemic content.

Group Control of Language and Logic: Precisely because progressive ideology tends to eschew rational objectivity and, by extension, a commitment to universally intelligible language, it tries to advance its goals by imbuing words and statements with whatever meaning the identity groups believe will best advance their political interests. The ideology's creation of "in group" language intended for "out group" consumption often results in contradictory claims (e.g., "Colorblindness is racism," "Property destruction is peaceful protest," "All lives matter is bigotry," or as "antiracism" activist Ibram X. Kendi has asserted, "The only remedy to racist discrimination is antiracist discrimination,"[38] which is another way of saying that racial discrimination is both unjust and just at the same time).

A Tendency to Generate Neologisms: Relatedly, progressive ideology frequently generates words and slogans whose meaning is entirely dependent on the will of the identity group yet whose moral authority must be obeyed by those outside the group. Examples include "love is love," "non-binary," "misgendering," "unconscious bias," "mansplaining, "cultural appropriation," "believe all women," "white/male privilege," "patriarchy," "heteronormativity," "cisnormativity," "dead naming," "silence is

---

38. Ibram X. Kendi, *How to Be an Antiracist* (New York: One World, 2019), 19.

violence," "microaggression," "Latinx," "equity," "birthing person," "allyship," "whitewash," "queer bating," "pansexual," "toxic masculinity," "intersectionality," and "gender-affirming care," among *many* others. Questioning the meaning, coherence, or selective applicability of these terms can generate the charge that one has a "phobia" or is motivated by "hate."

A Conflation of Opposing Viewpoints with "Harm" and "Danger": Again, because progressivism tends to reject rational standards of truth, falsity, and coherence as tools for advancing their positions, the only principle to which they can appeal to criticize competing viewpoints and advance their own is "safety." Progressivism thus frequently tags speech with which it disagrees as "unsafe," which, in turn, generates a moral imperative to "be protected" from that speech—which means silencing the speaker or speakers.

Focused on Attaining Power: Progressive ideology tends to reduce all forms of knowledge to an assessment of "power dimensions," specifically construed as identifying (a) which group is most dominant in society and (b) how to oust that group from its sociopolitical perch. In this sense, progressivism is mercantilist in nature; it asserts there is a fixed, limited supply of power in the world, and if one group has it, that means it has been stolen from another group. It also tends to interpret all empirically observable inequalities among groups (as *they* define "group") as ipso facto evidence of oppression. Moreover, the existence of people who question the causal relationship between "oppression" and "inequality" is, for progressivism, itself dispositive evidence that the "system" is oppressive.

Offer Catch-22 "Solutions": Progressivism tends to offer "out group" individuals a Catch-22 scenario: either (a) submit to our demands and thereby admit that you are in fact an oppressor or (b) refuse our demands and thereby reveal that you are in fact an oppressor because your refusal to admit your guilt proves you are an agent of the oppressive system. The two options are redolent of the late medieval practice of "witch testing": if the accused woman cast into the water by the mob submitted and drowned, she was no longer a communal threat and thus could be counted as "on *our* side"; if, however, she struggled and survived, her very resistance proved she was "on *their* side"—and needed to be punished.

INTERSECTIONALISTS UNITE!

Reading this summary, it may be difficult to comprehend how such a hodgepodge of disparate assertions could ever fit a unified body of beliefs that could be accurately described as a single ideology. To be sure, these elements by themselves, like fragments of different puzzles tossed together into a single box, cannot and will not fit together on their own. They need a binding agent, a political glue, to hold them all together. That glue takes the name of the final characteristic of progressivism: intersectionality. "Intersectionality" recognizes overlapping interests among different identity groups. So, for example, a feminist-racialist identity group could find a common cause with (i.e., intersect with) a feminist sexual-orientation identity group on the issue of, say, access to abortion, free medical care, or federal employment law. However, it is important to keep in mind, given progressivism's underlying particularist epistemology, that any agreement among identity groups is accidental in nature, meaning it just happens to be the case that the groups have a common interest. There cannot be shared rational agreement on anything because there is no such thing as universally shared rationality.

This framework, however, immediately generates problems: How do identity groups handle situations in which there is a conflict of group interests? For example, say one identity group believes that its members should get X number of seats on a corporate board while another identity group believes that *its* members should have the same number (or more). Since negotiation based on rationally objective principles is not an option, what is the alternative to (physical) confrontation? Intersectionality lights the way forward: competing identity groups can pause the fighting among themselves and turn their opprobrium to a common "oppressor." If the cooperative of identity groups can take out this shared threat to their interests, then that will open more opportunities (e.g., more seats on corporate boards) for all the members of the heretofore competing identity groups.

Once a common enemy is removed, however, the problem of dominance or oppression doesn't go away. It just gets shifted to a new set of players in a game that everyone who is committed to identity politics cannot *not* play and yet can never win, because the logic of intersectionality permits a limitless permutation of identity groups, each with equal authority to claim that the interests of their group trump all others because they say so. In the end, the only alternative left to settle disputes among identity groups is thus the old-fashioned one: the threat of violence and ultimately violence itself. The shadow side of "Diversity, Equity, and Inclusion," in other words, is "Destruction, Elimination, and Implosion." It is a fitting mantra for an ideology that promises peace by intentionally and systematically pitting human beings against each other.

(NOT) THINKING IN CIRCLES

With all this background in place, consider how we might go about mapping the different dimensions of progressive ideology on the Thinking in Circles map. Here it is again:

THEOLOGY

ONTOLOGY

ANTHROPOLOGY

EPISTEMOLOGY

MORALITY

APPLIED
MORALITY:
POLITICS

As with Kantianism, the most instructive place to begin mapping the levels of progressivism is in the realm of the epistemological, answering the question "What can I know and how can I know it?" First, note that progressive ideology shifts the "I" to a "we" and then answers, "We know whatever our lived experiences tell us that we know and we are the ones who tell ourselves what our lived experiences are." This claim about knowledge reveals the answer to every other rung on the map. Moving upward/ outward, what is the progressive understanding of human nature? Whatever the identity group says it is, though with the added proviso that human beings are either bad (oppressors) or good (oppressed and *maybe* allies of the oppressed)—and some elite layer of people are *really* good, those progressive saints who have the special insight into which anthropological category everyone else fits. How about the progressive definition of reality (ontology) and ultimate reality/God (theology)? That, too, is defined by whatever the identity group says it is. After all, saying is believing, and believing makes it true.

The same pattern follows when moving inward/downward from epistemology. What, then, is ethics? Whatever the identity group says it is, which means that applied ethics and politics will not only be a product of the group's self-defined interests but also, consequently, be defined by strategic questions about how to get what the group wants most efficiently rather than asking questions like "What, actually, is good?" In sum, the whole progressive worldview emanates from the epistemological core, and that core is defined by what the identity group determines its political interests to be, which, in turn, means that the whole progressive worldview is defined by—wait for it—identity politics.

HOW TO WIN "FRIENDS" AND SILENCE PEOPLE: A SIMPLE FORMULA FOR SUCCESS

One of the questions that arises when exposing progressivism's incoherence is this: How did ideas this asinine become so politically and culturally potent? Although largely a question for future historians, much of progressive ideology's success comes down to implementing a simple formula:

- **Step #1:** Identify a morally obvious position that virtually no one in society would disagree with, for example, "It is bad to hate."

- **Step #2:** Using the powers invested in you by your identity group, redefine the meaning of the terms in the morally obvious position in a way that aligns with your identity group's political interests, for example, "Denying trans women [biological men] the opportunity to compete against biological women in sports is a form of hate."

- **Step #3:** Combine step #1 with step #2. Since society has already rightfully agreed that "hate is bad," you now have those outside your identity group exactly where you want them. By a neat trick of woke logic, they must now support the view that biological men should be allowed to compete in women's sports in order to maintain that "it is bad to hate." If they don't take this position, then they are rejecting that "hate is bad," which implies that they believe that "hate is not bad" or, even, "hate is good." That, in turn, would mean that they are "haters"—and no one wants to be friends with haters or give them a job or let them speak freely online.

- **Step #4:** Repeat steps 1–3 ad infinitum, ad nauseam with any other combination of a generally held moral view and a redefinition of the terms of that view. Watch people squirm then comply.

Here are more examples of this rhetorical strategy, which could also be described as the weaponization of moral language:

1. Weaponizing "Discrimination"

Morally obvious position: Discrimination is morally bad.

Progressive redefinition of terms: "Failing to give favorable treatment to someone on the grounds of her/his/[invented possessive pronoun] race, ethnicity, gender, or sexual preference is a form of discrimination."

Progressive reformulation of the original position: Failing to give favorable treatment to someone on the grounds of her/his/[invented possessive pronoun] race, ethnicity, gender, or sexual preference is morally bad.

The trick: To disagree with this reformulation means that you disagree with the position that "discrimination is bad," which implies that you believe that discrimination is morally acceptable—which means, in turn, that you are a bigot.

The win: People will say they support giving favorable treatment to individuals based on their race, ethnicity, gender, or sexual preference to avoid being called a "bigot."

2. Weaponizing "Social Justice"

Morally obvious position: Social justice is morally good.

Progressive redefinition of terms: "Permitting and celebrating the destruction of public and private property is a form of social justice."

Progressive reformulation of the original position: It is morally good to permit and celebrate the destruction of public and private property.

The trick: To disagree with this reformulation means that you disagree with the position that "social justice is morally good," which implies that you are *against* social justice and *for* social injustice—in other words, you are an oppressor.

The win: People will say they support the destruction of public and private property to avoid being called "an oppressor."

3. Weaponization of "Mental Health"

Morally obvious position: Good mental health entails not having a phobia (an irrational fear).

Progressive redefinition of terms: "Believing that marriage only pertains to the union of one biological woman and one biological man, also known as traditional marriage, is homophobia (an irrational fear)."

Progressive reformulation of the original position: Good mental health entails rejecting the belief that marriage only pertains to the union of one biological woman and one biological man, also known as traditional marriage.

The trick: to disagree with this reformulation means that you disagree that good mental health entails not having a phobia, which implies either (a) you are ignorant and/or mentally ill because you do not understand what defines good mental health or (b) you are *against* good mental health—in other words, you are a bad person (for who else would be against mental health?).

The win: People will say that they reject traditional marriage to avoid being charged with having a phobia (that is, being mentally ill) and/or being an ignoramus and/or bad person.

4. Weaponization of "Black Lives Matter"

Morally obvious position: Supporting the belief that "black lives matter" is morally good.

Progressive redefinition of terms: "Believing that black lives matter entails supporting the defunding and dismantling of police departments."

Progressive reformulation of the original position: Supporting the defunding and dismantling of police departments is morally good.

The trick: To disagree with this reformulation means that you disagree that the belief "black lives matter" is morally good, which means that you believe that black lives do not matter, which means you are a racist.

The win: People will say they support the defunding and dismantling of police departments to avoid being called a racist.

In short, with this formula, any term can be redefined to align with the identity group's desires. That even includes the definition of "violence," as is evident in this progressive syllogism:

Premise 1: Violence should always be outlawed.

Premise 2: Some speech is violence to its hearers.

Conclusion: Some speech should be outlawed.

In other words, by getting people to accept the redefinition of "speech" as an act of "violence," you can, in short order, get them nodding approvingly, even enthusiastically, in support of legally outlawing some forms of speech. And which forms in particular? The favored identity group gets to choose.

That's how this game works. It is linguistically rigged by design and, as such, *the only way to avoid losing is to refuse to play.* "Not playing," however, is easier said than done, especially as the ideology's anti-logic bleeds into every facet of mainstream culture: when preschool television shows on preschool television networks start showing pride parades hosted by an animated man in drag, when rainbow flags bedeck every corner of your downtown shopping district, when your breakfast cereal box starts preaching about the value of "acceptance," when your boss says that your job depends upon attending diversity trainings, when your social media platform blocks your account for posting biological facts, when you discover that your child's elementary school can report you to Child Protective Services for not supporting her gender transition, then compliance might not sound so bad after all. Indeed, you might begin to wonder whether *you* were the one who was confused in the first place. Maybe treating all people with equal moral regard *is* racist. Maybe talking about fundamental human biology *is* transphobic. Maybe asking for evidence to support an accusation of sexual misconduct *is* misogynistic. Yes, maybe *I am* just as bad as they say I am. Maybe I deserve their opprobrium. In fact, maybe I should be grateful for it, grateful for the opportunity they're giving me to become a better person. Maybe I should thank them. At the very least, I should give them my money. Sure, some might call this emotional abuse in the service of a totalitarian nightmare. But, for me and my house, we will take a knee, raise a fist, and call out all the enemies of progress, starting with the people next door.

(Just please don't hurt us.)

THE CATHOLIC RESPONSE

It has probably become apparent that I find progressive ideology to be a distinctively poisonous form of thinking, which has evoked in me a distinctively forceful, even personal, response. Perhaps I can attribute that to working in higher education for close to a decade. However, I do not intend to condemn the people who call themselves "progressives." As a basic act of respect and charity, it is always important to recognize that, just as people with ill will can hold very good ideas, people with good will can hold very bad ideas. I'll leave it to others to determine whether I have good will or not, but I can certainly say that I have held some very bad ideas over the course of my youth and adulthood, including a brief period in my twenties in which I was (oh man, this hurts to say) *sympathetic* to many progressive ideas. What attracted me to some (not all!) of those ideas then was that they appeared to me to be the only political option that took issues of social justice seriously, both domestically and internationally. In addition to volunteering in some poor urban areas in the United States, I spent a year on a fellowship living in or near even poorer areas in Argentina, India, Poland, and Tanzania with the goal of learning about cross-cultural dimensions of poverty. These experiences taught me two things relatively early in life: (1) the problem of poverty is so immensely complex that it is difficult even to know where to begin in effectively addressing it in a just and durable way; (2) the reality of that complexity does not mean either that nothing should be done or that the whole issue should be left only to altruistic individuals doing good deeds. Moreover, I learned that, personally speaking, just going about my life ignoring, in biblical language, the "cry of the poor" on the grounds that "it's not my problem" is a delusionally self-righteous and callously complacent way to live, one that would lead to my perdition. Looking around, it appeared to me at that time—especially because I was such a poorly catechized Catholic—that the progressives were the only ones who really cared about the problem, and so I started leaning in that direction.

I no longer consider myself a progressive in any way. I believe it to be the most wrongheaded and dangerous of the four ideologies this book considers. But it is also fair to say that there are a great number of people in the progressive movement who are there because they sincerely feel called to act on behalf of a great number of individuals whose suffering could be mitigated if we were to implement better social policies. It is this authentic concern, this recognition of the unnecessary and avoidable suffering of others fused with a desire to do something about it, that unites the Catholic social thought tradition with some—again, not all—basic elements of progressive ideology. Indeed, the Catholic social thought tradition locates the pursuit of social justice at the heart of its comprehensive moral vision. For example, as the *Catechism of the Catholic Church* states as a gloss on the Seventh Commandment, "Thou shall not steal,"

The Church makes a moral judgment about economic and social matters, 'when the fundamental rights of the person or the salvation of souls requires it.' . . . The Church is concerned with the temporal aspects of the common good because they are ordered to the sovereign Good, our ultimate end. She strives to inspire right attitudes with respect to earthly good and in socioeconomic relationships.[39]

And:

Economic life is not meant solely to multiply goods produced and increase profit or power; it is ordered first of all to the service of persons, of the whole man, and of the entire human community. Economic activity, conducted according to its own proper methods, is to be exercised within the limits of the moral order, in keeping with social justice so as to correspond to God's plan for man.[40]

And:

In its various forms—material deprivation, unjust oppression, physical and psychological illness and death—*human misery* is the obvious sign of the inherited condition of frailty and need for salvation in which man finds himself as a consequence of original sin. This misery elicited the compassion of Christ the Savior, who willingly took it upon himself and identified himself with the least of his brethren. Hence, those who are oppressed by poverty are the object of a *preferential love* on the part of the Church, which, since her origin and in spite of the failings of many of her members, has not ceased to work for

39. *Catechism of the Catholic Church* 2420.
40. *CCC* 2426.

their relief, defense, and liberation through numerous works of charity which remain indispensable always and everywhere.[41]

And here is one of many examples of the Church speaking against the evils of racism and all other unjust forms of discrimination. Pope Benedict XVI stated to the United Nations Conference against "Racism, Racial Discrimination, Xenophobia and Related Intolerance,"

> Firm and concrete action is required at a national and international level, to prevent and eliminate every form of discrimination and intolerance. Above all, an extensive educational effort is needed, which exalts the dignity of the person and safeguards his fundamental rights. The Church, for her part, reaffirms that only the acknowledgement of human dignity created in the image and likeness of God, can constitute a reliable reference point for such a task. From this common origin, in fact, stems a common destiny of humanity that should inspire in one and all a strong sense of solidarity and responsibility. I express my sincere wishes that the Delegates present at the Geneva Conference will work together, in a spirit of dialogue and mutual acceptance, to put an end to every form of racism, discrimination and intolerance, thereby marking a fundamental step toward the affirmation of the universal value of human dignity and rights, in a horizon of respect and justice for every person and nation.[42]

In short, hearing and heeding the cry of the poor and those suffering injustice, in its many forms, is central to the Church's evangelical mission. As Pope Emeritus Benedict XVI explains in his encyclical *Deus Caritas Est* (*God Is Love*), "The Church's

---

41. CCC 2448.
42. Benedict XVI, Regina Caeli Address, April 19, 2009, vatican.va.

deepest nature is expressed in her three-fold responsibility: of proclaiming the word of God (*kerygma-martyria*), celebrating the sacraments (*leitourgia*) and exercising the ministry of charity (*diakonia*). These duties presuppose each other and are inseparable."[43] Catholicism is not Catholicism without its mission to care for the poor, and its mission to care for its poor is incomplete without its pursuit of social justice. In this sense, the Church can ally with progressivism insofar as it works to mitigate human misery and overcome real oppression.

That said, profound differences remain. As in previous chapters, I will summarize and categorize those differences using the "problems" below. As usual, keep in mind the Thinking in Circles map to help understand the contrasts and their implications.

- the problem of truth

- the problem of perfection

- the problem of human dignity

- the problem of moral hierarchies

- the problem of free speech

- the problem of idolatry (which includes the problem of false mutual exclusivities and the problem of too high / too low human nature)

The Problem of Truth

Progressive ideology has a dual problem with telling the truth: it denies that universal objective truth exists yet asserts that the truth claims made by identity groups should apply to all people. So, for example, if an identity group believes that criticism of their values is a form of hate speech, then that lived experience

43. Benedict XVI, *Deus Caritas Est* 25, encyclical letter, December 25, 2005, vatican.va.

is not only true for them but true for everyone else as well. As explained above, this rhetorical move highlights the impossible position progressivism puts people in, particularly those who do not belong to politically favored identity groups. It is ultimately equivalent to the groups having the authority to say, "We believe what we believe because we believe it and you must believe it too, even though you can never understand what we believe (because you do not have our lived experience)." In other words, just do what we say and don't ask any questions. This is tyrannical. It is a virulent form of moral relativism that allows groups to shield their claims from rational scrutiny while concurrently enabling them to be imposed on others.

As I have argued throughout, the Catholic social thought tradition categorically rejects all forms of moral relativism, including the relativistic group epistemologies of progressivism. All moral claims, especially those that apply to the sociopolitical realm, should be open to the most rigorous rational scrutiny possible. Indeed, that is the entire epistemic premise beneath the Church's argument that natural law must lie at the foundation of the political order. The presupposition is that all people, independent of their race, class, sex, etc., can both understand and evaluate the moral principles embedded in natural law. It is precisely for this reason that Martin Luther King Jr., fighting against truly systemic racism on behalf of black Americans, appeals to an objective and universal moral law, even citing St. Thomas Aquinas as he does it:

> How does one determine when a law is just or unjust? A just law is a man-made code that squares with the moral law, or the law of God. An unjust law is a code that is out of harmony with the moral law. To put it in the terms of St. Thomas Aquinas, an unjust law is a human law that is not rooted in eternal and natural law. Any law that uplifts human personality is just. Any law that degrades human personality is unjust. All segregation

statutes are unjust because segregation distorts the soul and damages the personality.[44]

This kind of objective thinking is alien to progressive ideology, yet it is, both philosophically and practically speaking, the only way that claims about social justice can be both universally intelligible and universally morally binding. The Catholic social thought tradition recognizes that, without a floor of objective truth, one group's demands for justice are another group's definition of tyranny.

Indeed, this is precisely what Pope Benedict XVI means when he refers to the "dictatorship of relativism." In a 2011 conversation with journalist Peter Seewald, Benedict says the following about the relationship between relativism, truth, and authentic justice. It is worth quoting at length because his words encapsulate the Catholic view of how and why objective truth is essential and what role it must play in both morality and politics:

> It is obvious that the concept of truth has become suspect. Of course it is correct that it has been much abused. Intolerance and cruelty have occurred in the name of truth. To that extent people are afraid when someone says, "This is the truth," or even "I have the truth." We never have it; at best it has us. No one will dispute that one must be careful and cautious in claiming the truth. But simply to dismiss it as unattainable is really destructive.

> A large proportion of contemporary philosophies, in fact, consist of saying that man is not capable of truth. But viewed in that way, man would not be capable of ethical values, either. Then he would have no standards. Then he would only have

44. Martin Luther King Jr, "Letter from Birmingham Jail," California State University Chico website, https://www.csuchico.edu/iege/_assets/documents/susi-letter-from-birmingham-jail.pdf.

to consider how he arranged things reasonably for himself, and then at any rate the opinion of the majority would be the only criterion that counted. History, however, has sufficiently demonstrated how destructive majorities can be, for instance, in systems such as Nazism and Marxism, all of which also stood against truth in particular.

That is why we must have the courage to dare to say: Yes, man must seek the truth; he is capable of truth. It goes without saying that truth requires criteria for verification and falsification. It must always be accompanied by tolerance, also. But then truth also points out to us those constant values which have made mankind great. That is why the humility to recognize the truth and to accept it as a standard has to be relearned and practiced again.

The truth comes to rule, not through violence, but rather through its own power.[45]

To deny the possibility of objective truth is to deny the possibility of objective morality; and to deny the possibility of objective morality is to make power, and power alone, the arbiter of all disputes. Groups may be able to fight for power and attain it, but without objective truth on their side, their victory will be without any moral merit—and always temporary.

This passage points to another important dimension of the Catholic conception of truth. Benedict recognizes that "one must be careful and cautious in claiming the truth." Truth is indeed fixed, but our pursuit of it must be carried out ever anew in profoundly different cultural and socioeconomic circumstances. Recognizing this relationship between fixity and flexibility,

---

45. Benedict XVI, "The Dictatorship of Relativism," September 12, 2011, https://lst.edu/articles/the-dictatorship-of-relativism-pope-benedict-xvi/.

objectivity and subjectivity, opens a space in the epistemology of Catholic social ethics for, yes, "lived experience." Indeed, there is absolutely no reason why a natural law framework cannot accommodate experience, not in the derivation of its principles—again, those, by definition, must be fixed—but in the *application* of those principles carried out in practicing the virtue of prudence. For example, Catholic social thought derives from the natural law the principle that all workers must be paid a fair wage. That's fixed. But what amount of money plus benefits defines a fair wage? That's dynamic. Indeed, we cannot come to that answer a priori—we have to look around, get a good sense of the economic and cultural landscape. In other words, we have to rely on experience. And not just our own experiences, but the experiences of the many. The experience of "getting a good-paying job" for someone who went to private school in the suburbs and then any ivy league university will likely look very different from the experience of someone who went to an inner-city public school followed by community college. So too with the experience of getting to work every day without a car, or coming from a non-English-speaking household, or getting good grades if you have a learning disability, or looking different from most other people, or having an alcoholic father at home, or having parents who are fighting all the time, or having to sleep in the bathtub to protect yourself from bullets, or spending months on end sleeping in a car because the income from your twelve-hour-a-day job no longer covers the rent, or having to cross a border illegally because you found out the cartels were going to murder you and your family. None of these experiences tell us anything about what is right and wrong, good and bad, at the level of basic moral principles. But we cannot build a just society without taking them into account, without listening to each other and doing the best we can to imagine what it's like to be other people in all of their different circumstances.

The Catholic social thought tradition recognizes both the diversity of human experience and the need to incorporate those experiences into moral and political decision-making. Yet it also maintains that unless these conversations take place within a horizon of fixed, objective, universal moral truths, they won't ultimately be conversations but rather an unintelligible emoting of noise that will inevitably rise into cacophonous shouting and, eventually, violence. To adapt a cliché, politics without the truth is merely war by other means—on its way to an actual war.

The Problem of Perfection

Progressivism tends toward utopianism because it contains no limiting principles either at the level of epistemology (what can be known) or at the level of anthropology (the potential perfectibility of human nature). Because knowledge is determined exclusively by identity groups' lived experience—with the additional proviso that that experiential knowledge must be accepted as unquestionably true by non-group members, particularly if they are deemed to be "oppressors"—identity groups can continually recalibrate their experience to demand ever greater political concessions. For example, despite the fact that there is strong empirically verifiable evidence that the US has made substantial and abiding progress in combatting the evils of racism[46]—and also despite empirical evidence that American police do not, in fact, disproportionally use unjust force against black individuals[47]—the identitarian politics at the heart of progressive ideology take it as a matter of undisputed dogma that American society is as racist as it has ever been.[48] As a consequence of its relativistic view of truth,

46. See, for example, Jason L. Riley, "Race Relations in American Are Better Than Ever," *The Wall Street Journal*, April 27, 2021, https://www.wsj.com/articles /race-relations-in-america-are-better-than-ever-11619561751.

47. See, for example, Martin Kaste, "New Study Says White Police Officers Are Not More Likely to Shoot Minority Suspects," NPR, July 26, 2019, https://www .npr.org/2019/07/26/745731839/new-study-says-white-police-officers-are-not -more-likely-to-shoot-minority-suspe.

48. See, for example, Robin Wright, "To the World, We're Now America the Racist and Pitiful," *The New Yorker*, July 3, 2020, https://www.newyorker.com /news/our-columnists/to-the-world-were-now-america-the-racist-and-pitiful.

progressivism shuts down all avenues of rational scrutiny into the content of its claims and can therefore make unending demands on society to fulfill its limitless vision of social perfection.

This epistemic shape-shifting is dangerous enough on its own; yet combined with the power of progressivism's Manichaean anthropology, all the necessary ingredients for outright totalitarianism fall into place. Within this anthropological paradigm, progressivism tends to divide individuals—whatever personal particularities might define them and whatever actions they may or may not have committed in their lives—into one of two categories: "good" (victim, non-white, non-heterosexual, non-male, non-cisgendered, non-immigrant, etc.) and "bad" (white, heterosexual, cisgendered—which means you identify with the gender you were assigned at birth—native born, etc.). This is not a sensationalist exaggeration or hyperbolic charge of reverse discrimination in the key of Robin DiAngelo's "white fragility." Contemporary progressivism rhetorically attacks "whiteness" and other associated "hegemonic" and "oppressive" characteristics in ways that are analogous to how Stalin described the Kulaks[49] (whom he largely later exterminated), how the ethnic Hutu described the ethnic Tutsi[50] (which eventually led to the Rwandan genocide), and how ethnic Turks have described ethnic Armenians[51] (which, despite Turkish government efforts to block the designation as such, led to genocide in the early twentieth century).

49. See, for example, Patrick J. Kiger, "How Joseph Stalin Starved Millions in the Ukrainian Famine," History, April 16, 2019, https://www.history.com/news /ukrainian-famine-stalin.

50. See, for example, Kennedy Ndahiro, "In Rwanda, We Know All About Dehumanizing Language," The Atlantic, April 13, 2019, https://www.theatlantic.com /ideas/archive/2019/04/rwanda-shows-how-hateful-speech-leads-violence /587041/.

51. See, for example, "Turkey's Armenians keep heads down after genocide recognition," France 24, April 27, 2021, https://www.france24.com/en /live-news/20210427-turkey-s-armenians-keep-heads-down-after-genocide -recognition.

Think of it this way. Though he was temporarily fired from Viacom CBS for his comments (the company later rehired him as host of a new show, *Wild 'N Out*[52]), Nick Cannon, a former co-host of America's Got Talent, one of the most mainstream shows on American television, felt sufficiently emboldened to share the following views in a 2020 interview. Speaking of "white people" and "Jews," he said,

> They're acting out of fear, they're acting out of low self-esteem, they're acting out of a deficiency. . . . So, therefore, the only way that they can act is evil. They have to rob, steal, rape, kill in order to survive. So then, these people that didn't have what we have—and when I say we, I speak of the melanated people—they had to be savages . . . I say all that to say, the context in which we speak, whether it's Jewish people, white people, Europeans, the illuminati, they were doing that as survival tactics to stay on the planet. We never had to do that.[53]

Notice the *moral* difference Cannon marks between "we the melanated" (e.g., "we never had to do that") and the Jewish and white "they" (e.g., "the only way that they can act is evil."). There is no interpretation or connecting-of-the-dots or making the implied explicit necessary here: the former host of *America's Got Talent* believes it is legitimate to say, in public, that Jews and white people are evil for no other reason than because they are Jews and white people. Sadly, this is not an isolated event, as the Smithsonian guide to whiteness examined above and many other

52. See Cydney Henderson, "Nick Cannon rejoins 'Wild 'N Out' as host after getting fired for anti-Semitism," *USA Today*, February 5, 2021, https://www.usatoday.com/story/entertainment/tv/2021/02/05/nick-cannon-rejoins-wild-n-out-after-apology-anti-semitic/4411401001/.

53. See Adam White, "Nick Cannon fired by US media giant for 'hateful speech' and calling white and Jewish people 'savages,'" *The Independent*, July 15, 2020, https://www.independent.co.uk/arts-entertainment/tv/news/nick-cannon-fired-antisemitism-savages-youtube-professor-griff-a9619501.html.

similar instances demonstrate. Among wide swaths of contemporary culture, entertainers, teachers, business leaders, professors, and even government officials are eager to denounce groups of individuals for indelible characteristics that they have never chosen nor could possibly choose. That used to be called racism. Now it is called "social justice." And we know how this shadow version of a morality tale—a tale of good and evil not told in the language of conflicting ideas but in conflicting peoples—ends: once you start seeing evil in a group, you'll soon start to speak that evil, first in private but then, once it becomes acceptable, in public; and once you start speaking that evil in public, you're going to start calling for someone to do something about it; and once enough people start making the same call, a critical mass forms to implement a solution to the problem, a solution whose only form, by the very logic of Manichaean anthropology, can be the removal of the source of evil from society. The good groups of people must suppress if not purge the bad groups of people. Identitarian "justice" can call for nothing less.

The Catholic social thought tradition, in contrast, brooks no such division among human beings. First, as noted above, it vehemently rejects the claim that some groups have access to a special knowledge that is otherwise inaccessible to others outside the esoteric group of right-knowers. This belief in the existence of special knowledge and of special people who can know this special knowledge is just another expression of Gnosticism—and the Church has been fighting Gnosticism since its very inception. Second, Catholic social thought's understanding of original sin prevents any individual or group of individuals from claiming moral superiority by dint of birth, race, sex, ethnicity, or any other indelible characteristic for which the individual is not responsible. It is human action—and the character generating that action— alone that determines guilt and innocence and viciousness and virtue. And even within the recognition that individuals can choose to be better or worse persons (and that societies can make choosing to be a good person easier or harder) is the even more fundamental recognition that, in St. Paul's words, "all have sinned and fall short of the glory of God" (Rom. 3:23). Just as no individual can declare himself or herself free from sin, neither can any group.

In sum, for the Catholic social thought tradition, all human beings, without exception, are made morally equal in the image and likeness of God, and all human beings, without exception, are mired in sin—chief among them the sin of pride. We can and should, as individuals, do everything possible to avoid the temptations of our broken nature. We can and should, as societies, also do everything possible to prevent the temptations of our broken nature from becoming socialized and encrusted in injustice, including, but by no means limited to, racial injustice. We should become the best we can in all our complex diversities, moving closer to the kingdom of God without forgetting for a moment that we are not gods and that it is, in the end, not our kingdom to achieve. Having chosen sin, we have chosen to break ourselves, every one of us. God help us from ever falling into the delusion that we can completely fix ourselves or, even worse, that "we" can fix "them" by creating a utopianly perfect temporal heaven.

The Problem of Human Dignity

The previous section notes how progressive ideology imposes moral bifurcation on human beings, dividing us into camps of good and evil. This division cuts all the way down into the bedrock of human dignity, opening the door for the possibility that some lives are more valuable than other lives. The contemporary toxification of the claim "All lives matter" is emblematic of the progressive willingness to abandon the belief that all human beings are morally equal by virtue of being human. Indeed, according to progressive ideology, the affirmation that "all lives matter" can itself be racist—meaning that it demeans the value of black individuals.[54] If that also sounds nonsensical—by definition, "all lives" is inclusive of "black lives"—recall that progressive ideology authorizes itself the power to redefine both logical relationships between terms and the meaning of the terms themselves. To be fair, some progressive activists argue that, while they agree with the content of the claim "All lives matter," using the term in political discourse obscures the specific injustices suffered by black people. This response, however, is a non sequitur. There is nothing mutually exclusive about believing "All lives matter" and "There is racial injustice specifically against black individuals." One can hold both ideas at the same time without contradiction. The silencing of the public expression of "all lives matter"—so much so that individuals have been fired for saying it on their private social media accounts[55]— is thus purely political in nature, serving as a rhetorical weapon against the expression of views that an identity group finds inimical to its political interests. Even worse, however, removing "all lives matter" from acceptable mainstream political discourse undercuts the idea of universal human dignity and, correspondingly, universal human equality.

The Catholic social thought tradition's view of dignity as both objective and universal remains steadfast, however. Indeed, it supplies the necessary moral logic and motivation for why we as individuals and societies should fight against injustice toward any individual or group. If all lives don't matter equally, then only some injustice counts, and if only some injustice counts, some lives can be disposed of without concern or recourse. To be sure, when an identity group is experiencing political ascendency, the belief that "all lives matter" may seem dispensable

54. See, for example, Ashley May, "#AllLivesMatter hashtag is racist, critics say," *USA Today*, July 13, 2016, https://www.usatoday.com/story/news/nation-now/2016/07/13/why-saying-all-lives-matter-opposite-black-lives-matter/87025190/.

55. See, for example, Mark Fischer, "NBA announcer Grant Napear fired over 'All Lives Matter' comment," *New York Post*, June 2, 2020, https://nypost.com/2020/06/02/nba-announcer-grant-napear-fired-over-all-live-matter-comment/.

if not an obstacle to gaining greater power. But when—not if, when—another group begins clamoring that it is their lives that matter the most and then they start gaining power based on that claim, the belief that "all lives matter" will start coming in handy again. For these reasons, the Catholic social thought tradition recognizes that the best way to protect minorities from tyrannical majorities is to hold fast to the belief in equal human dignity. It recognizes that equal dignity because it is the truth about human beings, independent of whatever particular identities we may also have or ascribe to. In sum, upholding universal human worth protects us all—and the moment it becomes controversial to say "All lives matter" is the moment when everybody's lives become most vulnerable.

The Problem of Moral Hierarchies

Despite the clouds of moral dust progressive ideology produces with its unrelenting political demands, it is, at its core, relativistic in nature. As argued throughout the chapter, it does not—because it cannot—believe in universally objective moral truth. This moralistic nihilism means, among many other implications, that progressivism rejects the existence of moral absolutes, either in the form of categorical prohibitions ("Thou shall not") or positive injunctions ("Thou shall"). In this sense, the ideology tends to embrace a consequentialist model for moral calculations, but instead of applying it to society as a whole it applies it specifically to the political interests of the identity group—namely, how do "we" get more power. Consequently, progressivism has no conceptual mechanism to identify or criticize hypocrisy because it contains no objectively fixed standards that it could violate either in belief or action.

I noted above how this approach entails jettisoning members of an identity group who do not toe the ideological line, but it also applies to any other "threat" the identity group perceives to its interest. For example, progressive democrat Representative

Maxine Waters of California once said the following to an agitated crowd about how to engage with members from then President Trump's administration: "If you see anybody from that Cabinet in a restaurant, in a department store, at a gasoline station, you get out and you create a crowd and you push back on them, and you tell them they're not welcome anymore, anywhere."[56] In other words, she is instructing her followers to physically harass and threaten members of the opposing political party, even when they are doing private, personal activities. The same representative also later called for protestors to get "more confrontational" with police in the streets and to ignore any curfews that may be imposed—meaning, *break the law*—if the jury did not return the verdict she wanted against Derick Chauvin, a police officer who was indeed found guilty of killing George Floyd.[57] These and other similar examples show how progressivism can readily justify calls not only for protest but for violence if it supports a desired ideological outcome.

However, other self-identified progressive politicians—who have never criticized Waters for her inflammatory remarks—have denounced as "violent" or "calling for violence" even the quotation of their own words. For example, in 2021 a pro-Israel political action group paid for advertisements criticizing progressive Representative Ilhan Omar of Minnesota for morally equating the United States and Israel with the Taliban and Hamas by using Omar's exact words from one of her tweets: "We have seen unthinkable atrocities committed by the US, Hamas, Israel, Afghanistan, and the Taliban."[58] In response to the advertisement,

56. See, for example, Jamie Ehrlich, "Maxine Waters encourages supporters to harass Trump administration officials," CNN, June 25, 2018, https://www.cnn.com/2018/06/25/politics/maxine-waters-trump-officials/index.html.

57. See, for example, Kathianne Boniello, "Maxine Waters attends protest over police killing of Daunte Wright," *New York Post*, April 18, 2021, https://nypost.com/2021/04/18/maxine-waters-attends-protest-over-police-killing-of-daunte-wright/.

58. See, for example, Matt McNulty, "Ilhan Omar's spokesman claims pro-Israel group has 'put her life at risk' over new ad reminding her that she compared

Representative Omar's office tweeted, "'Make no mistake: AIPAC [the political advocacy group that published the ad] is putting Rep. Omar's life at risk with repeated Islamophobic attack ads."[59] In other words, progressives can refrain from criticizing Maxine Waters for calling for *actual* political violence while denouncing their critics as "violent" merely for quoting, verbatim, their own words.

To be sure, there is no political movement without hypocrisy, and all of it should be identified and condemned as such whenever and wherever it occurs (which is a full-time job). However, that points to the main problem at the heart of progressive ideology: it has made itself immune to the charge of hypocrisy because it has given itself carte blanche to define and redefine terms and logical relationships. Thus, progressivism can call for spray-painting public spaces as an act of free speech when it is in support of Black Lives Matter yet support the arrest of pro-life activists who write "Black Pre-Born Lives Matter" in public spaces *with chalk*.[60] The calls for "tolerance" and "diversity, equity, and inclusion" can be weaponized to mean coercively shutting down businesses that disagree with progressive views on sexuality and gender.[61] And people can be fired because of their skin color in the name of combating racism.[62] It is crucial to recognize that, according to

America to the Taliban," *Daily Mail*, August 12, 2021, https://www.dailymail.co.uk /news/article-9886127/Ilhan-Omar-spokesman-says-AIPACs-attack-ads-putting -life-risk-death-threats-continue.html.

59. Ibid.

60. See, for example, Elissa Graves, "Washington D.C.'s Free-Speech Double Standard Blesses BLM but Punishes Pro-Lifers," *National Review*, August 10, 2021, https://www.nationalreview.com/2021/08/washington-d-c-s-free-speech-double -standard-blesses-blm-but-punishes-pro-lifers/.

61. See, for example, Caleb Parke, "Colorado Christian cakeshop sued a third time for discrimination," Fox News, June 11, 2019, https://www.foxnews.com/us /colorado-christian-cakeshop-sued-discrimination.

62. See, for example, Emma Colton, "Chicago Museum Fires All of Its Mostly White Female Financially Well-Off Docents for Lack of Diversity: Report," *New York Post*, October 21, 2021, https://nypost.com/2021/10/18/chicago-museum-fires -all-of-its-mostly-white-female-financially-well-off-docents-for-lack-of-diversity -report/.

the shadow logic of progressivism, these examples and countless more like them are not hypocritical and therefore do not deserve any moral scrutiny. They are justified because they serve the identity group's political aims.

As I have argued throughout, the Catholic social thought tradition stands diametrically opposed to this relativistic and tyrannical political paradigm. Are there Catholic hypocrites out there? Oh, you bet, some of the best in the business. But I'll take a hypocrite over a nihilist any day. Hypocrites might, at the very least, be professing good beliefs, even if their actions stink to high heaven. Progressive ideology's moralistic nihilism, on the other hand, will congratulate itself for practicing nonviolence as it dons its ski masks, tightens its military boots, stuffs its Molotov cocktails, and pours out into the dark streets, looking to save the world by burning it to the ground.

The Problem of Free Speech

Unsurprisingly, and as the chapter has already highlighted, progressive ideology has zero interest in protecting free speech. It is worth highlighting once again how important the embrace of metaphysical and moral realism is as an antidote to the threat progressive ideology poses to free speech (and, correspondingly, the freedom of religion). If there is ultimately no ontological or metaphysical connection between words and reality—meaning that language is purely a social construct fabricated by the most powerful—then words will mean anything that the powerful want them to mean. Within this relativistic paradigm, moreover, if you happen to be in one of the groups that has less power than the dominant group or affiliation of groups, there is no argument you can make, no rational case you can build, against the threat of aggression. The progressive conception of reality can be nothing more than a dog-eat-dog world in which power—raw, coercive power—is the only principle of social organization.

As we have seen, moreover, the classical liberal/libertarian conception of procedural rationality fails to stand up to this threat despite its best intentions because it cannot say anything about the nature of the "the good" and thus cedes those definitions to the most powerful. There are also no allies to be found among the utilitarians because they'll only protect your free speech as long as it tends to produce the most aggregate pleasure—and there's nothing that ruins a good buzz like hearing the truth.

In the end, then, it is only a political paradigm that both recognizes the existence of objective rationality and invests that objective rationality with the power to identify objective goods in existence that can stand up both for the truth itself and for the search for truth, which includes a fundamental right to say and believe things that are wrong. In other words, for all the criticism secularity heaps on Catholicism for being "politically intolerant" or "against free thinking" or "desiring to impose its views on others" (all inaccurate, by the way), it is precisely the "Catholic" part of the Catholic social thought tradition that supports the right to say, "Catholicism is completely wrong and I want nothing to do with it." Try finding that freedom in progressivism—or, for that matter, any other ideology.

The Problem of Idolatry

Of the four ideologies this book examines, there is none more idolatrous than progressivism. Utilitarianism makes an idol out of pleasure, which is false and destructive but at least understandable given our human weakness to desire comfort above all else. Classical liberalism and libertarianism make an idol out of the self, which, though also false and destructive, at least preserves some semblance of rational order and imposes moral limits on human action. It is progressivism that is most old-school in its idolatry, with roots reaching all the way back to the primordial garden. What did the serpent tell Eve when the forbidden fruit first caught her eye? "You will certainly not die; for God knows that when you eat of it your eyes will be opened, and you will be like God, knowing good and evil" (Gen. 3:4–5). That is the original attraction of sin—you will be like gods, you will determine good and evil, you will never die. In dismantling barriers imposed by classical liberalism and libertarianism and appropriating to its own will even the definition of pleasure itself, progressivism, among all the other ideologies, seeks to fulfill the serpent's promise. You get to redefine lies as the truth; you get to trounce through the garden of humanity damning whom you will and saving whom you will; you get to do whatever you want while cursing those who do exactly the same as you. In short, you get to be temporal gods, demanding worship for your unearned virtue and sacrifice for your never-ending wrath.

To be sure, every god wishes he/she/[invented pronoun] were the only god. But progressivism teaches that the second-best alternative, since wannabe divinities so crowd the landscape, is to ally with those who look like you and talk like you and dress like you and are from the same place as you, and to fight, with every means necessary, against your competitors, those who have what you want or are trying to get what you already have. Fighting fire with fire and beating the dominant tribes at their own game may indeed lead to a victory here and there. But it's never going to last. All tribal wars are eventually lost. And they're lost not only because there is always another tribe coalescing against you and your tribe, ready and motivated to take all the ground you've just (re)conquered; they're lost because the whole war is being fought entirely on the serpent's terms and entirely for his pleasure. The snake's first trick was to turn men and women against each other; his second was to sever blood brothers; his third, to divide the human family itself. His fourth—to convince us all that the active threat of mutual destruction is the only thing we have in common.

Progressivism promises the oppressed tribe du jour a rousing and humiliating defeat of their oppressor; yet it does so while winking at the oppressors, whispering that they ought not to worry because they'll have their revenge soon enough—all while signaling to the neutral tribes that they better pick a side and do it quickly if they hope to survive the coming hostilities. The Catholic social thought tradition, in contrast, teaches that the only way to win this internecine war of tribal supremacy is not to fight it in the first place. Indeed, if we could all just pause the circular firing squad for a moment, we'd see that the real enemy isn't each other. Hell, it's not even ourselves. Look down. It's that damned snake. And fighting his false promises is what can and should unite us all.

CHAPTER 9

The God of Fortune: Non-Theistic Conservatism

Money talks—and no matter what it has to say, it's guaranteed an audience. And why not? Money may not be able to buy you love, but it can supply everything else under the sun: power, pleasure, health, fame, and, if you are willing to sacrifice a little off the top, even some honor as well. Everyone knows that everyone (except fools and liars) wants more money. So best get your piece before someone beats you to it.

But perhaps you find this candor a bit too candid. Too crass. Too vulgar. Too consumeristic. Too *common*. If so, I have an ideology that might interest you. What if you could preserve and augment your primal acquisitive drive, yet do so in a way that makes you appear civilized, educated, and even wise? What if you could cultivate a systematic neglect of, if not invigorating disdain for, the plebs who clean your house, cut your lawn, serve your food, and unclog your toilet (even though the latter might be making more than you are) in the noble name of tradition, stability, and/or individuality? What if you could shake the nickels and dimes loose from the pockets of your subordinates while chastising them for their lack of industry as your peers enviously long to mimic your efficiency? What if, in short, you could convince everyone that you actually *deserved* that unmerited spot in the skinny part of the socioeconomic pyramid? It's the deal of the centuries and yours for the taking—provided you can afford it.

And if you can't? Too bad. Life's not fair, after all, right? Better luck next time.

SETTING THE TARGET RIGHT

As with previous chapters, the explanation and critique of non-theistic conservatism best begins with a dive into its conceptual foundations. It is important to specify the target at the outset, however. This chapter is on "non-theistic conservatism," not "political conservatism" per se, which, like all political traditions, is internally diverse. The adjective drastically alters the noun in this case, so much so that "conservatism," depending on its specific formulation, and "non-theistic conservatism" can be categorically different political animals, not so much like a duck and goose, but rather a horse and a pig. To describe this form of conservatism as "non-theistic" is to say that its justification finds its grounding in custom and/or self-interest—not the reality of God and God's relationship with humanity. This is not to claim that individuals in this ideological camp are necessarily atheists (i.e., principled believers in the statement "God does not exist"); they very well may believe in God and, in fact, be regular church-goers. Rather, it is to say that they have severed their belief in God (if any) from their political values in a way that renders God's existence as, at best, indifferent to the socioeconomic character of society. As such, their political values can, by definition, have no other foundation than self-interest and/or tradition. And the specific form of self-interest and/or tradition that defines non-theistic conservatism, notwithstanding its erudite pretensions, is ultimately bound by one golden thread: preserving and advancing the social and material interests of the monied classes.

Three qualifications are in order. First, to critique the worship of the accumulation of wealth is not to critique wealth itself, which is, as St. Thomas Aquinas observes, not only a good but a necessary good, insofar as possessing wealth is instrumental to possessing any other material good, including necessities.

Second, it is also not to critique "free markets" or "capitalism" as intrinsically immoral. To the contrary, notwithstanding the fact that economic questions often fall within the realm of prudential judgment and, therefore, can be debated by people of good will, Catholic social thought has long defended the right to private property and, its corollary, the right to freely engage in commerce.[1] Catholic social thought has also firmly rejected both communism and socialism as contrary to natural law.[2] There is no ambiguity on this point: free people engaging freely in free markets is a good to be defended, even celebrated. Third, many of the values associated with navigating and excelling in the free market—for example, thrift, competence, hard work, ingenuity, flexibility, resilience, self-reliance, and, even, the profit motive itself (desiring to improve one's material well-being)—are also not under suspicion. All those are good, too, in their proper place. Moreover, I will argue that the Catholic social thought tradition provides a stronger and more coherent foundation for "individualism" than any of its ideological rivals, including non-theistic conservatism.

However, things go awry when the acquisition of wealth and "the market" transmute from an instrumental good into being the good in and of itself. *That* is this chapter's target. And like every other ideology, non-theistic conservatism does not pop into existence out of a moral and historical vacuum. It has deep intellectual roots, perhaps deeper than any other ideology in this book. Indeed, a case can be made that the father of non-theistic

---

1. Pope Benedict XVI writes in his encyclical *Caritas in Veritate*, for example, "Economy and finance, as instruments, can be used badly when those at the helm are motivated by purely selfish ends. Instruments that are good in themselves can thereby be transformed into harmful ones. But it is man's darkened reason that produces these consequences, not the instrument *per se*. Therefore it is not the instrument that must be called to account, but individuals, their moral conscience and their personal and social responsibility" (*Caritas in Veritate* 36, encyclical letter, June 29, 2009, vatican.va).

2. Pope Leo XIII, for example, directly condemns socialism in his 1878 encyclical, *Quod Apostolici Muneris* (encyclical letter, December 28, 1878, vatican.va).

conservatism is a figure that Catholic social thought, by way of St. Thomas Aquinas, rightfully reveres: the classical Greek philosopher Aristotle. The connection between Aristotle and non-theistic conservatism is not because Aristotle advocated for the adoration of wealth. Far from it; as a virtue theorist par excellence, he understood, like Aquinas many centuries later, that wealth is only instrumental to attaining the good, not the good itself. However, unlike Aquinas, Aristotle embraces metaphysical, anthropological, and, by extension, political principles that establish a conceptual foundation for non-theistic conservatism. As we will see below, the principles take this syllogistic form:

> Premise 1: Living a good life—a properly human life—depends on where in the socioeconomic hierarchy you are born and how you are raised.

> Premise 2: Where in the socioeconomic hierarchy you are born and how you are raised depend on fortune/chance.

> Conclusion: Therefore, living a good life—a properly human life—depends on fortune/chance.

And there's nothing, according to Aristotle, that anyone or any society can or should do to fix that.

Aristotle lays down one pillar of contemporary non-theistic conservativism. The Enlightenment philosopher John Locke—whose ideas are deeply embedded in the United States Declaration of Independence and Constitution—lays another one. It takes the form of the myth of the pre-societal individual existing in a "state of nature." All individuals, according to Locke, naturally possess an inherent freedom and inviolable self-sovereignty; thus, no person, group, or state can justly coerce an individual to do anything he does not want to do. However, the individual can freely choose to surrender some of his natural freedom to a centralized authority on the grounds that belonging to society will empower him to pursue his desires with greater security and probability of success. This contractual arrangement is, for Locke, the *only* foundation of a just government, one whose sole legitimacy lies in protecting individual liberty and property from other individuals and the state.

As we'll see, Locke's social contract theory provides non-theistic conservativism ersatz moral legitimacy in the form of a faulty anthropology, one that can be especially seductive to those born into privilege: since, according to Lockean anthropology, we all start out as equals in the game of life, the unequal outcomes that emerge in the competition for resources can be exhaustively explained by individuals' unequal talents and/or moral defects. In other words, socioeconomic disparity, including acute poverty, is a priori an individual problem, not a social one, which means there is scant justification for pursuing social justice properly defined. Moreover, since self-interest, rather than the pursuit of an objectively rational good, constitutes the sole standard for determining the meaning of "happiness," Lockean individualism provides no limiting principle to defining happiness as the pursuit of endless wealth. This is not only a recipe for personal greed; it also lays the foundation for the formation and preservation of a society that enables the most powerful to take advantage of the less powerful in the name of "freedom."

These two strands of non-theistic conservativism—Aristotelian aristocracy and Lockean hyper-individuality—also appear in the work of the contemporary political philosopher George F. Will, whose recent oeuvre, *The Conservative Sensibility*, includes a chapter entitled "Conservatism without Theism." As we'll see, Will's thought shows that some elements of non-theistic conservatism overlap substantially with Catholic social thought. However, it also reveals how rejecting theism ultimately and ineluctably leads conservatism to another ideological dead-end: being prostrated before a golden calf (or, better, golden bull) bearing the moniker, "god of fortune."

Moving forward it will be helpful, as in previous chapters, to keep the Thinking in Circles map in mind:

THE FEW, THE PROUD, THE LUCKY

Aristotle should be an uneasy target for Catholicism not only because Aristotle rightly retains the title, shared, perhaps, only with Plato (and his teacher, Socrates), of being the most influential philosopher in the history of ideas, but also because, as noted above, the philosophy and theology of St. Thomas Aquinas—the Angelic Doctor of the Church—would be unrecognizable without Aristotelian forms of reasoning, something St. Aquinas happily acknowledges throughout the *Summa* by referring to Aristotle simply as "the Philosopher." However, Aristotelianism also has its shadowlands, and one of them is his philosophical defense of, in contemporary language, social and political elitism.

To understand Aristotle's morality and, by extension, politics, we must first turn to his epistemology, which, unsurprisingly because of his intellectual consistency, contains anthropological and ontological presuppositions embedded within it. Aristotle divides all human knowledge into what he calls two "sciences": "theoretical science" and "practical science." The theoretical sciences seek knowledge about the nature of existence and the explanation for the changes that take place in existence. "Existence," in this context, means not only physical existence (what Aristotle would call the "natural sciences") but also "mathematics" and "theology," the latter meaning the rational study of "eternal causes," which does not include revelation or scripture. Indeed, it is important to highlight upfront that while Aristotle does affirm the existence of what he calls the "unmoved mover," this divine mover does *not* have a will and is not engaged in the affairs of existence, including, but not limited to, human affairs. In other words, Aristotle's "God" is radically different from a biblical conception of God and even the God that St. Thomas Aquinas believes is accessible to human reason. For Aristotle, the "universe" and everything within it was not created but, rather, is eternal. What is always has been and always will be; the universe has no purpose, direction, or meaning and is completely outside of human control. It does not care about anything or anyone and it does not infuse anything with value or goodness.

That said, Aristotle maintains that existence as such, including divine existence (the unmoved mover), is knowable by human reason precisely because it is permanent and invariable. The function of theoretical science, and its underlying epistemic grounding, theoretical reason, is to ascertain fixed truths about the nature of existence and to teach those truths to others who, assuming they possess healthy rational capacities, should be able both to comprehend and ascent to those truths. It is important to note, here, that both the human body and human rational soul, for Aristotle, fall within the domain of theoretical science because both belong to the order of existence as such and, therefore, do not change. Reason qua reason is thus capable of identifying and understanding the nature of the human being.

But what about the *purpose* of the human being or, more specifically, on *attaining* that purpose? Unlike the nature of the human being per se, this question belongs within the domain of "practical science," which, unlike theoretical science, pertains not to the way things are (e.g., the invariably fixed nature of the Aristotelian universe), but rather the way they should be. Moreover, unlike theoretical science, the subject matter of practical science *is* under human control and, therefore, subject to change. This variability leads Aristotle to conclude that, unlike the theoretical sciences, which can apprehend certain truths, practical science can only ascertain probable and thus tentative truths. He writes,

> We must be content, then, in speaking of such subjects [of practical science] and with such premises to indicate the truth roughly and in outline, and in speaking about things which are only for the most part true and with premises of the same kind to reach conclusions that are no better.[3]

In other words, the conclusions of the practical sciences are subject to change, which becomes an especially important point to consider when asking *who* has the authority to change those conclusions and on what grounds.

The practical sciences include what Aristotle calls the "productive sciences," which encompasses the study of how to make things, including both physical objects like pottery, weapons, and sculptures, and literary works (Aristotle's examination of rhetoric and poetics, for example, falls in this category). Our focus, however, is on practical science as it pertains to what Aristotle calls "ethics" and "politics." Ethics and politics answer the question,

---

3. *Nicomachean Ethics*, 1094b.

What is the purpose of human existence and, crucially, how do human beings attain that purpose?—a question Aristotle also formulates as, What is the efficient cause of attaining the final cause of all human beings?[4] "Ethics" studies the *individual* human good or final cause; "politics" studies the common human good or final cause.

There are two characteristics of the relationship between ethics and politics that need highlighting here: (1) ethics and politics are different yet are both mutually implicative and mutually dependent—the good of the whole necessarily implies the good of the individual, yet there can be no good of the whole if there is not also a good of the individual; and (2) both ethics and politics pertain directly to *human action* and, in particular, how human action both instantiates and attains the final good of human beings both individually and collectively. While there remains ongoing debate about Aristotle's conception of what defines the final human good, it is sufficient, for our purposes, to say that it includes living a life of virtue in service of the political community (the "polis") and in contemplation of the eternal truths of the unmoved mover (the subject matter of the theoretical sciences). Aristotle writes, for example,

> Now, since politics uses the rest of the sciences, and since, again, it legislates as to what we are to do and what we are to abstain from, the end of this science must include those of the other, so that this end must be the good for man . . . though it

4. Aristotle divides everything in existence, including human existence, into four causes: (1) material, (2) formal, (3) efficient, and (4) final. In shorthand form, the material cause of something is what it is made of; the formal cause of something is what makes it unique among all other things in existence; the efficient cause is that which enacts the change within something to move it from being potentially what it is (its existence) to what it actually is intended to be (its essence); and the final cause is the final end or purpose of a thing, that is, what it is *for* and what explains, orders, and structures all the changes that ought to be taking place with a being to realize its full potential and, thus, become fully what it is.

is worthwhile to attain the end merely for one man, it is fine and more godlike to attain it for a nation or city-states.[5]

And:

Happiness extends, then, just so far as contemplation does, and those to whom contemplation more fully belongs are more truly happy, not as a mere concomitant but in virtue of the contemplation; for this is in itself precious. Happiness, therefore, must be some form of contemplation.[6]

Aristotelian scholars can work out how these two definitions of the final human good relate to each other. For our purposes, here's what matters: for Aristotle, the final human end includes a life of virtue as part of a properly constituted political community, and a life of virtue entails *good action*, which is the subject matter of practical science, which, Aristotle affirms, can only be probable rather than certain. So, how does practical science *determine* what defines the good actions that, in turn, define the virtues whose practice, in turn, leads to the attainment of the final individual good (ethics) as part of a properly formed community (politics)? Or, put more colloquially, how does anyone know what they are supposed to do to be happy? It is in answering this question that Aristotle's aristocratic elitism most clearly emerges. He ultimately defends a position that limits both the apprehension and attainment of a good life—that is, a fully human life—to those born and raised in the right kinds of families and communities.

In the *Nicomachean Ethics*, Aristotle claims that determining what constitutes good action must begin with an examination of the "facts." In his words, "The fact is the primary thing or first principle [of morality]."[7] "Facts" are that which empirical

5. *Nicomachean Ethics*, 1094b.
6. *Nicomachean Ethics*, 1178b.
7. *Nicomachean Ethics*, 1908b.

observation reveals to be true (probably so) about the nature of individual and social morality. Facts are not, however, just "out there" waiting to be gathered up by anyone passing by; rather, they require that the observer have the right kind of moral habituation—the right kind of moral upbringing and training—for them to be observed and, even more so, heeded. Aristotle writes,

> We must begin with things known to us. Hence anyone who is to listen intelligently to lectures about what is noble and just, and generally, about the subjects of political science must have been brought up in good habits. For the fact is the starting point, and if this is sufficiently plain to him, he will not at the start need the reason as well; and the man who has been brought up has or can easily get starting points.

And then comes the elitist proviso:

> As for him who neither has nor can get them [i.e., good habits], let him hear the words of [the poet] Hesiod: "far best is he who know all things himself. Good, he that [heeds] when men counsel right; But he who neither knows nor lays heed to another's wisdom, is a useless [person]."[8]

In other words, if you are not born into and/or brought up within a community that instills within you *good habits* from early childhood, it's not only the case that you won't be able to act virtuously—*you won't even be able to comprehend what "virtue" is.*

The elitist consequences of this conclusion for Aristotle's moral and political vision become even more apparent when we see his definition of "virtue":

---

8. *Nicomachean Ethics*, 1095b.

Virtue is a state of character concerned with a choice, lying in a mean, i.e., the mean relative to us, this being determined by a rational principle, and by the principle by which the man of practical wisdom would determine it.[9]

It is the last claim here—"by which the man of practical wisdom would determine it"—that gives substance to every other claim in this definition: the condition for the possibility of knowing what defines the "mean" that should govern the "choices" that, collectively, constitute the state of character, that, ultimately, defines virtue is the example the man of practical wisdom provides. And how do we know which men are men of practical reason and which men aren't? It depends on whether your practical reasoning is functioning as it ought to, meaning whether it is properly apprehending relevant moral facts—and having that capacity, in turn, depends upon being born and/or raised in a community that instills "good habits" within you. How, then, do you ensure you get born into and/or raised by a community that instills good habits? You don't. It's blind chance. You either have it or you don't. And if you don't? Tough luck—you are, by birth, relegated to the classes of "useless persons," at least as far as acting virtuously and thereby realizing your full humanity is concerned.

Given this anthropological divide, it should come as no surprise that Aristotle recognizes what he calls "natural slaves" among human beings. He writes in the *Politics*, for example, "For he who can be, and therefore is, another's, and he who participates in rational principle enough to apprehend, but not have, such a principle, is a slave by nature."[10] Or, as he later explains in more detail,

9. *Nicomachean Ethics*, 1107a.
10. *Politics*, 1.5, 1254b.

Almost all things rule and are ruled according to nature. But the kind of rule differs; the free man rules over the slave after another manner from that in which the male rules over the female, or the man over the child; although the parts of the soul are present in all of them they are present in different degrees. For the slave has no deliberative faculty at all; the woman has, but it is without authority, and the child has, but it is immature. So it must necessarily be supposed to be with the moral virtues also; all should partake of them, but only in such manner and degree as is required by each for the fulfilment of his duty.[11]

Note the radically hierarchical nature of "humanity" that Aristotle presents here. Some humans are more fully human than others merely by dint of their birth and/or physical characteristics—not because of any free choices they make. Men with good habits (that is, those born and raised in the right kind of communities living according to right practical reason) are at the top; women with good habits are beneath them; and children with good habits are beneath the women (though male children, it is important to note, can and will surpass women once their rationality "matures"). At the very bottom, however, are the slaves—the women and men who, according to Aristotle, have only enough rationality to obey orders but not enough to understand why the moral content of the order is, in fact, good. The only purpose they serve for the political community, therefore, is utilitarian in nature: they're the ones who till the fields, and pick the olives, and sweep the marble, and rinse the latrines, and dig the graves, and otherwise provide the basic goods and services that make the civilized life of the political community possible but are otherwise "useless." In this sense, they're necessary for the good of the "true human beings" but not fully human themselves—and never could be.

11. *Politics*, 1.13,1260a.

There is some insult to add to the injury here as well. While Aristotelianism contains tremendous intellectual resources for understanding both the nature and purpose of virtue, moral action, and the final human good, there is a strong case to be made that the whole ethical *and* political edifice is built on sand, if not thin air. While, again, there is debate among interpreters of Aristotle whether an objectively rational foundation to his moral theory can be found in his conception of the unmoved mover, Aristotle's argument within his *Ethics* itself can be read as a form not only of elitism but of conventionalism as well—that is, an ethic built on custom and custom alone. This circularity of Aristotelian ethics, which many critics have pointed out, can be seen in the following representation of his definition of virtue:

What is virtue?

Virtue is that which the man of practical wisdom determines it to be.

What defines the "man of practical wisdom"?

He who is virtuous.

In short, the critique—a justified one, in my view—is that Aristotle simply embraces the customs of the literate, educated, and, thus, wealthy elite and then repackages those customs as "virtue." The work of both the *Ethics* and the *Politics* is thus an intellectual refinement of moral principles that, rather than being axiomatic or deduced from some metaphysical truth, are merely reflections of a particular people living in a particular time who happened to be holding the reins of cultural and political power. In Aristotle's defense, at least historically speaking, his philosophy did not make all the powerful happy; he was forced to flee his beloved Athens towards the end of his life because of a shift in the political winds. However, it remains the case that the substance of Aristotle's argument is built upon the epistemological *and* anthropological belief that only some people—those fortunate enough to be rightly habituated—have any hope of being virtuous and, thus, contributing to the individual and communal good. Politics is, consequently, of the elite, by the elite, and for the elite.

RAISING A PINKY TO THE GOOD OF TRADITION

While contemporary non-theistic conservatism categorically rejects Aristotelianism's moral justification for slavery and misogyny, it nevertheless adopts some of its elitist elements and, more importantly, some of the anthropological, epistemological, and even theological assumptions that justify that elitism. We'll see some of these elements in George F. Will's *The Conservative Sensibility* below; however, let me highlight five general features of Aristotelianism present in non-theistic conservatism as a primer:

An a priori moral justification for deep and widespread socioeconomic inequality

Given the epistemic and anthropological presuppositions of Aristotelianism (i.e., only those who have been born into the right kinds of families and properly habituated can both know and effectively pursue what is truly good), the explanation for the existence of socioeconomic inequality can be known without any empirical examination—to wit, the poor classes are penurious and powerless because their nature and/or upbringing dictates that that be their station in life. It is not the fault of the properly habituated; indeed, it's not the fault of the poorer classes, either, insofar as they neither chose their low station in life nor are capable of choosing any higher station. It is just the way things are, a consequence of the nature of reality. To be sure, the poorer classes do lack moral virtue; they are certainly not as good as the higher classes. However, this deficiency is akin to the kind of deficiency we see in a person who has a disability that prevents his body from extracting nutrients from food: it's just how he came into the world, sadly so, perhaps, but certainly no one's fault and, consequently, no one's responsibility. The lack of moral responsibility also applies to the "nurture" category, as well: expecting individuals who weren't raised right to do better with their own children is like holding a blind man morally accountable for not teaching his blind child how to see. It is all very *unfortunate*, yes. But that's just the way it is, and some things will never change.

An a priori moral justification for the belief "Nothing can be done to help these people"

As a consequence of the epistemic and anthropological determinism that divides humanity into the rightly and not rightly habituated, both the questions (a) What *can* be done to reduce socioeconomic inequality? and (b) What *should* be done to reduce socioeconomic inequality? have ready-made answers even before they are asked: nothing. If, as Immanuel Kant famously averred, "ought implies can" (meaning, a moral duty can only rightly be considered a duty if individuals are capable of fulfilling it), then the "problem" of inequality is akin to the "problem" of the universe's eventual heat death: there's simply nothing anyone *can* do about it and, therefore, there's nothing anyone *should* do about it. Consequently, the only, and thus best, option the rightly habituated have is to protect and augment their own material interests without worrying about those who could never be helped anyway.

An a priori justification for viewing manual labor as morally and economically inferior

Given that (a) the highest human good is a life devoted to the practice of virtue (in and through a correctly formed political community) and the comprehension of eternal truth and (b) attaining this good requires being properly habituated, then it is not only the case that there are two classes of people that correspond with two classes of human dignity (the properly habituated and the non-properly habituated). There are also two classes of *labor* that correspond with these two classes of people: the work of the mind of the rightly habituated (e.g., statecraft, law, philosophy, education, art, medicine, journalism, etc.) and the work of the hands of the deficiently habituated, for example, those who watch dirt and grime spiral down the drain when they shower after their shift. It's not that manual workers are morally bad because they do manual labor; it's just that they are not, and never could be, as morally *good*, because their work, unlike the mental labor of the virtuous, isn't fully human and thus cannot move them any closer to attaining the true human good. It should thus come as no surprise that manual laborers aren't going to earn the most money or social respect. Their work may be essential for society, but that doesn't mean it's valuable. Your HVAC technician may be good at keeping your house livable in the summer, in other words—but there's no way he has anything useful to say about politics, theories of civil governance, or the unmoved mover.

A theological justification for believing that God has no concern for socioeconomic inequality and poverty

It is important to remember that Aristotle is not an atheist or an agnostic. There is a God in the Aristotelian universe. However, much like the Platonic, Epicurean, and, later, Stoic conception of God, that God does not have any concern for the good of humanity or the good of an individual person. To the extent that God has any effect on existence it is purely ontological, sustaining the order of things as they are but otherwise remaining radically remote and uninterested. There are, then, two dispositions to take when answering the question, "What does God 'think' about socioeconomic inequality and the travails of the poor?" Either (a) God endorses socioeconomic inequality and poverty since, to the extent that there is any intentionality to God at all, that is the way that God has "set up" the universe, or (b) God is disinterested in socioeconomic inequality and poverty because God is disinterested in all human affairs. God can thus be interpreted as "being on the side" of those who have more power and money in society either as (a) a metaphysical ally or (b) a completely impartial spectator, on no one's side at all. Either way, theology favors the fortunate.

A moral and political methodology based solely on tradition and the preservation of tradition

The Aristotelian elements above pertain to the substance of non-theistic conservativism—that is, the content of its beliefs about the nature of existence, humanity, knowledge, morality, and politics. Non-theistic conservatism also adopts Aristotelian *methodology* as well—that is, how it reasons and reaches conclusions. As noted, there's a good case to be made that Aristotle's ethics and politics are logically circular, starting and ending with the same premise ("the man of practical wisdom"). Setting aside whether this critique of Aristotle holds up in light of his analysis of the unmoved mover in Book X of the *Nicomachean Ethics*, Aristotle's definition of virtue, taken by itself, represents a form of conventionalism, one that embraces the customs and mores of a particular class of people (the properly habituated), baptizes them as axiomatically normative representations of "practical reasoning," and then employs them to reach all other moral and political conclusions—for example, about the nature of justice, the proper form of government, and who is included/excluded from deliberations in civil affairs. The appeal of conventionalism, especially in politics, is that it gives an intellectual and moral veneer to beliefs, actions, and practices that, at their core, are reducible to sheer custom: people doing things a certain way because that's the way they do them where they live. What Aristotelian conventionalism provides non-theistic conservatism in particular—again, setting aside whether Aristotle fixes the logical problem elsewhere in his work—is a façade of intellectual and moral legitimacy that is, in fact, merely a cover to protect and advance the economic, social, and political interests of those who are already powerful in the community. In other words, the political game is rigged even before it begins: whoever ends up playing on the socioeconomic field, Aristotelian conventionalism ensures that the best-funded team (even though they may not have the best players) is not only guaranteed to win but also to feel vindicated in doing so because it is protecting "tradition"—that is, the good of the game itself.

FROM ARISTOTELIAN ARISTOCRACY TO THE STEALTH ELITISM OF JOHN LOCKE'S EGALITARIANISM

Some non-theistic conservatives may be scoffing at this point, saying something like, "Aristotelianism does *not* represent my conservative values because I believe in the freedom and equality of *all* individuals, not just the economically and socially elite." Fair enough. Non-theistic conservatives need not be Aristotelians. They could also be devotees of John Locke, the seventeenth-century political philosopher who disdained the power of "class" and "tradition" as justifiers and arbiters of the political order and who was, perhaps, the single greatest intellectual influence on the American Declaration of Independence and Constitution. But here's the thing: whether Aristotelian or Lockean in nature, non-theistic conservatism *always* ends up serving as an ideological cover for protecting and advancing the interests of the most prosperous. The reason is because Lockean conservatism—like Aristotelian conservatism—is built upon a faulty metaphysics and anthropology that, despite its egalitarian intentions, leads it back to one common denominator: power.

As with all great thinkers, understanding Locke's political project requires digging into his beliefs about the nature of existence, human nature, and knowledge. As we'll see, Locke's thought can sometimes appear similar, if not identical, to libertarianism, which we examined in chapter 7. Indeed, Robert Nozick, one of the paradigmatic representatives of libertarianism, explicitly draws on Lockean political theory to develop his conception of the state in *Anarchy, State, and Utopia*. However, while there is significant overlap between the libertarian and Lockean conceptions of individual freedom, especially as it relates to the freedom from state interference and the freedom to define one's own conception of the good, Locke's political vision is pre-Kantian both historically and conceptually. Unlike Kant and the libertarian legacy that finds its roots in Kantian thought, Locke affirms that the human mind *can* apprehend metaphysical truth that is "out there" in existence, specifically in the form of the "natural law" and a "fixed human nature." Because of Kant's radical separation between phenomena (the way we experience the world) and noumena (the way the world actually is), these "natural" categories are epistemically and, thus, politically prohibited from a Kantian-grounded political theory. That is not the case for Locke; the "natural" remains alive and well and, in fact, is the foundation of his entire view of politics.

So how, then, can we account for the similarity between the conception of "autonomy" at the heart of libertarianism and the conception of "freedom" at the heart of Lockeanism? The answer has as much to do with Locke's epistemology and anthropology as it does with his metaphysics. Like both the later David Hume (1711–1776) and Immanuel Kant (1724–1804), Locke (1632–1704) is deeply interested in marking the *limits* of human knowledge. He writes in the *Essay Concerning Human Understanding*,

> Thus men, extending their inquiries beyond their capacities, and letting their thoughts wander into those depths where they can find no sure footing, it is no wonder that they raise questions and multiply disputes, which, never coming to any clear resolution, are proper only to continue and increase their doubts. . . . Whereas were the capacities of our understandings well considered, the extent of our knowledge once discovered, and the horizon found which sets the bounds between the enlightened and dark parts of things; between what is and what is not comprehensible by us, men would perhaps with

less scruple acquiesce in the avowed ignorance of the one, and employ their thoughts and discourse with more advantage and satisfaction in the other.[12]

In this passage, Locke asserts that there are some questions that human reason cannot answer and thus should not seek to answer (i.e., "those depths where [men] can find no sure footing"). These "depths," for Locke, as we will see, include the nature of the ultimate human good. However, it is important to stress that, unlike Hume and Kant, Locke does *not* argue that the existence of God is within "these depths." In fact, he employs a rational argument to demonstrate God's existence by appealing to the principle that a "non-cogitative being" (i.e., a non-thinking being) could not produce a "cogitative being"—that is, a human being. He writes in the same essay, "It [is] evident that something necessarily must exist from eternity, it is also [therefore] evident that that something must necessarily be a cogitative being: for it is as impossible that incogitative matter should produce a cogitative being, as that nothing, or the negation of all being, should produce a positive being or matter."[13] At first blush, this conclusion would seem to place Locke in league with the philosophical foundations of Catholic social thought—namely, the belief that (a) God exists and (b) is knowable by human reason as both the eternal law and the ground of the natural law. If this is the case, however, why does Locke's view of individual freedom end up being more similar to Kant than to Catholicism?

Providing a satisfying answer to this question is difficult because it enters into what the Stanford Encyclopedia of Philosophy has called the "puzzle" of Locke's moral philosophy.[14] On the

12. John Locke, introduction to *An Essay Concerning Human Understanding*, https://www.gutenberg.org/files/10615/10615-h/10615-h.htm#link2HCH0001.

13. *An Essay Concerning Human Understanding*, 4.10.11.

14. Patricia Sheridan, "Locke's Moral Philosophy," Stanford Encyclopedia of Philosophy, June 10, 2016, https://plato.stanford.edu/entries/locke-moral/.

one hand, Locke affirms the existence of God and, based on that premise, believes human reason can deduce the existence of an objective natural law and an objectively real human nature that corresponds with that law. On the other hand, Locke, sounding like David Hume, also seems to affirm that human reason, in the form of empirical analysis, can only identify *physical pleasure* as the highest human good, which relativizes the definition of the good into sheer individual preference. He writes,

> Things then are good or evil, only in reference to pleasure or pain. That we call good, which is apt to cause or increase pleasure, or diminish pain in us; or else to procure or preserve us the possession of any other good or absence of any evil. And, on the contrary, we name that evil which is apt to produce or increase any pain, or diminish any pleasure in us: or else to procure us any evil, or deprive us of any good.[15]

While Locke scholars continue to debate how to interpret this apparent contradiction between metaphysical realism and empirical subjectivity as it relates to human nature and the good, for our purposes the inconsistency helpfully explains why Locke's conception of human freedom drifts into Kantian and, by extension, libertarian territory. This is the basic takeaway: for Locke, reason can know enough about existence to ascertain that there is a God, a natural law, and an objectively fixed human nature, but *not* enough to know that there is, correspondingly, an objectively fixed human good. In other words, for Locke, human beings can rationally know *what we are*; however, we cannot know *what we are for*. As such, the final human good ultimately becomes a matter of arational (neither rational nor irrational) preference—some define it one way, others another, and there is no rational standard to adjudicate who is right and who is wrong. It is this *preferential*

---

15. John Locke, *An Essay Concerning Human Understanding*, 2.20.1.

character of the good that explains why Locke sounds more like Kant than Catholicism about the relationship between individual freedom and the ultimate good, notwithstanding the overlap between Lockean and Catholic metaphysics. It also explains, as we'll see below, why he describes the function of the state as only pertaining to protecting life and property.

Freedom, Consent, and Convenience: The State of Nature and the Makings of the State

Like political theorists Thomas Hobbes before him and Jean-Jacques Rousseau after him, Locke employs a "state of nature" trope to identify both (a) the normative nature of human beings before entering into any formally organized political community and (b) the rational justification for why human beings would consent to "leave nature" to join a political community, which, in turn, establishes the justification for legitimate government. Locke develops his full theory of the state of nature and its relation to the formation of government in *Two Treatises of Government*. However, he provides an apt summary of the argument in the much shorter work *A Letter Concerning Toleration*. The relevant passage is worth quoting at length:

> But besides their souls, which are immortal, men have also their temporal lives here upon earth; the state whereof being frail and fleeting, and the duration uncertain, they have need of several outward conveniencies [sic] to the support thereof, which are to be procured or preserved by pains and industry; for those things that are necessary to the comfortable support of our lives, are not the spontaneous products of nature, nor do offer themselves fit and prepared for our use. This part, therefore, draws on another care, and necessarily gives another employment. But the pravity of mankind being such, that they had rather injuriously prey upon the fruits of other men's labours than take pains to provide for themselves; the necessity

of preserving men in the possession of what honest industry has already acquired, and also of preserving their liberty and strength, whereby they may acquire what they farther want, *obliges men to enter into society with one another*; that by mutual assistance and joint force, they may secure unto each other their properties, in the things that contribute to the comforts and happiness of this life; leaving in the mean while [sic] to every man the care of his own eternal happiness, the attainment whereof can neither be facilitated by another man's industry, nor can the loss of it turn to another man's prejudice, nor the hope of it be forced from him by any external violence. But forasmuch as men thus entering into societies, grounded upon their mutual compacts of assistance, for the defence of their temporal goods, may nevertheless be deprived of them, either by the rapine and fraud of their fellow-citizens, or by the hostile violence of foreigners: the remedy of this evil consists in arms, riches, and multitudes of citizens: the remedy of others in laws: and the care of all things relating both to the one and the other is committed by the society to the civil magistrate. *This is the original, this is the use, and these are the bounds of the legislative, which is the supreme power in every commonwealth. I mean, that provision may be made for the security of each man's private possessions; for the peace, riches, and public commodities of the whole people, and, as much as possible, for the increase of their inward strength against foreign invasions.*[16]

In short, the emergence of the state, or what Locke calls "society" under the "civil magistrate," takes place in two steps, both freely consented to by all: First, individuals in a state of nature realize that they cannot produce all the goods and services they need and want by their individual labor alone (a situation

16. Excerpt from *A Letter Concerning Toleration*, Natural Law, Natural Rights, and American Constitutionalism website, https://www.nlnrac.org/american /bill-of-rights/primary-source-documents/locke-toleration (emphasis added).

Locke summarizes as "inconveniences"); the individuals thus freely enter into agreements with other individuals to exchange goods and services, thereby forming a voluntary cooperative. However, the same individuals, now loosely affiliated with others in economic arrangements, subsequently discover that they remain vulnerable to both domestic and foreign threats to their lives and property. This realization leads to the second step in the exit from nature: the exchange of additional individual freedom to a centralized government that alone possesses the legitimate authority to employ coercive power, including violence, to enforce voluntary contracts and to protect individuals and their property from harm. The creation of the state, according to Locke, is thus a result of self-interested individuals determining that it is in their best interests to surrender some of their self-sovereignty to a centralized authority in exchange for protection.

It is important to highlight that providing this protection is not only the primary function of government for Locke—it is the *only* function. He writes,

> The commonwealth [is] a society of men constituted *only* for the procuring, preserving, and advancing their own civil interests. Civil interest I call life, liberty, health, and indolency of body [that is, bodily comfort]; and the possession of outward things, such as money, lands, houses, furniture, and the like.[17]

In other words, the entire legitimacy of the state rests on it performing one task alone: protecting individuals' lives and property, which, in turn, permits them to seek their "civil interests" with greater security and confidence. This task, moreover, should be interpreted in entirely materialistic terms. The state has no concern for any individual's moral or, even less, spiritual well-being; it is only concerned that the individuals honor their

---

17. Excerpt from *A Letter Concerning Toleration* (emphasis added).

contracts and refrain from physically harming each other. The "public good" is thus nothing more than a civil structure that enables each individual to do whatever she or he wants within the limits of the law.

It is important to keep in mind that Locke's reasoning about the sole legitimate function of the state emanates not only from his anthropology (i.e., all humans are born free and equal and can only give up their freedom by consent) but also from his epistemology: although we can, according to Locke, rationally agree that there is a fixed definition of human nature, we cannot rationally agree that there is a fixed purpose to that nature beyond protecting individual life and property. To be fair to Locke's position, he does believe affirming God's existence is a prerequisite for a just civil order. He argues in *A Letter Concerning Toleration*, for example, that the state has no duty to tolerate atheists because they have no reason, morally speaking, to uphold the contracts they make with others. Moreover, Locke frequently identifies "salvation," in the general Christian sense of "going to heaven," as an individual's greatest possible good. Locke's political theory is thus not opposed to religion, and he is not seeking to create a state that is hostile to the practice of religion, so long as it does not violate civil laws.

Yet—and this is a subtle but crucial point—his understanding of the meaning of "religion" is limited to what he calls "opinion," which, in turn, means beliefs that reason can neither confirm nor deny. As such, "religion" has nothing to do with civil government. He writes, for example, "The business of laws is not to provide for the truths of opinion, but for the safety and security of the commonwealth and of every particular man's goods and person."[18] This claim may sound commonsensical when applied to, for example, the Catholic dogma of Mary's Assumption into

18. John Locke, *A Letter Concerning Toleration*, Online Library of Liberty, https://files.libertyfund.org/files/2375/Locke_1560_EBk_v6.0.pdf.

heaven or the Real Presence of Christ in the Holy Eucharist; there's no reason these, and other revealed dogmas, should have any influence on civic matters. Yet that points to what's precisely at issue here: Locke conflates all revealed truths—truths, say, Catholics know by virtue of Scripture and the Magisterium of the Church—with all ultimate truth per se, that is, truth about the purpose of existence, including human existence. All those "truths," for Locke, are gathered up and tossed into one "religious" basket, given the title "faith," and summarily segregated from civil relevance. The upshot is that the political order, by design, leaves every individual free to define and pursue the good any way he or she desires so long as that pursuit does not interfere with other individuals' life, liberty, or property. For Locke, a just government dares not do anything more. Or less.

Sounding Familiar—with a Twist

Using this language, it can be difficult to distinguish between Lockean liberty and Kantian liberty, and Lockean government and libertarian government. In other words, despite their different underlying epistemologies, anthropologies, and metaphysics, the Kantian and Lockean traditions end up fundamentally agreeing that the meaning and purpose of human life lies completely outside the bounds of rational apprehension and, thus, has no political relevance. It should come as no surprise, then, that the critiques that apply to the Kantian political model (present in both libertarianism and classical liberalism as examined in chapter 7) also apply to the Lockean model: summarily, when the state is defined as purely *procedural* and, thus, only a vehicle for individuals to carry out their own arational desires, then there's no rational basis for a common substantive civic morality; and if there is no rational basis for a common substantive civic morality, then the civic "morality" will, by default, be whatever the dominant powers in society want it to be; and since "morality" as it pertains to the human being's final good has been expunged from the domain of the rational, there is nothing that the minority or the less powerful—all those who disagree with the majority's desires—can do to resist it as long as their bodies, livelihoods, and personal beliefs are left unmolested.

On the surface, that may not sound like a bad civic deal: letting the majority have its sociocultural way while protecting minority rights to life, property, and to practice their own beliefs in private sounds like the *solution* to the problem, not the problem itself. Yet the foundation on which this compromise is built— divorcing public morality based on a shared, substantive vision of the human good from public rationality—belies a profound naïveté about individual liberty, the meaning of consent, and the condition for the possibility of maintaining civic cohesion. In the chapter on Kantianism, for example, I noted how a libertarian or classical liberal state could defend implementing a school policy that requires that students be taught that the meaning of the terms "boys" and "girls" are entirely interchangeable and enforce that policy on pain of expulsion for anyone who disagrees. From a libertarian or classical liberal perspective, the meaning of "biological sex" is entirely preferential, and so if the majority of people (or, at least, a minority with the most power) want to pass a rule that says you must abide by that belief, at least publicly, in order to attend public school, so be it—children aren't fully autonomous (and thus not full bearers of individual rights) and their parents can choose to send them elsewhere or, if there is no "elsewhere" because they can't afford it, just keep them at home. While justifying such a policy may be more challenging with a Lockean framework because Locke, unlike Kant, upholds the epistemic and ontological category of "the natural," it remains the case that the Lockean model also permits an arational majority—or a minority with majority power—to impose its will on society without the possibility of rational contestation.

Indeed, this is precisely the connection I wish to draw between Lockeanism and the ideological cover it provides for maintaining and advancing the power of the monied elite. More broadly, the Lockean state, grounded in Locke's anthropology and epistemology, offers non-theistic conservatism three tools to engender and maintain the creation of a society that exalts the material interests of the monied class as its highest good. (Some of these characteristics also appear in the thought of George F. Will, which we will soon turn to.)

An Empirically False Socioeconomic "Starting Line"
While Locke admits that his description of a pre-societal and pre-civic "state of nature" is not meant to convey a historical truth about the human condition (i.e., humans have never actually lived this way), it nevertheless establishes a baseline of human equality not only in terms of dignity and rights—which is certainly praiseworthy—but also with regard to *socioeconomic* opportunity. The Lockean presupposition is that people start off with roughly the same potential to succeed materially; therefore, all or most inequality in society can be explained, a priori, by individual moral failure (e.g., being lazy, insufficiently industrious, wasteful, etc.). Conversely, those who have wealth in society can be causally explained—again, a priori given the anthropological presuppositions—as having their wealth because they "earned it" either by "mixing their labor with land," which is the justificatory ground of owning private property in Lockean thought (and, it is important to note, Catholic thought, as well), or because they acquired it using a common currency—i.e., money. As Locke writes in *The Second Treatise of Government*,

> But since gold and silver, being little useful to the life of man in proportion to food, raiment, and carriage, has its value only from the consent of men, whereof labour yet makes, in great part, the measure, it is plain, that men have agreed to a disproportionate and unequal possession of the earth, they having, *by a tacit and voluntary consent, found out, a way how*

a man may fairly possess more land than he himself can use the product of, by receiving in exchange for the overplus gold and silver, which may be hoarded up without injury to any one; these metals not spoiling or decaying in the hands of the possessor. This partage of things in an inequality of private possessions, men have made practicable out of the bounds of society, and without compact, only by putting a value on gold and silver, and tacitly agreeing in the use of money.[19]

To be sure, Locke condemns the hoarding of perishable goods on the grounds that they unnecessarily go to waste, which, he believes, violates the natural law. However, as we see in the quote above, hoarding—Locke's word, not mine—non-perishable wealth (i.e., "gold and silver") falls perfectly within the bounds of natural law. There is thus no principled reason why individuals cannot hoard wealth themselves and also use that wealth to acquire more property that, in turn, reduces opportunities for other individuals to acquire property, which in turn necessitates more individuals having to "consent" to the property-owner's terms in order to trade her or his labor for a wage in exchange for working on another individual's property. There is also no principled reason this hoarded wealth cannot be transferred to subsequent generations who can profit from its material and social benefits even though they have not earned it.

I want to stress that I am not highlighting this dimension of Locke's thought to leverage it into an argument against private property or in favor of high taxes. As I noted at the outset of this chapter, the Catholic social thought tradition unequivocally upholds an individual right to private property, which includes the right to employ that property to make profits, and even to become "rich." I am also not adopting a mercantilist view of economics that posits that there is a fixed amount of wealth in the world and,

19. John Locke, *Two Treatises of Government*, 2.5.50 (emphasis added).

thus, if one person has it that must mean that another person lost it. Wealth can obviously be created.

Rather, my critique of Locke's thought is both anthropological and sociological—namely, (1) the claim that individuals "start off" more or less with the same socioeconomic potential is empirically false, and (2) justifying the existence of inequality on an implicit right to hoard wealth establishes the theoretical and practical conditions for the creation of a profoundly socioeconomically unequal society, one in which those with the most wealth (and thus, likely, the most property) are able to set the terms which everyone else must "consent to" in order to make a living. In other words, so long as wealth and property are not explicitly stolen from anyone, there is no reason, in a Lockean society, why a wealthy cadre of individuals cannot increasingly constrict the socioeconomic opportunities of all in the name of their own individual freedom—an added insult to the injury of insisting that, to use contemporary language, everyone starts off on an even playing field in society.

Reducing the Definition of the "Public Good" to Agglomerated Self-Interest

While Locke recognizes the legitimacy of setting aside some land as "public"—provided individuals consent to create such lands[20]—it is important to remember that the *only* purpose of government, and thus every civil institution tied to government, is to serve individuals in their "procuring, preserving, and advancing their own civil interests." Recall, also, that he defines "civil interests" in entirely material terms, even including "furniture." Given these definitions, it is not clear how the "public good" could have any substantive content beyond preserving and advancing private interests. But how is this "public"? How can a society organized around these principles be spoken of as a "people"?

20. cf. John Locke, *Two Treatises of Government*, 2.5.35.

How can they be united in one common civic vision if the only substance of what defines that common vision is "individuals pursuing their own desires"? Indeed, how could such a "people" show any kind of *patriotism*? Isn't love of country, under such a model, merely just an extension of love of self? How could it be anything else? Even worse, when asking men and women to die for their country so defined, how can we honestly tell them that they are not sacrificing their lives so that *others*, especially those already high on the socioeconomic perch, can become rich(er)?

I don't want to overplay my hand on this point; the Lockean principles that define "civil interests" in exclusively material terms still provide a bulwark against state tyranny and that is an unqualified good. However, it is important to keep in mind that that's *all* a Lockean government is designed to do—protect lives and property from others and from the government. Yet think of everything that does not fall into these categories: for example, a civic commitment to the education of children; a civic commitment to the well-being of families; a civic commitment to encouraging the development of a virtuous citizenry (e.g., people interested in pursuing justice for the sake of justice and not only as a requisite tool to advance their own interests); a civic commitment to mitigate poverty; a civic commitment to care for the elderly and others who are no longer (or never were) "worth" anything to the economy; a civic commitment to assist foreign peoples, to the extent it is prudent, in their own struggles against tyranny and/or penury; indeed, even a civic commitment to teaching "civics" itself. While a Lockean people *could* support these policies politically, they would, according to Locke's underlying anthropology and epistemology, have no reason to do so beyond sheer individual preference. Since "the common good" can only mean "the individual good writ large," the citizen who lives to maximize his own health and wealth within the bounds of the law and the citizen who lives to maximize others' wealth and health within the bounds of the law are rationally and, thus, morally indistinguishable. Or to put a finer point on it, Lockean government cannot mark a rationally defensible evaluative difference between those who choose to die for their country and those who choose only to use it as an ATM.

Defining God as Indifferent to Individual Flourishing and the Common Good

It is important to keep in mind that Locke's argument has a theistic foundation: government's sole function is to protect rights that human beings possess by virtue of God having endowed them with those rights in and through reason and the natural law. To remove "God" from Locke's political theory would thus be to pull the rug out from underneath it. The whole thing would fall.

How, then, is it justified to say that Lockeanism represents a form of non-theistic conservatism? Recall that non-theistic conservatism, as I defined it at the beginning of the chapter, does not necessarily deny God's existence. However, it does maintain, either explicitly or implicitly, that God, to the extent his existence can be known, is *indifferent* to the moral character of the political order. A non-theistic conservative may appeal to "God" as an ontologically real ground of some fundamental truth claim—for example, that a natural law exists and that humans possess rights by virtue of that law. However, the same God within this theological framework is devoid of all agency (God does not have a "will" or, if he does, it does not have political relevance) and is thus devoid of any interest in the moral and material wellbeing of any individual, society, or humanity as a whole. Indeed, this is what distinguishes "theism," as it is typically defined, from "deism": the former describes belief in the existence of a personal God that both creates the world and maintains an ongoing interest in its flourishing, especially human flourishing, while the latter describes belief in the existence of God as a causal first principle—an unmoved mover, in Aristotelian terms—that makes the world metaphysically possible but is otherwise remote from, and uninterested in, everything in it, including human beings. Thus, analogous to how the principles of mathematics can justify the existence of apodictically true answers yet have no "concern" or "interest" in whether answers are known or if anyone is getting them right, the God of non-theistic conservatism may be able to justify the existence of a natural law conceptually, but it has no concern for whether those laws are respected. Moreover, such a God would be indifferent to anyone who surpasses their minimal natural-law duties (refraining from harming others and respecting contracts) to create a society that assists individuals in realizing their full economic and moral potentials.

This is precisely the God that Lockean thought offers to non-theistic conservatism—just enough divinity to justify the existence of an objectively fixed human nature and, derivatively, objective individual rights, but not enough to justify the formation of a society that has any common interest in seeking a substantive common good. Indeed, recall that the identification of the existence of a common good—a good that is inclusive of but transcends the individual good—is epistemically impossible from a Lockean perspective because both the substantive nature of, and means to, attaining the "final purpose" of human beings is relegated to the realm of "faith," which is, from his theological perspective, rationally indistinguishable from private opinion and preference and, therefore, of no relevance to the justification and proper functioning of the state. In short, what Lockeanism offers non-theistic conservatism is the ability to talk about "God" and "the natural law" and "divinely endowed individual rights" while being functionally indistinguishable from a libertarian who sees the comprehensive purpose of the state as reducible to one-part armed security guard and one-part tort judge.

A MARRIAGE OF CONVENIENCE

Yet how does all this support the claim that Lockeanism enables socioeconomic elitism? And how, given their substantial, even diametrical differences, is it fair to say that *both* Lockeanism and Aristotelianism support non-theistic conservatism?

In response to the first question, the three features of Lockean thought highlighted above provide both theoretical and practical conditions for the creation of a deeply unequal society. For example, taking as a sociological presupposition that all individuals start off life on a relatively even playing field is not only empirically false (in the United States, for example, 16% of children were living in poverty in 2020[21]; the percentage goes as high as 42% when poverty is defined as "episodic"[22]); this false starting line also obscures a proper understanding of "merit" and "desert" as it relates to the top socioeconomic brackets in society. There is a very strong statistical correlation, for example, between the income of parents and the income of their adult children: the wealthier the household the children are born into, the more likely they are to earn high incomes themselves in adulthood. The opposite is also true: the poorer the household children are born into, the less likely they will earn high incomes as adults. The nonpartisan data analysis site FiveThirtyEight summarizes this relationship between poverty and future income as "Rich Kids Stay Rich, Poor Kids Stay Poor."[23]

I do not spotlight these figures to suggest that being born into poverty destines someone to be poor; my own father-in-law was abandoned as a child and spent years living alone on the streets of Buenos Aires before, slowly and with great sacrifice, building a life

21. Emily A. Shrider, Melissa Kollar, Frances Chen, and Jessica Semega, "Income and Poverty in the United States: 2020," United States Census Bureau website, September 14, 2021, https://www.census.gov/library/publications/2021/demo/p60-273.html.

22. Abinash Mohanty, "Seniors and Children Typically Remained in Poverty Longer Than Working-Age Adults," United States Census Bureau website, August 30, 2021, https://www.census.gov/library/stories/2021/08/children-experienced-episodic-poverty-at-higher-rate-than-adults.html.

23. Ben Casselman and Andrew Flowers, "Rich Kids Stay Rich, Poor Kids Stay Poor," FiveThirtyEight, February 1, 2016, https://fivethirtyeight.com/features/rich-kids-stay-rich-poor-kids-stay-poor/.

that could support a middle-class family. I'm also not suggesting that individuals living in poverty have no responsibility for their condition; that, too, is insulting to all those who fought and fight their way to stability and, even, prosperity. Rather, the point of noting these basic statistics is to mark the general empirical truth that being born into poverty substantially negatively affects your opportunities to flourish, economically and otherwise, in life. Moreover, the greater point to stress for this context is that, whatever the specific causes that explain these statistics, *the statistic itself is not a politically relevant problem to Lockean non-theistic conservatism.* In other words, non-theistic conservatives have no principled reason, based on their non-theistic conservative beliefs alone, to be concerned about socioeconomic inequality or even poverty.

To be fair, Locke does argue that people have an individual duty of charity towards each other. He argues in the *First Treatise*,

> But we know God hath not left one man so to the mercy of another, that he may starve him if he please: God, the Lord and Father of all, has given no one of his children such a property in his peculiar portion of the things of this world, but that he has given his needy brother a right to the surplusage of his goods; so that it cannot justly be denied him, when his pressing wants call for it: and therefore no man could ever have a just power over the life of another by right of property in land or possessions; since it would always be a sin, in any man of estate, to let his brother perish for want of affording him relief out of his plenty. *As justice gives every man a title to the product of his honest industry, and the fair acquisitions of his ancestors descended to him; so charity gives every man a title to so much out of another's plenty as will keep him from extreme want, where he has no means to subsist otherwise*: and a man can no more justly make use of another's necessity to force him to become his vassal, by withholding that relief God requires him

to afford to the wants of his brother, than he that has more strength can seize upon a weaker, master him to his obedience, and with a dagger at his throat offer him death or slavery.[24]

Locke does, therefore, show some concern for the welfare of the poor. He argues that one with abundant resources must never "let his brother perish for want of affording him relief out of his plenty." However, without downplaying the importance of this passage in evaluating the overall Lockean conception of a just state, keep these two qualifiers in mind, which the passage also makes clear: (1) the duty to assist the poor is an individual duty based not on justice but rather on charity (which, in turn, is grounded in private faith—cf., "God the Lord and Father of all"); (2) even if assisting the poor could be interpreted societally from a Lockean perspective, it still only applies to severe material deprivation—i.e., "extreme want" that is analogous to "death or slavery." A society founded on Lockean principles of justice thus has no general obligation, to the extent it has any obligation at all, to mitigate poverty and socioeconomic inequality that does not fall into the category of basic survival, which means that most of the markers of poverty used by the US Census Bureau to generate the numbers cited above would be of no common political concern. To be sure, Lockean individuals may take a private interest in supporting the poor, but such interest would merely be an individual preference with no rational or moral connection to any civically shared conception of justice.

All of this is to repeat the main point here: the Lockean society is made for those who are best able—not only by merit and effort but *by birth*—to take advantage of their good fortune to create the conditions that further empower them to make an even better fortune. Indeed—and this highlights the second and third features of Locke's thought in non-theistic conservatism—there

---

24. Locke, *First Treatise*, 2.42 (emphasis added).

is no reason, no rational limiting principle, why the fortunate could not deliberately and explicitly engineer a society in such a way. Locke clearly defines the purpose of the state as protecting life and property. Given this is the *sole* function of the state, what prevents those with socioeconomic advantage from using the state not only to preserve their advantage but to augment it by, for example, paying lobbyists to butter up politicians who then pass tax laws that make it easier for corporations to sell their products at cheaper prices than their "Main Street" competitors, which puts "Main Street" out of business, which, in turn, increases corporate profits and the financial capacity to lobby for more control of the market? Or what prevents massive real estate companies from buying up tens of thousands of properties—turning once-single-family homes into rental units—and then raising the rent on all of them simultaneously, thus forcing tenants in local rental markets either to pay the higher rent or move out, further from their jobs and extended families? What prevents entire industries from shuttering factories and moving them overseas where they can pay a fraction of the wages they used to pay while those laid off back home can no longer afford their mortgage, even while they watch the value of their home plummet? Or what would prevent a corporation from laying off an employee with a sterling service record for the company after 25 years because it is cheaper, both in salary and benefits, to divide her/his job into two part-time positions? Or what would prevent the CEOs of all the major banks and credit card companies from coming to an agreement that they will not permit consumers to use their products to "undermine reproductive rights" (i.e., support pro-life causes) while also ensuring that there are no other viable alternatives for consumers to use in the market? Notwithstanding the complex economic and corporate-governing-structure questions embedded in these examples, the Lockean strand within non-theistic conservatism looks at each of these scenarios and says, "Too bad, but them's the breaks; market's gotta do what the market's gotta do." Since everyone has ostensibly consented in these examples—e.g., the corporations consented to offer you a job, you consented to take it—what happens in the aftermath is of no societal concern. No one was murdered, nothing was criminally stolen, no contracts were even violated (you can ask the lawyers). So what's the big deal?

The big deal is that economically and socially eviscerating entire cities is not a moral problem for non-theistic conservatism. And it's precisely not a problem because the whole system is designed so that the good of the market—and, more specifically, the good of those who have the most power and influence over the market—becomes king, *the de facto ruler* of society. There is no limiting principle to prevent this outcome because, again, (a) the "public good" explicitly means nothing more than protecting individual life and property, and (b) there is no conception of God—no metaphysical ground not only of natural law and individual rights but also for a *common good*—coming to the rescue. Similar to Aristotelianism, "God" is either silent on the question of the moral character of society (at least outside the bounds of personal, preferential "faith") or tacitly endorses deep socioeconomic inequality, which means the most powerful get to speak for everyone by default.

Yet what about the other characteristics of Aristotelianism? How can they coexist with Lockeanism under the same ideological tent? Although the fit is awkward, incoherent even, it is in the combining of Aristotle and Locke that the comprehensive character of non-theistic conservatism comes into focus. Aristotle, though he defended private property,[25] would find it unbearably vulgar to say that the whole purpose of the state is to protect property (and its owners). For Aristotle, the purpose of the state—the purpose of politics—is to habituate citizens into a life

25. Lee Trepanier, "An Aristotelian Defense of Private Property in the Age of the Sharing Economy," Public Discourse, June 21, 2022, https://www.the publicdiscourse.com/2022/06/82939/.

of virtuous friends who collectively realize their individual moral potential in community. That is, the purpose of the state, for Aristotle, is to produce morally good people who mutually labor to produce a morally good state. For Locke, describing the purpose of the state in these terms would be unbearably aristocratic and a profound violation of natural liberty. It appears that we are at an ideological impasse here: individual freedom vs. communal virtue; economic prosperity vs. moral flourishing; ambition vs. wisdom; etc.

But what if we could find a way to unite the clans? What if we keep Locke's emphasis on freedom and property and combine it with the Aristotelian ideal of a rightly habituated citizenry that sees itself as the unique repository of correct moral thinking? What if, even better, we could say that living for the advancement of your own socioeconomic interest is the definition of virtue itself and, therefore, those who fail socioeconomically are not only materially poorer but also morally inferior? What if, even better than that, we could say that this whole system, designed to favor the prosperous, is not only just but also divinely sanctioned by God's nature and nature's God? Now *that* would be a powerful ideology, one so potent it could transform moral lead into the appearance of gold: good fortune into moral desert, economic necessity into consent, and greed into patriotism.

GEORGE F. WILL'S *THE CONSERVATIVE SENSIBILITY*

These two conceptual pillars of non-theistic conservatism—high-minded aristocratic virtue on one side, pragmatic self-interest on the other—lie at the foundation of political theorist George F. Will's *The Conservative Sensibility*. Will's work is scholarly, comprehensive, exhaustively researched, and cleverly written. Indeed, it is fair to say that there is more in common between the Catholic social thought tradition and *The Conservative Sensibility* than any other contemporary secular text cited in this book. Will rejects both hedonistic utilitarianism and progressivism and, while sympathetic to some classical liberal/libertarian arguments, also eschews founding politics on Kantian autonomy. Consonant with Catholic social thought, Will also defends a universal human nature, the existence of a morally objective natural law (based on human nature), and the existence of inalienable individual rights. He also advocates for the creation of a virtuous society, to the extent it is possible. There is, in short, significant overlap between Will's conservative sensibility and the Catholic sensibility. The problem, however, is that Will builds his political vision atop a *non-theistic* foundation, which, as we will see, ineluctably leads his project into the conceptual and moral mishmash of Aristotelianism and Lockeanism that is the hallmark of non-theistic conservatism.

Will begins by framing American history as an ongoing ideological battle between Madisonians (after James Madison, one of the drafters of the Constitution and the fourth president of the United States) and Wilsonians (after Woodrow Wilson, the twenty-eighth president of the United States and the individual, in Will's mind, most responsible for first turning the US away from its constitutional principles of limited government and toward a progressive expansion of state power). Without delving into the nitty gritty of this historical record, a task Will deftly accomplishes, *The Conservative Sensibility*'s case against both Wilsonian policies and their underlying progressive ideology is persuasive. Will effectively frames Wilson as the country's first culturally and politically progressive figure—and chapter 7 of this book has already said its piece about the merits of progressivism (though, to be fair, the progressivism of Woodrow Wilson would hardly be able to recognize today's progressivism, even though they have the same theoretical foundation). What is most relevant for our purposes, therefore, is not Will's argument against progressivism but rather his argument *for* conservatism.

Will emphasizes that the brand of conservatism he defends has little in common with "European conservatism," which he writes is "descended from, and often is still tainted by, throne-and-altar, blood-and-soil nostalgia, irrationality, and tribalism."[26] In contrast, Will's conservatism—"American conservatism," as he calls it—not only has a different historical genealogy to "throne and altar" conservatism; it is antagonistic to it. Describing the fundamental task of American conservatism as being the "custodians of the classical liberal tradition,"[27] Will writes,

> The label "liberal" was minted to identify those whose primary concern was not the protection of community solidarity or traditional hierarchies, but rather was the expansion and protection of individual liberty. Liberals were then those who considered the state the primary threat to this. Liberals espoused the exercise of natural rights within a spacious zone of personal sovereignty guaranteed by governments instituted to serve as guarantors of those rights.[28]

What makes American conservatism's embrace of liberalism distinct, for Will, is that it is written into the very DNA of America's founding. As he writes,

> Unique among all nations, the United States knows precisely when and exactly why it was founded. American conservatism is an ongoing meditation on America's Founding, which means on the Declaration of Independence and on the Constitution, which should be construed in the bright light cast by the Declaration's affirmation of natural rights. The American project, distilled to its essence was, and the conservative project is, to demonstrate that a government constructed on the assumption of natural rights must be limited government. The

26. George F. Will, *The Conservative Sensibility* (New York: Hachette Books, 2019), xxv–xxvi.
27. Will, xxvi.
28. Will, xxvi.

natural rights theory is that individuals in the state of nature possess rights that pre-exist government; that the government is created for the limited purpose of securing those rights; and that the individual surrenders some sovereignty to government on the basis of a rational calculation that government secures more sovereignty than it requires to be surrendered.[29]

The echoes of John Locke's theory of government are deliberately palpable here. For Will, "classical liberalism," properly defined, emerges from a Lockean conception of natural law and human nature, not a Kantian conception of autonomy (it is no accident that Immanuel Kant is only mentioned once in the six-hundred-page book). The reason the difference between the origins of liberalism matters—even if, as I'll argue below, the sociopolitical outcome is similar (individuals defining the good however they like with no rationally common, fixed reference point)—is that, unlike Kant who rejects all classical metaphysics, Locke (and, therefore, Will) has no philosophical objection to using "nature" to justify a political theory.

On the surface, this should provide Will's position an advantage over Kantian liberalism because the capacity to appeal to "human nature" can ostensibly provide the rational possibility of identifying objectively fixed human goods that, in turn, can order the political system in a way that prevents it from devolving into a collection of rationally arbitrary expressions of individual will, a problem we examined in chapter 7. However, keep in mind that Will's conception of human nature is specifically *Lockean*, which means, as we saw above, that it lacks the intellectual resources to identify a rationally accessible common human good. Indeed, it is this feature of Lockean natural law—that it explicitly excludes a common "summum bonum" for human beings—that most attracts Will to Locke's conception of human nature over rival

29. Will, xxx–xxxi.

versions of human nature (for example, the kind we see in the Catholic social thought tradition). Comparing John Locke to Thomas Hobbes (Will rejects Hobbes's thought, but embraces Locke's), he writes,

> Hobbes and Locke differed—but not about the important point, which is that there is no single *Summum bonum*. There are as many as there are palates. *It is a matter of taste.* This is, in two senses, the beginning of the political philosophy of modernity, the dawn of the modern enterprise. The challenge of modernity is to argue that a broad spectrum of tastes exist, and many tastes should be accommodated, even though not all tastes are equally admirable or socially beneficial. Regarding the ultimate good, Locke said "men may chuse [sic] different things, and yet all chuse right." This proposition was the point of embarkation for what would become what now is called classical liberalism.[30]

Note that, insofar as Will is defending "classical liberalism," he is thus explicitly rejecting, by his own reasoning, a unified, substantive, and comprehensive human good. Indeed, he reduces "the good" to "taste," which is another way of saying that each person's conception of the good is arational—neither consonant with reason nor contrary to reason, but rather an arbitrary expression of individual preference.

It is important to pause here and flag the puzzling claim that Will nestles within this description and endorsement of classical liberalism—namely, that, on the one hand, conceptions of the good are merely "tastes," but, on the other hand, not all "tastes" are equally "admirable" or "socially beneficial." The problem is that Will is seeking to retrieve an ideal with one assertion that he has just discarded with another: namely, that there is a

30. Will, 5–6.

non-preferential principle for objectively distinguishing between "tastes" that are "admirable" and "less admirable" and "useful" and "less useful." Upholding the existence of an objective summum bonum *could* do that moral work by, for example, identifying actions and habits of character that instantiate the highest good as "admirable" and those that contradict the highest good as "less admirable" (or just plain "bad"). Indeed, that's the role that "virtue" plays in these kinds of teleological moral systems: virtue is the name given to habits individuals develop, by means of performing good actions, that propel them towards the objective final good.

But that's precisely the issue here: as a conservative classical liberal, Will *rejects* the existence of a final objective good and, thus, obliterates any rational standard for distinguishing among "tastes." Indeed, Will confirms this interpretation—that there is no final human good or objective definition of "happiness" (another term Will uses to describe the good)—in the following passage. Note that his whole justification for limited government is founded on this claim, which, in turn, sets him up to argue that the state's only proper function is to create the largest civic space possible for individuals to pursue their own desires:

> The case for limited government is grounded in the empirical evidence that human beings have something in common— human nature—but are nevertheless incorrigibly different in capacities and aspirations. From this it follows, not logically but practically, that government cannot hope to provide happiness to all. Rather, the most it can reasonably expect to provide are the conditions under which happiness, as each defines it, can be pursued, as each is equipped, by nature or nurture, to do so.[31]

31. Will, 8.

The chain of reasoning here is difficult to follow. Even if it is the case that no government can "provide happiness to all," that does not mean that "happiness" cannot be objectively defined. In fact, Will seems to make a category error by conflating the problem of *attaining* a common societal good—which, indeed, is impossible given individuals' varied capacities and their penchant to sin—with the problem of *defining* an objective societal good, which is not only possible but necessary in order to distinguish conservatism from libertarianism. However, it seems that's precisely Will's goal here: to create a justification for government in which each person can define the good however she or he desires with no restrictions so long as the pursuit of that good does not violate the rights of others. Yet if that is the case, why doesn't Will skip "nature" and the "American Constitutional tradition" and the "wisdom of the founders"? His detour through history and natural law is precisely that—a detour—if the final destination of his argument is the justification of a government of, by, and for the autonomous self. So why doesn't he just quote some Kant and leave it there?

Perhaps the answer is that Will still desires to incorporate some account of politically relevant virtue in his theory, even if he knows, deep down, that his reduction of happiness to "tastes" renders all permitted actions (that is, actions that do not violate anyone's rights) as equally morally arbitrary and thus neither praiseworthy (virtuous) nor condemnable (vicious). In support of this interpretation, it's important to note that, much earlier in his career, Will wrote a book entitled *Statecraft as Soulcraft: What Government Does* in which he sharply criticizes an excess of "individualism" and argues that the government should play an essential role in producing good citizens. Will also cites none other than *Aristotle* to make his case for a conservatism that seeks to ennoble the populace. He writes,

Aristotle was the first consciously conservative philosopher because of his premise that what is generally predominates over what ought to be. But he is a founder of conservatism, properly understood, because his realism did not preclude a politics that takes its bearings from what ought to be. The United States acutely needs a real conservatism, characterized by a concern to cultivate the best persons and the best in persons. It should express renewed appreciation for the ennobling functions of government. It should challenge the liberal doctrine that regarding one important dimension of life—the "inner life"—there should be less government—less than there is now, less than there recently was, less than most political philosophers have thought prudent.[32]

How can we square the George Will of this passage, who calls for government to enter the "inner life" of its citizens to bring out the best of them, with the George Will who emphatically rejects the existence of a *summum bonum* in politics and identifies the good with "tastes"? One answer is that Will just changed his mind. Fair enough. I've changed my mind on some fundamental issues too. However, there are arguments in *The Conservative Sensibility* that suggest that Will is not quite ready to jettison the goal of producing virtuous citizens. He writes, for example, "A government [overseeing a society composed of self-determining individuals] need not be uninterested in improving the souls of its citizens, but it must do so by respecting their reasonableness and thereby encouraging them to subordinate passion to reason."[33] Will then cites the Founders to argue that the condition for the possibility of having citizens who do, indeed, subordinate passion to reason, which is necessary for constitutional government to

32. George F. Will, *Statecraft as Soulcraft: What Government Does* (New York: Touchstone Books, 1983), 24.
33. Will, *The Conservative Sensibility*, 20.

function, is that citizens must have "good motives" that are manifestations of "good character." He writes,

> [The] Founders [did not] presuppose that America could prosper without good motives. Such motives are manifestations of good character, and America's Founders did not suppose that freedom can thrive, or even survive, without appropriate education, broadly understood to include not just education by schools but also by all the institutions of civil society that explain freedom and equip citizens with the virtues freedom requires. These virtues include industriousness, self-control, moderation, and responsibility, virtues that reinforce the rationality essential to human happiness.[34]

Will also writes, "This, then, is the crux of the conservative project: to advocate those practices—political, economic, and cultural—that are conducive to flourishing, understood as living virtuously."[35]

It thus seems that Will *does* believe that the government should be in the virtue business: If the government's job is to protect individual freedom, and individual freedom can only exist if it is governed by rationality, and rationality can only function properly if it is governed by virtue, then it would seem to be government's job to protect virtue. Although Will does not put it this way, his argument about the relationship between individual freedom and the correct function of government seems unavoidably to lead to this conclusion. In this sense, then, Will sounds much more like Aristotle than John Locke.

There is another strand of Will's argument that also sounds Aristotelian: there appear to be classes of individuals who, because of their defective upbringing, *cannot* develop the virtues that are

---

34. Will, 21.
35. Will, 506.

necessary for the proper functioning of reason and, therefore, cannot be expected to participate fully in democratic society. To be sure, Will never claims that there exists an inequality of dignity among human beings; much the opposite, he praises the founders for repudiating moral distinctions among individuals with regard to their fundamental nature. He writes,

> The classical idea of human nature is . . . aristocratic: all men are human, but some are more so, and that is the crucial political fact. The modern idea of human nature is democratic: no difference among us can reach so far as to alter our naturally equal humanness, and *that* is the crucial fact.[36]

Will also argues in favor of limited government by maintaining—with support from extensive empirical evidence—that concentrating power in government ends up exacerbating social inequalities by enabling those with the time and resources—that is, the wealthy and well-connected—to lobby government to serve their private interests. "Regulation," Will writes, drawing on insights from James Madison, "inherently confers advantages on those who have the education and time to 'watch' and the skill, or perhaps the hired representation, to 'trace' what goes on in the government's labyrinthine interior."[37] There is, then, a case to be made for conservatism, according to Will, on the grounds that it is more *egalitarian* than competing political theories.

Yet this "egalitarianism" does not necessarily translate into the realm of virtue, which, recall, Will believes is necessary for the protection of freedom and the proper functioning of government. In his chapter "The Aims of Education," Will distinguishes between "values," which he believes are democratic in a negative

---

36. Will, 27.
37. Will, 267–268.

sense (i.e., plebian), and "virtues," which are, by definition, reserved for the few. He writes,

> How very democratic values talk is. Unlike virtues, everyone
> has values; everyone has as many as they choose. . . . Values
> are an equal-opportunity business; they are mere choices. In
> contrast, virtues are habits, difficult to develop and therefore
> not equally accessible to all. Speaking of virtues rather than
> values is *elitist*, offensive to democracy's egalitarian ethos,
> which is precisely why talk of virtues should be revived and
> talk of values should be devalued.[38]

Will goes on to argue that it is the task of education, higher
education in particular, to cultivate virtue, especially those virtues
that are necessary for the healthy functioning of a democratic
society: "The purpose of education, especially higher education,
for young citizens of democracy is to help them identify a rarity—
excellence—in various realms, and to study what virtues bring it
about and make it excellent."[39]

Combining the claims in these passages, Will generates a
syllogism that would make Aristotle proud:

Premise 1: The proper functioning of democracy depends
upon the cultivation of virtue.

Premise 2: The cultivation of virtue depends upon a
proper moral education.

Conclusion: Therefore, the proper functioning of democracy depends upon a proper moral education.

The next question for Will would be (we already know Aristotle's answer) whether the "proper moral education" is equally

38. Will, 380–381 (emphasis added).
39. Will, 381.

accessible to all both in terms of capacities *and* opportunities. By explicitly associating virtue with "elitism," the answer already appears to be "no"—virtue (and thus having the capacity to serve as a guardian of democracy) is a rarity that belongs only to those who have been appropriately habituated in both the nature and pursuit of "excellence" rightly understood. Will's chapter on "Culture and Opportunity" seems to confirm this conclusion. While exhibiting great sympathy for individuals born into material poverty and social dysfunction, Will remains pessimistic about their long-term prospects to flourish in society. He writes, for example,

> At least 15 percent of IQ points are experientially rather than genetically based, and the preschool experiences of some children can cost them a significant portion of those points. Studies of "failure to thrive" babies and their mothers suggest a strategy for combating the syndrome. Very early intervention, involving close and protracted supervision of young mothers, can "jump start" their mothering skills. There are, however, too many single mothers who need this long, labor-intensive, and therefore expensive attention. *An America in which a majority of mothers under thirty are not living with the fathers of their children is simply not going to be able to supply a social policy that can compensate for the defects of fragmented families.*[40]

It is important to stress that Will is not claiming, on principle, that civil society should abandon the poor. Indeed, the chapter concludes by advocating for a government that "concerns itself with a minimum of what can be called moral essentials."[41] Rather, he is basing his minimalist view of government in relation to the poor on what he takes to be an empirically grounded belief: that

40. Will, 321–322 (emphasis added).
41. Will, 351.

the state has little capacity to improve society and, therefore, should generally refrain from trying to do so. In addition to this argument, however (the argument that government shouldn't do that which it is incapable of doing, which is compelling if shown to be true), Will adds that social policies that aim for equality of opportunity are often based on "envy":

> The issue of inequality has become more salient as affluence has increased, which suggests two conclusions: People are less dissatisfied by what they lack than by what others have. And when government engages in redistribution in order to maximize the happiness of citizens who become more envious as they become more comfortable, government is apt to become increasingly frenzied and futile.... Besides, envy is not something that should be encouraged by being rewarded.[42]

Thus, though Will's conservatism carves some minimal space for addressing the worst of socioeconomic inequality, the facts that (a) there isn't much the state can do to diminish poverty or inequality, and (b) such acts would likely be based on, and further aggravate, the envy of the "have nots" and "have lesses," his overriding conclusion is that the state should generally steer clear of trying to foster equality of opportunity. He recognizes that the cost of creating such a society is that many, perhaps most, people will have to deal with substantial economic and social unpredictability. Yet such unpredictably, for Will, is to be welcomed, if not celebrated. He writes, "To the conservative sensibility, much of the pleasure of life derives from the fact that in an open society, events, and the future, are splendidly beyond control."[43]

42. Will, 278–279.
43. Will, 298.

COSMIC LUCK

In the end, then, Will resigns himself—"splendidly" so—to what he takes to be the way things are in life in general and, therefore, in civic life, as well: everyone's born morally equal, but some people are fortunate enough to have the opportunity to become full flourishing democratic citizens (i.e., those who are not consigned to poverty and are educated in virtue), and some don't—and there isn't much the former can, or, even if they could, should do for the latter, lest they enflame the vice of envy. The best we can thus hope for in an unpredictable existence is to let everyone do what they want to as long as they respect the rights of others to do the same (Locke) and, if possible, inculcate some civic virtue in those who are properly disposed to receive it along the way (Aristotle). That is as good as it gets.

Yet how is it possible to unite these two disparate visions of politics, one paradigmatically aristocratic, the other paradigmatically individualistic? Answering this question ultimately points to the greatest weakness in Will's argument: it *isn't* possible, because "American conservatism," as Will describes it, lacks both a metaphysical *floor* to hold the anthropological weight of a Lockean morally equal human nature and a metaphysical *ceiling* to justify the Aristotelian vision of politics inculcating moral "excellence." The consequence of this incoherence is not only conceptual; it paves the way for the implementation of a political system that structurally favors the fortunate, those who are born into material and social opportunity, under the aegis of both "individualism" and "civic virtue." In other words, it is precisely because Will jettisons the necessity of a theistic definition of "God" from his theory that he ends up representing the tenets of non-theistic conservativism.

In a break from the thought of John Locke, who otherwise receives fulsome praise in *The Conservative Sensibility*, Will argues that American conservatism does not require a theological foundation to be coherent, even if religion can be "helpful." He writes,

Regarding the question of our government's logic, the idea of natural rights does not require a religious foundation, and the Founders did not uniformly think it did. It is, however, perhaps the case that natural rights are especially firmly grounded when they are grounded in religious doctrine.... So religion is helpful and important, but not essential. This formulation ... is neither hypocritical nor self-contradictory precisely because of the character of the American tradition.[44]

Will goes on to argue that those who claim that atheists cannot, on principle, defend the existence of natural rights are making a logical error, to wit: the empirical fact that there are people, like Will, a self-declared "amiable low-voltage atheist,"[45] who *do* affirm the existence of natural rights disproves the claim that atheism and the affirmation of natural rights cannot coherently coexist. Will argues,

It is false, and politically ruinous, for conservatives to assert that conservatism requires a shared religion or even ubiquitous religiosity. The assertion that particular virtues depend, or that virtue generally depends, on religion is an empirical claim, and demonstrably false. There are many virtuous unbelievers, and many virtues with no religious provenance, and many religious people who are not virtuous.[46]

In other words, Will is appealing to the "good atheist" syllogism in response to the question "Can atheists be good people?" It takes the following form:

Premise 1: A good person is someone who acts like a good person.

44. Will, 473.
45. Will, 479.
46. Will, 481.

Premise 2: There are atheists who act like a good person.

Conclusion: Therefore, there are atheists who are good persons.

The syllogism also cuts the other way:

Premise 1: A good person is someone who acts like a good person.

Premise 2: There are believers in God who do not act like a good person.

Conclusion: Therefore, there are believers in God who are not good persons.

Will's argument on the "logic" of the non-necessity of God for the existence of natural rights merely modifies this syllogism to attain the same conclusion.

Premise 1: An American conservative is someone who believes in natural rights and virtue.

Premise 2: There are atheists who believe in natural rights and virtue.

Conclusion: Therefore, there are atheists who are American conservatives.

The problem with all these syllogisms, however, is that they all beg the fundamental question: Are "natural rights" and "virtues" *true*? Or, to use ontological language: Are "natural rights and virtue" *real*? Notwithstanding Will's admirable desire to make the conservative tent as inclusive as possible, the "good atheist" argument as it applies to natural rights makes a fundamental category error by conflating *belief* (and acting in accordance with that belief) with *justification for belief* (and justification for acting in accordance with that belief). The empirical fact that anyone, atheist or non-atheist, believes in something or acts in accordance with their beliefs tells us *nothing* about whether those beliefs are true. The relevant question, then, is not *Does any particular atheist believe in natural rights and virtue?* but *Does atheism itself support that belief?*

Reframed this way, it's not clear how Will can coherently justify his conception of American conservatism. Atheism, as a doctrine, is not only the belief that God does not exist but also, and consequently, that there is no universal, objectively real meaning or purpose in existence, including human existence. Therefore, all "values" and "virtues" are reducible either to the arbitrary will of a group (cultural relativism) or to the arbitrary will of an individual (subjectivism). Consequently, if atheism is true, the statement "Individual rights objectively exist" is false; the statement "Individual rights objectively exist *and* we have a universal duty to respect those rights" is comically false. The same goes with "virtue": if atheism is true, the statement "It is objectively good to pursue moral excellence" is objectively false precisely because there is no "objective good." Whether any self-described atheist happens to believe this about natural rights and virtue is irrelevant; just as a flat-earther believing that the earth is flat does not, in fact, make the earth flat, an atheist believing in individual rights and virtues does not, in fact, make those values true.

Though they have their own logical issues, there are two possible escape hatches to this predicament Will could have taken: (1) he could adopt a form of Kantianism and claim that individual rights are embedded in the operation of human reason itself, or (2) he could adopt some form of utilitarian materialism and claim that believing in natural rights and virtue may not correspond with the actual existence of rights and virtue but acting as if they did exist is socially useful. However, Will's embrace of both Lockean "nature" as ontologically real and morally dispositive *and* Aristotelian virtue as the condition for, and result of, a properly functioning civil society disqualifies the

Kantian route as a solution because Kant rejects the possibility of knowing anything at all about "nature." With regard to the second option, materialistic utilitarianism, Will does, at times, refer to his political theory as a form of utilitarianism, like when he states, for example, that the Founders "were, without quite knowing it, rule utilitarians . . . saying that certain behaviors, practices, and conventions are, as a general rule, conducive to happiness and flourishing."[47] Yet embracing utilitarianism would also entail dropping the affirmation that individual rights are *inalienable* (i.e., they must never be violated no matter what the consequences), which remains at the heart of Will's argument. It would also entail embracing materialism itself and the consequent belief that, since "freedom" is not a kind of matter, there is no such thing as free will. Yet Will rejects this, too, writing,

> Yes, the mind is an emanation of the brain, it *is* the brain. This, however, does not make each of us . . . "just a soft machine." And none of this means that our reasoning is beyond our control, or that we are, at bottom, beyond the control of our reasoning.[48]

So, if not Kantianism, utilitarianism, Lockeanism, or Aristotelianism, what *philosophically coherent* foundation is supporting Will's political theory? In the end, it's just not clear. Once you sift through the erudite and keenly insightful historical, sociological, and public policy analysis in *The Conservative Sensibility*, it seems that the whole edifice of "American conservatism" is ultimately constructed upon two disjointed pillars, whose respective foundations are lost in a murky intellectual cloud beneath (1) self-interest (government only exists to protect individuals from each other and to enforce contracts) and (2) the American

47. Will, 12.
48. Will, 500.

democratic "tradition"—yet since "tradition" in Will's argument is not grounded in objective moral reality (despite his argument to the contrary), it is indistinguishable from sheer custom. The custom, moreover, also happens to correspond with the values of those with the right kind of education, the moral elite who truly understand what "virtue is" and why it's necessary for civic society.

It should thus come as no surprise that the "conservative sensibility" seems to be found predominantly among those who occupy the upper echelons of the socioeconomic pyramid, where life is, on the whole, stable and comfortable and predictable; where the thought of having to choose between heating your (rental) home or eating three meals a day is as remote—as ridiculous—as the thought of ever stepping foot in a corner payday loan store; where you always buy new things when they break and have never once anxiously thought, "If my car breaks down again today, I'm going to lose my job." To be sure, there are many rich and powerful who pay their moral tithe by embracing progressive-wokeist ideology, an ideology that offers the public appearance of concern for the "marginalized" without having to change how you live. Yet non-theistic conservatism, like that which we see in *The Conservative Sensibility*, offers another attractive ideological option: being able to tell yourself that you are who you are and have everything you do because you are virtuous and, conversely, the reason that others aren't as successful is because they just don't have the moxie, good habits, and (since we're being honest here) high IQ that you do. To non-theistic conservatism, that's just the way the world works: some people got it, and some people don't; some people know how to seize an opportunity, others don't; some people know how to leverage the markets, some don't; some can afford their kid's medicine, and some can't. It's just the "natural law" playing itself out in real time. The winners win and the losers lose and there's nothing we can or should do to modify the rules of the game.

And to those who think some of the rules might be rigged? Tough luck.

WELCOMING NATURE AND VIRTUE
BACK TO THE PUBLIC SQUARE

Notwithstanding the differences between the Catholic social thought tradition and non-theistic conservatism, which I'll identify below, it's important to note that there is deep, even foundational, overlap on several points. First, Catholic social thought not only agrees that all individuals possess inalienable rights that precede the existence of the state; it also agrees that those rights are grounded in *nature* and not in "autonomy" or some other disembodied rational capacity. This matters because it permits the public discussion of goods that universally pertain to human nature and thus removes "consent" as the sole moral standard adjudicating public policy. Second and related, the Catholic social thought tradition wholeheartedly supports the idea that "virtue" is of public and not merely private concern. It also supports the belief that it is impossible, both theoretically and practically, to sustain a free society absent the cultivation and practice of virtue, since freedom, left to operate in a moral vacuum, has no limiting principle that prevents it from degrading and eventually destroying the common good. Third, Catholicism unequivocally supports a right to private property and a right to the material goods that one's labor produces. There is also overall agreement that the good of the state should always be *instrumental* to the good of individuals and families and never construed as a good in and of itself. In combining Locke and Aristotle, in short, non-theistic conservatism ends up addressing many of the problems in other secular ideologies: the Aristotelian elements help fix the deficiencies of classical liberalism and libertarianism, while the Lockean elements help fix the (much more dangerous) deficiencies of utilitarianism and progressivism-wokeism. Of all the ideological poisons to pick from, in other words, non-theistic conservatism is the least noxious.

That, of course, is damning with the faintest of praise; for notwithstanding the agreements between non-theistic conservatism and the Catholic social thought tradition, there remain deep divergences. As in previous chapters, I will summarize and categorize those differences using the "problems" below—and as usual, keep in mind the Thinking in Circles map to help understand the contrasts and their implications.

- the problem of truth

- the problem of perfection

- the problem of human dignity

- the problem of moral hierarchies

- the problem of free speech

- the problem of idolatry (which includes the problem of false mutual exclusivities and the problem of too high / too low human nature)

The Problem of Truth

Non-theistic conservatism considers itself to be grounded in "reality." However, it's not clear what the metaphysical ground of that "reality" is. The Aristotelian side of non-theistic conservatism finds its epistemological core not in abstract "human reason" but rather in reason grounded in a specific moral tradition. Indeed, that's one of Aristotle's greatest anthropological insights: "reason" can only properly be understood when it is seen as nested within a full account of what it means to be human, including what comprehensively defines human nature and the ultimate human good. However, to escape the charge of cultural relativity, the moral tradition within which reason makes its claims about what is "true" must somehow be grounded in a reality *beyond* the tradition itself. Without this metaphysically fixed point, each moral tradition produces different patterns of moral reasoning, all of them equally arbitrary. The "American democratic tradition" would thus be just as morally legitimate as the "Aztec imperial tradition" or the "Marxist-Stalinist communist tradition." The only way to provide a normative and not merely descriptive moral standard to distinguish among these and all other traditions is to ask which one of them is *true*. Setting aside the question of whether Aristotelian thought can fix the apparent circularity in the *Nicomachean Ethics* cited above, it is certainly not clear how George Will establishes the truth of the American democratic tradition (what he also calls "American conservatism") as he interprets it. He could—and does—appeal to a pragmatic epistemic standard and say the American democratic tradition is useful for "flourishing" and "happiness"; however, that begs rather than answers the question "What is the *true* standard of 'flourishing and happiness'?" Moreover, without an account of the truth of the American democratic tradition, all the virtues Will cites as necessary for the preservation of that tradition are also completely relativized. They may be a necessary means to an end, but if the end is arbitrary then the means to the end are ultimately arbitrary as well.

The Lockean side of non-theistic conservatism could be more promising for explaining how the ideology can escape the charge of moral relativism. Locke, recall, grounds his account of natural rights in a doctrine of God. Yet two problems remain. One, even if we preserve the theological foundation at the base of the Lockean conception of individual rights, recall that Locke denies that human beings can, based on that foundation, identify a rationally knowable universal common human good. In other words, Locke believes that human beings can rationally know what we *are* (free individuals bearing natural rights), but we cannot rationally know what we are *for*. Yet answering the

question *What are human beings for?* is necessary for being able
to identify a common human good; and if we cannot identify a
common human good, then Lockeanism becomes functionally
indistinguishable from libertarianism (autonomous individuals
pursuing arational desires, only limited by the consent of others)
and thus suffers from the same problems examined in chapter 7.

The second problem is that Will deliberately excises "God"
from the Lockean natural rights framework, which renders the
question of whether it is possible to identify a "Lockean common
good" moot from the get-go and, indeed, vitiates any rational
claim to the existence of "individual rights" at all. In other words,
Locke may be able to defend the existence of individual rights but
not the existence of a common good; Will, however, can neither
defend the existence of individual rights nor the existence of a
common good. As such, his theory, representative of non-theistic
conservatism in general, cannot escape the charge of cultural
relativism.

In contrast, and as argued throughout, the Catholic social
thought tradition upholds both the rational existence of individual rights *and* the rational existence of a common human good. It
is important to reaffirm that the Catholic position is *not* that all
human beings can, for example, attain rational knowledge that
Jesus is Lord or that Mary was assumed into heaven or that the
Holy Spirit descended on the Apostles on Pentecost. Catholics
take these claims about God and their implication for human life
as true but also *revealed*; that is, God chose to disclose these truths
about himself and his mother and his action in the world in a way
that reason otherwise would not have been able to ascertain using
its own lights. However, Catholicism maintains that we all can
know, by virtue of human reason itself, (a) that God exists and (b)
that a relationship with God constitutes the highest human good.
As the *Catechism* puts it, "The Church . . . holds and teaches that
God, the first principle and last end of all things, can be known
with certainty from the created world by the natural light of

human reason. . . . Man has this capacity because he is created in the image of God."[49] From this rationally accessible knowledge of God's existence as both first principle and last end, Catholicism maintains that we can deduce a natural law that *both* establishes natural individual rights *and* orients those individual rights to a common human good. This combination of rights and the common good, in turn, forms the basis for any just political order. As the *Catechism* summarizes these points,

> The natural law is a participation in God's wisdom and goodness by man formed in the image of his Creator. It expresses the dignity of the human person and forms the basis of his fundamental rights and duties.[50]

> The natural law is immutable, permanent throughout history. The rules that express it remain substantially valid. It is a necessary foundation for the erection of moral rules and civil law.[51]

In short, Catholicism maintains that we can say all of this, and much more, without once referencing "dogma" or "scripture" or "faith."

This distinction between reason and revelation also uncovers the flaw in both Locke's and Will's conception of "religion," especially as it relates to the nature and purpose of government. Will writes, "Locke's principle [is] that religion can be useful or can be disruptive, but its truth cannot be established by reason."[52] Many apologists today would dispute this claim, arguing, for example, that there is ample historical evidence not only that Jesus was a real historical figure but also that his followers saw

49. *Catechism of the Catholic Church* 36.
50. *CCC* 1978.
51. *CCC* 1979.
52. Will, *The Conservative Sensibility*, 464.

him both die and return to life.[53] However, let's assume (contrary to evidence) that there is no rational warrant for believing in one religious doctrine over another. *That does not mean that there is no rational warrant either for believing in God or for believing in a natural law deduced from God's existence.* Indeed, that is precisely what the *Catechism* is affirming: believing in God and the natural law doesn't make you "religious" (unless by "religious" we mean "naturally oriented to ultimate reality"); it constitutes the very definition of what it means to be rational, since all other truths about both reality and morality are deduced, proximately and remotely, from the truth of God. Thus, in maintaining that human beings can know both that God exists and that God is the final end of all things—including, by definition, human beings—Catholicism preserves the necessary metaphysical grounds for justifying the existence of individual rights *and* the existence of a rational common human good, which, in turn, provides justificatory grounds for the existence and purpose of virtue (developing the interior habits that correspond with living according to the external natural law).

In sum, Locke gives us equal natural rights, but at the expense of virtue and the common good. Aristotle gives us virtue and the common good, but at the expense of equal natural rights. Catholicism says: Why not have it all?

The Problem of Perfection

To its great credit, non-theistic conservatism stands opposed to all utopian political projects. That opposition is embedded, first, in its affirmation of natural individual rights that precede the existence of the state and which thus act as a non-negotiable bulwark against state power. However, there is an additional restraint on utopianism that is apparent in Will's thought. Within

---

53. See, for example, Anthony Maas, "Resurrection of Jesus Christ," in *The Catholic Encyclopedia*, vol. 12 (New York: Robert Appleton, 1911), newadvent.org.

his account of an objectively fixed human nature is a recognition that humanity is morally static; people do not get morally worse, but they do not get morally better either. That does not mean, however, that human beings are "morally neutral" blank slates. Rather, in Will's view, human nature contains a universal drive toward conflict. He writes in his chapter on foreign policy, "What is the essential, unchanging nature of human beings? Conservatism's answer is: Human beings are desirous and competitive, hence they often are anxious, and hence they [are] given to conflict."[54] This incorrigible brokenness in humanity drives Will's conception of American conservatism to the conclusion that the correct disposition toward all attempts at social progress should be pessimism. Will writes,

> The study of history should be an immersion in the realities of contingencies. This immersion should lead to a talent for pessimism: Things can, and frequently do, go wrong. . . . Pessimism does not entail fatalism. On the contrary, it is a form of activism, of perpetual wariness born of historically informed realism. Pessimism, far from promoting passivity, should be a constant spur to political engagement.[55]

Will then clarifies that his endorsement of pessimism does not mean that he thinks history is morally circular (i.e., every moral zenith will eventually lead to an equal and opposite moral nadir); yet he insists that he does not endorse the notion of moral progress either. He writes, "Pessimism informs the conservative sensibility by eschewing 'both progress and circularity as guiding temporal frames.'"[56] The model he chooses to illustrate this ostensible compromise position is the mythical figure Sisyphus, who was condemned for eternity to roll a giant boulder up a

54. Will, *The Conservative Sensibility*, 413.
55. Will, 400.
56. Will, 402.

mountain only to watch it go tumbling back down the moment he reached the summit. Will approvingly quotes the French existentialist philosopher Albert Camus, author of *The Myth of Sisyphus*, writing, "The important thing . . . is not to be cured but to live with one's ailments."[57]

Will's argument paradigmatically illustrates the "Pessimist" model of moral progress I described in chapter 4. The model does not describe moral history as circular; it recognizes some minimal possibility for moral improvement. However, precisely because it is *pessimistic*, whatever moral improvement human beings can attain in history is as fragile as it is minute, barely detectable when seen from both historical and global perspective. This conclusion, for Will, is not only empirical; it is a consequence of his anthropology: Humans are primarily selfish, and so, overall, we cannot expect—cannot hope—that they will be anything more than desirous creatures engaged in near constant conflict doing whatever they think they can get away with to get what they want.

To be sure, the Catholic social thought tradition recognizes human depravity and its inexhaustible capacity, indeed desire, for destruction. It calls that "original sin." However, unlike Will's anthropology, it does not see human nature as, say, 60% bad and 40% good (or an even higher "bad-to-good" ratio). Rather, it sees human nature as 100% good, that is, as *naturally* good, because each individual bears the image and likeness of God (the *imago Dei*). Consequently, sin is a freely chosen deviation from a 100% good anthropological baseline. That does not mean that Catholicism minimizes sin's existence or its viciousness. Quite the opposite, it recognizes the fall and its effects on human nature as so devastating that it made it impossible for any individual to become whole again without God's direct intervention in the form of grace. That's what marks the upper limit of the asymptote in chapter 4's "Hope Model" of moral progress: a perfect person

---

57. Will, 402–403.

and/or society is *impossible* to attain in space and time because of sin. However, it remains the case that "sin" is to "human nature" in Catholicism as "disease" is to "health": *Health* is the more fundamental category and, indeed, the necessary standard for even knowing what a "disease" is in the first place. So, too, human goodness is the more fundamental category that makes it possible for us to know what a deviation from that goodness is. Humans are sinful, yes, but the condition for the possibility of being sinful is *the goodness* in our nature that we willfully deviate from.

This difference between Will's anthropology and the Catholic social thought tradition's anthropology may seem abstract. However, choosing one over the other has profound political consequences. Will rightly, based on his anthropological premises, embraces pessimism as the base disposition to take toward moral progress. But what can such pessimism say or, even less, do in the face of injustice? Will marks the end of the discriminatory Jim Crow laws as an important point in American history. Yet wouldn't the pessimistic political disposition he defends have said something like "People are racist, and they always will be racist, and there isn't much we can do about that, certainly at the level of government"? Or think of the 2022 *Dobbs v. Jackson Women's Health Organization* Supreme Court ruling that overturned the constitutional "right" to an abortion. Would a pessimist ever have imagined such a moment in American politics? More to the point, would a pessimist ever have *worked to achieve* such a moment? The same line of reasoning applies to every other moral issue of this or any other time in history. If we define politics as synonymous with rolling boulders up mountains only to watch them somersault down again, it's not clear why we all wouldn't just say, "What's the point? Why try in the first place?" While the Catholic social thought tradition appreciates the non-theistic conservative's caution, even suspicion, when hearing calls for moral progress, it shows equal caution, even suspicion, in the face of being told moral progress is nigh impossible. There's a third way between "Yes, we can" and "No, we can't." It's called "Do what's right, expect the worst, and hope for the best."

The Problem of Human Dignity

Non-theistic conservatism gets two fundamental characteristics right about human dignity; however, it has no conceptual mechanism either to justify the existence of each characteristic individually or to coherently unite them into one unified account of human worth. The first characteristic, as also explained in chapter 4, is that dignity is objectively inherent and universally equal, possessed by all human beings simply by virtue of being human. As such, dignity is invulnerable to all harm (i.e., no individual can strip herself or himself of dignity nor can others take it away or diminish it). The second characteristic is that dignity is something that is attained in the form of being a potential that can be realized or fail to be realized. As such, dignity *is* vulnerable to harm, both in the form of the individual's own actions and the actions done (or not done) by others. Recall that both characteristics of dignity are necessary in order to explain how dignity is (a) universally equal among all human beings and (b) capable of coherently providing a guide for action (if dignity is only invulnerable, then it is morally moot, since nothing anyone does or fails to do can affect it).

The Lockean strand of non-theistic conservatism, specifically its affirmation of individual natural rights, provides a possible grounding for the first characteristic of dignity—that is, its invulnerable universal equality. The Aristotelian strand of non-theistic conservatism, specifically its account of virtue as it relates to the realization of the individual's good, provides a possible grounding for the second characteristic of dignity—that is, its status as a vulnerable good that can be attained or not attained depending on an individual's own actions and the actions of others. Non-theistic conservatism, however, has several obstacles to explaining how it can coherently combine these two strands. First, if, like George Will's account of conservatism, it removes God as the moral foundation of dignity, then there is no justification either for the claim that all individuals have equal worth (humans are patently *unequal* from an empirical perspective) or that the realization of that worth entails virtuous action and developing a good character (if there is no God, then all accounts of "virtue" are equally arbitrary). Second, if non-theistic conservatism jettisons its Aristotelian side and relies only on its Lockean roots, including Locke's argument that natural rights are based on a doctrine of God, it may be able to give an account of how dignity is universally equal; however, since Locke cannot identify a rational final good that all individuals ought to pursue because it is the authentically true human good, non-theistic conservatism renders dignity a morally moot concept. Conversely, third, if non-theistic conservativism jettisons its Lockean side in order to adopt a conception of dignity that entails the pursuit of virtue, it may be able to account for how dignity is a morally and politically relevant concept because it is a good that is vulnerable to harm; however, the same move would pull the rug out from under the claim that dignity is universally equal (recall that Aristotle explicitly argues that some humans are more fully "human" than others). In short, non-theistic conservatism needs *both* Lockeanism and Aristotelianism to justify a universally equal and morally/politically relevant account of dignity. But how can it pull this off?

It can't—and the reason points to the fundamental incoherence at the heart of non-theistic conservatism. If you want individual dignity/rights *and* virtue then you need *both* a rational account of human dignity based on a doctrine of God *and* a rational account of the human good based on an objective natural law founded, in turn, in a doctrine of God. The problem, in other words, is that non-theistic conservatism wants both dignity/rights *and* virtue but doesn't want to pay the full philosophical and theological price for it.

As explained in chapter 4, the Catholic social thought tradition offers an alternative. Catholicism affirms that all of the following are rationally accessible: (1) God's existence, (2) God as first principle and last end of everything in existence, (3) God as first principle and last end of human existence in particular, (4) humankind's unique relationship with God in the form of the *imago Dei*, and (5) the recognition that the *imago Dei* is both an ontological fact about all humans (which establishes equal human dignity) *and* a potential to be realized in the form of virtuous action (which establishes the vulnerability of dignity and, consequently, its moral and political relevance). These are the conceptual parts that are necessary to build a coherent account of human worth, and the Catholic social thought tradition, unlike non-theistic conservatism, provides all of them.

It is important to note that these same components provide a coherent account of the meaning of "individualism" as well. Non-theistic conservatism, like libertarianism, champions individual rights and the ultimate sovereignty of the individual over and against the state. However, unlike libertarianism, non-theistic conservatism affirms that individual virtue not only leads to, in George Will's words, individual "flourishing" and "happiness" but is also necessary for the creation and maintenance of a free society. In other words, individual virtue is socially and politically indispensable. This relationship between virtue, individual flourishing, and the public good should, if non-theistic conservatism seeks to be coherent, place a limiting principle on the meaning of "individualism." The implication is that individuals should be radically free to live their lives as they choose so long as their choices (a) do not violate others' rights and (b) help preserve and advance individual flourishing and the public good. To be sure, this model of individualism does not necessarily entail making "non-virtuous" acts *illegal*. However, it does generate a civic model that would encourage some behaviors and discourage others in the name of protecting and fostering virtue.

This conception of individualism is remarkably similar to the conception of individualism within the Catholic social thought tradition. The difference, akin to the difference we see on the question of dignity, is that Catholicism, unlike non-theistic conservatism, can *coherently* explain this relationship between individualism, virtue, individual flourishing, and the public good. As noted previously, there is an uneasiness in George Will's discussion of virtue: on the one hand, he recognizes it as necessary for the preservation of a free society; on the other hand, he affirms—for example, by claiming that American conservatism is one and the same as "classical liberalism"—that civil society should entirely privatize virtue and leave it to individuals' own subjective definitions. This tension, if not contradiction, is a result of the lack of a unifying metaphysical and anthropological foundation beneath Will's thought specifically and non-theistic conservatism in general. Once again, the *only* way to coherently affirm both that individuals have rights that entail certain inviolable freedoms and that individuals ought to use their freedom to act virtuously for their own good and the good of society is to locate both individuality and virtue within a rational moral framework that upholds both individual rights *and* a common good.

In sum, if you only want individual rights and near absolute individual sovereignty, then there's no reason to call yourself "conservative. "Libertarian" will do just fine. If you want both individualism and virtue, then the Catholic social thought tradition has something to offer.

The Problem of Moral Hierarchies

One of the basic critiques this chapter makes against non-theistic conservatism is that it ultimately reduces the purposes of the state *either* to self-interest, which ends up benefiting those with the most money and power, *or* to an arbitrary tradition created by those with the most money and power. Given these two options

(with both leading to the same outcome), the only possible definition of the "common good" is "that which most benefits the
monied class," which, of course, is not "common" at all. Perhaps
this dimension of non-theistic conservatism is most palpable in its
devotion to the "good of the market," which is usually shorthand
for both the US stock market (e.g., the S &P 500, Nasdaq, etc.)
and for business/corporate profits in general. For example, the
well-known conservative commentator Ben Shapiro—who I hes-
itate to identify as a non-theistic conservative, yet still, I believe,
represents the ideology's undue praise of "markets"—wrote the
following words criticizing the TV commentator Tucker Carlson,
who gave a widely circulated monologue critiquing "the market"
from a conservative point of view:

> [Market capitalism] is not a tool. It is not a "creation" of a
> centralized decision making process. It is a reality of free and
> voluntary interactions among human beings. It is an outgrowth
> of the unique value of each individual, and of each individual's
> right to use his labor as he sees fit, and to alienate that labor
> in exchange for the labor of someone else. And markets don't
> exist to "serve us." They exist to allow us to act in liberty.[58]

It's these words that are most telling: "markets don't exist to
'serve us.'" For Shapiro, the good of the "us"—meaning the common good of society as a whole—does not constitute the market's
final purpose. Rather, the "liberty" of the individual is the real "us"
("They exist to allow us to act in liberty"). The whole purpose of
the market, according to Shapiro, is to *serve* that liberty. Thus, if

---

58. Ben Shapiro, "Tucker Carlson Claims Market Capitalism Has Under-
mined American Society. He's Wrong," The Daily Wire, January 4, 2019, https://
www.dailywire.com/news/tucker-carlson-claims-market-capitalism-has-ben
-shapiro. For an interesting critique of Shapiro's critique, see Matthew Walther,
"Tucker Carlson has fired the first shot in conservatives' civil war over the
free market," *The Week*, January 8, 2019, https://theweek.com/articles/816134
/tucker-carlson-fired-first-shot-conservatives-civil-war-over-free-market.

the purpose of the market is to serve liberty and the purpose of liberty is to be able to engage in the market, then *the purpose of the market is ultimately the market itself.* To be sure, that doesn't mean that anyone *must* live as if the market were her or his highest good. However, the problem with non-theistic conservatism is that it contains no limiting principles on individuals choosing to create a *state* that conflates the good of the market with the public good. Indeed, insofar as we conflate "liberty" with the "free market" that seems to be what a Lockean definition of limited government explicitly calls for. Recall Locke's definition of the nature and purpose of government from above:

> The commonwealth [is] a society of men constituted only for the procuring, preserving, and advancing [of] their own civil interests. Civil interest I call life, liberty, health, and indolency of body [that is, bodily comfort]; and the possession of outward things, such as money, lands, houses, furniture, and the like.

If we accept Shapiro's premise that the purpose of the market is to serve individual liberty and the protection of individual liberty—especially the liberty to pursue material goods—is the only function of the state, then we could, combining both Locke and Shapiro, conclude that the purpose of the state is to serve the market. And *that's* the problem with non-theistic conservatism's moral hierarchy: by its own logic, every other value that a society could pursue must be *subsumed* within, and placed in service of, the good of the market in such a way that that market and the state become substantively indistinguishable.

As I noted at the beginning of this chapter, the Catholic social thought tradition is *not* against free markets. Indeed, it recognizes them as a positive, even essential good, and unequivocally morally and economically superior to socialist and communist economic systems. But it is also unequivocally against defining markets as good in and of themselves. The United States Conference of

Catholic Bishops provides this helpful summary of the Catholic view of markets and their proper role in a just society:

- The economy exists for the person, not the person for the economy.

- All economic life should be shaped by moral principles. Economic choices and institutions must be judged by how they protect or undermine the life and dignity of the human person, support the family and serve the common good.

- A fundamental moral measure of any economy is how the poor and vulnerable are faring.

- All people have a right to life and to secure the basic necessities of life, such as food, clothing, shelter, education, health care, safe environment, and economic security.

- All people have the right to economic initiative, to productive work, to just wages and benefits, to decent working conditions as well as to organize and join unions or other associations.

- All people, to the extent they are able, have a corresponding duty to work, a responsibility to provide for the needs of their families and an obligation to contribute to the broader society.

- In economic life, free markets have both clear advantages and limits; government has essential responsibilities and limitations; voluntary groups have irreplaceable roles, but cannot substitute for the proper working of the market and the just policies of the state.

- Society has a moral obligation, including governmental action where necessary, to assure opportunity, meet basic human needs, and pursue justice in economic life.

- Workers, owners, managers, stockholders and consumers are moral agents in economic life. By our choices, initiative, creativity and investment, we enhance or diminish economic opportunity, community life and social justice.

- The global economy has moral dimensions and human consequences. Decisions on investment, trade, aid and development should protect human life and promote human rights, especially for those most in need wherever they might live on this globe.[59]

Again, free markets are good. Profits are good. Material prosperity is good. Dynamism and innovation and entrepreneurship and continually growing GDPs and GNPs—all very, very good. But note, they're not the *highest* good. The highest good is the common good, which, for the Catholic social thought tradition, necessarily includes the individual good properly defined. To define this hierarchy of goods otherwise is not only to confuse means with ends. It is to misidentify the whole purpose of being human.

The Problem of Free Speech

Non-theistic conservatism, like classical liberalism and libertarianism, provides uncompromising protections for freedom of speech. It has its Lockean insistence on individual rights to thank for that (even if Locke himself thought the state did have limited but real authority to suppress speech that is "contrary to human society" or contrary to "those moral rules which are necessary to the preservation of civil society.")[60] This protection of free speech and its corollary, the freedom of religion, is to its credit.

---

59. Adapted from "A Catholic Framework for Economic Life," United States Conference of Catholic Bishops website, https://www.usccb.org/resources/catholic-framework-economic-life-0.

60. John Locke, *A Letter Concerning Toleration*.

However, non-theistic conservatism's conception of free speech contains the same flaws as the classical liberal/libertarian view: individuals are free to make whatever arguments they want about the human good; however, all those arguments, by definition, are equally arational since all three of these ideologies presuppose that the final human good cannot be rationally identified. Thus, to talk about the purpose of human life is indistinguishable from talking about your favorite type of pizza: it's merely a sharing of preferences. So, too, talking about the purpose of government beyond its procedural role of protecting individual rights. There is literally nothing more to say, at least rationally, than "government exists to protect individual rights." Everything else one might say is just emoting.

As I argued in chapter 7, this substantive vacuum at the heart of the formal right to free speech engenders the conditions for a tyranny of the majority on political questions that do not directly pertain to individual rights. Since no "viewpoint" can be more rational than any other "viewpoint," those with the dominant viewpoint by sheer majority and/or cultural influence will be able to impose theirs without the possibility of rational contestation from the minority. Since all points of view are equally preferential, the moral tie goes to the team with the most (powerful) players who, in turn, get to write (and rewrite) the rules for everyone else.

As I've argued previously, the Catholic social thought tradition, in contrast, both upholds a right to free speech *and* the possibility of the use of that speech to identify real, substantive truth in the moral and political sphere. That does not mean, of course, that "the truth" will always win or even often win. But, unlike the ideological alternatives, at least it has a fighting chance.

The Problem of Idolatry

In the end, as laid out in the beginning, non-theistic conservatism ultimately commits the one sin it was ostensibly designed to prevent: the unjust concentration of power in the hands of a few. Whether it's by morally authorizing the state to become the private vehicle of the wealthy or by segregating the understanding and practice of the "virtue" necessary to sustain the state to those with the right kind of education (or both), politics becomes a cover for the materially comfortable to morally justify their elevated position on the socioeconomic hierarchy. There is one additional irony to point out in this justificatory move. If it is true, as George Will and other non-theistic conservatives say, that human nature is so corrupt, then why would we assume that individuals, left to their own profit-seeking devices alone, will be able to construct a just socioeconomic system for everyone? How does non-theistic conservativism think that the sum total of individuals fulfilling their material desires will somehow produce a virtuous civil society? How, in other words, does an anthropology so low suddenly become an object of praise and even celebration when viewed through the lens of "the market"? If we are so bad, in short, why trust us to create anything other than another Tower of Babel when left to do as we please?

The answer, once again, lies in the alchemy of idolatry and its power to invert the true and the good. Sin hijacks our reason, to be sure. But it doesn't disable it. We may blind ourselves to the truth, but our capacity to lie, to others and to ourselves, remains firmly intact. Utilitarianism tells the lie that god can be defined by pleasure; classical liberalism and libertarianism, the lie that the self can be its own god; progressivism corporatizes the self and lies that our identity group can be god. Among these ideological imposters, non-theistic conservatism may think that it alone speaks the truth, yet it, too, is engaged in its own self-soothing tall tale: god, if he exists, favors the fortunate, and I am among the chosen.

CHAPTER 10

Conclusion: Practical Advice
for Evangelists
in the Political Sphere

Evangelization and Ideology has, up until this point, talked a lot about ideology. But what about evangelization? I hope that it has become apparent through these many words that the "evangelization" part is embedded within the conclusions to the arguments in each chapter. What unites all political ideologies is that they are all ultimately dead ends—wildly diverse paths through fantastically different terrain that all end up smacking into the same wall. Notwithstanding all the alternatives that exist within the ideological bazaar, there is in the end, as the African Cardinal Robert Sarah has written, only God or nothing.[1] Either our politics is grounded in and oriented to God as our true good and true source of happiness or it is grounded in and oriented to something other than God, which is tantamount to grounding it in an idol. And the thing about idols is that they all eventually decay and crumble, even if their demise takes centuries or even millennia. If our politics is based on an idol, the best we can hope for is a slow decline into ossified philosophical and practical senescence and eventual obsoletion. The worst we should expect is total violent collapse. Either way, things will fall apart. It is not hyperbole to

---

1. Robert Sarah and Nicolas Diat, *God or Nothing: A Conversation on Faith*, trans. Michael J. Miller (San Francisco: Ignatius Press, 2015).

say that politics is ultimately a matter of life and death, of (eternal) happiness or (eternal) misery. The call to evangelize the culture, therefore, must include the call to evangelize the political culture as well, not only for the good of the individual souls who could hear the Good News from an unexpected source but also for the temporal good of society.

To wrap up and synthesize the book's arguments, I'd like to end by offering some suggestions on how to carry out this work from within the ideological fray based upon my own experiences as a professor working in a secular and often hostile political and religious environment. The suggestions below are intended to help steel evangelists' nerves while also offering tips on how to have a decent shot at conversing with detractors in a way that doesn't leave hearts (including our own hearts) more hardened. This advice is just as much for me as it is for anyone else.

Try to avoid attacking "bad people" and focus on attacking bad ideas instead. As noted above, bad people can have good ideas and good people can have bad ideas.[2] Without denying that there is an abundance of ill-willed people in the world who desire to cause others harm, and also recognizing that proclaiming "All of us are sinners," while true, does not mean "All people sin equally," it is crucial to remember that some of heaven's greatest saints were once some of the world's worst sinners. Think, for example, of St. Mary Magdalene, or St. Paul, or St. Augustine, or St. Ignatius of Loyola—all of them not only held wrong ideas but were also doing bad things. And now they are certifiably in heaven. People are complex creatures whose mixture of beliefs, motivations, fears, desires, ambitions, kindnesses, and cruelties can be difficult to

2. This echoes former Supreme Court Justice Antonin Scalia's observation (and advice to others). He is reported to have said, "I attack ideas. I don't attack people. Some very good people have some very bad ideas. [laughter] And if you can't separate the two, you gotta get another day job." See Ruth Bader Ginsburg, "Eulogy for Justice Antonin Scalia," Iowa State University Archives of Women's Political Communication, March 1, 2016, https://awpc.cattcenter.iastate.edu/2017/03/21/eulogy-for-justice-antonin-scalia-march-1-2016/.

understand and categorize. Indeed, that is why a good confessor gets into the nitty gritty of each action to examine the relative culpability of our sins. Judging intentions, while not impossible (courts of law must do it all the time), is a messy business. Judging ideas, on the other hand, can be done with much greater confidence, especially if performed with the humility that comes from knowing that we are caretakers and ambassadors of the truth, not its creators or owners. So try—again, to the extent it is prudent—to stick with battling ideas, and let God sort us people out.

Employ the Socratic method to engage in debate. Directly criticizing an idea in the abstract can be effective in clarifying and strengthening your convictions, especially if you are among people who generally agree with you. However, directly criticizing the ideas of someone who disagrees with you—e.g., saying to them, "This position is completely incoherent"—will likely shut down the conversation before it can even get started. For this reason, the Socratic method is usually the best technique for engaging in a conversation that you hope will lead to an agreement. The Socratic method entails asking sincere questions and looking for sincere answers with the goal of attaining both definitional and logical clarity. Chapters 2 and 3 of this book provide a conceptual foundation for how to engage in such a conversation, but it really is as simple as making inquiries, seeking clarification, and looking for common ground along the way.

For example, one point of agreement that I've often been able to find with people from radically different political and religious perspectives is on the claim that "all human beings are equal and should be treated with equal moral regard." It is a rare person, in my experience, who will openly contradict this statement, even if they will also say things like "life has no meaning or purpose" or "all moral and political values are relative." Standing on this common platform of human dignity, you can then begin to ask questions about both the presuppositions of dignity (e.g., "What must be true in order for human dignity to be real?") and the implications of human dignity (e.g., "If it is true that humans have dignity, what kinds of things should and should not be permitted in society?")[3] As we've seen, the conversation can quickly become complex because of the potentially different meanings of terms within different ideological outlooks (see the next point below), but real philosophical and evangelical progress can be made even atop the narrowest points of contact. The Socratic method is one of the best methods to find those points and build on them.

Seek clarity, not simplicity. A common misconception is that complex ideas must be ambiguous ideas. To be sure—as a slog through the mind of Immanuel Kant reveals—political theories can be like a spider web: intricately woven with interconnected, hierarchically organized structures that can easily catch and bind your mind due to their complexity, leaving you wondering how you got stuck and whether there's any way out besides tossing the whole thing to the wind. Any great philosopher or theologian worth his or her salt is going to build complex systems of thought because those systems of thought, if they're any good, are going to be trying to reflect, and provide a constructive response to, reality, including moral reality, which can be and often is profoundly complex. If the task is living truthfully, then complexity is the name of the game.

However, complexity need not entail ambiguity; nuance need not be gauzy; working step-by-step through a system of thought need not be the same as wandering through a maze. The goal in all endeavors of the mind should be arriving at or at least approximating the truth of the matter. In this sense, it is important, like the character Westley in *The Princess Bride*, to build up a

---

3. The Jesuit academic Fr. Robert McTeigue provides another useful framework for understanding and evaluating competing points of view that he calls "thinking in four dimensions." It involves identifying and examining the antecedents, consequents, supports, and objections to any truth claim. See *Real Philosophy for Real People: Tools for Truthful Living* (San Francisco: Ignatius Press, 2020), 40.

tolerance to tough, multi-layered ideas, which can indeed be mentally toxic in high doses, especially to the un-inured. Yet both within that complexity and at the end of that complexity should be the final goal of clarity. Indeed, the whole point of trafficking in and embracing complexity is not to sound smart or even be smart; it is to get to the point where you can honestly say, both to yourself and to others, "I get it!" That's the gift of clarity, and it is a gift that we should seek for ourselves and seek to offer others whenever we can. The evangelist's work thus demands being able to understand and communicate the full schematics of competing political ideologies while communicating that the whole point of the intellectual exercise is to get to "aha." Our minds love to run not because they like movement but because they like a properly earned rest.

Be disposed to learn something new. Some truths are fixed. They are permanent, immutable, eternal. They cannot not be. And, consequently, the human mind cannot not know them, despite our best rebellious efforts otherwise. The Catholic social thought tradition is made up of those truths (and for those who scoff at the idea of "truth," ask them if they believe that the claim "There is no universal objective truth" is true). However, as discussed previously, there are expansive territories within human life, both individually and socially, in which "discovery" is the proper disposition to take. It will never be the case, for example, that the intentional taking of innocent human life is morally acceptable or, God forbid, morally praiseworthy; however, we have much to learn from each other about how to create a society in which, as the pro-life movement puts it, abortion is not only illegal but unthinkable, akin to how most view slavery today. It will always be the case that every child deserves to be born to and raised by a loving mother and father; however, we have much to learn from each other about both how to create societies that embrace and sustain natural marriage and how to support children who come from less-than-ideal family structures, always with the goal of seeking what is best for the children—not conforming to the desires of the adults. It will always be the case that deliberately ending one's own life and asking others to facilitate your death is morally wrong and should be illegal; however, we have much to learn from each other on how to create societies where no one ever feels so hopeless as to contemplate and, even less, carry out acts of self-destruction.

All of us have limitations not only by virtue of being human but by virtue of being ourselves. There is nothing we can or should do about the first set of limitations. But there is much we can and should do about the second. Have strong opinions on crime? Be sure to talk with some people who have been incarcerated as you form your point of view. Strong feelings about "red tape" and "government regulation"? In addition to the horror stories of governments having gone too far, read up on some of the great harm that can result when government fails to regulate or follow through with its regulations—harms like pollution-poisoned drinking water, dishonest predatory lending, harmful chemicals in food, lead poisoning of children, dirty medical clinics, unsafe bridges, overfishing, the wanton destruction of habitats, etc. Absolutely sure you know what immigration policy should be? Get to know someone who left his friends, family, home, and lucrative career in Mexico to escape, in the middle of the night, from regional cartel thugs who were seeking to punish him and his family because he refused to be bribed. Ever seen someone buying groceries with food stamps and then notice that they've packed all the bags into the back of a $60,000 SUV in the parking lot? Me too. But before drawing conclusions about "the poor," it would be good to go to your local food bank and chat with the people who work full time in minimum-wage work yet are living in their cars, or who lost everything because of medical bankruptcy, or who lost a bread-earning spouse with no life insurance and are unable to work due to disability, or who made some really poor choices in life that they are working to make up for but are having a hard time finding an escape. Think America should never get involved in any way in the affairs of other countries? Talk to some war refugees. Etc. Maybe these conversations won't change your position. Maybe they will reinforce what you imagined to be the case all along. But at least, by talking with each other, by learning from each other, we can stop imagining and—to a limited but still profoundly morally relevant degree—*start knowing.*

Be a happy warrior. Being a happy warrior entails two things. First, be a warrior; that means not only acting in self-defense but going out into the world, seeking and making opportunities to spread the Good News no matter what the nature of the opposition. Although it became unpopular in the wake of Vatican II (which is not to blame Vatican II itself), the Church has long used militant language as an umbrella term to define every Christian's mission: to be a *spiritual* warrior, fighting sin in ourselves and in the world in the name of Jesus Christ and calling ourselves and the world to repent and trust in the Lord. The *Catechism of the Catholic Church* states, for example,

> Because man is a composite being, spirit and body, there already exists a certain tension in him; a certain struggle of tendencies between "spirit" and "flesh" develops. But in fact this struggle belongs to the heritage of sin. It is a consequence of sin and at the same time a confirmation of it. It is part of the daily experience of the spiritual battle.[4]

To be a Christian certainly means trusting in Christ's ultimate and final victory, but we must do our part in the interim. If you believe Jesus is Lord, there is no sitting this one out. It's a fight. And we're all in it, all the time.

Yet precisely because it is a spiritual battle and precisely because it is in the name of the Lord, it is a battle fought not only

---

4. *Catechism of the Catholic Church* 2516.

willingly but also joyfully, no matter what we may be feeling at any given moment. There is no shortage of callousness, viciousness, and sardonic cruelty in the political arena. As evangelists, we should do everything possible not to increase the supply, no matter how tempting it may be. Even prophetic denunciations, which are indeed sometimes necessary (see below), should be done in the spirit and tone of charity. That does not mean using namby-pamby speech or otherwise avoiding saying hard truths. It means speaking to others as if your greatest hope for them is their unmerited salvation rather than their just damnation. Think of family members doing an intervention for someone they love who has fallen into addiction and created havoc in everyone's lives as a result. They tell it like it is for the sole sake of getting the person back on track, not to punish him for his waywardness. May we always speak to others this way, if for no other reason than to avoid being hypocrites when it's our turn to be on the receiving end of a much-needed intervention.

Don't be afraid of courage. It is often forgotten that sins of omission can be just as grave as sins of commission. We are justly judged not only for what we do but for what we don't do. Writing these words makes me nervous because I know they are true and because they make me aware of just how much good I *don't* do in addition to the sinful things I *do* do. But our weaknesses do not diminish our individual and collective duty to do the right thing, come what may. The internet and social media have provided a false sense of valor by allowing us to take pot shots at our rivals from behind the protection of anonymity or, even when we do share our identities, from the improbability of digital "fighting words" ever causing negative consequences in our lives besides a temporarily bruised ego (though digital egos, like video game characters, regenerate endlessly and with remarkable speed). But digital valor is not real valor, just as the digital world is not the real world. To be sure, speaking up in defense of the truth online is admirable, but it's not, ultimately, going to lead to any significant durable changes. Indeed, isn't that precisely the criticism embedded in the charge that someone is merely "virtue signaling"—that he or she is merely trying to score moral points by communicating that they are on the "right side of history" in a way that doesn't require a scintilla of sacrifice?

So what am *I* willing to sacrifice to stand up for the moral law? If my only answer is "to brook the mean words of online commentators," then I am not being courageous. Indeed, I am no doubt committing sins of omission, even if my moral hands are relatively clean of commissions. Am I forgetting that there are martyrs who still die for the faith every day?[5] Has it slipped my mind that there are Christians who are risking everything right now to practice their faith in North Korea, where the punishment for being caught believing in Christ is death?[6] What am I doing? Writing a book. Well, swell job there, Matt, but not quite enough to march in with the saints. I am sadly not only speaking about myself when I say that Christians in the West, especially Catholic Christians, have lost our collective spine in a half-virtuous effort not to be "offensive" to others. (To be fair, others have grown a hard head—which they confuse with a hard spine—by delighting in being offensive to others.) I can keep deluding myself into thinking that I'm doing everything I can to fight what Pope St. John Paul II has rightly called the culture of death. But, as the sage says, there ain't no foolin' God. Not for me. Not for any of us.

Don't compromise the faith to gain a (temporary) ally. The temptation to water down—if not completely ignore—Church teachings in the political realm is often overwhelming. I'm not talking about the problem of politicians who identify as Catholic openly contradicting Church teaching on abortion, homosexual

---

5. Open Doors, an advocacy group working to end religious persecution, estimates that thirteen Christians are martyred every day. See "13 Christians murdered for following Jesus—every day," Open Doors, January 18, 2021, https://www.opendoorsusa.org/christian-persecution/stories/13-christians-killed-every-day/.

6. See "World Watch List: 2. North Korea," Open Doors, https://www.opendoorsusa.org/christian-persecution/world-watch-list/north-korea/.

marriage, and transgenderism; that is a grave issue, but it is more a problem for the clergy to handle rather than the laity, at least with regard to the reception of the Eucharist and ensuring that the faithful are not scandalized. Rather, I am more broadly addressing those (like myself) who desire to be fully orthodox in belief and practice but who also want to be, yes, *relevant to the culture*. It's not so easy, especially when you are outnumbered in your place of work, your group of friends, or even your own family. The temptation to revert to highly generalized moral language with all the bite of a suckling newborn—saying things like "All that matters is that we try to be good people" or "We should be welcoming" or "We shouldn't be judgmental"—can be very strong when pressed on your beliefs by suspicious or hostile parties.

Fight it. You see, the thing about being a Christian, and a Catholic Christian in particular, is that the faith is invariably and uncompromisingly specific. We don't just worship a God become flesh. We worship Jesus of Nazareth, son of Mary and adopted son of Joseph. We don't just have a symbolic meal to signify human fellowship. We eat the Body and Blood of Jesus of Nazareth, son of Mary and adopted son of Joseph. The whole faith is incarnational and sacramental. All the images, statues, rosaries, candles, incense, vestments, and words in the liturgy are overflowing with the divine. They point beyond themselves to be sure; yet they are also saturated with the eternal. It should thus be no surprise that the Church's moral teachings are also very distinct, not in the sense of "idiosyncratic," but in the sense of "clearly mean this rather than that." Remember that line from the book of Revelation about God's feelings about people who are "lukewarm"? We get vomited out (Rev. 3:16). Being "lukewarm" doesn't just apply to our dispositions, attitudes, and actions. It applies to our words as well. Being mealy-mouthed in hopes of sounding less "religious" to someone whose approbation you would like won't win any friends, even fewer converts, and it certainly is not going to solve any long-term problems.

I hasten to add that not compromising the faith does not mean refusing to make political compromises. For example, let's say you think that a local electorate would be willing to support a ban on abortions in which a fetal heartbeat can be detected but aren't yet ready to "outlaw abortion," especially in light of the pro-choice movement calling such a law "anti-woman" (even though abortions also kill many baby girls—and in some places, like India, far *more* baby girls than boys[7]—otherwise known as future women). There is no reason why a pro-lifer, animated by Catholic social teaching, could not fully support such a fetal heartbeat law. That doesn't mean that she or he is not fully pro-life; it only means that she or he is making the prudential decision to advance the pro-life cause as much as possible in that given time and place. Making political compromises, in other words, does not have to entail compromising the faith. How can we know the difference? The first (making political compromises) entails giving up a greater good in order to attain a lesser, but nonetheless still good, good—like a partial ban on abortions. The other (compromising your faith) entails giving in to an evil in order to attain a good—like supporting a poverty-relief program that includes funding for abortion providers. As St. Paul reminds us, Christians should never give cause to anyone to say that we "do evil so that good may come" (Rom. 3:8).

Be ready to make strategic retreats and take shelter. The history of Christianity is marked by two general movements: (1) moving from the center outward into the world to spread the Gospel to all nations, and (2) moving from the center deeper inward to purify and fortify the faith. It is the centrifugal and centripetal power of Christ, simultaneously spreading and concentrating. Sometimes, in some historical periods in some places, both of

7. Amrit Dhillon, "Selective Abortion in India Could Lead to 6.8m Fewer Girls Being Born by 2030," *The Guardian*, August 21, 2020, https://www.theguardian.com/global-development/2020/aug/21/selective-abortion-in-india-could-lead-to-68m-fewer-girls-being-born-by-2030/.

these movements could occur at the same time. Sometimes, however—indeed, many times—the world became so aggressive, so violent, so inhospitable to Christians that the faithful had no choice but to withdraw from the world and form parallel and even underground societies. That is the current state of the Church in many places right now. It may become so in many more places, including regions where the Church once enjoyed great cultural respect and influence. If and when that happens, all of us should be ready to make the move inward, in whatever ways we can, to protect the faith.

How can we know when to pull back? It will always be a prudential judgment, but a good test is to examine to what degree publicly practicing your faith makes you a target not just for public criticism and derision but for active persecution—things like not being able to practice medicine unless you are willing to kill children in the womb; not being able to teach in public schools unless you are willing to ask kindergartners for their pronouns; not being able to work in a corporation unless you confess your racial guilt; or, more generally, not being able to share moral teachings from natural law, the Bible, and the *Catechism of the Catholic Church* without fear of getting fired. If your fourteen-year-old daughter must share a locker room with an eighteen-year-old man in the name of inclusivity; if your son's teacher uses her or his position of authority to insist that the belief that biological sex is real is "hateful" and a sure sign of "toxic masculinity"; if your children in general have great difficulty finding a peer group in which belief in God and objective morality is not openly mocked; if waiting to have sex until marriage is interpreted as a mental pathology by peers and teachers alike; if, more broadly, your circle of acquaintances cannot understand why you or any other "religious people" would care that a satanic baby goat demon was installed next to the Nativity Christ Child in the Illinois

Statehouse as part of the state's "Holiday celebrations"[8]—if you find any or all of these walls closing in on you and those whom you love, it might be time to escape the Michael Bay–worthy scene of the secular world violently imploding under its own weight and jump back on to the Barque of Peter.

What does such a leap entail? Building everything from new schools to new faith-friendly businesses to new sources of entertainment to new sporting leagues, even new faith-friendly social media. The Orthodox Christian author Rod Dreher provides much good food for thought on this theme in his widely read book *The Benedict Option*.[9] The "option" Dreher lays out is one all Christians should take seriously and, in the midst of an increasingly hostile culture, will likely have no choice but to take seriously if things continue on their current trajectory. As St. Augustine observed 1600 years ago, the City of God cannot and should not be entirely independent of the City of Man in the temporal realm. But its ties and modes of cooperation can be stronger or weaker, its differences can be more or less visible, and its respective citizens can be harder or easier to tell apart. Now may indeed be a time for the creation of new Christian-friendly, or at least religious-friendly, civic structures.

Apart from the certainty of the eschaton itself, it is hard to say what the future holds for the once-Christian West. Perhaps there will be a revival. Perhaps there won't. Either way, the Church's job is to be faithful to Christ, and being faithful to Christ entails caring for and protecting the bodily and spiritual good of the "least of these" (Matt. 18:6), which especially means our children. If the sociocultural soil that feeds both Christians and non-Christians alike grows too toxic to support the healthy

8. Jakob Emerson, "Satanic holiday display installed at Illinois Capitol," ABC News Channel 20, December 20, 2021, https://newschannel20.com/news/local /satanic-holiday-display-installed-at-illinois-capitol.

9. Rod Dreher, *The Benedict Option: A Strategy for Christians in a Post-Christian Nation* (New York: Sentinel, 2017).

growth of new generations of Catholic Christian disciples, then it may be time to pull back, move in, band together, and let yet another historical storm pass—never abandoning the missionary call to go out into the world but doing so in a way that ensures the missionaries always have a safe haven to return to. The doors of the Church were made to be open, yes. But the great thing about doors is that they have a dual function.

Remember: God does the sowing and the harvesting—but we tend to the ground. One of the most poignant parables Christ employs to describe his relationship to the world is the parable of the sower. For example, Jesus says in the Gospel of Matthew,

> And he told them many things in parables, saying: "Listen! A sower went out to sow. And as he sowed, some seeds fell on the path, and the birds came and ate them up. Other seeds fell on rocky ground, where they did not have much soil, and they sprang up quickly, since they had no depth of soil. But when the sun rose, they were scorched; and since they had no root, they withered away. Other seeds fell among thorns, and the thorns grew up and choked them. Other seeds fell on good soil and brought forth grain, some a hundredfold, some sixty, some thirty. Let anyone with ears listen!" (Matt. 13:3–9)

As Jesus soon after explains to his disciples, God is the farmer who casts the seeds—that is, the Gospel—into the hearts of the people. Jesus makes clear in the following parable, "The Parable of the Weeds," that God is also the one who harvests the good wheat that comes from the growth of the seed (and separates it from the "weeds" that grow among it). In other words, the primary actor in the story of salvation is the Trinitarian God—not us. We did not create the seed. We did not bring the seed into the world. Indeed, the parable makes clear that we are not even the ones who disperse the seed; that, too, is the work of the "farmer." In other words, the salvation story is for us and about us but not by us. What, then, is our role? Are we mere passive props that God moves to and fro as he builds his kingdom?

Not at all. With roots all the way back in Genesis' primordial garden, the Christian's proper role and duty is to *tend to the soil*, to do everything within our power to foster and maintain the conditions in which the seed, the Word of God, cannot only take root but grow and flourish. It is our job to clear the rocks, to soften and fertilize the ground, to ensure the earth has the nutrients to feed the sprouts, and to perform the endless task of trimming back the thorns. This is our work. And if we don't do it, it's not that anything is going to happen to the farmer and his seeds; no, the tragedy will be—the tragedy is—that there could have been such an abundant harvest if we just would have been willing to do our work rather than leaving the fields barren and dry.

It is for this reason that the evangelist's work includes evangelizing the political culture. Although God is and always will be the agent of salvation, the kind of world we choose to build has eternal significance. What we do and what we fail to do, both individually and communally, makes, to borrow language from the Jesuit theologian Karl Rahner, the choice to say yes to God either easier and more natural or harder and more alien. Bad ideologies can cause temporal harm, including temporal hell, but they can lead to spiritual hell as well, inducing us, like the serpent in the garden, to embrace death over life.

Sound hyperbolic? Imagine the despair that must permeate a culture for it to be able to produce 91,799 drug overdose deaths (251 per day),[10] 45,900 suicides (125 per day)[11]—of which there were 6,062 in the *ten- to twenty-four-year-old* age group alone in

---

10. See "Drug Overdose Deaths Remain High," Centers for Disease Control and Prevention, June 2, 2022, https://www.cdc.gov/drugoverdose/deaths/index .html.

11. See "Suicide," National Institute of Mental Health, June 2022, https:// www.nimh.nih.gov/health/statistics/suicide.

2020—and 24,576 homicides (67 per day)[12] *in one year.* Imagine the epidemic of internal instability it takes to produce a population in which over 10% of individuals over age twelve take antidepressants.[13] Imagine the state of families in a society in which, according to one survey, 44% of men and 11% of women watch pornography on a monthly basis[14] and 40.5% of children are born to women out of wedlock[15]—and yet that 40.5% is, in fact, lucky to have made it out of the womb, given that there have also been 629,898 abortions (1,725 per day) in a recent year as well.[16] All is not well in the temporal kingdom, and it is not getting better on its own. To be sure, the Church can and should take shelter to protect the faith; but the whole purpose of protecting the faith is to strengthen it, and the whole purpose of strengthening the faith is to introduce it (back) to the world, again and again, as an invitation to escape moral, spiritual, and even bodily death. How many will accept the invitation? Not ours to know. But as Jesus warns us, we better not be caught standing still in the fields, or worse, asleep when he returns (Mark 13:23–37).

For God's sake, don't make everything about politics. These may sound like rich words coming at the end of a book about . . . politics. But if there's one human activity that Jesus Christ was careful

12. See "Assault or Homicide," Centers for Disease Control and Prevention, September 6, 2022, https://www.cdc.gov/nchs/fastats/homicide.htm.

13. See "Antidepressant Use in Persons Aged 12 and Over: United States, 2005–2008," Centers for Disease Control and Prevention, November 6, 2015, https://www.cdc.gov/nchs/products/databriefs/db76.htm.

14. See Daniel A. Cox, Beatrice Lee, and Dana Popky, "Politics, Sex, and Sexuality: The Growing Gender Divide in American Life: Findings from the March 2022 American Perspectives Survey," Survey Center on American Life, April 27, 2022, https://www.americansurveycenter.org/research/march-2022-aps/#Views_About_Premarital_Sex.

15. See "Unmarried Childbearing," Centers for Disease Control and Prevention, May 16, 2022, https://www.cdc.gov/nchs/fastats/unmarried-childbearing.htm.

16. See "Abortion Surveillance—United States, 2019," Centers for Disease Control and Prevention, November 26, 2021, https://www.cdc.gov/mmwr/volumes/70/ss/ss7009a1.htm.

to put in its proper place and keep there, it was politics. Remember this one?

> Then they sent to him some Pharisees and some Herodians to trap him in what he said. And they came and said to him, "Teacher, we know that you are sincere, and show deference to no one; for you do not regard people with partiality, but teach the way of God in accordance with truth. Is it lawful to pay taxes to the emperor, or not? Should we pay them, or should we not?" But knowing their hypocrisy, he said to them, "Why are you putting me to the test? Bring me a denarius and let me see it." And they brought one. Then he said to them, "Whose head is this, and whose title?" They answered, "The emperor's." Jesus said to them, "Give to the emperor the things that are the emperor's, and to God the things that are God's." And they were utterly amazed at him. (Mark 12:13–17)

Our Lord has a good reputation for drop-dead one-liners, but this one ranks among the top. In a handful of words, Jesus de-divinizes politics and the political realm by making it clear that Caesar is not and never can be God. Yet he does so in a way that also clearly communicates our properly belonging within a temporal political order. In other words, everyone, including the world's most powerful temporal rulers, are under God's authority, yet no one is exempt from paying taxes to temporal authorities. And that's all Christ has to say about the role of government in this scene. Politics is important enough, sure, but really not that important.

Indeed, if there's any doubt about the ultimate role that politics should play in our lives, take another look at the Beatitudes:

> When Jesus saw the crowds, he went up the mountain; and after he sat down, his disciples came to him. Then he began to speak, and taught them, saying: "Blessed are the poor in spirit,

for theirs is the kingdom of heaven. Blessed are those who mourn, for they will be comforted. Blessed are the meek, for they will inherit the earth. Blessed are those who hunger and thirst for righteousness, for they will be filled. Blessed are the merciful, for they will receive mercy. Blessed are the pure in heart, for they will see God. Blessed are the peacemakers, for they will be called children of God. Blessed are those who are persecuted for righteousness' sake, for theirs is the kingdom of heaven. Blessed are you when people revile you and persecute you and utter all kinds of evil against you falsely on my account. Rejoice and be glad, for your reward is great in heaven, for in the same way they persecuted the prophets who were before you." (Matt. 5:1–12).

What's not on the list is just as important as what is. The powerful do not receive a special blessing, nor do those who seek power, nor do those, for that matter, who do community organizing, or who appear on cable TV news programs, or who conduct voting campaigns, or who craft public policy, or who write about religion and politics. It's not that any of these activities are bad. It's just that, well, *they're not blessed*, and they don't, by themselves, lead to blessedness. What makes us happy, what gets us to heaven, is having humility, loving others, orienting our whole lives to be in conformity with God's commands, forgiving others so that we might be forgiven, opening and reopening ourselves to God's cleansing grace, doing everything we can to bring authentic peace to those around us, and being willing to risk every worldly good out of love for the Lord.

What does any of this have to do with politics? In the end, a little—but that little matters a lot. The shape and character of the political order, as I've argued throughout, either helps or harms us individually and collectively in our pursuit of the highest good. It is a tool, an important tool, that can be used to help fashion ourselves and each other into the best possible expressions of who we are called to be. But it can also be used as a weapon to tear us down, both individually and collectively. In this sense, it is not a question of whether politics will impact us; it is only a question of what impact it will have. And the Catholic social thought tradition, I believe, offers the best instructions for building something good, something true, and perhaps even something beautiful in the political realm, to the extent that is possible in a fallen world this side of the eschaton.

Yet all this work has one final purpose and one final purpose alone: to enable individuals to hear the good news of the Gospel and to facilitate an encounter with Jesus Christ and his Church. The dominant political ideologies of today are blocking wide swaths of the culture from receiving this invitation and all of its blessings. Evangelizing the political culture is thus ultimately not about ideology and even less about politics. It is about opening the widest and straightest path possible for making the pilgrimage to the Lord.

Index of Names

Index of Subjects